C000252787

The Sound Patterns of Syntax

OXFORD STUDIES IN THEORETICAL LINGUISTICS

GENERAL EDITORS: David Adger, *Queen Mary College London*; Hagit Borer, *University of Southern California.*

ADVISORY EDITORS: Stephen Anderson, *Yale University*; Daniel Büring, *University of California, Los Angeles*; Nomi Erteschik-Shir, *Ben-Gurion University*; Donka Farkas, *University of California, Santa Cruz*; Angelika Kratzer, *University of Massachusetts, Amherst*; Andrew Nevins, *Harvard University*; Christopher Potts, *University of Massachusetts, Amherst*; Barry Schein, *University of Southern California*; Peter Svenonius, *University of Tromsø*; Moira Yip, *University College London.*

RECENT TITLES

For a complete list of titles published and in preparation for the series, see pp. 386–387.

The Sound Patterns of Syntax

Edited by
NOMI ERTESCHIK-SHIR
and
LISA ROCHMAN

OXFORD
UNIVERSITY PRESS

OXFORD

UNIVERSITY PRESS

Great Clarendon Street, Oxford OX2 6DP

Oxford University Press is a department of the University of Oxford.
It furthers the University's objective of excellence in research, scholarship,
and education by publishing worldwide in

Oxford New York

Auckland Cape Town Dar es Salaam Hong Kong Karachi
Kuala Lumpur Madrid Melbourne Mexico City Nairobi
New Delhi Shanghai Taipei Toronto
With offices in
Argentina Austria Brazil Chile Czech Republic France Greece
Guatemala Hungary Italy Japan South Korea Poland Portugal
Singapore Switzerland Thailand Turkey Ukraine Vietnam

Oxford is a registered trade mark of Oxford University Press
in the UK and in certain other countries

Published in the United States
by Oxford University Press Inc., New York

© Editorial matter and oranization Nomi Erteschik-Shir and Lisa Rochman 2010
© The chapters their authors 2010

The moral rights of the author have been asserted

Database right Oxford University Press (maker)

Reprinted 2011

All rights reserved. No part of this publication may be reproduced,
stored in a retrieval system, or transmitted, in any form or by any means,
without the prior permission in writing of Oxford University Press,
or as expressly permitted by law, or under terms agreed with the appropriate
reprographics rights organization. Enquiries concerning reproduction
outside the scope of the above should be sent to the Rights Department,
Oxford University Press, at the address above

You must not circulate this book in any other binding or cover
And you must impose this same condition on any acquirer

ISBN 978-0-19-955686-1

Printed in the United Kingdom by
Lightning Source UK Ltd., Milton Keynes

Contents

Notes on Contributors

Tor A. Åfarli is Professor in Scandinavian Linguistics at the Norwegian University of Science and Technology NTNU, Trondheim. His research interests are theoretical linguistics and micro- and macrocomparative syntax. He is currently involved in a collaborative research effort mapping and analyzing the syntax of Scandinavian dialects, as well as a project investigating the macrocomparative syntax of Norwegian and Mandarin Chinese, including problems of second language acquisition. He is working on a book on the microcomparative syntax of subjects in Norwegian.

João Costa is a Professor of Linguistics at the Linguistics Department of Universidade Nova de Lisboa, in Portugal. He received his Ph.D. in Linguistics from Leiden University in 1998. He works on theoretical syntax, language acquisition, and educational linguistics. His research focuses primarily on word order and on interface issues.

Isabelle Darcy completed her Ph.D. dissertation about phonological assimilation and word recognition at the Laboratoire de Sciences Cognitives et Psycholinguistique at CNRS/EHESS in Paris (France) in 2003. Subsequently, she held postdoctoral research and teaching positions at Potsdam University and Tübingen University (Germany). She is currently an Assistant Professor in the Department of Second Language Studies at Indiana University in Bloomington.

Katalin É. Kiss is a Research Professor at the Research Institute for Linguistics at the Hungarian Academy of Sciences, and Chair of the Doctoral School in Linguistics of Pázmány Péter Catholic University. She is the author of *The Syntax of Hungarian* (CUP, 2002), and editor and co-author of *Event Structure and the Left Periphery* (Springer, 2006), and *Adverbs and Adverbial Adjuncts at the Interfaces* (Benjamins, 2009), among others.

Nomi Erteschik-Shir is Professor of Linguistics in the Department of Foreign Literatures and Linguistics at Ben-Gurion University, Israel. Her publications include *The Dynamics of Focus Structure* (1997), *Information Structure: The Syntax-Discourse Interface* (2007), and *The Syntax of Aspect* (2005) co-edited with Tova Rapoport. She is currently extending her work on the syntax–phonology interface to elliptical constructions. She is also working on a book with Tova Rapoport on the lexicon–syntax interface, *The Atoms of Meaning*.

Caroline Féry is Professor of Phonology at the Department of Linguistics at the University of Potsdam. Her main interests lie in the prosodic and tonal structure of languages, the interface between syntax and intonation, and the theory of grammar. She is the director of the Collaborative Research Center 632 on Information Structure.

Steven Franks is Professor of Linguistics and Chair of the Department of Slavic Languages and Literatures at Indiana University. Franks is editor-in-chief of the *Journal of Slavic Linguistics*, author of *Parameters of Slavic Morphosyntax* (OUP, 1995), and co-author of *A Handbook of Slavic Clitics* (OUP, 2000). In 2004, Franks held the Fulbright Distinguished Chair in Linguistics and Philosophy at Ca' Foscari, Venice.

Sam Hellmuth is Lecturer in Linguistics in the Department of Language and Linguistic Science at the University of York, UK. Her research focuses on prosodic variation among spoken varieties of Arabic, with a particular interest in variation in the distribution of intonational pitch accents and its relation to the phonological and syntactic grammar.

Charles W. Kisseberth taught at the University of Illinois from 1969 to 1996, and at Tel Aviv University from 1996 to the present. His main research interests have been in the areas of theoretical phonology, the interface of phonology and syntax, Bantu tonal systems, field linguistics, and long-distance phonological phenomena such as vowel harmony. The book *Generative Phonology: Theory and Description*, co-authored with Michael Kenstowicz (1979), played a significant role in graduate linguistics education into the 1990s. Kisseberth's paper on 'The functional unity of phonological rules' (1970), as well as a number of other papers in the 1970s challenging generative phonology orthodoxy, provided the foundation for the emergence of Optimality Theory. His work on Optimal Domains Theory over the past fifteen years has sought to push OT towards a more representational solution to problems such as opacity.

Emily Nava is a Ph.D. student in Linguistics at USC (degree to be completed in 2010) with a concentration on Hispanic Linguistics. Her research area is second language acquisition and bilingualism, with a focus on the acquisition of prosody. Her current research project examines the relation between rhythm and main phrasal prominence.

Lisa Rochman is a Ph.D. candidate at Ben Gurion University. Her research focuses on the role of intonation and information structure in word order in English, with a focus on floating quantifiers. Lisa also works on the prosodic structure of Hebrew.

Mamoru Saito is Professor of Linguistics in the Department of Anthropology and Philosophy at Nanzan University, and Distinguished Visitor in the Department of Linguistics at the University of Connecticut. Among his recent publications are 'Notes on East Asian Argument Ellipsis' (*Language Research* 43, 2007: 203–27) and 'N'-Ellipsis and the Structure of Noun Phrases in Chinese and Japanese' (with T.-H. Jonah Lin and Keiko Murasugi, *Journal of East Asian Linguistics* 17, 2008: 247–71).

Tobias Scheer is currently Directeur de Recherche at the CNRS in France. He works at the laboratory Bases, Corpus, Langage (UMR 6039) in Nice, of which he is the director. Being a phonologist, his main interests lie in syllable structure thematically speaking, and in the (Western) Slavic family as far as languages are concerned. He is committed to Government Phonology and hence to the idea that representations contribute an independent and unoutrankable arbitral award: a linguistic object may be well- or ill-formed in absence of any comparison with other objects. In 2004, he published a book on a particular development of GP, so-called CVCV, and he is currently preparing the second volume, which will be entirely devoted to the interface of phonology and morphosyntax.

Mohinish Shukla has a background in molecular genetics, and holds a Ph.D. in cognitive neuroscience from SISSA, Italy. He is currently a post-doc at the University of Rochester, NY. He is interested in infant development, particularly the development of linguistic abilities from phonology to syntax. He is also interested in neural measures of development, particularly using optical imaging and eye-tracking.

Kriszta Szendrői is a Lecturer in linguistics and psycholinguistics at University College London. Her research interests include the interfaces between syntax and phonology and between syntax and discourse. She has published articles on the syntax of focus and on the acquisition of focus by typically developing children.

Hubert Truckenbrodt wrote his Ph.D. thesis about the syntax–phonology interface at MIT in 1995. He has since taught in the US and in Germany, won a teaching award, and coordinated a circle of Lab-Phon-oriented projects in Germany. He is currently a researcher at the Centre for General Linguistics (ZAS) in Berlin and holds a Habilitation and Prof. title at the University of Tübingen.

Maria Luisa Zubizarreta is Professor of Linguistics and director of the SLA Laboratory at the University of Southern California. Her research interests include (but are not limited to) the interaction of syntax and the lexicon; the relation between syntax, prosody, and information structure; second language acquisition; and second language speech.

Abbreviations

ACC	Accusative
A-deacc	Lexical Anaphora Deaccenting
AgrOP	Agree Object Phrase
AgrSP	Agree Subject Phrase
BCS	Bosnian/Croatian/Serbian
CP	Complementizer Phase
DP	Determiner Phrase
EA	Egyptian Arabic
ENC	Native English speakers
FF	formal features
FQ	floating quantifier
I-phrase	Intonational phrase
IS	information structure
ITL	Iambic-Trochaic Law
L2	second language
LCA	Linear Correspondence Axiom
LF	Logical Form
LP	Lexical Phonology
NF	narrow focus
NOM	Nominative
NP	noun phrase
NSR	Nuclear Stress Rule
O	object
PF	Phonetic Form
PhPh	Phonological Phrase
PIC	Phase Impenetrability Condition
PTT	Phrasal Prominence Transfer
QUIS	Questionnaire on Information Structure (Skopeteas *et al.* 2006)

SA	sentence adverbial
SAAR	Sentence Accent Assignment Rule
SCC	Strict Cycle Condition
Spec	Specifier
T	Tense
TP	Tense Phrase
V2	verb second
VP	verb phrase
WF	wide focus

1

Introduction

NOMI ERTESCHIK-SHIR AND LISA ROCHMAN

The impetus for the workshop[1] and the resulting volume was the work we were each doing on phonological effects on word order (Erteschik-Shir 2005a, b and Rochman 2007b, in prep, forthcoming). Erteschik-Shir came to the surprising conclusion that object shift in Scandinavian was best accounted for by prosodic constraints on the linearization of adverbs and pronouns. Even more surprising was that this account afforded an explanation of the differences between the Scandinavian languages with respect to object shift—the shift of full DPs in Icelandic but not in the other Scandinavian languages, and the optionality of object shift in Swedish but not in Danish. These differences turned out to hinge on the different prosodic properties of the languages in question. Rochman's investigation of the placement of so-called floating quantifiers turned out to be determined, at least in part, by purely prosodic factors. These conclusions were surprising in that we had each assumed working hypotheses in which these word orders were in fact triggered purely by information-structural constraints. As it turned out, both information structure (and its intonational effects) and independent prosodic properties of the languages in question turned out to determine word order. These results raised serious architectural questions, some of which had been raised independently by others in different contexts.

The syntax–phonology interface has attracted interest since the beginning of generative grammar. Initially this interest focused on the prosodic marking of constituent structure and the syntactic and phonological manifestation of focus. More recently it has also been observed that certain constraints on word order are best viewed as phonological as well (e.g., Heavy NP Shift,

[1] We thank the Israel Science Foundation Grant No. 1228/07 for funding the workshop.

Right Node Raising, Stylistic Inversion, Second Position Clitics, and Object Shift). Bobaljik (2002), for example, proposes a copy theory of movement which allows for the pronunciation of copies as well as the head of the chain. In this framework, word order is accounted for by syntactic movement, yet morphophonological constraints determine which copy is pronounced. This allows for a syntactic account of word order which is sensitive to PF properties such as adjacency. At the other extreme, Erteschik-Shir (2005a, b) proposes the radical view that word order is determined solely by phonological properties. Between these two extremes lie approaches which utilize a post-syntactic, 'stylistic', component to account for phenomena such as word order which seem to be syntactic, yet do not comply with well-established syntactic constraints. Such post-syntactic or stylistic components seem particularly suited to those cases where word order is determined by information structure. Taking such a tack has the advantage of leaving syntax unperturbed by 'messy' phenomena, but it has the disadvantage of creating a new component, post-syntax, which is undefined and therefore merely provides a dumping ground for unaccounted-for data. Moreover, the issue of mapping from the syntax to this post-syntactic component requires explanation. The papers in this volume explore these and similar issues on the syntax–phonology interface in order to examine the theoretical consequences of their accounts.

Very different conclusions from a wide range of data and languages (Chmwiini, Danish, Egyptian Arabic, English, European Portuguese, German, Hungarian, Japanese Norwegian, South Slavic languages) are to be found in this volume. The first eight papers deal with word-order phenomena in a range of different languages and question whether these word orders are to be accounted for in the phonology or not. The phenomena are varied and so are the theoretical perspectives and the conclusions concerning the interface. The next six papers deal with various prosodic issues with several papers dealing with issues relating to the phonological phrase and accent. Papers in both of these groups deal with information structure, considering the impact of information structure both on word order and on prosody. Since information structure potentially interacts with both syntax and phonology, it may therefore play a deciding role as to whether a particular phenomenon is to be accounted for in the syntax or in the phonology. Here it is again critical where information structure fits in to the architecture of grammar. Some of the papers position information structure strictly in the syntax (e.g., Saito) whereas others view it as playing an instrumental role in the process of phonological linearization (Erteschik-Shir) while others yet view it as having purely phonological effects. The last paper brings evidence from word stress for an intermodular grammar.

The four first chapters of the volume all deal to some extent with the placement of adverbials and all adhere (explicitly or implicitly) to the view that adverbials are merged in a third dimension and are then linearized. They differ as to which principles determine linearization and also with respect to where interpretation fits into the picture. The basic idea of 3D derivation of adverbials and their subsequent linearization is however strongly supported by the range of phenomena accounted for.

Åfarli spells out the basis for a three-dimensional analysis of sentential adverbials (and for adjunction in general), which provides the basis for accounting for some well-known facts about the special behavior of adverbials. According to Åfarli, adverbials are 'bent' into their linear position by a process of bending defined in the paper. The constraints on bending, in turn, provide an account of a number of important word-order puzzles in Norwegian. Åfarli argues that in view of the scopal effect of their linear position, 3D to 2D conversion cannot take place in the phonology, since the 2D structure must also provide the input to interpretation. The conversion therefore could take place before Spell-Out, but Åfarli suggests instead that Spell-Out should be construed as an integral part of 3D to 2D conversion (or vice versa) allowing for linearization in the phonological component and interpretation in the semantic component.

Erteschik-Shir argues that linearization is responsible for the placement of MON, a Danish adverbial typing particle, as well as V2 and overt performatives. Although inspired by Åfarli's (1997) original idea that adverbs are merged in a third dimension, Erteschik-Shir views linearization as a purely phonological process. This is possible under her view because scope is calculated on Information Structure and not in the semantic component. Erteschik-Shir adopts Speyer's (2005) analysis of the disappearance of V2 concomitantly with topicalization in English as being due to the trochaic requirement: a topicalized DP followed by a verb and then another DP forms a trochee in view of the lack of stress on the verb. Without V2, topicalization would form the sequence DP, DP, V which violates the trochaic requirement, hence topicalization in modern English is rare. An examination of the historical development of V2 in Danish provides an explanation for the lack of V2 with MON, one of the questions the article sets out to explore. Phonology is thus argued to play a major role in determining word order. The interplay of linearization and prosody is accounted for at the syntax–phonology interface in which phonological factors such as sentence-initial position as well as prosodic factors are expected to play a significant role.

É. Kiss argues that the free constituent order attested in the postverbal section of the Hungarian sentence is a PF operation. Her main argument comes from the placement of adverbials which she too argues are adjoined in a third dimension (following Åfarli 1997 among others) and are then linearized in the phonology. Linearization follows Behaghel's Law of Growing Constituents that lighter constituents precede heavier ones, clearly a phonological principle. In order to account for the scopal properties of the postverbal adverbials (which in fact mirror those of the preverbal ones), É. Kiss argues that they too c-command the syntactic projection over which they scope, but from a right-adjoined position which is then linearized into the postverbal string. The fact that the word order in this domain depends on the size of the constituents is clear evidence for her phonological account in terms of linearization.

Rochman is concerned with the placement of so-called floating quantifiers which she argues are in fact also adverbials which are linearized at the phonological interface. She argues that these quantifiers mark the element following them as a focus, usually a contrastive one. It follows that quantifiers will tend to float from a subject topic.

Rochman's methodology is an interesting one: she examines speakers' judgments as well as corpora of naturally occurring discourse with respect to the position of floating quantifiers and particles. Surprisingly, the results of these two investigations conflict. According to Rochman the naturally occurring discourse predicted by the focus-marking hypothesis overrides the phonological preference for sentence-final floating quantifiers evidenced by the speaker-judgment results. This is an important finding both theoretically and methodologically: Rather than finding fault with the methodology itself, one can look for a theoretical explanation for such conflicts. Naturally occurring discourse is supported by context, the judgment experiment was not. Out of context, the sound of a sentence will influence judgments more than information structure which is contextually determined. Theoretically, Rochman concludes that information structure interfaces both phonology and syntax.

Costa reaches a similar conclusion to Rochman with respect to the role of prosody in determining word order. He demonstrates that the prosodic and interpretive constraints on the relative order of adverbs and direct objects in European Portuguese fail to obtain in out-of-the-blue contexts. It follows, according to Costa, that prosody cannot be viewed as the trigger for movement. Costa supports this conclusion with further data as well as acquisition facts. He then argues for a syntax which generates multiple outputs. Which output is selected depends on post-syntactic filters. If none apply, true optionality results. Architecturally, Costa's approach to the interaction between prosody, word order, and focus takes focus information out of the syntax and views it as a discourse matter. The information-structure component of the grammar, however, communicates with both the prosodic and the semantic components (following Valldduví 1992 and Erteschik-Shir 1997), thus allowing for both prosodic and semantic effects of focus.

Franks employs South Slavic clitics to argue that Spell-Out subsumes a complex of operations, including at least deletion, linearization, and prosodification, and examines how these three processes interact. He argues for Multiple Spell-Out (different from Costa's multiple outputs) with linearization done cyclically, reapplying at different points in the derivation, making use of different kinds of information. Initial linearization exploits c-command along the lines of Kayne's (1994) 'Linear Correspondence Axiom'. Later relinearization, however, exploits prosodic properties of specific lexical items. Franks's later relinearization should thus be compared to the approaches to linearization presented in the previous papers. Franks outlines a formalization of the reassembly of the pieces sent to Spell-Out independently in terms of subarrays which are spelled out as lexical items, making the sentence itself just one big word. In presenting and analyzing the rich data in his paper, Franks proposes a variety of conceptual alternatives, leaving their resolution for future research.

Franks concludes that 'linearization, copy selection, ellipsis, and possibly even movement are defined in an effort to pronounce'. It follows that a growing number of processes which were previously thought to be purely syntactic should now be viewed as phonological.

Saito discusses the discourse properties of Japanese scrambling and argues for a purely syntactic account of these in terms of a new set of features projecting at the left periphery. From the scopal interaction of scrambling and negation, Saito argues for a PredP projection at the left periphery with the Pred head attracting an arg(ument) feature. This is the final landing site of scrambled elements and of subjects when no scrambling occurs. Elements in this position necessarily take wide scope.

Saito goes on to demonstrate how the information-structural role of elements in this position is derived, namely that nominative phrases are focused, whereas topic-marked phrases become thematic topics. Saito compares his view of the left periphery to that of Rizzi and shows that they cannot be reconciled. He therefore suggests that these two views of the left periphery should be compared in order to uncover crosslinguistic variation in the left periphery.

Saito demonstrates that an optional, discourse-motivated word order such as the scrambled order in Japanese, can be accounted for syntactically without recourse to phonological linearization. Saito's view is therefore diametrically opposed to that of Erteschik-Shir (2005b) and this volume which accounts for information-structure-motivated word order in the phonology.

Shukla and Nespor are concerned with the acquisition of word order by infants. Their view is decidedly phonological. Infants, they argue, acquire word order prelexically on the basis of the rhythmic patterns within the phonological phrase (PPh). While phonological constituents are not in direct communication with syntactic units (Selkirk 1984; Nespor and Vogel 1986 [2008]), one level of the prosodic hierarchy, the phonological phrase, does reflects the underlying head complement order of the syntactic structure. They propose that since infants are sensitive to the rhythm within the phonological phrase (Christophe et al. 2003), and the placement of the accent is determined by branching direction, infants can use this information to determine the direction of branching. In left-branching languages the prominence in the PPh is initial while in right-branching languages the prominence is final (Nespor and Vogel). Following Shukla and Nespor, infants would know the correct word order of their language without having to have any lexical knowledge of the words in the sentence. Shukla and Nespor's work raises important questions regarding the issue of language acquisition and the crucial role the phonological phrase plays in informing the infant about the syntactic structure of the language in question.

Truckenbrodt and Darcy look at phrasal stress and syntax in German, in particular extraposition. They consider Gussenhoven's (1983b, 1992) Sentence Accent Assignment Rule's (SAAR) success in predicting phrasal stress in these cases. Following the SAAR, as originally formulated, a final verb will be stressless when adjacent to a stressed DP argument. The question Truckenbrodt and Darcy investigate is whether a following object clause exempts the verb from being stressed as a preceding object does. The underlying question being whether extraposition allows for stress reconstruction, if it is allowed then the verb should be able to remain stressless.

The results of their production and perception experiment support the hypothesis that there is no stress reconstruction for the extraposed elements as the verb is stressed in these cases. Truckenbrodt and Darcy's work explores an aspect of the role that syntax has on the manifestation of the prosodic structure.

Kisseberth's paper deals with the construction of the phonological phrase, accounting for its construction by arguing for two Optimality Theoretical (OT) constraints, Align XP and Wrap XP. Adding to the evidence present in the previous papers for the existence of the phonological phrase, Kisseberth provides more evidence from Chmwiini vowel length and accent. Kisseberth discusses the well-established claim that the PPh is not the same as the syntactic phrase (Selkirk), thus requiring some mechanism to convert the latter into the former. The recursive nature of prosodic structure is argued for based on the need for both Align XP as well as Wrap XP to work in the language without conflict. Kisseberth's paper argues for the existence of mapping constraints to function between the syntax and phonology and further shows the need for a recursive prosodic structure. His paper reinforces the importance of the phonological phrase and its role in the marking of focus.

Hellmuth's paper argues against the claims that syntactic and phonological marking of focus is complementary in language. The language she uses for exploring this issue is Egyptian Arabic (EA). In EA, focus can be marked through either prosodic or syntactic means. The exception to this is thetic sentences, which can only employ syntactic focus marking, and this sentence type is the subject of the paper. Hellmuth argues that this is not a result of the complementary nature of focus-marking systems in which focus is either marked by syntactic or phonological devices and not both, but instead is the result of the phonological system of the language. She concludes that a lack of a phonological (or syntactic) device for focus marking in a language is due to the nature of the phonological (or syntactic) system of that language and not due to the presence of another focus-marking strategy by another component of the grammar.

Hellmuth's paper suggests that the model of architecture does not have a specific information-structure component. Instead surface IS markings are a result of the interaction of other components of the grammar.

Féry explores another aspect of focus marking by looking at accenting and the influence of focus on the height of a given accent. Arguing against the belief that pitch accents are changed on an individual basis, usually because of IS, Féry proposes that accent heights are interpreted in relationship to other accents in the phrase, and thus their heights are relational. IS does not create pitch accents but instead raises and lowers the register of the accents and IS does not influence PPhs. She separates the effects of syntax from those of information structure. It is the syntax that is responsible for determining the shape of the prosodic phrases while the IS determines the realization of the accents and the relative height of the accents. Information structure does not create the accents nor determine the absolute height of an accent. What it does do is enlarge the pitch range for new information and compress it for given information.

Nava and Zubizarreta also discuss the relation between focus and prosody. They show that there are crosslinguistic differences in the prosodic marking of focus: The Germanic stress pattern in wide-focus contexts is the output of the interaction of two rules: the Nuclear Stress Rule and an Anaphoric Deaccent-ing Rule. The latter rule is missing in Spanish. Furthermore, the Nuclear Stress rule, which is present in both languages, operates differently in Ger-manic and Spanish. In the former, it applies to a metrical structure in which the functional nodes are invisible, whereas in the latter, it applies to a structure isomorphic to S-structure.

The paper shows, on the basis of experimental data, that Spanish learners of English apply the Spanish version of the Nuclear Stress Rule to English, and the learning of the Anaphoric Deaccenting Rule precedes the restructuring of the Spanish Nuclear Stress Rule.

Szendrői's paper also provides experimental evidence for the proposal that focus marking is a language-specific rule as opposed to being an exclusively communicative, extragrammatical device. Szendrői notes that while there is vast theoretical knowledge supporting this approach, there is very little experimental evidence to support it. Her data come from an experiment on an autistic child. Members of this population would likely find focus marking and identification quite difficult if focus marking is extralinguistic because the deductive steps needed require the theory of mind which they lack. Yet the lack of this communicative deductive step would not pose a hindrance if focus marking was part of grammar.

Scheer's paper explores the interactionalist nature of grammar. He shows that Phrase Impenetrability Condition (PIC), which is a fundamental com-ponent of phase-based syntax, plays a deciding role in determining the validity of phonological theory. Scheer argues for an intermodular grammar, where the material sent to Spell-Out must be the same as regards the syntax and PF with Phase Impenetrability (the PIC) operating the same on both sides. With this in mind he discusses the different approaches to affixes in English.

Scheer compares the offspring of morpheme-specific phonologies and Kayne's (1992, 1995) supplemented approach of Halle and Vergnaud's (1987) approach with selective Spell-Out and no look-back device. Scheer argues that Kayne's approach is the better one as he feels it is compatible with phase-based syntax. Scheer's paper adds to the body of work supporting interactionalist approaches to grammar and shows the benefits of employing intermodular argumentation, a fitting conclusion to this volume.

2

Adjunction and 3D phrase structure: A study of Norwegian adverbials

TOR A. ÅFARLI

2.1 Introduction

Chomsky (2001a, 2004) discusses the example given in (1).

(1)   Which picture of Bill that John liked did he buy.

Whereas *he* may be co-referent with *John*, *he* cannot be co-referent with *Bill*. The latter fact follows from reconstruction and principle C of the binding theory. However, reconstruction and principle C should also have prohibited co-reference between *he* and *John*, contrary to fact. On the other hand, if the adjunct relative clause is somehow not fully integrated into the structure, it could nevertheless be possible to explain why co-reference between *he* and *John* is not excluded by principle C.

Chomsky uses this example to motivate a proposal to the effect that adjuncts and non-adjuncts are introduced into structures in radically different ways. Specifically, whereas structure building normally takes place by the free symmetrical operation set-merge, adjuncts are introduced by the asymmetrical operation pair-merge, which means that adjuncts are attached to the structure 'on a separate plane' (Chomsky 2004: 118). Attachment of an adjunct thus leaves the structure formed by set-merge on the primary plane unaffected, and the adjunct is basically 'invisible' to operations taking place on that plane, thus facilitating an explanation of the puzzle presented by (1).

In previous work (Åfarli 1995, 1997), I made a similar proposal based on the behavior of Scandinavian adverbial phrases, proposing a three-dimensional (3D) analysis of phrase structure, where adverbial phrases are introduced in a third dimension as compared to the 2D basic structure of the clause. In this paper, I want to update and explore my arguments further, showing that they support Chomsky's distinction between set-merge and pair-merge in a quite striking manner, and at the same time, I contend that the set-merge—pair-merge distinction should be interpreted in terms of dimensions of phrase structure.[1]

The paper is organized as follows. After the present introductory section, section 2.2 concentrates on Norwegian sentence adverbials, showing that they are readily analysed given a 3D approach to phrase structure. Section 2.3 concentrates on the more tricky problems of predicate (or verb phrase) adverbials, showing that they too should be analyzed as originating in the third phrase-structural dimension. Section 2.4 concludes the paper.

2.2 Sentence adverbials as 3D phrases

2.2.1 *Basic distribution of SAs in Norwegian*

The most elementary observation to be made about a sentence adverbial (henceforth SA) in Norwegian is that it typically occurs immediately to the right of the finite verb in a subject-first main clause. This is shown in the a-versions in (2)–(3). Since Norwegian is a V2 language, this means that the SA occurs immediately to the right of the V2 position. Usually, the SA can also occur in extraposition, in which case it is set apart from the rest of the clause by special intonation, cf. the b-versions. The term extraposition is here used purely descriptively, with no particular implications about how extraposition phenomena should be analyzed.

(2)   a.   Ola korrigerte **truleg** feilen.
            Ola corrected probably the error

      b.   Ola korrigerte feilen, **truleg**.
            Ola corrected the error probably

      c.   ***truleg** Ola korrigerte feilen.
            probably Ola corrected the error

      d.   *Ola **truleg** korrigerte feilen.
            Ola probably corrected the error

(3)   a.   Ola kan **truleg** korrigere feilen.
            Ola can probably correct the error

---

[1] Boeckx (2008: 100–1) argues that adjunction should be identified with set-merge and non-adjunction with pair-merge, i.e. the opposite of Chomsky's construal. My analysis is compatible with both alternatives. See also Rubin (2003) for further ideas on the mechanism of merge and the analysis of adjunction structures.

   b.   Ola kan korrigere feilen, **truleg.**
        Ola can correct the error probably

   c.   **Truleg** Ola kan korrigere feilen.
        probably Ola can correct the error

   d.   *Ola **truleg** kan korrigere feilen.
        Ola probably can correct the error

   e.   *Ola kan korrigere **truleg** feilen.
        Ola can correct probably the error

Notice in particular that an SA cannot easily occur in between non-finite verbs in a longer verb sequence, cf. (4).

(4)   a.   Ola vil **truleg** kunne ha korrigert feilen (før klokka 8 i morgon tidleg).
          Ola will probably can have corrected the error (before 8 o'clock tomorrow morning)

      b.   *Ola vil kunne **truleg** ha korrigert feilen (før klokka 8 i morgon tidleg).
          Ola will can probably have corrected the error (before 8 o'clock tomorrow morning)

      c.   *Ola vil kunne ha **truleg** korrigert feilen (før klokka 8 i morgon tidleg).
          Ola will can have probably corrected the error (before 8 o'clock tomorrow morning)

In embedded clauses, the SA typically occurs immediately to the left of the finite verb, as expected since embedded clauses do not observe the V2 constraint, cf. (5).

(5)   (a)   ... at Ola **truleg** korrigerte feilen.
          ... that Ola probably corrected the error

      (b)   ... at Ola **truleg** kan korrigere feilen.
          ... that Ola probably can correct the error

In addition to the patterns shown above, Norwegian SAs can be topicalized, as shown in (6).

(6)   a.   **Truleg** korrigerte Ola feilen.
        probably corrected Ola the error

      b.   **Truleg** kan Ola korrigere feilen.
        probably can Ola correct the error

Adopting a CP + TP + vP + VP basic structure of Norwegian, where the C-position is the V2 position, and where auxiliary verbs are generated between TP and vP, the patterns shown above indicate that an SA in Norwegian is generated attached to the T-projection (in addition to occurring possibly in extraposition). Thus, Norwegian seems to be more restricted as to possible positions that an SA can occupy than for instance English is. Notice in particular that the data in (4) indicate that an SA cannot easily be attached to the projection of an auxiliary or main verb, contrary to occasional claims in the literature that the position of an SA indicates the edge of VP. In fact, given the patterns presented thus far, it can be hypothesized that an SA in Norwegian is left-adjoined to T' on the assumption that subjects are at least raised to <Spec, TP>.[2]

Generally, even though a given language may have a relatively fixed overall word order, SAs are typically quite flexible as to the linear position that they may occupy in the sentence. This is exemplified in English for instance, but the data given in (2)–(6) indicate that Norwegian is not very flexible in that respect. However, it turns out on closer inspection that SAs are a little more flexible even in Norwegian. This is most readily seen in main clauses where the subject remains in <Spec, TP> (because another phrase has been moved to <Spec, CP>). Consider (7)–(8), where it is shown that the SA can occur on both sides of the subject.

(7)   a.   Feilen korrigerte <u>Ola</u> **truleg** (for to dagar sidan).
           the error corrected Ola probably (two days ago)

      b.   Feilen korrigerte **truleg** <u>Ola</u> (for to dagar sidan).
           the error corrected probably Ola (two days ago)

(8)   a.   Feilen kan <u>Ola</u> **truleg** korrigere (på to dagar).
           the error can Ola probably correct (in two days)

      b.   Feilen kan **truleg** <u>Ola</u> korrgiere (på to dagar).
           the error can probably Ola correct (in two days)

The flexibility seen in (7)–(8) is still quite limited. Nevertheless, these data suggest that Norwegian SAs do not occupy absolutely rigid phrase-structural positions.[3]

---

[2] I use an old-style three-level X'-notation (X-X'-XP) for expository purposes, but it might be that a two-level distinction between X and XP (head and non-head) would be more appropriate, in which case any qualms about adjunction to the intermediate category X' would be irrelevant.

[3] Given the data in (7)–(8), it is also expected that an SA may occur on either side of the subject in an embedded clause, assuming that the subject is raised to <Spec, TP>. This prediction also seems to be correct, cf. (i).

The hypothesis about the flexibility of SAs is sometimes contended. Many linguists have assumed that the linear position of adverbial phrases may be used as a diagnosis for movement, the idea being that the position of an SA serves as a fixed point that may be used in determining the structural position of other constituents. For instance, Holmberg (1993: 32) notices that an adverbial phrase may occur either to the right or to the left of a subject in Swedish, cf. (9).

(9) a. Har <u>nogon student</u> **möjligen** läst boken?   (Swedish)
         has any student possibly read the book

     b. Har **möjligen** <u>nogon student</u> läst boken?   (Swedish)
         has possibly any student read the book

Assuming a CP + AgrSP + TP + AgrOP + VP structure, and furthermore assuming that *möjligen* 'possibly' adjoins to TP, Holmberg argues that all subjects move obligatorily to <Spec, TP> in overt syntax. In addition, according to Holmberg a weak subject pronoun obligatorily moves on to <Spec, AgrSP>, whereas other subjects may optionally make this additional step from <Spec, TP> to <Spec, AgrSP>, thus producing either (9a), if the step is taken, or (9b), if it is not taken.

However, there is solid empirical evidence that data like (9) cannot be used to motivate noun phrase movement in this manner, since an SA may simultaneously occur to the immediate right and left of a subject noun phrase, as illustrated in (10).[4]

(10)   Har **möjligen** <u>nogon student</u> **inte** läst boken?   (Swedish)
       has possibly any student not read the book

Thus, whatever specifier position the subject occupies, it must be possible for an adverbial phrase to adjoin to categories on both sides of that position, and therefore the subject in (9a) and the subject in (9b) might very well occupy

(i) a. ...om/at <u>Ola</u> **kanskje** kan korrigere feilen (på to dagar)
         ...if/that Ola maybe can correct the error (in two days)

     b. ...om/at **kanskje** <u>Ola</u> kan korrigere feilen (på to dagar)
         ...if/that maybe Ola can correct the error (in two days)

However, in contrast to main clauses like (7) and (8), the b-version type, where the SA occurs to the left of the subject, is often somewhat degraded in embedded clauses. I have no explanation of this fact, which must be due to some intervening factor. It suffices for my purposes that both orders subject + SA and SA + subject are attested at least in some main and embedded clauses.

   [4] I assume that the negation element is an SA in both Norwegian and Swedish in contrast to e.g. English where it originates in NegP, cf. Helgå (2008).

the same specifier position.[5] Comparable data exists corresponding to the Norwegian (7) and (8), cf. (11).

(11)   a.   Feilen korrigerte **derfor** <u>Ola</u> **truleg** (for to dagar sidan).
            the error corrected therefore Ola probably (two days ago)

       b.   Feilen kan **truleg** <u>Ola</u> **kanskje** korrigere (på to dagar).
            the error can probably Ola maybe correct (in two days)

Given my assumptions thus far, the data discussed in this subsection indicate that an SA in Norwegian may be adjoined either to T' or to TP, thus being able to occur on either side of a subject in <Spec, TP>. However, adopting pair-merge and a 3D analysis, a more interesting interpretation of the data is possible.

2.2.2 *A 3D analysis of Norwegian SAs*

Many linguists have observed that the distribution of adjuncts tends to be more flexible than the distribution of arguments. For instance, Boeckx (2008: 100) mentions the more 'flexible mode of attachment' that adjuncts show as compared to non-adjuncts. Also, Keyser (1968) made a similar observation four decades ago. He proposed a special Transportability Convention applying to adverbials, which 'permits a particular constituent to occupy any position in a derived tree so long as the sister relationships with all other nodes in the tree are maintained' (op. cit.: 368). Thus, whereas the transportability property allows for variation in the first place, the range of the variation is restricted by the fact that the constituent is attached to a fixed category type.

Taking Keyser's general idea of constrained flexibility as a point of departure, I will first assume that the fixed category an SA is attached to is TP. Thus, I assume that TP licenses an SA, which is a reasonable assumption given that T may be said to facilitate the temporal anchoring of the situation described by the clause. Adopting Chomsky's notion of pair-merge, I further assume that the adverbial is pair-merged with TP, which means that the adverbial is merged on another plane as compared to the basic CP + TP + vP + VP structure. In other words, the adverbial is merged in a third dimension as compared to the rest of the structure. Thus, an essential consequence of

---

[5] As pointed out by an anonymous reviewer, it is of course possible that there are *both* multiple subject positions *and* multiple positions where an SA can be adjoined, but in the absence of compelling evidence to the contrary, I will assume the more restrictive hypothesis that there is only one designated subject position outside the verb phrase, namely the <Spec, TP> position. Still, the analysis I am going to propose should be able to accommodate the assumption of two (or more) designated subject positions outside the verb phrase, *mutatis mutandis*.

pair-merge is that adverbials originate on a z-axis in a 3D phrase-structure system, i.e. beyond the 2D plane defined by the x-axis and the y-axis of the basic CP + TP + vP + VP structure. The 3D system is illustrated in (12), where the subject, TP, and T′ are nodes in the plane, with SA being added on the z-axis in the third dimension.

(12)

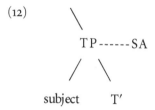

Crucially, I assume that, in the initial cognitive representation of a string, a z-axis node is not ordered as to precedence in relation to the node it is attached to or in relation to nodes dominated by that node. Thus, in (12) the SA is not ordered w.r.t. the other nodes given. However, the 3D representations are representations of strings of leaves that are eventually ordered linearly, since they must be produced/perceived by the speaker/hearer in linear time. Therefore, there are at the outset exactly three possibilities for the eventual linear ordering of the nodes in (12), namely (13a, b, c).

(13)   a. subject < SA < T′   b. SA < subject < T′   c. subject < T′ < SA

To use a metaphor, I will refer to the process of ordering z-axis elements with elements in the 2D plane as 'bending'. Thus, the adverbial phrase is either bent downward, to the left, or to the right, illustrated in (13a, b, c), respectively. In other words, in this 3D system Keyser's transportability effect is explained as bending of a 3D z-axis element into the 2D plane. It is at the outset expected that an adverbial may occupy any of the various positions that bending allows for. This seems in fact to be the case. (13a) is exemplified by (7a) or (8a), (13b) by (7b) or (8b), and (13c) by extraposition structures as e.g. in (2b) or (3b).

Thus far, it seems that bending gets the ordering facts pertaining to Norwegian SAs right, but what exactly is bending? First, I assume that the bending process itself is not part of the feature-regulated merging system of the basic CP + TP + vP + VP structure, cf. also Boeckx (2008: 100–1): '...adjunction does not involve any featural transaction of the *Agree/* checking sort...'. In fact, assuming that it is part of the nature of the 2D CP + TP + vP + VP structure to be formed by feature-regulated Merge and Move, the 3D-attached elements could be exactly those that are *not* introduced into the structure by feature-regulated Merge or Move, but are introduced in a 'looser' manner as z-axis elements in a third dimension.

Next, if an SA is attached to TP on a z-axis before bending, what is the phrase-structural status of SA after bending, and where during the derivation does bending take place? Let's first try to find out what kind of configuration might be the output of bending. Chomsky (2004: 118–19) assumes that the pair-merged structures are eventually turned into set-merged structures at Spell-Out. In Chomsky's words: 'α of <α, β> is integrated into the primary plane' (Chomsky 2004: 119). Adopting this idea, I will depict the result of integration into the primary plane as traditional adjunction structures, as illustrated in (14). Given economy, I further assume that adjunction is to a licensing phrasal category (TP or T') which is configurationally local relative to the initial attachment category, i.e. TP. This formulation constrains bending so that a z-axis element cannot be adjoined to *any* phrasal category, and it excludes that the adjunction structures that result from bending have crossing branches. Thus, downward bending can only result in left-adjunction to T' in (14a); leftward bending can only result in left-adjunction to TP in (14b); and rightward bending can only result in right-adjunction to TP in (14c), or in right-adjunction to T' (not shown). Notice that the notion of adjunction adopted here is quite simple. The term just denotes the phrase-structural status of 3D constituents after bending into the 2D plane.

(14)   a.   b.   c.

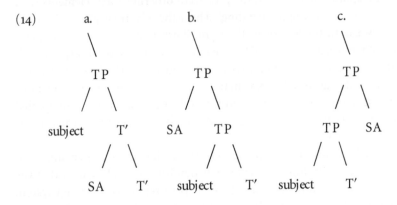

Now, where during the derivation does the bending and adjunction operation of the 3D to 2D conversion take place? It is tempting to argue that since linearization is a precondition for (linear) pronunciation, 3D to 2D conversion must take place in the phonological component, i.e. after Spell-Out. However, this doesn't necessarily follow, since phonological linearization is also compatible with 3D to 2D conversion taking place *before* Spell-Out. I will show later (in section 2.2.4) that articulated hierarchical representations like those depicted in (14) are projected into the semantic component, where they form a configurational basis for the interpretation of scope. Thus, it seems that 3D to 2D conversion is required to take place before Spell-Out, since bending into the plane is a condition both for the phonological and semantic interpretation of adverbials. However, instead of construing 3D to 2D conversion as a pre-Spell-Out operation, I suggest that Spell-Out should be construed as an integral part of 3D to 2D conversion (or vice versa). Therefore, at the point of 3D to 2D conversion, the derivation is handed over to the phonological component (Spell-Out) and the semantic component, respectively. As a result, SAs are linearized in the phonological component and get scope interpretations in the semantic component. We will see some of the ramifications of these assumptions in subsequent sections.

2.2.3 *SAs and the distribution of weak pronouns*

It might not be immediately clear that the 3D analysis that I have proposed above is better than a traditional adjunction analysis. Therefore, I will now present some independent evidence for the 3D analysis. However, before I present the evidence, notice that the 3D analysis has an edge over a traditional adjunction analysis at the outset, since an adjunction analysis must stipulate several adjunction nodes as well as adjunction directions, whereas on the 3D analysis the possible adjunction nodes and adjunction directions follow in a more principled way, as a consequence of bending given initial attachment to TP.

Consider now the data in (15), where (15b, c) illustrate the behavior of weak object pronouns in Norwegian. As can be seen by comparing (15a) and (15c), the weak object pronoun is displaced as compared to the full noun phrase object.

(15) a. Ola korrigerte **truleg** <u>feilen</u> i dag.
          Ola corrected probably the error today

      b. *Ola korrigerte **truleg'<u>n</u>** i dag.
          Ola corrected probably it$_{clitic}$ today

      c. Ola korrigerte'<u>n</u> **truleg** i dag.
          Ola corrected it$_{clitic}$ probably today

If the clause contains an auxiliary verb, the weak object pronoun must cliticize to the main verb and there is no linear displacement as compared to the full object phrase, cf. (16).

(16)   a.   Ola kan **truleg** korrigere <u>feilen</u> i dag.
            Ola can probably correct the error today

     b.   *Ola kan'<u>n</u> **truleg** korrigere i dag.
            Ola can it$_{clitic}$ probably correct today

     c.   Ola kan **truleg** korrigere'<u>n</u> i dag.
            Ola can probably correct it$_{clitic}$ today

According to some linguists, weak object pronouns in Mainland Scandinavian (including Norwegian) should be explained in the same way as object shift of full object phrases as found in Icelandic, see e.g. Holmberg (1993). However, such an analysis has some conceptual and empirical drawbacks, some of which are pointed out in Hellan (1994). To mention only one empirical drawback (not mentioned by Hellan), Holmberg (1993) construes the displacement of the weak pronoun in a clause like (15c) as obligatory movement of the weak pronoun to <Spec, AgrOP> (in his analysis), assuming the adverbial to be adjoined to VP. However, in face of data like (17), it must also be assumed that SAs may adjoin to TP as well as to VP (given Holmberg's assumptions).

(17)   I dag har **truleg** Ola korrigert feilen.
       today has probably Ola corrected the error

But then it is predicted that a weak object pronoun should manage to occur to the right of an adverbial adjoined to TP, and clauses like (15b) are therefore wrongly predicted to be grammatical.

Although there are some quite striking parallels between the displacement of weak object pronouns in Mainland Scandinavian and the shift of full noun phrase objects in Icelandic, I take it that Bobaljik and Jonas (1996: 207) are correct in assuming that movement of weak pronouns is distinct from the movement called object shift: 'We will thus further restrict the use of the technical term *object shift* [...], excluding A-movement of (weak) pronominals as a distinct process', see also Erteschik-Shir (2005a) for a partly similar view. Furthermore, I will follow Hellan (1994) (and others) in analyzing weak pronouns as *simple clitics* basically in the sense of Zwicky (1977).

In fact, the descriptive generalization seems to be that a weak pronoun in Norwegian must form a prosodic unit together with some other phonetically realized host adjacent (typically left-adjacent) to it, where that host may be an element belonging to any category (verb, noun, adjective, preposition, complementizer, etc.), as long as it is *not* an adverbial (cf. also Holmberg and Platzack 1995: 165). This is illustrated in (15), (16), and (18) for weak *object* pronouns (cliticization to the verb in the first two examples and to the subject noun phrase in the last example). (19) shows that weak *subject* pronouns behave in a similar fashion, i.e. it is obligatorily a clitic on the finite verb in C, not on the SA, even though a full subject phrase may occur to the right of the SA.

(18) a. I dag korrigerte Ola **truleg** <u>feilen</u>.
          today corrected Ola probably the error

      b. *I dag korrigerte Ola **truleg'<u>n</u>**.
          today corrected Ola probably it$_{clitic}$

      c. I dag korrigerte Ola'<u>n</u> **truleg**.
          today corrected Ola it$_{clitic}$ probably

(19) a. I dag kan <u>Ola</u> **truleg** korrigere feilen.
          today can Ola probably correct the error

      b. I dag kan **truleg** <u>Ola</u> korrigere feilen.
          today can probably Ola correct the error

      c. I dag kan'<u>n</u> **truleg** korrigere feilen.
          today can he$_{clitic}$ probably correct the error

      d. *I dag kan **truleg'<u>n</u>** korrigere feilen.
          today can probably he$_{clitic}$ correct the error

In all these cases, cliticization ignores the adverbial.[6] Given mainstream analyses, this exceptional role of adverbials constitutes virtually

---

[6] Cliticization to adjective, preposition, and complementizer is illustrated in (i)–(iii), respectively.

(i)   Han er redd'n.
      he is afraid + clitic

(ii) Han ser på'n.
      he looks at + clitic

(iii) a. ...at'n truleg korrigerte feilen.
          ...that + clitic probably corrected the error

      b. *...at truleg'n korrigerte feilen
          ...that probably + clitic corrected the error

I'm assuming that predicative adjectives as in (i) are part of the initial 2D representation, cf. the non-distinction between verbs and predicative adjectives in many languages. On the other hand, attributive adjectives seem to be adjunctlike, and they are probably introduced as 3D elements. I know of no way of testing the interaction of attributive adjectives and weak pronouns in Norwegian.

the only reason for *not* analyzing weak pronouns as simple clitics, i.e. as clitics leaning onto an adjacent host, which would be an extremely plain analysis, and therefore an attractive one, were it not for the adverbials.

Now, the virtue of the 3D approach is of course that it provides a framework for assigning the desired exceptional role to adverbials, so that a simple clitic analysis of weak pronouns may be maintained. Assuming that cliticization of weak pronouns is a pre-bending process, adverbials are effectively made 'invisible' for cliticization, as desired. Notice that if cliticization of weak pronouns is a pre-bending process, the restrictions that govern that type of cliticization are of a syntactic nature. Still, the actual prosodic integration of weak pronouns with their hosts may very well take place in the phonological component. Thus, I assume that syntactic cliticization juxtaposes the weak pronoun (marked as a clitic) and its host in the syntax, and the juxtaposed unit receives its appropriate prosody in the phonological component. In other words, cliticization as a syntactic process takes place before 3D to 2D conversion and the concomitant bending and adjunction of 3D elements into the structure, and therefore 3D elements are invisible for the cliticization process. Thus, the 3D approach facilitates a simple clitic analysis of weak pronouns. The simplicity of the analysis in turn lends strong support to the very assumption of a 3D construal of adverbials. Notice that the reasoning here is in relevant respects parallel to Chomsky's reasoning regarding (1). In both cases the 3D or pair-merged constituents are invisible to operations on the 2D plane.

To conclude, notice that a traditional adjunct analysis of adverbials or an analysis like that proposed in Cinque (1999) would have to stipulate that adverbials are invisible to cliticization of weak pronouns. On the other hand, given the 3D analysis, the distribution and displacement of weak pronouns follow immediately on a simple clitic analysis. Therefore, a 3D analysis is preferable to the other analyses.

2.2.4 *SAs, multiple attachment, scope, and interpretation*

There is no principled phrase-structural limitation as to the number of SAs that can be attached simultaneously to a given TP node as z-axis elements. If more than one SA is attached, it is predicted at the outset that any of those SAs can be bent in any direction, giving rise to many different word-order variants. Multiple SAs with absolutely no ordering restrictions are hard or impossible to find. The examples in (20) present one possible case where any ordering of the two SAs is more or less equally good (see also

Østbø 2003: 83). However, there are obscure differences in interpretation and felicitousness that seem to correlate both with word order and intonation.

(20) a. Slike feil korrigerer **kanskje** Ola **vanlegvis** (på to dagar).
such errors corrects maybe Ola usually (in two days ago)

b. Slike feil korrigerer **vanlegvis** Ola **kanskje** (på to dagar).

c. Slike feil korrigerer **kanskje vanlegvis** Ola (på to dagar).

d. Slike feil korrigerer Ola **kanskje vanlegvis** (på to dagar).

e. Slike feil korrigerer **vanlegvis kanskje** Ola (på to dagar).

f. Slike feil korrigerer Ola **vanlegvis kanskje** (på to dagar).

Usually, when two (or more) SAs occur in the same sentence, there are ordering restrictions among them, sometimes weaker, sometimes stronger; see Østbø (2003) for an investigation based on Norwegian data. The fact that some SA orders are more natural than others, should probably be explained as an effect of co-occurrence restrictions among semantic types of SAs, see Ernst (2002) for a detailed analysis.

There is also reason to believe that scope properties resulting from configurational architecture play a role in the interpretation of SAs. Recall that the 3D representations are transformed and projected into the semantic component as 2D adjunction structures, which means that bending in different directions results in the SAs being adjoined to TP or T' (see section 2.2.2). Thus, scope relations between the SAs are expected to exist. For instance, an SA preceding a subject noun phrase is adjoined to TP and will end up higher in the structure than an SA immediately following the subject, which is adjoined to T'. It is therefore predicted that the former has scope over the latter. This prediction seems to be correct. Thus, (21a) means that it is almost the case that Jon always has disliked books, whereas (21b) means that it has always been the case that Jon almost has disliked books.

(21) a. Bøker har **nesten** Jon **alltid** mislikt.
books has almost Jon always disliked

b. Bøker har **alltid** Jon **nesten** mislikt.
books has always Jon almost disliked

Furthermore, it is predicted that it should be possible for a rightward-bent SA to have scope over a downward-bent SA immediately following the subject. This is so since the downward-bent SA must be left-adjoined to T', whereas the rightward-bent SA may be right-adjoined to TP. Thus, the latter has scope over the former. This prediction also seems to be correct, cf. (22).

(22) a. Bøker har <u>Jon</u> **nesten** mislikt, **alltid.**
          books has Jon almost disliked, always

      b. Bøker har <u>Jon</u> **alltid** mislikt, **nesten.**
          books has Jon always disliked, almost

(22a) means the same as (21b), whereas (22b) means the same as (21a).

These readings are directly predicted by the analysis proposed here, on the assumption that bending of z-axis elements into the 2D plane and subsequent adjunction is not just part of Spell-Out, affecting only the phonological component. Actually, the data presented above support the claim made in section 2.2.2 that both bending/adjunction and Spell-Out are essential aspects of 3D to 2D conversion with consequences both in the phonological component (linearization) and in the semantic component where the hierarchical adjunct structures receive scope interpretations.

Two points should be noticed here. First, the data discussed above constitute further evidence for the 3D analysis of adverbials. This is so since the mirror effects shown in (21) and (22) are directly predicted on the 3D analysis (see Barbiers 1995: 102 ff. for a similar mirror effect in Dutch). Second, the claim that adjunction resulting from bending has semantic scope effects seems to be at odds with the claim by Chomsky referred to in the introduction to the effect that 3D elements are invisible to binding. If both scope interpretation and binding take place in the semantic component, both phenomena should relate to 3D elements in comparable ways, i.e. both should either ignore or be sensitive to 3D elements, depending on assumptions about where in the derivation bending takes place. However, I hypothesize that binding relations are determined instantly, i.e. once the appropriate configurations are brought into existence (e.g. as a result of movement), which means that the particular binding relations involved in Chomsky's example are resolved in the syntax, i.e. in the 2D representation before the 3D elements are integrated into the plane. Thus, binding ignores 3D elements, while at the same time semantic scope relations can exist among adverbials having been adjoined into the 2D plane as a result of bending.

2.3 Lower adverbials as 3D phrases

I have been arguing that SAs are pair-merged to TP resulting in attachment in a third dimension as compared to the 2D structure of the basic clause. I will refer to such adverbials as higher adverbials. In this section, I will tentatively argue that

VP is the attachment point for pair-merge of so-called predicate adverbials, which I will refer to as lower adverbials. In other words, I will argue that both higher and lower adverbials are attached in a third dimension. Like the 3D higher adverbials, I assume that the 3D lower adverbials are subsequently integrated into the 2D plane, facilitating linear pronunciation and scope interpretation.

Before I discuss the relevant data, I want to point out that I do not assume a rigid partition between higher and lower adverbials in the sense that some individual adverbials or adverbial types are always of the higher type and others always of the lower type. Many individual phrases can be used equally well as a higher or lower adverbial, whereas others show different degrees of preference for one of the attachment nodes. Thus, even an adverbial normally used as a higher adverbial may be attached as a lower adverbial and vice versa (with interpretation varying accordingly). Still, some adverbials show a quite strong preference for only one of the two attachment nodes.

2.3.1 *Lower adverbials and active vs passive participles*

Consider the contrasts in (23) and (24), where the a-versions are active and the b-versions are passive.

(23) a. *Han har **grundig** lurt tanta mi.
          he has thoroughly fooled my aunt

      b. Tanta mi vart **grundig** lurt.
          my aunt was thoroughly fooled

(24) a. *Han skal ha **ofte** fornærma tanta mi.
          he shall have often offended my aunt

      b. Tanta mi har blitt **ofte** fornærma.
          my aunt has been often offended

These contrasts show that a lower adverbial may occur to the left of the participle if it is a passive participle (the b-versions), but not if it is an active participle (the a-versions). Notice that *grundig* 'thoroughly' in (23) is not easily analyzed as a higher adverbial. If it were, (23a) would have been grammatical since it occurs immediately after the V2 position, i.e. in a position where it could have been analyzed as attached to TP if it could in principle be used as a higher adverbial. On the other hand, *ofte* 'often' is easily used both as a higher and lower adverbial, but in (24) it can only be interpreted as a lower adverbial since it is too far down to be possibly analyzed as attached to TP.

As to other distributional possibilities, *grundig* 'thoroughly' in (23) can be positioned immediately to the right of the object, but not between the verb and its object, cf. (25). *Ofte* 'often' in (24) shows a comparable distribution, cf. (26).

(25)   a.   Han har lurt tanta mi **grundig**.
            he has fooled my aunt thoroughly

     b.   *Han har lurt **grundig** tanta mi.
            he has fooled thoroughly my aunt

     c.   Tanta mi vart lurt **grundig**.
            my aunt was fooled thoroughly

(26)   a.   Han skal ha fornærma tanta mi **ofte**.
            he shall have offended my aunt often

     b.   *Han skal ha fornærma **ofte** tanta mi.
            he shall have offended often my aunt

     c.   Tanta mi har blitt fornærma **ofte**.
            my aunt has been offended often

The crucial observation that can be made on the basis of the above data is that a lower adverbial may occur on both sides of a passive participle, but only to the right of an active participle.

Now, this puzzling fact can be explained on the assumption that lower adverbials are 3D elements attached to VP. Assuming the verb phrase to consist of vP + VP, the passive facts are explained if the passive participle does not move out of VP, which is quite reasonable on the assumption that an abstract passive morpheme (PASS) occupies the v head of vP so that V to v raising does not happen. Bending of the adverbial will then take place to the left or right, producing the b-versions in (23) and (24), or the c-versions in (25) and (26). The partial pre-bending structure of (23b)/(25c) is shown in (27).

(27)

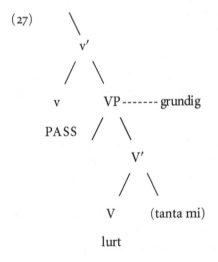

Consider now the active version, where the adverbial can only occur to the right of the participle. Assuming that active participles undergo V to v raising, an adverbial attached to VP will end up to the right of the participle irrespective of the direction of bending. That an active participle should raise to v seems natural given that no passive morpheme occupies the v head position.[7] A partial structure of the relevant configuration is shown in (28).

(28)

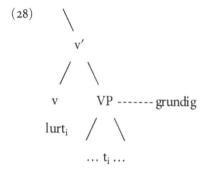

Given V to v raising of the active participle as depicted in (28), it is easily seen that the adverbial must occur to the right of the participle on any of the bending options.

However, there is one serious problem with this account. Recall that a lower adverbial is not permitted to occur between a verb and its object, as seen for instance in the b-versions in (25) and (26). Unfortunately, precisely that possibility is allowed by the analysis sketched in (28). This is so since the object remains in VP even though the participle is raised. Therefore leftward or downward bending would wrongly result in the adverbial intervening between the participle and its object.

Now, there is reason to believe that leftward and downward bending are excluded for independent reasons in configurations like (28). Specifically, I claim that there is a restriction that prohibits that an adverbial is enveloped by a verbal chain sequence whose head is in a position lower than C. Thus, the adverbial cannot be bent from VP to the left or downward in (28), because that would mean that the adverbial would be enveloped by the v + V chain. Therefore, only rightward bending is available. Since there is no corresponding

---

[7] It is tempting to speculate if it would be possible to relate the proposed raising difference between active and passive participles to thematic properties of <Spec, vP> since in active structures, the <Spec, vP> position is typically a thematic position, whereas it is always de-thematized in passives, see Pollock (1989) and Bowers (1993), where analyses making verb movement dependent on thematic properties are proposed.

v + V chain in (27), leftward, downward, or rightward bending can take place there.

The restriction prohibiting an adverbial being enveloped by a verbal chain has a stipulative flavor as it stands, and at present I cannot provide any knockdown independent evidence for this restriction. However, it should be understood as a restriction against adverbials breaking up (possibly extended) head–complement relations, which seems natural enough. In any case, it turns out that the restriction against enveloping proposed above gets additional support by being extended to another empirical domain, as I will show in the next section.

2.3.2 *Lower adverbials and indirect objects*

Consider object-shift phenomena involving full noun phrases. Usually, Icelandic is used to illustrate this type of object shift. However, it appears that something resembling object shift with a full noun phrase is also found in Mainland Scandinavian, notably in Norwegian and some varieties of Swedish, but then only with *indirect* objects. This phenomenon is discussed in Holmberg and Platzack (1995: 172), where the pair in (29) is given.[8] (30) shows an additional example.

(29) a. Jeg viser <u>gjestene</u> **gjerne** mine bilder.
          I show the guests gladly my pictures

      b. Jeg viser **gjerne** <u>gjestene</u> mine bilder.
          I show gladly the guests my pictures

(30) a. Eg gir <u>gjestene</u> **ofte** nokre bilde.
          I give the guests often some pictures

      b. Eg gir **ofte** <u>gjestene</u> nokre bilde.
          I give often the guests some pictures

These data are strikingly similar to the data in (7) and (8), where it was shown that an adverbial may occur on both sides of the subject. The data above show that an adverbial may occur on both sides of an indirect object as well.

Assuming that indirect objects are generated in <Spec, VP> in a vP + VP structure (cf. Åfarli 2008), these data are in fact predicted by my analysis, on the assumption that the adverbials in question are of the lower type. The

---

[8] (29) is written in the Norwegian *Bokmål* orthography, in contrast to all the other Norwegian example sentences in this paper, which are given in the *Nynorsk* orthography.

representation in (31) of the relevant partial structure of (30) indicates how
the analysis explains the data.

(31)

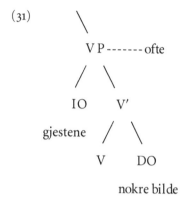

If the adverbial is bent downward, we get (30a), and if it is bent leftward, we get
(30b). Moreover, if the adverbial is bent rightward, we get the grammatical (32).

(32) Eg gir gjestene nokre bilde **ofte**.
      I give the guests some pictures often

Given that lower adverbials attached to VP are 3D elements, it is predicted
that indirect objects that are weak pronouns will ignore the adverbial. This
prediction is also correct, cf. the contrast in (33).

(33) a. Eg gir <u>dei</u> **ofte** nokre bilde.
          I give them_clitic often some pictures
      b. *Eg gir **ofte** <u>dei</u> nokre bilde.
          I give often them_clitic some pictures

As expected, the weak pronoun indirect object cannot occur to the right of the
adverbial, even though the corresponding full noun phrase indirect object
can, as shown in (30b). This fact strongly supports the claim that lower
adverbials are 3D elements, according to the reasoning in section 2.2.3.

   Notice that most speakers find that the b-versions in (29) and (30) are
slightly better than the a-versions. The reason for this is that the adverbial to
the left of the indirect object may not only be analyzed as a VP-attached lower
adverbial that has been bent leftward. It can also be analyzed as a TP-attached
higher adverbial that has been bent downward or leftward. For many individual adverbials the latter option is preferable. Thus, even though a typical
higher adverbial like *muligens* 'probably' can also be used as a lower adverbial

to some degree, most speakers clearly prefer to treat it as a higher adverbial, so that (34b) will in general be judged as better than (34a).

(34)   a.   Eg gir <u>gjestene</u> **muligens** nokre bilde.
             I give the guests probably some pictures

        b.   Eg gir **muligens** <u>gjestene</u> nokre bilde.
             I give probably the guests some pictures

In the examples shown in this subsection, the verb raises all the way to C, from V via v and T, so bending leftward or downward is permitted both for VP-attached and TP-attached adverbials. Recall that leftward and downward bending is only prohibited if the adverbial is enveloped by a verbal chain whose head is *not* in C. That means that a TP-attached adverbial will *never* be enveloped by a verbal chain in such a way that leftward or downward bending is prohibited. If the verb raises only to T (embedded clauses), the area to the left of the T-projection is not enveloped by a verbal chain so leftward or downward bending can take place, and if the verb moves to C (main clauses), the link between T and C doesn't count as an enveloping chain of the prohibitive sort. However, a VP-attached adverbial bent leftward or downward will be enveloped by a prohibitive verbal chain if the verb raises to v or to T, and not higher. We will see in the next subsection what happens to bending of a VP-attached adverbial in such cases.

2.3.3 *Holmberg's generalization*

Holmberg's Generalization captures the fact that the object-shift phenomenon seems to be dependent upon raising of the main verb to C. Thus, object shift involving the direct object in Icelandic is not found in structures with both auxiliary and main verb, i.e. in cases where the main verb has *not* moved out of the verb phrase. I hypothesize that this illustrates the prohibition against adverbials being enveloped by a verbal chain whose head is not in C. In other words, I assume that object shift is not a consequence of movement of the object, but rather of the flexibility of the adverbial resulting from bending.[9] I will not go into (so-called) object shift in Icelandic here. Rather, I will consider Holmberg's Generalization in relation to object shift of indirect objects in Norwegian as discussed in the previous subsection.

---

[9] This suggests that the so-called shifted object is an argument in an A-position. Regarding the A- versus A′-movement discussion about object shift, this is compatible with the conclusion of most linguists that Scandinavian object shift seems to have more A-movement properties than A′-properties, cf. Thráinsson (2001: 180). This is in line with my analysis, except for the movement part.

Even though object shift of an indirect object is possible in simple clauses like (29) and (30) given earlier, it becomes impossible when an auxiliary verb is added, as seen in (35).

(35) a. *Eg vil gi <u>gjestene</u> **ofte** nokre bilde.
          I will give the guests often some pictures

    b. *Eg vil gi **ofte** <u>gjestene</u> nokre bilde.
          I will give often the guests some pictures

In both cases the main verb moves from V to v and stops there, so that a prohibitive verbal chain is brought into existence. Thus, the adverbial attached to VP is enveloped by a chain sequence whose head is not in C, and the adverbial cannot be bent in the directions that would produce (35a, b).

Now, consider embedded clauses with just a main verb (i.e. with no auxiliary verb). In Mainland Scandinavian the finite verb does not move to C in embedded clauses, C being empty or filled by a complementizer. Suppose the finite verb moves to the head of T. Then, in Mainland Scandinavian embedded clauses, VP is always enveloped by a verbal chain sequence whose head is not in C, and consequently a VP-attached adverbial can never be bent to the left or downward in an embedded clause. On the other hand, the TP is not enveloped by any prohibitive chain sequence at all in embedded clauses, and TP-attached adverbials may be bent leftward or downward. This correctly predicts the grammaticality judgments in (36).

(36) a. ...at eg **ofte** gir <u>gjestene</u> nokre bilde.
          ...that I often give the guests some pictures

    b. *...at eg gir **ofte** <u>gjestene</u> nokre bilde.
          ...that I give often the guests some pictures

    c. *...at eg gir <u>gjestene</u> **ofte** nokre bilde.
          ...that I give the guests often some pictures

As can be seen, there is no adverbial flexibility around the indirect object here, even though there is no auxiliary verb.[10] In general, unlike what is the case in main clauses, it is correctly predicted that an adverbial never occurs to the right of the finite verb in embedded clause, unless the adverbial is bent to the right, of course.

---

[10] The judgment is for the embedded clause word order; notice that main clause word order is sometimes possible in that-clauses, in which case (36b, c) would be grammatical with the adverbial analyzed as attached to TP or VP, and with the finite verb in the (lower) C-position, creating no prohibitive verbal chain.

2.3.4 *A paradox*

It was seen in subsection 2.3.1 that a lower adverbial may occur on both sides of a passive participle, but only to the right of an active particple, cf. (37) and (38), respectively.

(37) a. Han skal ha blitt **ofte** slått.
           he shall have been often beaten

      b. Han skal ha blitt slått **ofte**.
           he shall have been beaten often

(38) a. *Han skal ha **ofte** slått.
           he shall have often beaten

      b. Han skal ha slått **ofte**.
           he shall have beaten often

This difference was explained by assuming that the active participle is raised from V to v, whereas the passive participle remains in V.

I have been assuming that indirect objects are situated in <Spec, VP>. Therefore, assuming that passive participles remain in V, it is predicted that an indirect object will precede a passive participle. However, that prediction is not correct, cf. (39).

(39) a. Det vart gitt gjestene nokre bilde
           it was given the guests some pictures

      b. *Det vart gjestene gitt nokre bilde.
           it was the guests given some pictures

What is shown by (39) is that a passive participle is raised from V to v, just like active participles. In other words, we are faced with the following paradox: The earlier data show that passive participles do not raise from V to v, whereas the data in (39) show that they do.

This paradox is solved if passive participles are raised just in case the structure contains an indirect object. My hypothesis is that the presence of the indirect object triggers raising of a passive participle for licensing purposes (the exact nature of the licensing at work will not be investigated here). The data in (40) indicate that this hypothesis may be correct. Notice that the adverbial cannot be analyzed as a TP-attached higher adverbial in any of the examples in (40) since it is too far down in the verb sequence.

(40) a. Det har blitt **ofte** gitt nokre bilde
           it has been often given some pictures

b. *Det har blitt **ofte** gjestene gitt nokre bilde
    it has been often the guests given some pictures

c. *Det har blitt gjestene **ofte** gitt nokre bilde
    it has been the guests often given some pictures

d. *Det har blitt gitt **ofte** gjestene nokre bilde
    it has been given often the guests some pictures

e. *Det har blitt gitt gjestene **ofte** nokre bilde
    it has been given the guests often some pictures

(40a) has no indirect object, therefore the passive participle is not raised, and the VP-attached adverbial may be bent leftward/downward (no prohibitive verbal chain is created). (40b, c) are ungrammatical because the indirect object has not been licensed, since the passive participle has not been raised, as witnessed by the word order. (40d, e) are ungrammatical even though the indirect object is licensed through the raising of the passive participle, because the raising has created an enveloping verbal chain, thus excluding that the adverbial can be bent leftward/downward, as it must have been given the word order.

2.4 Conclusion and further research

The distributional flexibility shown by adverbials has been explained by assuming a 3D phrase structure, where adverbials originate in the third dimension and are eventually bent in different directions into the 2D plane of the basic CP + TP + vP + VP structure. Apart from the flexibility itself, an important type of motivation for this proposal was that cliticization is blind to the presence of adverbials, but sensitive to the presence of any other category. Bending of 3D constituents into the 2D plane means that the 3D constituent is linearized in relation to the constituents in the 2D plane, thus facilitating linear pronunciation (Spell-Out to the phonological component). Bending also means that 3D constituents are hierarchically ordered in adjunction structures, thus facilitating scope interpretation of the 3D constituents in the semantic component.

Notice that given their flexibility, the position of adverbials cannot be used as diagnosis of movement (of other constituents) to the extent that have been done in some accounts previously. However, the flexibility allowed by my analysis is nevertheless quite limited, and also both constrained and principled, so the position of adverbials can still be used to diagnose movement, given that due attention is paid to the constraints that obtain. This is an important result in my view, since adverbials have sometimes been used to diagnose movement without enough attention being paid to their flexibility.

It might be argued that a model that assumes that adverbials originate as 3D constituents that are eventually integrated into the overall phrase structure by adjunction is uneconomical. Why not assume adjunction in the first place, avoiding the 3D phase? My answer to that is that cognitive reality, to the extent that it can be hypothetically identified through the empirical data, seems to support the idea of 3D origin and eventual 2D integration of adverbials. An adjunction analysis would have been theoretically simpler, but at the same time it would have to resort to quite blatant stipulation e.g. to account for the restricted distributional flexibility that is observed, or to account for the peculiar interaction between adverbial distribution and the distribution of weak pronouns. The 3D-analysis provides a more principled approach.

I want to emphasize that the 3D-analysis is intended as a *basis* for explanation, and I think the motivation for that basis is fairly convincing. However, constituting a basis for explanation implies that various factors may intervene to blur the data, a phenomenon that is not uncommon, especially as regards adverbials, it seems. The properties of such intervening factors have scarcely been discussed in this exploratory article, but they constitute an important theme for future research, as do further investigation of the theoretical status of 3D representations and what I have metaphorically referred to as bending.

3

The phonology of adverb placement, object shift, and V2: The case of Danish 'MON'*

NOMI ERTESCHIK-SHIR

3.1 Introduction

A prominent topic among researchers of Germanic languages in particular is the availability of main clause word order (verb second) in subordinate clauses and the conditions that license it.[1] The Danish illocutionary particle MON presents the opposite problem: When it appears sentence-initially in main clauses, the sentence presents with subordinate clause word order, i.e., the verb does not appear in second position. I argue that this follows from an implicit main clause representing the particular illocutionary force associated with MON.

The paper takes the following form. First I examine the illocutionary properties of MON and show its similarity with German 'ob' described in Truckenbrodt (2006b). I proceed to examine the syntax of MON (which differs totally from that of the complementizer 'ob'). I then propose an account in which both V2 and the position of MON in the sentence are accounted for at the Articulatory–Perceptual Interface. I also propose a theory of speech acts which interacts with this interface.

* The research for this work was funded by the Israel Science Foundation Grant No. 1012/03. I thank Anita Mittwoch, Lisa Rochman, and the audience of the ZAS 2006 Workshop 'How to refer to one's own words: Performatives between grammar and pragmatics' for their helpful comments.

[1] See e.g. Meinunger (2005) and the references cited therein.

3.2 Speech acts

3.2.1 *The illocutionary force of MON*

Since the early days of performative theory, the syntactic embedding of clauses with illocutionary force and the constraints on such embedding has been a burning issue. Wechsler (1991) renewed the interest in this issue by showing that there is a correlation in Germanic languages between V2 and illocutionary force and that exactly those embedded clauses which allow V2 also function performatively. Truckenbrodt (2006b) is a recent addition to this discussion. He argues that the illocutionary force of V2 is "correlated with the presence of a specification of the *addressee* in the meaning of a sentence type:

(1)   'S wants (**from x**)$_1$ (that it is common ground)$_2$ that/whether....'
      'S wants that it is common ground that/whether....'"

According to Truckenbrodt, the most palpable effect of the presence of the addressee (x) in (1) is that it presupposes that x controls whether the proposition is true. V2 interrogatives are therefore predicted to presuppose that the addressee knows the true answer to the question.

Truckenbrodt tests this property of V2 interrogatives by comparison with the non-V2 interrogatives.[2] (2) shows that a V2 question is infelicitous in a context in which it is made clear that addressee does not know the answer.

(2)   Stefan: Ich hab seit Jahren nichts mehr von Peter gehört.
                'I haven't heard from Peter in years.'
      Heiner: Ich auch nicht.
                'Me neither.'
      Stefan: # Mag er immer noch kubanische Zigarren?
                'Does he still like Cuban cigars?'

Heiner's first sentence in (2) makes it clear that he knows nothing about Peter. Stefan's question to him therefore violates the requirement on V2 questions that the addressee (Heiner) control whether it becomes common ground whether Peter still likes Cuban cigars. Since this requirement is not fulfilled, the question is infelicitous.

Since non-V2 question do not have this requirement the sequence in (3) is unproblematic.

---

[2] I use V2 as a way of referring to raised V word order, even if the verb is in fact sentence-initial.

(3) Stefan: Ich hab seit Jahren nichts mehr von Peter gehört.
              'I haven't heard from Peter in years.'
     Heiner: Ich auch nicht.
              Me neither.'
     Stefan: Ob er immer noch kubanische Zigarren mag?
     Lit.:   'Whether he still likes Cuban cigars?'
              Interpretation ≈ 'I wonder whether he still likes Cuban cigars.'

Here Stefan's non-V2 question with 'ob' does not presuppose that the hearer
know the answer. Therefore the question is appropriate in the context given.
   The distinction between (2) and (3) also holds in Danish:

(4) Mon Peter kommer?
     mon Peter comes
     'Do you think Peter is coming?'

(5) *Mon du   kommer?
      mon you come?
     'Do you think you're coming?'

(6) Mon du når det?
     mon you reach it?
     'Do you think you'll make it?'

The difference between (4) and (5) is that the addressee is not assumed to
know whether *Peter* is coming but is assumed to know whether s/he herself is
coming.[3] In view of the fact that the addressee cannot know for sure whether
s/he will make it on time, the 'mon' question in (6) is fine. It follows that not
only does the question with 'mon' not presuppose that the addressee knows
the true answer to the question, as do V2 questions, this question type strictly
requires that the addressee NOT know the answer.

3.2.2 *Typing of speech acts*

I follow Brandner (2004: 1), who extends Cheng's (1991) notion of typing to
declaratives and argues 'that V-2 is a strategy to specify a FORCE value in an
explicit way' in languages which do not have typing particles. According to
Brandner, V2 languages mark every FORCE value, including the declarative,
(whereas in other languages the declarative is the default case). In such
languages the verb moves because of the need for FORCE specification and

---

[3] Although one cannot predict for sure whether one is going to make it on time, one can 'think' that
one will since a person has some control over an event concerning oneself. This is not the case,
however, for a third person.

the value is delivered by a subsequently moved constituent. If the moved constituent is a wh-phrase, the FORCE value will be interrogative; if a DP, it will be declarative. Brandner treats verb-initial structures as underspecified for FORCE. Their interpretation depends on intonation and discourse strategies. V-initial Yes-No questions, get their illocutionary force by its characteristic intonation and not by syntactic means.

Brandner distinguishes languages that encode FORCE values with lexical means via the insertion of a relevant particle. It seems though that Germanic languages can use both methods. When a particle is used, FORCE can be directly read off the particle. Brandner argues that the FORCE feature must have scope over all verbal projections. It follows that FORCE particles occur either at the left or at the right periphery of the clause.[4] MON is indeed (usually) initial.

What, then, does MON type? The dictionary entry in Becker-Christensen (1995) describes MON as an interrogative adverb. According to Allan et al. (1995), MON expresses strong uncertainty or doubt by the person who poses the question. It is usually translated as *I wonder,* but this translation does not reflect the request for an answer associated with it.[5] The closest translation is therefore *Do you think that X?* It seems, then the MON types a deliberative question.

MON can occur on its own as in (7):

(7)   A: Det går nok!
        It   goes PRT
        'It'll be OK'

      B: Mon?
        Really?

B's answer expresses that he is uncertain about A's assertion.

3.3 Syntax

The adverbial particle MON occurs sentence-initially with subordinate clause word order. In Danish, adverb position distinguishes main and subordinate clause word order. In main clauses adverbs follow the verb in second position, in subordinate clauses the adverb is positioned between the subject and the

---

[4] Both cases are attested.

[5] MON is a short version of 'monstro' which includes the verb 'tro' = believe. Like 'maybe', it can be seen as a main clause without a subject.

verb. The verb can therefore be seen not to be in second position. This is shown in

(8)   a.   Main Clause: S V Adv O

       b.   Subordinate Clause: ... S Adv V O

In (9) the adverb follows the subjects and precedes the verb. The initial MON blocks V2 and the sentence has the order of a subordinate clause as in (8b).

(9)   Mon han *stadigvæk* ryger   cigarer?
       mon he   still   smokes cigars
       'Do you think he still smokes cigars?'

Compare (9) to (10) and (11):

(10)   Ryger   han *stadigvæk* cigarer?
       smokes   he   still   cigars
       'Does he still smoke cigars?'

(11)   *Mon ryger han stadigvæk cigarer?

In the yes-no question in (10), inversion has raised the V to first position, but the position of the adverb is still that of main clauses if one assumes that inversion across an adverb is blocked.[6]

One explanation proposed for the lack of V2 in MON questions is that little words including MON are base-generated in C blocking V to C (e.g., Vikner 1995; Bayer 2004). This solution would be an elegant one, if it weren't the case that Spec,C cannot be filled in the presence of MON. One would expect the occurrence of topics and wh-phrases in Spec,C preceding MON, but in fact this position must remain empty as shown in (12a) and (12b).

(12)   a.   *Disse   cigarer mon   Peter ryger?
             These   cigars MON Peter smokes

       b.   *Hvilke cigarer mon   han   ryger?
             which cigars MON he   smokes

(12a) could be explained away as a conflict between topicalization and questioning, yet (12b) should then be perfect, especially in view of (13) in which the

---

[6] Traditional topological grammar positioned the verb in the second linear position. The first position (the German 'vorfeld') contains a variety of elements including topics, wh-elements, and may also be empty as in the case of yes-no questions. The initial position of the verb as in (10) is still considered to be V2, but with an empty first position. This is also reflected in generative theories in which the position of the V is raised to the same position in yes-no questions, as it is in V2 declaratives.

subject is questioned and the sentence with MON is fine and (14) which is identical to (12b) except that MON occurs sentence-finally:[7]

(13)   Hvem (mon)   kommer?
       Who   (MON)   comes
       'Who (MON) is coming?'

(14)   Hvilke cigarer ryger   han mon?
       Which cigars   smokes he   (MON)
       'Which cigars does he smoke (MON)'

The asymmetry between (12b), (13), and (14) will be examined below in section 3.4. Meanwhile, we can conclude that the lack of V2 with MON remains unexplained.

3.3.1 *V2 in Subordinate clauses—root phenomena*

According to Hooper and Thompson (1973), root clauses can be embedded under verbs which enable their interpretation as main assertions. Such clauses have the syntax of main clauses including the possibility of topicalization and V2. The existence of V2 in embedded clauses is a problem for syntactic analysis. The following Swedish and English examples are from Wechsler (1991). Wechsler shows that embedded V2 is optional in indirect assertions under verbs such as: *claim, report, assume, guess, imagine, believe.*

(15)   a.   Hugo påstod att [du aldrig *kommer* att läsa den här boken]

       b.   Hugo claimed that [you never *will* read this book]

(16)   a.   Hugo påstod att [du *kommer* aldrig att läsa den här boken]

       b.   Hugo claimed that [you *will* never read this book]

The examples in (15) have subordinate clause word order; those in (16) have V2. According to Wechsler, roots and non-roots have different syntax: Roots are CPs, whereas non-roots are simple S. Another approach to distinguishing V2 root complements from regular complements is to attach them in different syntactic positions (e.g., Reis 1997; McCloskey 2005; Meinunger 2006; Truckenbrodt 2006b).

We are now left with two opposite problems:

1. Accounting for V2 in certain embedded clauses
2. Accounting for non-V2 in direct MON questions

---

[7] I return to non-initial occurrences of MON in section 3.4.

Both questions relate to the relation between V2 and illocutionary force: Embedded V2 depends on whether the matrix verb allows the subordinate clause to have the force of the main assertion of the sentence and the lack of V2 order may have to do with the difference in illocutionary force between regular questions and MON questions.

3.3.2 *Speech-act theory and syntax*

Sigurðsson (2004) takes a somewhat radical position concerning the relationship between meaning and what is pronounced. According to Sigurðsson, UG features are radically universal: they are common to all languages and so are not selected. Languages differ, however, in what is pronounced. As a result, meaningful elements may not be pronounced and pronounced elements may be meaningless, i.e., languages demonstrate variability with respect to 'meaningful silence' and 'meaningless sounds'. Not only may features be silent in individual languages, there are also meaningful features that are silent in *all* languages. Sigurðsson introduces the *silence principle*:

(17)   Languages have meaningful silent features; any meaningful feature, 'formal' or not, may be non-prominent, hence silent.

According to Sigurðsson, any finite clause is computed in relation to a speech event, containing the speech participants (logophoric features Λ) and the time and location of speech (ST/L).

(18)   Speech Event ε {ST/L = Fin, $\{\Lambda_n, \Lambda_{n+1}, \ldots\}, \ldots\}$

That these speech-event elements are part of language is uncontroversial.

   But Sigurðsson argues that they belong to syntax since they have PF effects as illustrated in (19):

(19)   a.   He said to **me** that **he** loved **me**.

       b.   He said to **me**: 'I love **you**.'

Subordinate clauses (19a) have a secondary, anaphoric speech event; its speech features inherit their values from preceding elements which may be 'silent'. In (19b), the embedded Λ-features have 'shifted values': they are not identical with the silent matrix Λ-features but with the overt matrix arguments.

   It follows, according to Sigurðsson, that silent speech-event features *are* syntactically active, unless, of course, 'we want to say that pronominal reference (and temporal reference) are not decided in syntax.' Sigurðsson assigns the speech-event features an architecture along the lines of Rizzi (1997):

(20) $[_{CP} \Lambda_A \ldots$ Force .. Λ_P .. S_T .. S_L $[_{IP}$ ..Pers .. T..$[_{vP}$ ..E_T .. θ .. ..

For Sigurðsson, the speech-act features on the left periphery are silent.[8]

3.3.3 *Extending the approach to embedded V2*

Assume that the types of verbs that allow embedded V2 clauses (bridge verbs), are overt instantiations of FORCE and so the matrix of a V2 complement is an overt instantiation of the 'performative' speech-event features. V2 embedded clauses and matrix clauses would then differ only in that the performative matrix in the former is pronounced whereas it is silent in the latter. This would be a rather elegant way of unifying V2 in main and subordinate clauses. (V^* represents the class of verbs under discussion.):

(21)   a.   (I V you) [Main clause, V2]

     b.   I V^* You [Subordinate clause, V2]

But working out the syntax so as to get the correct word orders is anything but simple since the 'silent' matrix necessarily triggers raising of the V, but with the overt matrix, V2 is optional and is restricted to the small class of bridge verbs. This may be sufficient reason to reject the analysis.

3.3.4 *What about MON?*

If Sigurðsson's idea is extended further to account for the subordinate word order in MON questions, then these would have a silent performative matrix:

(22)   a.   (I ask you) [MON Main clause, no V2]

     b.   (I ask you) MON han kommer

Bayer (2004) discusses similar German root clauses with illocutionary force in which V2 is suppressed. His examples, like the German example with 'ob' in (3), have a complementizer in C which blocks V2. Bayer also suggests that the source of such sentences may be a sentence with an *elided matrix*. There are, however, a number of problems with this approach. First of all, MON is not a complementizer; it is an adverb. Evidence that MON is indeed an adverb, and not a complementizer (as is clearly the case for 'ob' in German), is the fact that it triggers object shift as shown in (23).

---

[8] A, P, T, L refer to argument, participant, tense, and location features, respectively.

(23)   a.   Så   Peter   hende   mon?
            saw   Peter   her   MON
            'Did Peter see her?'

       b.   Så   Peter   mon   *hende/Susanne?
            saw   Peter   MON   her/Susan
            'Did Peter see her/Susan?'

Object shift in Mainland Scandinavian applies only to pronouns which must precede adverbs. Full DPs, however, necessarily follow the adverb.

Second, 'internal' MON also occurs in embedded clauses:

(24)   Gad   vide   om   Peter   mon   kommer   i morgen.
       Like-to   know   if   Peter   MON   comes   tomorrow

Third, MON can occur sentence-internally in questions as shown in above (12b) and (13) and also below in the direct yes-no question in (25). There is no significant difference in interpretation between (25) and the one with left peripheral MON in (26).

(25)   Så   Peter   mon   Mette?
       saw   Peter   MON   Mette
       'Did Peter see Mette (do you think)?'

(26)   Mon   Peter   så   Mette?
       MON   Peter   saw   Mette
       'Did Peter see Mette (do you think)?'

Note that the force of V2, that the addressee controls the truth of the answer, conflicts with the interpretation of MON and is suppressed:

(27)   *Så   du   mon   Mette?
        saw   you   MON   Mette
        'Do you think you saw Mette?'

As noted above in section 3.2.2, Brandner (2004) allows for typing either by V2 or by a particle, but not by both. Under this view, non-initial MON does not function as a typing particle. This approach works, but predicts that sentences such as (27) should be good, since the force of the sentence should be that determined by V2 and not by the presence of MON.

The idea of allowing both overt and silent performative matrices in the syntax, although initially promising, does not account for the full array of facts concerning V2 and the distribution of MON.

3.3.5 *Silent syntax: turning Sigurðsson's idea on its head*

In this section I pursue the opposite of Sigurðsson's idea, namely the avail-ability of overt, pronounced elements which are inactive in syntax.[9]

Mittwoch (1976: 31–2) argues that performatives cannot function syntac-tically as a higher clause as proposed in Ross (1970). Instead, she suggests, their properties are akin to those of parentheticals, juxtaposed to the uttered sentence. And, according to Mittwoch (1977: 182), 'parenthetical elements are not constituents of sentences to which they are attached.' So, according to Mittwoch, performatives, like parentheticals, are inactive in syntax, what I call syntactically 'silent'. Where then are these 'invisible' parentheticals? I argue in Erteschik-Shir (2005a) following Åfarli (1997) (and see also Åfarli this volume; Chomsky 2001a; Bobaljik 2002), that adjuncts are not represented hierarch-ically in the syntactic tree but are rather merged on a separate plane. It is plausible, then, that parentheticals are also adjoined on a separate plane, and that they therefore do not interact with the core syntactic constituents of a sentence, i.e., they are inactive in syntax, or syntactically silent. The site of adjunction of adjuncts is the phrase they modify, in the case of parentheticals the maximal projection. According to this view performatives are invisible in syntax AND in phonology.

Before we discuss the repercussions of this approach, it is useful to examine the properties of overt parentheticals since those of silent ones should be analogous.

According to Reis (1995) and Bayer (2005) certain matrix clauses should be analyzed as parentheticals. Bayer shows that this explains the that-t effect:

(28)   <u>Wh-object</u>
    a. Who did John believe Susan will meet?
    b. *Who did John believe Susan will meet?

(29)   <u>Wh-subject</u>
    a. Who did John believe will meet Susan?
    b. Who did John believe will meet Susan?

(28) shows that the main clause material intervening between the wh-phrase and the subordinate clause cannot be left out, and so cannot be considered to be parenthetical when the object is extracted. Object extraction is therefore not predicted to depend on the presence or absence of an overt complementizer

---

[9] This idea is inspired by the work of Anita Mittwoch on the syntax–speech-act interface from the 1970s including Mittwoch (1979) not cited above.

as is indeed the case. (29) shows that when the subject is extracted, it is possible to leave out the main clause, and therefore it can be analyzed as a parenthetical.

Embedded subjects extract in the absence of an overt complementizer in cases where the matrix functions parenthetically. As noted in Erteschik-Shir (1997: 234), the complementizer is optional in English only with 'bridge' verbs. These are the verbs which make for natural matrix 'parentheticals' and the same verbs allow for subordinate V2.

The merger of adjuncts on a separate plane allows for the free linearization of adjuncts within the domain of the constituent to which they are attached, modulo-independent phonological processing and pronunciation constraints.[10] The particular linearization patterns of adjuncts are language-specific and depend among other things on their prosodic properties. Parentheticals form independent phonological phrases. It follows that they can only be linearized in positions which allows for a prosodic break. This is shown in (30) for English:

(30)   a.   I think Peter smokes cigars.
       b.   Peter, I think, smokes cigars.
       c.   Peter smokes cigars, I think.
       d.   *Peter smokes, I think, cigars.

The matrix of V2 complements is adjoined in syntax and linearized in phonology.[11]

We now have a reasonable explanation of embedded V2: The matrix of V2 subordinate clauses is analyzed as a parenthetical, adjoined to its clause in a separate dimension. The clause is therefore syntactically a matrix and V2 word order follows. Linearization allows for the adjunct to be linearized as in (30a), thus deriving a subordinate clause with main clause syntax.

3.3.6 *Silent phonology*

Parenthetical performatives are analyzed in the same way. They are adjoined on a third plane. They are interpreted but remain unpronounced. They are in fact *phonologically silent*. To account for this option, I propose the following addition to Sigurðsson's Silence principle:

---

[10] Erteschik-Shir (2005a) argues that this view of adjunct placement explains Scandinavian object shift. Scandinavian adverbs are necessarily linearized after unaccented object pronouns and before full DPs.

[11] According to Vikner (1995) languages differ as to whether embedded V2 occurs with overt complementizers. I have nothing to say about why complementizers are allowed in sentences which are in fact analyzed as matrix clauses (see also Wechsler 1991).

(31)   Silence principle (addition): Meaningful elements can be *syntactically* silent or phonologically silent, but not both.

Remember that Sigurðsson's Silence principle refers to formal features as shown in (32) repeated from (17).

(32)   Languages have meaningful silent features; any meaningful feature, 'formal' or not, may be non-prominent, hence silent.

The view I take represents the relevant meaningful elements as well-formed parenthetical clauses adjoined in a third dimension. This allows for a unified approach to overt and implicit 'parentheticals' with similar meanings and properties. These clauses can account for the pronominal properties of the sentence as proposed by Sigurðsson and the choice of verb determines its force.

In order to implement this proposal it is necessary to investigate what determines the ultimate silence of these parentheticals which consist of a verb as well as subject and object pronouns. The first requirement is that the pronouns represent the speaker and the hearer (first and second person). The second is that the verb indicate little more than the force of the sentence (e.g., *say, think, ask*).

3.4 Back to MON

The question we set out to answer was why V2 does not occur with initial MON. So far we have argued above that MON is an adverbial. If so, it is adjoined on a separate plane and linearized in the phonology. We have also shown that the interpretation of MON, *Do you think that . . . ?*, indicates the force of the sentence, namely a question albeit one which lacks the presupposition that the hearer know the answer. Although this interpretation is constant over all occurrences of MON, we also have to explain the occurrence of internal MON with V2.

Let us first examine initial MON and compare it to sentences with the matrix *gad vide om* (see (24) above) which has a similar interpretation as well as with the matrix *Do you think that*:

(33)   Mon   Peter kommer i morgen?
        MON Peter comes   tomorrow
        'Is Peter coming tomorrow?'

(34)   Tror   du   at   Peter kommer i morgen.
        think you that Peter comes   tomorrow
        'Do you think that Peter is coming tomorrow?'

(35) Gad   vide   om Peter kommer i morgen.
     Like-to know if Peter comes   tomorrow

In (33) MON performs the same function as does the matrix in (34) and
the expression in (35). If we implement the idea that MON represents a
silent matrix discussed in section 3.3.4 ((22)), together with the idea that
the silent matrix is adjoined and linearized, we will get around the problems raised in that section. MON is silent in the syntax, hence does not
trigger V2; it is interpreted as a typing particle and pronounced in the
phonology. MON thus behaves exactly like the matrices in (33) and (34), a
good result.

Turning now to internal MON and its placement, as observed in section
3.3.4, internal MON behaves like an adverb and undergoes object shift. This
was demonstrated in (23) repeated here:

(36) a.   Så   Peter hende mon?
           saw Peter her   MON
           'Did Peter see her?'

      b.   Så   Peter mon   *hende/Susanne?
           saw Peter MON   her/Susan
           'Did Peter see her/Susan?'

Internal MON thus behaves just like any other Danish adverb. Due to its
interpretation, however, it occurs only with questions. What types the
sentence as a question is either the intonation, in the case of yes-no questions
(see section 3.2.4 above) or else it is the wh-element preceding the raised verb.
MON does not function as a typing element in these cases. What MON adds
here is the uncertainty associated with it, i.e., it removes the presupposition
that the hearer know the answer.

MON also occurs in the embedded yes-no question (37) repeated from (24)
above.

(37) Gad   vide   om Peter (mon)   kommer i morgen.
     Like-to know if Peter (MON) comes   tomorrow

Here again its position is that of an adverb which (as mentioned in section
3.3) is placed between the subject and the verb in embedded clauses.[12]

---

[12] Note that MON cannot be inserted in any subordinate question:

(i)   *Jeg ved ikke om   Peter MON kommer i morgen.
       I know not whether Peter MON comes tomorrow

Note that this matrix is incompatible with the uncertainty associated with MON since it asserts
'not-knowing'.

Mon also occurs in adverbial positions in main clause questions:

(38)   Kommer Peter mon/ikke?
       comes   Peter MON/not
       'Is Peter MON/not coming?'

(39)   *Kommer mon/ikke Peter?
       comes   MON/not Peter

(38) and (39) show that MON occurs in the same position as the adverb *ikke*.
From what we have seen so far we can conclude that MON either occurs
sentence-initially as a typing particle or else it occurs sentence-internally in
the same positions any other adverb would.[13]

In view of the fact that MON can function as a typing particle, typing
sentences as uncertainty questions, and in view of the fact that it also occurs in
yes/no question and wh-questions which are independently typed (by intonation and by the wh-element), the question arises as to whether MON can
function as a typing particle in questions. It turns out that MON does not
occur sentence-initially in questions of either type:

(40)   *Mon   kommer Peter?
        MON   comes   Peter
        'MON is Peter coming?'

(41)   *Mon   hvem kommer?
        MON   who   comes
        'MON who is coming?'

This follows nicely if we assume that double typing is ruled out and that
typing with MON is unnecessary when regular question typing is present.
However, this leaves the following example unexplained:[14]

(42)   Hvem mon   kommer?
       who   MON   comes
       'Who MON is coming?'

Note that MON is not in a possible adverb position here as shown by the
ungrammaticality of (43):

---

[13] Rochman (this volume) argues that the placement of floating quantifiers is sensitive to focus.
When several positions for MON are available, the choice may also depend on focus properties of the
sentence. Further research into this question is warranted.

[14] MON does not occur in second position in yes-no questions:

(i)   *Kommer mon Peter?

(43) *Hvem ikke kommer?
      who   not comes

The position of MON in (42) therefore requires an explanation: MON is not sentence-initial as it is when it functions as a typing particle, neither is it in an internal adverb position. I propose that the wh-word *hvem* and MON invert for prosodic reasons: MON + hvem is ruled out as a prosodic constituent whereas hvem + MON is not.

It is a property of adverbs in Danish that they cannot stand alone and must form a prosodic unit with some other element in the sentence as discussed at some length in Erteschik-Shir (2005). This fact lies at the basis of my explanation of object shift in Mainland Scandinavian. Interestingly the adverb can either be the host of prosodic incorporation or else it can itself prosodically incorporate in the other element. Object shift with MON illustrated in (44) (repeated from (23)) shows the incorporation of MON into a host (the host is capitalized):[15]

(44) a. Så PETER + mon Susanne?
          saw Peter MON Susanne
          'Did Peter see MON Susanne?'

      b. Så PETER + hende + mon?
          saw Peter her MON
          'Did Peter see her?'

In (44a) MON incorporates into the subject, MON is prosodically weak whereas the subject is strong. In (44b) the subject is a pronoun and therefore it must incorporate in some host. Here MON incorporates into the unit formed by the subject and the incorporated pronoun.

In (45) with initial MON, there are two options depending on whether the subject is a pronoun or not. In (45a), MON incorporates into the subject, but on the left. In (45b) MON plays the role of the host and the pronoun is prosodically weak as expected.

(45) a. mon + PETER ryger cigarer?

      b. MON + han   ryger cigarer?

With this in mind, let us reexamine the problematic (42) repeated here as (46) and compare it to the unacceptable order in (47):

---

[15] The host has stronger stress than the incorporated element. Incorporation is similar to compounding in this respect. Note that the capitals refer to word stress, not focus stress.

(46)   Hvem mon kommer?
       who   MON comes
       'Who MON is coming?'

(47)   *Mon hvem kommer?
       MON who comes?
       'MON who is coming?'

Since both *hvem* and MON function as typing elements, either one could be initial in the sentence and since both mark the sentence as a question there is no conflict between them. One possible explanation for why the wh-phrase must come first could be the fact that wh-phrases are much more frequent than MON as question marker and therefore are better for typing purposes. However, this would leave the following facts unexplained:

(48)   Hvad MON han ryger?
       what MON he smokes
       'What does he smoke?'

(49)   *Hvad MON ryger   han?
       what MON smokes he

(50)   Hvad ryger   han MON?
       what smokes   he   MON
       'Which cigars MON does he smoke?'

In (48) as in (46), MON inverts with the wh-phrase. But here we also have evidence that MON functions as an initial typing element, because V2 is blocked as it is in all non-initial occurrences of MON. (49) shows that V2 order is indeed unacceptable. (50) in turn shows that V2 is required with internal MON. We can therefore conclude that (48) is a bone fide case of initial MON that has inverted with the wh-phrase. Since this ordering could not be syntactically motivated, a phonological explanation must be sought. (49) provides further evidence that phonology is at stake:

(51)   ??Hvilke cigarer MON han ryger?
        Which cigars MON he   smokes

(51) is identical to the grammatical (48) except for the fact that the wh-phrase in the former is complex. I propose that the reason for the reduced acceptability of (51) is that the complex wh-phrase does not provide a good host for the prosodic incorporation of MON. It seems that one requirement on the host of incorporation is that it is stressed and that the stress cannot occur too far away. Therefore contrastive stress

on the noun preceding MON helps, whereas stress on the wh-element makes the sentence even worse:

(52)   a.   ?Hvilke CIGARER + mon han ryger?
          which cigars   MON he smokes

       b.   ?*HVILKE cigarer + mon han ryger

Another argument for the prosodic basis for the placement of MON is illustrated in (53).

(53)   a. ?Hvem MON er kommet?
          who   MON is   come
          'Who MON has come?'

       b.   Hvem er MON kommet?
          who   is MON come
          'Who has MON come?'

(53a) illustrates the case where initial typing MON inverts with a wh-element as in (48). This is OK according to my informant, but (53b) in which MON is placed after the auxiliary in a 'normal' adverbial position is much better. This has to do with the prosodic properties of the auxiliary which must prosodically incorporate into a host just as MON must. The order of incorporation in (53b) is better because the auxiliary reduces phonologically and is pronounced like a clitic whereas MON does not. It retains lexical stress. The sequence in (53b) therefore adheres to the trochaic requirement to be discussed in the next section, whereas the one in (53a) does not.[16]

     This section has argued that the placement of both typing MON and internal MON is determined by prosodic considerations. An explanation of the lack of V2 with typing MON is still missing, however.

3.5 V2 phonology

In Erteschik-Shir (2005b) I argued that V2 is a phonological operation which linearizes the matrix verb to the left edge of its phonological domain. There I adopted the traditional view that V2 is topological, i.e., it has to do with linear order. I argued that the V-adjacent position is good for prominence since verbs are not normally focused and are therefore not accented. V2 thus

---

[16] See Rochman (2007a) and Rochman (in prep) for similar facts about the placement of floating quantifiers in English.

enables the phonological prominence of the initial typing element (*wh* for questions; topic DP for declaratives).

Stronger evidence that V2 is phonologically motivated comes from Speyer (2005). According to Speyer, the verb-second constraint was lost in English in the course of the Middle English Period. During the same time frame, the rate at which direct object noun phrases topicalize also declines.[17]

Speyer poses the question as to why the rate of topicalization should decline parallel to the loss of V2? Speyer notes that topicalization is motivated by pragmatic reasons and that it is unlikely that the conditions of language usage change over time. The decline in topicalization is therefore surprising.

Speyer found that the decline of topicalization with full DP subjects is continual but the decline of topicalization with pronoun subjects is less pronounced and stops with the transition from Old English to Middle English Grammar. Since the decline affects pronoun subjects and full noun phrase subjects differently, Speyer figures that prosody must be a factor. He makes the following comparison between topicalization in German and English:

(54) a. **Hans** hasst **Bohnen. Erbsen** hasst **Maria.**

  b. **John** hates **beans. Peas,** Mary hates.

Topicalized elements are generally selected from a contextually evoked set and are therefore accented. This is the case in both languages. The German sentence (54a) is unobtrusive. The English sentence (53b) is awkward. It requires a little break between the two accents. This looks as if—at least in English—a weak element between two accents is compulsory. Speyer calls this requirement the 'Trochaic Requirement' (=TR). He views inversion in German as a handy way to avoid violation of the TR. Modern English, since it has lost the V2 constraint, no longer has this option. The loss of topicalization, according to Speyer, therefore follows naturally from the loss of V2 since topicalization without V2 violates the TR.

Although V2 is grammaticized in the languages in which it occurs, its original motivation can therefore be seen as purely phonological. Let us assume that this story applies to Danish as well. Then there is no motivation for V2 in sentences with typing particles since they are not accented and do not induce a violation of TR. Grammaticalization of V2 would therefore never be extended to such cases.

---

[17] Neither topicalization nor V2 are entirely lost but remain on a low level of usage until today.

3.5.1 *V2 in Danish*

According to Engberg-Pedersen et al. (2005) all old Scandinavian sentences present as V2. This is the case even in subordinate clauses.

(55)   Hvis du   tager ikke hævn...
       If   you take   not   revenge....
       'If you don't take your revenge....'

In modern Danish this sentence would be ordered as in (56):

(56)   Hvis du ikke tager hævn...

As noted in section 3.3 above, the adverb in modern Danish follows the verb in main clauses, but precedes it in subordinate clauses. (55) shows that old Danish subordinate clauses present with main clause word order and that the adverb is consistently postverbal, an indication of V2.

   In modern Danish adverb position thus identifies the subject in main clauses since there the subject precedes the adverb:[18]

(57)   a.   Peter elsker ikke   Mette. (Peter = subject)
       b.   Peter elsker Mette ikke.   (Mette= subject)

Such identification is useful in languages such as Danish which employ topicalization freely since without the adverb the DP V DP word order is ambiguous with the initial DP interpreted either as the subject or the object. In Old Scandinavian adverb placement was not needed since overt case marking was available and therefore ambiguity did not occur in these cases. The placement of adverbs with respect to the verb must have developed into its current form together with the loss of case. A careful investigation of the history of Danish examining these issues should shed more light on the function of V2 in the language.

   The identification of syntactic roles and illocutionary force together with other interpretive needs are now dependent solely on word order. This may lead to word order 'conflicts' in which one word order identifies the subject, and another the illocutionary force. At the same time word order is also constrained by prosodic forces. The interplay of linearization and prosody is accounted for at the syntax–phonology interface in which phonological factors such as sentence-initial position as well as prosodic factors are expected to play a significant role.

---

[18] For details see Erteschik-Shir (2005a).

3.6 Conclusion

My account of MON is therefore that it is adjoined to the sentence it modifies. It linearizes in first position as a typing particle. In the presence of a performative yes-no question (silent or overt), MON can not type as well. In this case it adverbially modifies the question and is linearized in the manner of weak adverbials. In the presence of a wh-question, MON can optionally linearize in first position, in which case it inverts with the wh-element, if it is prosodically licensed in inverted position. MON can also linearize in any adverbial position in matrix and subordinate clauses whose typing is compatible with MON, i.e., they must be questions, and their interpretation must be compatible with the uncertainty associated with MON. MON does not trigger V2 since V2 is not prosodically motivated. Under this analysis V2 is not seen as having illocutionary force. Illocutionary force is associated with performatives, typing particles, or, in the case of yes-no questions, with intonation.

Linearization has been shown to be responsible for the placement not only of MON, but also of V2 and overt performatives.

4

Is free postverbal order in Hungarian a syntactic or a PF phenomenon?*

KATALIN É. KISS

4.1 Introduction

This paper aims to identify the source of the free postverbal constituent order attested in the Hungarian sentence. It will examine whether it is the consequence of a base-generated flat VP, or the result of syntactic scrambling, or a PF phenomenon, the free linearization of a hierarchical syntactic structure.

The facts to be examined will support the latter hypothesis. In section 4.2 I introduce the basic facts of postverbal word order in Hungarian, and in section 4.3 I survey the major theories aiming to describe them. Sections 4.4 and 4.5 discuss two additional sets of phenomena to be addressed: postverbal adverbial adjuncts, and postverbal quantifiers. Section 4.6 will present a new proposal which can account for all the facts surveyed. Section 4.7 will demonstrate that the proposal can also explain further phenomena of Hungarian syntax: free extrapositon from NP, and the free mingling of matrix and embedded material in infinitival constructions.

* The research reported on in this paper has been partially supported by OTKA, the Hungarian National Research Fund, under grant TS 49873. I owe thanks to an anonymous reviewer, and to the participants of the Beer Sheva Workshop on the sound patterns of syntax in June 2007 for their comments.

4.2 Free constituent order in the postverbal section of the Hungarian sentence

As is well known, the Hungarian sentence displays a strictly fixed word order preverbally,[1] and a free constituent order postverbally. In the neutral sentence in (1a,b), the fixed preverbal section includes a quantified expression, an adverb, and a verbal particle, whereas the free postverbal section includes two definite noun phrases. (For perspicuity's sake, the verb will be spelled in boldface, and the quantifier and the adverb will be spelled in italics.)

(1)   a.   *Minden könyvet   idejében* vissza-**vittek** a   fiúk a   könyvtárba.
            every   book-ACC in.time   back   took   the boys the   library-to
            'The boys took back every book to the library in time.'

      b.   *Minden könyvet idejében* vissza-**vittek** a könyvtárba a fiúk.

If (1) is negated, the verb moves up next to the initial negative particle, whereby the quantifier–adverb–particle string becomes part of the postverbal free-word-order section. In other words, V-movement across the particle, the adverb, and the quantifier liberates their order relative to one another and to the postverbal noun phrases:

(2)   a.   Nem **vittek**ᵢ *minden könyvet   idejében* vissza tᵢ a   fiúk
            not took   every   book-ACC in.time   back   the boys
            a   könyvtárba.
            the library-to
            'The boys didn't take back every book to the library in time.'

      b.   Nem **vittek** vissza a könyvtárba *minden könyvet idejében* a fiúk.

      c.   Nem **vittek** *idejében* vissza a fiúk *minden könyvet* a könyvtárba.

Structural focus (to be spelled in capital letters), similar to the negative particle, also elicits V-movement into an adjacent functional head. V-movement to focus also frees up the order of the constituents that it crosses:

(3)   a.   RITKÁN **visznek**ᵢ *minden könyvet   idejében* vissza tᵢ
            rarely   take   every   book-ACC in.time   back
            a fiúk a   könyvtárba.
            the boys the library-to
            'Rarely do the boys take back every book to the library in time.'

      b.   RITKÁN **visznek** a fiúk *idejében* vissza a könyvtárba *minden könyvet*.

---

[1] More precisely, the order of topic constituents in multiple topic constructions is free.

The focus projection can be iterated. In multiple focus constructions the V moves up into a functional head right-adjacent to the highest focus, liberating the order of all the constituents crossed, including the lower foci:

(4) a. *Mindenki* CSAK EGY KÖNYVET **vitt** vissza
       Everybody only one book-ACC took back
       a könyvtárba.
       the library-to
       'Everybody took back only one book to the library.'

    b. MIÉRT **vitt** vissza *mindenki* CSAK EGY
       why took back everybody only one
       KÖNYVET a könyvtárba?
       book-ACC the library-to
       'Why did everybody take back only one book to the library?'

    c. MIÉRT **vitt** vissza a könyvtárba CSAK EGY KÖNYVET *mindenki?*

    d. MIÉRT **vitt** *mindenki* vissza a könyvtárba CSAK EGY KÖNYVET?

In fact, the different postverbal word-order variants are not always equally unmarked, but markedness is independent of the grammatical categories or grammatical functions of postverbal constituents; it is determined by their phonological weight. A postverbal string of constituents is felt to be optimal if it observes Behaghel's (1932) Law of Growing Constituents, i.e., if lighter (shorter and unstressed) constituents precede heavier ones. (5a), severely violating the Law of Growing Constituents, is unacceptable (even if not ungrammatical). Its optimal variant is (5b):

(5) a. ??MIÉRT **bukott** CSAK PÉTER *minden tantárgyból*
       why failed only Peter every subject-from
       az idén meg?
       this. year PRT
       'Why did only Peter fail every subject this year?'

    b. MIÉRT bukott meg *az idén* CSAK PÉTER *minden tantárgyból?*

4.3 Former theories of free word order

The question on which level of the derivation the freedom of postverbal word order originates has been given different answers in the literature.

    The most trivial way of predicting free postverbal order is to assume a flat VP, in which only the initial position of the head is fixed; the arguments and adjuncts are base-generated as sisters to it and to one another in an arbitrary order. Such is the VP-structure implicit in the work of Brassai (1863–5), and I also argued for such a VP in É. Kiss (1987, 1994, 2002, etc.) In the most recent version of this theory, É. Kiss (2006), I assume the Hungarian sentence structure in (6). The structure is intended to account not only for the freedom of postverbal order, but also for the fact that in the predicational part of the sentence, the V is preceded either by a verbal particle or by a focused constituent, but not both of them. In the proposed structure, the verbal particle is one of the postverbal complements in the flat VP. Verbal particles and focus-marked constituents are both claimed to have the feature [+ predicative], thereby representing potential, alternative fillers of the specifier of PredP.

(6) $[_{TopP} XP_j [_{PredP} XP_i [_{VP} V t_i t_j XP^*]]]$ (É. Kiss 2006)

The structure in (6) correctly predicts the fixed word order of the preverbal section and the free word order of the postverbal section of the Hungarian sentence; however, it leaves the subject–object–adverbial asymmetries attested e.g. in anaphora unexplained.[2]

In most partially free-word-order languages, e.g., in Japanese, free word order is derived from a hierarchical VP via Scrambling. This solution has been adopted to Hungarian by Surányi (2006); see also É. Kiss (2008c). The VP-adjunction of internal arguments, followed by V-to-T movement across them, not only yields the different postverbal argument orders attested but also correctly predicts binding possibilities unexpected in a standard hierarchical VP. However, in most languages Scrambling is a kind of internal topicalization, only affecting [+ specific] complements across languages (cf. e.g., Karimi (2003) about Persian, Kornfilt (2003) about Turkish, Dayal (2003) about Hindi, as well as the German facts in Diesing (1992)). This is not the case in Hungarian, where non-specific indefinites also participate in postverbal free word order. Observe (7), in which a non-specific bare plural has been preposed in front of both the subject and a manner adverb presumably adjoined to VP:

(7) $[_{FocP}$ CSAK ÍRÁSBAN vizsgáztatnak $[_{VP}$ nagy évfolyamokat
              only   writing-in   examine   great classes-ACC
        $[_{VP}$ *szívesen* $[_{VP}$ a   tanárok]]]]
              gladly   the   teachers
        'It is only in writing that teachers examine great classes gladly.'

In É. Kiss (2008a,b) I have sought to account for postverbal free word order in the framework of Phase Theory. I assume two phases in the derivation of a

---

2 The most detailed discussion of these asymmetries has been provided by Marácz (1989).

clause: a lexical phase and a functional phase. The head positions of both phases are filled by V-movement. When the V is raised into the head of the functional phase, the hierarchical structure constituting the domain of the functional phase is claimed to be flattened—as the silent copies of the V and their projections are deleted. In this framework, the major postverbal constituents become sisters to one another at the syntax/semantics/phonology interface. If the interface representation of the clause is visualized as a three-dimensional tree, its postverbal section consists of multiple branches spreading from a single node, which are not ordered, and can be linearized at will in the course of Spell-Out.

This approach can account both for the subject–object asymmetries and the subject–object symmetries attested in the language. The vP is subjected to semantic interpretation twice: first as the hierarchical domain of the lexical phase, then as part of the flattened domain of the functional phase. Observe example (8a), a neutral sentence. In PredP, the lexical phase, the vP is still hierarchical; however, once the verb has been removed into the head of the functional phase, PredP collapses and becomes freely linearizable.

(8)

a.

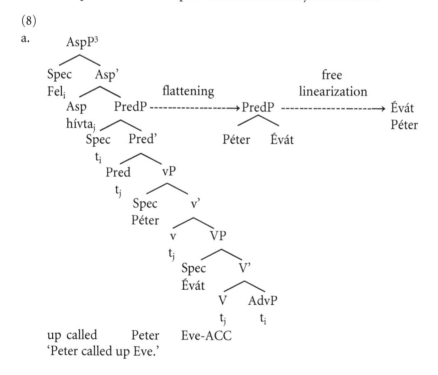

up called   Peter   Eve-ACC
'Peter called up Eve.'

---

[3] According to Csirmaz (2006), Spec, AspP has an EPP feature, which requires it to be filled by the closest potential filler, the verbal particle.

In non-neutral sentences, the functional projection also includes an NNP (Non-Neutral Phrase)⁴, and a FocP and/or a NegP. The V moves into the NN head, thereby reversing the 'particle, verb' order of neutral clauses. The head of the functional phase of a non-neutral clause is the V in NN (the highest overt head in the series of functional projections), and the phasal domain subject to flattening is AspP—see (8b). (Both neutral and non-neutral sentences can also involve a TopP.)

(8)

b.

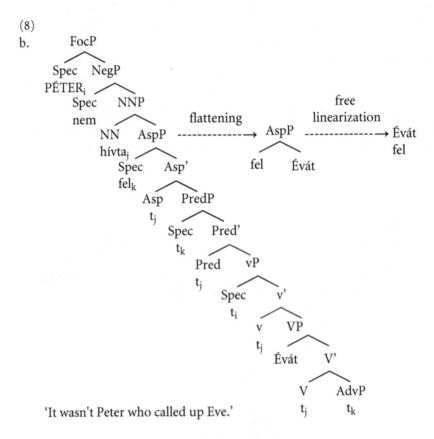

'It wasn't Peter who called up Eve.'

Grammatical phenomena which are indicative of a hierarchical structure, e.g., the anaphoric relation licensed in (9a) as opposed to (9b), are interpreted on the hierarchical domain of the lexical phase. Grammatical phenomena indicative of a flat structure, e.g., the lack of weak crossover effect in (10), are interpreted on the flattened domain of the functional phase, where the object

⁴ This functional projection has been argued for by Horvath (2006); the term is from Olsvay (2000).

variable c-commands (A-binds) the genitive specifier of the subject (for details, see É. Kiss 2008a).

(9)   a.   [$_{PredP}$ Fel hívták [$_{vP}$ a   fiúk [$_{VP}$ egymást]]]
            up called   the boys   each-other-ACC
        'The boys called up each other.'

      b.   *[$_{PredP}$ Fel hívták   [$_{vP}$ egymás [$_{VP}$ a fiúkat]]]
        'Each other called up the boys.'

(10) [$_{FocP}$ Kit$_i$ szeret [$_{PredP}$ [$_{DP}$ az   pro$_i$ anyja]   t$_i$?]]
        whom loves   the his   mother-NOM
        'Who does his mother love?'

Postverbal free word order, nevertheless, cannot be solely the result of domain flattening having taken place in the functional phase of the derivation. If postverbal free word order were nothing but the free linearization of sister nodes, then postverbal scope-bearing elements would all mutually c-command one another, and would all have identical scopes. Thus in a structure like (8b), postverbal quantifiers and adverbials would all have scope over AspP. In fact, however, postverbal quantifiers and adverbial adjuncts can also participate in the free postverbal order while having scope over NegP or FocP.

The facts to be accounted for will be summarized in sections 4.4 and 4.5.

4.4 The word-order position and scope of adverbial adjuncts

Preverbal adverbial adjuncts have scope over the sentence part that they precede and c-command. However, they can also follow the V, in which case their order among the postverbal constituents is free, and their scope is independent of their relative position within the postverbal string. (For further details of the placement of adverbial modifiers in the Hungarian sentence, see É. Kiss (2008b).)

In example (11), *figyelmesen* 'attentively' is a predicate adverbial, whereas *szerintem* 'in my opinion' is a sentence adverbial. The positions of preverbal adverbials correspond to their selectional/subcategorizational requirements and to their relative scope, assuming a right-branching structure; hence *szerintem* must precede *figyelmesen*.

(11) a.   [*Szerintem*   [János [*figyelmesen* [$_{AspP}$ el-**olvasta** a
            according.to.me John   attentively   PRT-read the
            könyvet]]]]
            book
        'In my opinion, John read the book attentively.'

b.   János *szerintem figyelmesen* [$_{AspP}$ el-**olvasta** a könyvet]

c.   *János *figyelmesen szerintem* [$_{AspP}$ el-**olvasta** a könyvet]

Postverbally, on the other hand, the word order of *figyelmesen* and *szerintem* is free. Their relative order does not affect the interpretation of the sentence: *figyelmesen* invariably takes scope over AspP, and *szerintem* invariably takes scope over the whole proposition:

(12)   a.   János el-**olvasta** *figyelmesen* a könyvet *szerintem*.

b.   János el-**olvasta** a könyvet *szerintem figyelmesen*.

c.   János el-**olvasta** *szerintem* a könyvet *figyelmesen*.

d.   János el-**olvasta** *figyelmesen szerintem* a könyvet.

Whereas in (11a) the structural positions of the two adverbs are determined by their lexical selectional properties, and their scopes follow from their structural positions, the variants in (12a–d) represent problems for the analysis.

In the theory presented in É. Kiss (2008a), it is the phasal domain c-commanded by the phasal head (the V) that is subjected to flattening and to free linearization at the syntax/semantics/phonology interface—however, in (12) neither *szerintem*, nor *figyelmesen* is part of the phasal domain. A predicate adverbial can become part of the phasal domain only in an extended functional phase, in which AspP is subsumed by a FocP projection, with the V (representing the phasal head) raised to the NN head. In such constructions, e.g. that in (13), the V moving from Asp to NN crosses the predicate adverbials preceding AspP, whereby they surface in the domain c-commanded by the V, to be flattened and to be linearized freely in PF. Since they are part of the presupposition, they undergo stress reduction. Observe the two postverbal predicate adverbials in (13a–c). Their position in the postverbal sentence part is free; they are understood to have scope over AspP, and they are destressed.

(13)   a.   [$_{FocP}$ CSAK 'JÁNOS [$_{NNP}$ **olvasta** [$_{AspP}$ el   a
            only   John   read   PRT   the

könyvet *végig   figyelmesen*]]]
book   end.till attentively
'It was only John who read the book through attentively.'

b.   [$_{FocP}$ CSAK 'JÁNOS [$_{NNP}$ **olvasta** [$_{AspP}$ el *figyelmesen végig* a
könyvet]]]

c.   [$_{FocP}$ CSAK 'JÁNOS [$_{NNP}$ **olvasta** [$_{AspP}$ el *figyelmesen* a könyvet
végig]]]

Whereas the word order and interpretation of the examples in (13) do not contradict the hypothesis that free postverbal order is the consequence of the deletion of the silent copies of the verb and their projections at the syntax/semantics/phonology interface, the examples in (12a–d) are not compatible with this framework. First, both postverbal adverbials in (12a–d) outscope the flattened phasal domain. Second, the two postverbal adverbials have different scopes (*figyelmesen* has scope over AspP, *szerintem* has scope over TopP). If they were sister nodes c-commanding each other at the syntax/semantics interface, the interpretive component would not be able to recognize their scope difference.

4.5 The word order position and scope of quantifiers

As is well known (cf. É. Kiss 1991), quantifiers precede and c-command their scope in the preverbal section of the Hungarian sentence, i.e., their scope order corresponds to their linear order. For example:

(14) a. *Mindenki több   cikket   is* [gyorsan [$_{AspP}$
          everybody several papers-ACC even quickly
          el-olvasott a vizsgára]]
          PRT read   the exam-for
          'Everybody quickly read several papers for the exam.' every > several

     b. *Több cikket is mindenki* [gyorsan [$_{AspP}$ *el-olvasott a vizsgára*]]
         'Several papers, everybody read quickly for the exam.' several > every

However, quantifiers can optionally also stand postverbally, where their word order is free, and their absolute and relative scope is independent of their word-order position. The word-order variants of (14a,b) listed under (15a–e), with one or both of the quantifiers in postverbal position, are scopally ambiguous: each of them has both the reading of (14a) and the reading of (14b):

(15) a. *Mindenki* gyorsan el-**olvasott***több cikket is* a vizsgára.

     b. *Több cikket is* gyorsan el-**olvasott** a vizsgára *mindenki.*

     c. Gyorsan el-**olvasott** a vizsgára *mindenki több cikket is.*

     d. Gyorsan el-**olvasott** *több cikket is* a vizsgára *mindenki.*

     e. Gyorsan el-**olvasott** *mindenki* a vizsgára *több cikket is.*

The interpretations of these sentences do not follow from the phasal theory presented in É. Kiss (2008a). In these examples, the projection subject to flattening and free linearization at the syntax/semantics interface is PredP. However, the postverbal quantifiers in (15a–e) cannot be part of PredP, as they outscope it. They have scope over the AspP modified by *gyorsan* 'quickly', hence they must occupy positions c-commanding AspP.

What the theory in É. Kiss (2008a) can handle in a straightforward way is postverbal quantifiers in the scope of a focus and/or negation. If an AspP with Q-raised quantifiers in front of it is extended by a focus and/or a negative particle, the verb is raised from Asp across the preposed quantifiers into the NN head, as a consequence of which the quantifiers crossed by the V will become part of the flattened phrasal domain, where they will c-command each other. The phrasal domain, representing the presupposition of the focus construction, undergoes stress reduction. The two destressed quantifiers are predicted—correctly—to have scope over AspP, and to be interpretable in either scope order. Indeed, such examples, e.g., (16a,b), are ambiguous:

(16)   a. A   SZINTAXIS- VIZSGÁRA **olvasott** el   *mindenki*
         the syntax exam-for   read   PRT everybody
         több   *cikket* *is.*
         several papers even
         'It was for the syntax exam that everybody read several papers.'
         every > several, several > every

      b. A SZINTAXIS-VIZSGÁRA **olvasott** el *több cikket is mindenki.*
         'It was for the syntax exam that everybody read several papers.'
         every > several, several > every

In non-neutral sentences, quantifiers can also have scope over FocP or NegP, and these wide-scope quantifiers can also stand either preverbally or postverbally. In preverbal position, they precede and c-command their scope, as expected, i.e., sentences with two or more preverbal quantifiers are never ambiguous:

(17)   a. *Mindenki legtöbb tárgyból* [$_{\text{FocP}}$ KÉTSZER **bukott** meg]
         everybody most   subject-from twice   failed   PRT
         'Everybody failed most subjects twice.'   every > most > twice

      b. *Legtöbb tárgyból mindenki* [$_{\text{FocP}}$ KÉTSZER **bukott** meg]
         'Most subjects, everybody failed twice.' most > every > twice

These quantifiers can also stand postverbally, where they do not lose their stress—unlike postverbal quantifiers in the scope of focus and/or negation. Their postverbal position, however, is independent of their scope. Focus constructions containing both a preverbal and a postverbal wide-scope (stressed) quantifier are ambiguous. Both (18a) and (18b) have the same two readings:

(18) a. *Mindenki* KÉTSZER **bukott** meg *'legtöbb tárgyból.*
'Everybody failed most subjects twice.' every > most > twice
'Most subjects, everybody failed twice.' most > every > twice

  b. *Legtöbb tárgyból* KÉTSZER **bukott** meg *'mindenki.*
'Everybody failed most subjects twice.' every > most > twice
'Most subjects, everybody failed twice.' most > every > twice

The variants in which both of the wide-scope (hence stressed) quantifiers follow the verb are also ambiguous in the same way:

(19) a. KÉTSZER **bukott** meg *'mindenki 'legtöbb tárgyból.*
'Everybody failed most subjects twice.' every > most > twice
'Most subjects, everybody failed twice.' most > every > twice

  b. KÉTSZER **bukott** meg *'legtöbb tárgyból 'mindenki.*
'Everybody failed most subjects twice.' every > most > twice
'Most subjects, everybody failed twice.' most > every > twice

Sentences containing a stressed postverbal quantifier are problematic for the theory in É. Kiss (2008a), deriving free postverbal order at the syntax/semantics/phonology interface, for the same reason as sentences containing a postverbal sentence adverb: namely, stressed postverbal quantifiers cannot form part of the flattened, freely linearizable phasal domain, as they have scope over (the whole or a part of) the left pheriphery of the phase, as well.

4.6 The proposal

4.6.1 *Postverbal adverbials*

According to mainstream generative tradition, adverbials enter the derivation via adjunction. They are adjoined to the syntactic projection that they have scope over. This is the view represented by Chomsky (2001b) and Ernst (2002), and this is the framework that has turned out to be most adequate for the description of adverbial modification in Hungarian (see the studies in É. Kiss 2008d). The widely accepted alternative theory, elaborated by Cinque (1999), Alexiadou (1997), Laenzlinger (2005), etc., treating adverbials as specifiers of designated functional projections participating in feature checking, provides no straightforward means of accounting for the position and interpretation of postverbal adverbials.

Adjunction serves the purpose of establishing a c-command relation between the adjunct and the syntactic projection it modifies. In standard generative syntax, nothing constrains the direction of adjunction,[5] i.e., not only left-adjunction, but also right-adjunction is allowed—see, e.g., Ernst (2002) and Fox (2003). In a version of the adjunction theory, developed by Lebeaux (1988), Åfarli (1997), and Chomsky (2001b),[6] among others, adjuncts are merged into the syntactic tree on a separate plane, in a third dimension, and are integrated into linear order only in PF. Third-dimension adjuncts can also be mapped onto the primary plane either on the left or on the right according to Åfarli (1997).

Adopting this framework, I assume that adverbials are merged into the Hungarian sentence via adjunction. Predicate adverbials (those modifying events) are typically adjoined to a functional projection in the predicational part of the sentence: AspP, NegP, or—rarely—FocP. Sentence adverbials are adjoined to TopP, or to a functional projection right below TopP (identified as Speaker Deixis Phrase (SDP) by Egedi (2008)). Observe the structure assigned to (11a):

(20)   [$_{TopP}$ *Szerintem*   [$_{TopP}$ János [$_{AspP}$ *figyelmesen* [$_{AspP}$ **el-olvasta**
          according.to-me   John   attentively   PRT read
        a   könyvet]]]]
        the book-ACC
        'In my opinion, John read the book attentively.'

The semantic interpretation of left-adjoined adverbials is determined by their c-commanding their scope at the syntax-semantics interface. The fact that postverbal adverbials have exactly the same reading as their preverbal counterparts suggests that they c-command the same projection from a right-adjoined position. That is, a right-adjoined adverbial is not part of the flattened phasal domain c-commanded by the V; it is integrated into the postverbal string to be linearized in accordance with the Law of Growing Constituents only in PF.

In (21), for example, the (a) sentence represents the the output of syntax and the input of the interpretive components, and the (b–e) sentences represent the output of PF. The optimal variant is (21b), but, since the postverbal constituents do not differ very much with respect to length, none of the PF variants violates the Law of Growing Constituents severely.

(21)   a.   [$_{TopP}$ [$_{TopP}$ János [$_{AspP}$ [$_{AspP}$ **el-olvasta** a könyvet] *figyelmesen*]]
             szerintem]

        b.   János **el-olvassa** a könyvet *szerintem figyelmesen.*

---

[5] I do not regard Kayne's (1994) Linear Correspondence Axiom, which excludes the possibility of right-adjunction, as a generally accepted, standard constraint.

[6] For a recent version of this theory, see Erteschik-Shir (2005).

    c.   János el-**olvassa** *figyelmesen* a könyvet *szerintem.*

    d.   János el-**olvassa** *szerintem figyelmesen* a könyvet.

    e.   János el-**olvassa** *figyelmesen szerintem* a könyvet.

4.6.2 *Postverbal quantifiers*

In standard generative syntax, quantifiers assume positions c-commanding their scope via Q-raising, an adjunction rule. At the same time, alternative theories have also been proposed in which quantifiers move to specifiers of designated functional projections, where they participate in feature-checking—cf. Beghelli and Stowell (1997). A version of this theory, based on facts of Hungarian, has been elaborated by Szabolcsi (1997), and Brody and Szabolcsi (2003).

    In the theory of Szabolcsi, and Brody and Szabolcsi, distributive quantifiers, among them universals, are moved into the specifiers of Distributive Phrases. DistP is an iterable functional projection located above FocP and below TopP.[7] A clause can contain several instances of the functional series FocP, DistP, TopP: above vP, above AgrOP, above TenseP, and above AgrSP. That is:

(22)

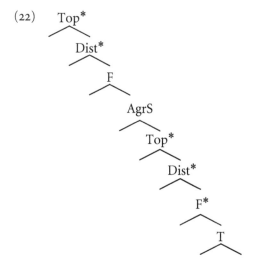

(* marks the iterability of the given projection.) Since the V raises across the functional heads AgrO and T into AgrS, the operators of the lower functional series will follow the V. The assumption of postverbal functional series

---

[7] In the theories of Szabolcsi (1997), and Brody and Szabolcsi (2003), the term TopP is replaced by RefP.

explains the presence of postverbal quantifiers; however, it does not explain the possibility of their having wide scope over a preceding sentence part, and inverse scope with respect to a preceding quantifier. This falls out from an additional component of the approach: Mirror Theory (cf. Brody 1997, and Baker 1985). According to Mirror Theory, syntactic heads precede their complement, whereas morphological heads follow it. Brody and Szabolcsi assume that Dist can be analyzed as either a syntactic or a morphological head. In a DistP with a morphological Dist head, a quantifier in Spec,DistP has scope over the projection which precedes it in the complement of the Dist head.

In addition to having several stipulative elements, the Szabolcsi–Brody theory also raises empirical problems. For example, it does not follow from anything that, whereas the highest quantifier and the highest topic can land in any of the lower, postverbal operator series, the highest focus must move up into the Spec,FocP position of the highest, preverbal, operator series. It also remains unexplained why FocP is recursive only in the lower operator series, but not in the highest one. The theory does not appear to be extendable to negative quantifiers. (For a more detailed criticism of the theory, see É. Kiss 2008b.)

These problems do not arise if we return to the standard, adjunction analysis of Q-raising, and we derive the wide scope of postverbal quantifiers by assuming right-adjunction, and we derive their free postverbal order by assuming free linearization in PF.

Quantifiers can be adjoined to any functional projection in the predicational part of the sentence. (The projections external to the predicational part, among them TopP and CP, are not possible landing sites of Q-raising).[8] Quantifiers adjoined to NegP are subject to negative concord, as a result of which their initial *minden* 'every' morpheme is replaced by *se-* 'no'.

If Q-raising is mapped on the two-dimensional syntactic tree as left-adjunction, the semantic and phonological interpretation of quantifiers in the preverbal domain is trivial: they c-command their scope, and they are pronounced in the order determined by their syntactic position. Observe the syntactic structures assigned to (14a) and (17a) (here renumbered (23a,b)):

---

[8] Left-adjunction to NNP is restricted by a PF-constraint: the focus and the finite verb must form one phonological word. Consequently, left-adjunction to NNP is only possible if it is dominated by NegP (rather than FocP), for example:

(i) [_NegP_ Nem [_NNP_ *mindenki* [_NNP_ jött [_PredP_ el   az   előadásra]]]]
          not   everybody   came   PRT the show-to
     'Not everybody came to the show.'

(23) a. [_{AspP} *Mindenki* [_{AspP} *több   cikket   is* [_{AspP} *gyorsan* [_{AspP}
              everybody   several papers even   quickly
          *el-*olvasott *a   vizsgára*]]]]
          PRT read   the exam-for
          'Everybody quickly read several papers for the exam.'
          every > several

     b. [_{FocP} *Mindenki* [_{FocP} *legtöbb   tárgyból* [_{FocP} KÉTSZER
              everybody   most   subject-from twice
          bukott *meg*]]]
          failed   PRT
          'Everybody failed most subjects twice.'   every > most

If Q-raising is mapped on the two-dimensional syntactic tree as right-adjunction, quantifiers will c-command, and take scope over, the very same syntactic domain as their left-adjoined counterparts. The right-adjunction of one or both of the quantifiers in (23a) yields the following syntactic structures:

(24) a. [_{AspP} [_{AspP} *Több   cikket   is* [_{AspP} *gyorsan* [_{AspP}
                      several papers even   quickly
          *el-*olvasott *a   vizsgára*]]] *mindenki*]
          PRT read   the exam-for   everybody

     b. [_{AspP}*Mindenki* [_{AspP} [_{AspP} *gyorsan* [_{AspP} *el-*olvasott *a vizsgára*]]
          több cikket is]]

     c. [_{AspP} [_{AspP} [_{AspP} *Gyorsan* [_{AspP} *el-*olvasott *a vizsgára*]] *több
          cikket is*] *mindenki*]

Each of these structures has the same interpretation as (23a), since the quantifiers have the same c-command domains, and, consequently, the same absolute and relative scopes. However, in PF the postverbal constituents of these strings are optionally reordered in observance of the Law of Growing Constituents. For example, (24c) can be pronounced as (25) (The stressed *mindenki* 'everybody' is phonologically at least as heavy as the one-syllable longer but unstressed *a vizsgára* 'for the exam'.)

(25) Gyorsan el-**olvasott** a vizsgára *mindenki több cikket is.*

At the same time (25) is also a possible linearization of the syntactic structure in (26), in which *több cikket* 'several papers' c-commands, and has scope over, *mindenki* 'everybody':

(26) [_{AspP} [_{AspP} [_{AspP} Gyorsan [_{AspP} el-**olvasott** *a   vizsgára*]]
                      quickly   PRT read   the exam-for

mindenki] több   cikket   is]
everybody several papers even

In this framework, the ambiguity of sentences containing both preverbal and postverbal quantifiers, such as (27a), also follows: the sentence is a possible PF-linearization of both (27b) and (27c):

(27) a. *Mindenki KÉTSZER bukott meg 'legtöbb tárgyból.*
         everybody twice   failed   PRT most   subject-from

      b. [_{FocP} *Mindenki* [_{FocP} [_{FocP} KÉTSZER **bukott** meg] *'legtöbb tárgyból*]]

      c. [_{FocP} [_{FocP} *Mindenki* [_{FocP} KÉTSZER **bukott** meg]] *'legtöbb tárgyból*]

In sum: the wide scope of right-adjoined adverbials and quantifiers, extending over a projection subsuming the overt verb, can be derived if the adverbial or quantifier c-commands its scope at the syntax/semantics interface. That is, its integration into the postverbal string must take place in PF; hence the free linearization of the postverbal string must be a PF operation.

4.7 A prediction

In the grammatical framework assumed, the output of the syntactic component is mapped on a prosodic structure in PF. However, there is no biunique relation between the two constructions; the former cannot be reconstructed from the latter. The prosodic hierarchy is expected to be less articulated than the syntactic hierarchy because of a Non-Recursivity constraint on prosodic representations. As formulated by Truckenbrodt (2007), this constraint requires that no constituent of level *l* be contained in another constituent of level *l*. Thus no phonological phrase can be contained in another phonological phrase; phonological phrases are to be directly dominated by an intonation phrase.

Phonological phrases are the PF equivalents of functionally extended lexical phrases such as noun phrases. Because of the Non-Recursivity constraint, a noun phrase (or postpositional phrase) embedded in another noun phrase like [_{DP}a *találkozás* [_{DP}a *régi barátnőjével*]] 'the meeting with his old girl-friend' is segmented into two adjacent phonological phrases (p-phrases) as follows: [_{pP}a *találkozás*] [_{pP}a *régi barátnőjével*].

If in Hungarian postverbal free linearization is a PF phenomenon, then it is expected to affect phonological phrases rather than syntactic phrases. This is exactly what happens. In (28) the syntactic structure is ambiguous: in the string *a találkozást a régi barátnőjével* 'the meeting-ACC with his old friend' *a régi barátnőjével* can be either the prepositional object of *a találkozás*, or a comitative adjunct of the verb:

(28) Péter   nagyon   várta   a   találkozást   a   régi
      Peter   very-much   looked-for the meeting-ACC the old
      barátnőjével.
      girlfriend-his-with
      'Peter was very much looking forward to the meeting with his old girlfriend.'

Under both structural interpretations of (28), *a találkozást a régi barátnőjével* is linearized as two independent units—in accordance with the fact that both syntactic structures underlying (28) are mapped on a prosodic representation in which *a találkozást* and *a régi barátnőjével* represent two distinct phonological phrases:

(29) a. Péter várta   a   **találkozást**   nagyon   a   **régi**
          Peter looked-for the meeting-ACC   very.much the old
          barátnőjével.
          girlfriend-his-with
          'Peter was very much looking forward to the meeting with his old girlfriend.'

      b. Péter várta a **régi barátnőjével** nagyon a **találkozást.**

The question arises what evidence we have that the disintegration of the complex noun phrase takes place in PF rather than in syntax. After all, the complex noun phrase cannot be focus-moved as a whole, either; the complement is obligatorily extraposed, which suggests that *a találkozást* and *a régi barátnőjével* are separated in syntax already. However, extraposition is obligatory only in the case of focusing, for the reason that Hungarian structural focus must be head-final. Topic movement is not constrained in this way; the complex noun phrase is topicalized as a whole, as in (30a). The PP complement of a topicalized noun phrase can only be extraposed if it has discourse features other than those of the host noun phrase (e.g., one of them is topic, and the other one is focus—see (30b,c)). If extraposition could take place in syntax automatically, without any trigger, (30d) should also be grammatical.

(30) a. [$_\text{TopP}$ **A találkozást**   a   **régi barátnőjével**
              the meeting-ACC   the old friend-his-with

[valószínűleg   nagyon   várta   Péter]]
presumably   very.   much   looked-for P.
'The meeting with his old girlfriend, Peter was presumably looking
forward to very much.'

b.   [TopP A **találkozást** [FocP csak **A RÉGI BARÁTNŐJÉVEL** [NNP
várta Péter nagyon]]]
'It was only his old girlfriend that Peter was looking forward to
meeting very much.'

c.   [FocP Csak **A RÉGI BARÁTNŐJÉVEL** [NNP várta Péter **a
találkozást**]]

d.   *[TopP **A   találkozást**   [TopP valószínűleg [TopP **a   régi**
          the   meeting-ACC   presumably   the   old
barátnőjével   [FocP PÉTER   várta   a   legjobban]]]]
friend-his-with   Peter   looked-for the   most
'The meeting with his old girlfriend, presumably PETER was
looking forward to the most.'

Infinitival constructions provide further evidence of free postverbal linearization taking place in the PF component. An infinitive phrase projects no CP in
Hungarian, and it does not represent a separate intonation phrase; it is
integrated into the matrix intonation phrase. If linearization in the postverbal
section of the matrix sentence takes place in PF, then the constituents of the
infinitive are expected to freely mingle with those of the matrix verb. This
prediction is borne out:

(31)   a.   Nem tudta   volna   **őket** János **egymással**
not   was.able PERF.COND them John   each-other-with
valószínűleg **kibékíteni**.
presumably   reconcile-INF
'John presumably wouldn't have been able to reconcile them
with each other.'

b.   Nem tudta volna **kibékíteni** János **őket** valószínűleg **egymással**.

In the syntactic component, the non-finite clause still forms a constituent
which can only be topicalized as a whole (see (32a,b)) unless its subconsti-
tuents are supplied with different discourse features (see (32c)).

(32)   a.   [TopP **Kibékíteni őket egymással** [valószínűleg [nem tudta volna
János]]]
'To reconcile them with each other, John presumably woudn't
have been able to.'

b.   *[$_{TopP}$ Kibékíteni [$_{TopP}$ János [$_{TopP}$ egymással [valószínűleg
[$_{TopP}$ őket [$_{NegP}$ nem tudta volna]]]]]]

c.   [$_{TopP}$ Kibékíteni [$_{TopP}$ János [$_{FocP}$ csak
       reconcile-INF   John   only
     EGYMÁSSAL   [$_{NNP}$ tudta   őket]]]]
     each-other-with   was.able them
     'As for making peace, it was only with each other that John could
     make them do that.'

4.8 Conclusion

It has been argued that the free constituent order attested in the postverbal
section of the Hungarian sentence cannot be either the result of random base-
generation, or the result of a syntactic operation, e.g., Scrambling, or flattening resulting from the pruning of the silent copies of the V. It must be a PF
operation, because it also affects postverbal adverbials and quantifiers which
c-command their scope from a right-adjoined position at the interfaces.
Further evidence of free linearization taking place in PF has been provided
by the fact that the units of reordering are the phonological phrases. Prosodic
representations are subject to a Non-Recursivity constraint, hence complex
noun phrases and infinitival phrases are segmented into strings of non-
recursive phonological phrases. PF-reordering affects these segments, yielding
the illusion of free extraposition. Postverbal phonological phrases are reordered according to their phonological weight.

5

Why float? Floating quantifiers and focus marking[*]

LISA ROCHMAN

This paper explores the connection between floating quantifiers (FQs) and information structure, arguing that there is a connection between the use of an FQ and the presence of a focused element following the FQ: Either the FQ or the following element is contrastive. Evidence comes from analysis of the f(ocus)-structure (Erteschik-Shir 1997) of sentences with FQs. Analysis of f-structure is done in conjunction with examining FQ behavior with particle verbs, FQs acceptability with different types of predicates, and the relationship between FQs and the nuclear accent. In exploring the motivation for using FQs, the meaning contributed by the FQ is also analyzed. FQs are shown to be relevant to the syntax–phonology interface as the phonology is sensitive to the presence of the FQ.

5.1 Introduction

The floating quantifiers in English are *all, both,* and *each.* These words can occur preceding the DP (hereafter called non-floating quantifiers) or in the so-called floated position, (1) and (2) respectively.[1]

(1)   **All** the kids left the party.

(2)   The kids **all** left the party.

---

* a. I would like to thank Nomi Erteschik-Shir for all her help with this paper. I'd also like to thank the workshop participants for their thought-provoking comments and input.
  b. Portions of this paper have been discussed in Rochman (forthcoming).

[1] As is commonly done, I will use the term *floating quantifier* in a theory-neutral way.

Of interest in this paper is the question of why speakers opt for the floated order and what role the FQ plays in sentences like (2). The majority of research on FQs in the past has concentrated on understanding the syntax involved in such sentences. The approach taken in this paper differs. I first set out to understand the discourse function of the FQ, and in doing so explore the f-structure of the utterances in relationship to the use of an FQ. Once the role of the FQ in the sentence is clear, we are then able to understand how it functions.

5.2 FQs and pronouns

The most outstanding indicator of a connection between FQs and information structure comes from the frequency of FQs found with pronouns as opposed to with full DPs. Natural speech readily shows that FQs are much more common with pronouns than full DPs. This raises the question of what the source of this difference in frequency stems from.

A randomly selected sample of sentences with FQs from the Santa Barbara Corpus (SBC) (Du Bois et al. 2000, 2003, 2004) showed that 97 percent of the sentences (that contained FQs) had FQs floated from a pronoun while less than 3 percent were floated from a full DP. The following examples are representative of what is commonly found in discourse.

(3)   **we** would **all** sit around the rug   (SBC 015)

(4)   **all the departures** seemed like they're going out the left   (SBC 022)

The sentence with the pronoun has the FQ (3) and the sentence with the full DP has the non-floated quantifier (4).

The choice between the use of a pronoun and a full DP is not random or stylistic, but is instead determined by the communicative needs of the speaker. The use of a pronoun is constrained by the fact that pronouns must be interpreted in relationship to information that has already been presented in the discourse (Erteschik-Shir 1997; Gordon, Grosz, and Gilliom 1993, among many others). In fact the use of a definite description for a topic that could host a pronoun causes difficulties in processing the utterance, as in (5c).

(5)   a.   Mike$_i$ just lost his job.

    b.   He$_i$ is quite upset about it.

    c.   ???Mike$_i$ is quite upset about it.

When (b) follows (a) the dialogue sounds much more natural than when (c) follows (a). With (c), it seems as if there are two separate *Mikes* while with (b) it is immediately clear that the *Mike* in (a) is the same in (b).

One may wonder if the choice between floated and non-floated quantifier is simply a by-product of the choice between pronoun and full DP which is driven by the discourse.[2] The data indicate very clear patterning with limited exceptions, pronouns have floated quantifiers while full DPs have non-floated quantifiers. Perhaps utterances that do not conform to this are simply flukes. A syntactic account based on the differing positions of pronouns and full DPs in the tree structure may be pursued. A phonological explanation, relating to phonological weight, arguing for the cliticization of pronouns but not full DPs leads to some interesting results (Bošković 2004a).[3] While a syntactic or phonological account as just mentioned could account for much of the data, what it misses is the fact that the non-conforming cases, limited as they may be, can be shown to form a unified group. We can find a clear pattern for the use of floated versus non-floated quantifiers, which is dependent upon the f-structure of the different constituents in the sentence. Thus an account of FQ should include the discourse function that determines whether or not the floating order should be used.

Analysis of the cases where FQs float from full DPs show one common trait with cases of FQs floated from pronouns; the subject is a topic. Building upon this finding, FQs can be expected to occur more frequently with pronouns as they are topics by nature. As for full DPs, they can be either topics or foci. As mentioned, speakers tend to use pronouns if the subject is a topic. Sentences with full DPs and FQs are not degraded, just less frequent.[4] In the rest of this paper further evidence for the claim that there is a relationship between FQs and information structure and that information structure governs the use of FQs is provided. I show that the significant issue is not the subject's status as a topic, but instead it is the quantifier's role in indicating focus that results in the use of FQs before foci and subsequently appearing frequently floated from topics.

5.3 FQs and particle verbs

In this section I explore the relationship between FQs and particle verbs in order to show that FQs indicate that what follows them is focused. In the next

[2] There is some basis for this possibility. It's noted in Buchstaller and Traugott (2006) that the Old English quantifier *eall* 'all' was a predeterminer with nouns but was generally a postdeterminer with pronouns. In light of the evidence showing that FQ usage is conditioned by information structure I will not pursue this line of questioning but I do note that perhaps this preference stemmed from the original use of the postdeterminer occurring with pronominal subject topics.

[3] See Bošković (2004a) for work on objects and floating quantifiers along these lines.

[4] If the FQ occurs directly after the full DP many speakers find these sentences degraded.

i. The children all have bought candy.

This is not because of information structure but because of the resulting intonation of the phrase. See Rochman (2007b) for discussion.

section these findings are compared to sentence-final findings for FQs. The relationship between FQ placement and particle verbs is interesting as placement of the particle is well established as being sensitive to information structure.

Before turning to particle verbs and FQs, a brief discussion of particle verbs is in order.[5] The particle, in particle verb complexes, can either occur before the object DP or after; cf. (6) and (7) below. Dehé (2005) argues that the unmarked order is the continuous order (6), and in the unmarked case the nuclear accent will fall on the direct object, the final constituent.[6]

(6)   [The boys drank up the BEER]$_{FOC}$.

(7)   [The boys drank the BEER up]$_{FOC}$.   (Dehé 2005)

The discontinuous order, seen in (7), results in the head of the phonological phrase, *the beer,* not being aligned with the right edge of the phrase. The focused constituent, which bears the nuclear accent, is favored as close to the right edge as possible and therefore the continuous order, (6), is preferred. Alternatively, if the nuclear accent is placed on the particle then the verb complex is the focus. The order of the DP and the particle is not random or stylistic but determined by f-structure. Dehé (2005) proposes that in sentence focus the order will be the continuous order with a full DP and discontinuous with a pronoun. Pronouns are ruled out after the particle unless they are contrastively focused. Only cases of object pronouns or verb focus give the discontinuous order.

In sentences with particle verbs and FQs, if the verb or the VP is the focus of the sentence then I speculate that we will find the quantifier floating. However, if the subject is the focus the quantifier should not be found floating.[7] The floated order results in the FQ preceding the particle and if FQs indicate that what follows them is focused, this word order would mark the particle (and thus the entire verbal complex) as the focus.

The following are examples taken from natural speech:

(8)   I want you to **pull them all out**.   (SBC 015)

(9)   . . . All he did is **send em all out**.   (SBC 022)

---

[5] For a more in-depth account of particle verbs and information structure see Erteschik-Shir (1979), Dehé 2005, and references therein.

[6] For the basis of the claim for the unmarked order the reader is referred to Dehe (2005) and references therein.

[7] Due to space constraints I will not deal with particle verbs, FQs, and full DPs. See Rochman (in prep) for an account of these.

(10)   I want you to **pull them all out.**   (SBC 015)

(11)   to **tear them all down**   (SBC 026)

(12)   ...and assignments and stuff so I had to **take them all up** (SBC 043)

All the above examples correspond to the pattern in (16) below. The alternative word orders, which were not found, are illustrated in the following:

(13)   a.   I want you to **pull all of them out.**
        b.   I want you to **pull out all of them.**
        c.   ???I want you to **pull out them all.**

In all cases of FQs with particle verbs found in the corpus, the FQ was floated and the discontinuous order for the particle and verb was used (see the pattern in (16)). Looking at an example in depth sheds light on the choice of this word order.

(14)   a.   Joanne: How many different types of pills do you have?
        b.   Ken: What's that?
        c.   Joanne: Let me see.
        d.   I want you to **pull them all out.**   (SBC 015)

In this sentence the focus is the verbal complex *pull out*. The nuclear accent is on the particle. The FQ is floated and precedes the particle. This in turn can mark the entire verbal complex as the focus. The FQ's position preceding the particle identifies the particle as the focus. Although the FQ does not precede the entire focus, since the verb is before the FQ, by marking the particle as the focus, the 'focal status' is transmitted to the entire verbal complex.

   The word order that is not expected to be found is the continuous order and a floated quantifier as in (15).

(15)   She pulled out them all.

The sentence in (15) has 'mixed signals'. The continuous order identifies the object *them/them all* as the focus, while the FQ indicates that there is a focus after the object, which is impossible in light of the fact that no overt material follows the FQ. This order serves no purpose in natural speech and did not turn up in the corpus search.

   In (16)–(19) I schematically show what each word order conveys in terms of focus structure.

(16)   S V O-pron FQ Part → FQ marks Part and thus whole verbal complex as focus

(17)   S V FQ O-pron Part → FQ marks object or entire VP as focus

(18)   S V Part Q of O-pron → no FQ (i.e. *all of them*)

(19)   S V Part O-pron FQ → FQ marks non-existent following material as focus (no basis for usage)

The acceptability of the word order in (21) is in contrast to the unacceptability of the continuous order with a pronoun and no quantifier, as in (20).

(20)   *?She pulled out them.

(21)   She pulled out all of them.

(20) is not a possible sentence. Non-contrastively stressed pronouns cannot follow particles. Dehé (2005) proposes that in non-particle verb sentences, weak object pronouns are clitics which cliticize onto the verb. The presence of the particle renders that attachment impossible as the clitic object pronoun is unable to cliticize onto the particle (Dehé 2005). The presence of the quantifier, floated or otherwise, redeems the sentence. In the example at hand, the pronoun and the quantifier can form a unit and the particle is no longer required as a host for the weak pronoun (22).

(22)   (She pull out)$_{iP}$ (them all)$_{iP}$.

The absence of the word order in (22) in natural speech is interesting. On the one hand its absence is expected since there is no material following that FQ that it could be marking as the focus. On the other hand, we know that in English, prosodically heavier material is favored rightmost. As the FQ is pitch-accented and the pronoun is intrinsically prosodically weak (as discussed, it attaches onto a host), in terms of phonology the quantifier could be expected to be floated. The absence of this word order therefore brings up a further issue of sentence-final quantifiers with pronouns. Thus far we have seen that FQs float from pronouns in order to mark the particle, and subsequently the verb as the focus. Next we turn to see how FQs and pronouns behave sentence-finally when there is no particle that could be identified as the focus.

5.4 Sentence-final FQs

In this section the contrast that is found in natural speech between FQs floated from object pronouns sentence-finally and FQs floated from object pronouns in sentences with particle verbs is explored. In particular, sentence-finally the floated word order occurs infrequently.

While judgments on FQs vary widely, one aspect is uncontroversial—FQs cannot be floated from full DPs sentence-finally as in (23). Only pronouns can float FQs in this position, (24).[8]

(23)   *The man fed the dogs all.

(24)   The man fed them all.

In addition, the word order in (24) is preferred by many informants over the non-floated order in (25).

(25)   The man fed all of them.

From the point of view advanced in this paper it is expected that the quantifier will float, but this is tempered by the phonological preference for heavier material close to the edge, leading to conflicting expectations. There are two competing hypotheses; the first I call the focus-structure hypothesis and the second the phonological hypothesis:

a. The Focus-structure Hypothesis: Q-float won't occur since it is unmotivated. There is no material following the quantifier and therefore nothing for the quantifier to mark as the focus.
b. The Phonological Hypothesis: The quantifier will float because the FQ is phonologically heavier than the pronoun and phonologically heavier material is preferred as close to the edge as possible.

In order to determine which hypothesis holds, I examine data from informants as well as natural speech. Starting with the former, data obtained from informants provides support for the phonological hypothesis. Informants were presented with sentences of the type illustrated in (26)–(27) and asked to choose which word order they preferred.[9]

(26)   a.   Sara hit them all.
       b.   Sara hit all of them.

(27)   a.   Ben broke them all.
       b.   Ben broke all of them.

---

[8] An account of why FQs cannot occur sentence-finally floated from full DPs will take us too far off base. For different views on this the reader is referred to Sportiche (1988), Bobaljik (1995), and Rochman (in prep).

[9] They were given no context since the pronoun ensures that the object is interpreted as a topic.

Another set of informants was asked to rate sentences of this type on a scale of 1–4.[10] The rating task was used in order to see if the sentences chosen by the first set of informants were perceived as 'better' or more likely to be used by the speaker than the disfavored sentence. If consistencies had been found across speakers this would indicate that there was some issue with the disfavored word order, be it phonological, syntactic, or semantic. While informants had mixed preferences, there was a slight preference for the floated order. Interestingly though, the ratings for the two orders were comparable. From this I conclude that there is a very slight favoring for the floated order although both sentences are perceived as acceptable English sentences.

These results are somewhat surprising in light of the focus hypothesis advanced in this paper. If the floated order is used to indicate that what follows is the focus then the floated order should not be used sentence-finally since obviously the focus of the sentence cannot be occurring after the FQ. This lends support to the Phonological hypothesis above.

Bošković (2004a) put forth an approach that argued that English has overt object shift for all objects, and an additional phonological cliticization of weak object pronouns. This additional movement of weak pronouns results in the quantifier being floated since the pronoun moves to a higher position.[11] The fact that informants do not find the (b) examples above degraded is consistent with this explanation. Since the cliticization of the weak pronoun is optional then sentences without it should be fully acceptable. Taking the cliticization to be optional in conjunction with informants having a slight preference for the floated order predicts that in natural speech there will be (close to) equal numbers of cases with the quantifier floated and not floated from the object pronoun, or even that the floated order will have a slight majority.

In order to verify this, the frequency of these two word orders in a natural speech corpus (first release of the Buckeye Corpus) was checked,[12] the expectation being that the floated order would be found in greater frequency

---

[10] One set of sentences was recited for the informants. This was because it became clear that informants were reading the (a) sentences such that the pronoun and the FQ were not prosodically incorporated and this was affecting their perception of the sentences. When the sentences were read in the more natural way with the FQ and pronoun prosodically incorporated ('emall) the informants' judgments of the sentences improved.

[11] This approach can also explain the lack of q-float in sentences where the object is a full DP. If the object is not phonologically weak, then it does not shift to a higher position. This provides a comprehensive account for the lack of sentence-final q-float with full DP and the consistent judgments in favor of it with pronouns.

[12] At the time this analysis was performed only a subset of the files were released to the public and so only those files were used in the analysis.

Table 5.1 Object pronoun

Sentence-final		Non-final	
Floated[a]	Non-floated	Floated	Non-floated
–	2101b	1001a	–
	2501a	1603a	
		1603b	
		3202b	
		3502a	

a. The transcript from file 1103b indicated that there was a floated FQ sentence-finally but the corresponding sound file did not contain an audible FQ and object pronoun. Evidently there was a mistake in the transcription or the sound file was cut or damaged.

than the non-floated order, or at least the two word orders would occur with (somewhat) equal frequency.

Contrary to expectation, quantifiers floated from object pronouns sentence-finally do not occur with a frequency equal to the non-floated quantifiers. The results are seen in Table 5.1.

These results are remarkably consistent. In contrast to informants' judgments, floating quantifiers are not found sentence-finally in natural speech, certainly not in the expected proportion.[13] While the sample used here is quite small, the nature of the corpus makes it relatively representative of natural speech.

The following are examples of sentence-final non-floating quantifiers:

(28)   Now wait, they both have advantages 'n disadvantages, **both of them**
                                                             (SBC 035 161–4)

(29)   how can you remember **all of them**
         . . .
         Lenore: I know **all of 'em,**   (SBC 15 516–19)

Natural speech challenges the phonological account since in sentences like (28) and (29) the motivation for cliticization is present yet the quantifier was never found floating. Additionally, with the non-floated order some examples with phonologically weak pronouns can be found, and even phonologically

---

[13] Note there is further evidence that it is not a purely phonological explanation as to why *all* does not occur sentence-finally. The word 'all' (in a different usage) can be used felicitously sentence-finally.

i. I didn't see him at all.

Additionally, binominal 'both' can occur finally while the FQ 'both' cannot.

ii. I gave the boys a nickel both.

reduced ones. In several cases, the corpus transcribers transcribed the pronoun as a reduced pronoun *'em* and not as *them*, (30).

(30)   **all of 'em** were at that age   (SBC 043)

Additionally, auditory analysis confirmed that in several non-floated utterances the pronoun was not stressed and was phonologically weak.

Following the cliticization approach one might expect that at least in the cases where the pronoun is weak, q-float would be found. Cliticization of the weak pronoun would produce the floated order and in doing so the phonologically heavy FQ would occur in the default sentential stress position—sentence-final position.

We are left in a bit of a conundrum here. On the one hand natural speech shows that FQs are favored non-floated in sentence-final position yet there is contradictory evidence from informants. At the outset of this section I proposed two hypotheses and it seems that both are correct depending on which type of data you look at. I take the gap between spoken language and judgments to indicate that while some speakers prefer the sound of the floated quantifier in natural speech, this preference is overridden by the discourse role of the FQ.

If the reason for the lack of sentence-final FQ is the f-structure requirements, this predicts that if there is a focus following the object pronoun then the floated order will be used. This is exactly what is found in the previous section where the behavior of FQs and particle verbs was looked at. In those cases there was material following the FQ that was focused and thus the floated word order was used.[14] In this section we have seen that syntax and phonology alone cannot predict the use of an FQ while information structure can. From this we can see that phonology is sensitive to f-structure, in fact f-structure can be seen as mediating between phonology and syntax.

5.5 Subjective opinion versus objective fact

Further evidence for the claim that FQs float in order to identify a following focus can be gleaned from the type of predicates that are preferred following FQs. FQs in sentences with a generic subject and a predicate expressing a subjective attitude are judged as better than sentences with a predicate expressing an objective fact. This difference can be accounted for if FQs are

---

[14] The complication of course is that if the problem relates simply to sentence-final position then the addition of material after the object removes this objection. Since there is no way to have a focus following the object and still have the quantifier sentence-final teasing apart these two possibilities is quite difficult. But see n. 11.

assumed to precede foci. Objective facts are less likely candidates for focus than subjective opinions which as the latter are more likely to contain focal material. This observation is attributed to Estling Vannestål (2004) (her 3:70) who provides the following judgments.

(31)   a.   Men are all the same/stupid.

     b.   ??Men are all mortal.

It was observed that when there is a generic subject, use of a floating quantifier is better with a predicative verb that expresses a subjective attitude, (31a) as opposed to an objective fact (31b).[15] This observation fits nicely into the f-structure approach advanced in this paper. In both cases the subject is the topic while the predicate is the focus. As the subject is a generic it is obligatorily a topic (Cohen and Erteschik-Shir 2002 among others). The quantifier forces one to look at the individuals within the set and evaluate the truth of the utterance with respect to all the individuals in the set. A subjective opinion is much more likely to be focused since it is an individual's opinion (not common knowledge). An objective fact, on the other hand, in the neutral case, would not be focused as it is a general truth and therefore evaluating each member of the set is awkward since it is a bit unnatural to do for a general truth. Sentence (31b) can be markedly improved through manipulation of the f-structure through context as in (32). If a contrastive focus is created, then there is 'reason' to focus the predicate and the oddness of the sentence is removed.

(32)   a.   Did you know that men are all immortal.

     b.   No they're not. Men are all mortal.

In this context, which forces a contrastive interpretation on the predicate in (b) with the contrast set being {immortal,mortal}, the sentence is equally good with or without the FQ. By manipulating the f-structure, the markedness of the sentence is removed. As we have seen thus far, floating quantifiers are found when a focus, in particular contrastive focus, follows it. The interchange in (32), which forces a contrastive reading on the predicate, is better than (32b) in a neutral context since in the former the redundancy of focusing a given fact is removed.

    In order to confirm these judgments with spontaneously produced data, a corpus search of the BYU Corpus of American English (COCA) (Davies 2008)

---

[15] While my own judgments do coincide I note that these judgments are extremely delicate.

was performed.[16] The search turned up very few hits, but of those that fit the target structure (generic noun with floated quantifier) all were subjective opinions and not objective facts.

(33)   Same old story. <u>Men</u> <u>are</u> <u>all</u> after one thing.
                                         (1994NEWSSanFrancisco- COCA)

(34)   ...men are incapable of valuing a woman's love—<u>men</u> <u>are</u> <u>all</u> raw in matters of love   (1995FICAntiochRev- COCA)

(35)   ...<u>men</u> <u>are</u> <u>all</u> scum, except for the ones...
                                         (1999FICCommentary- COCA)

In (33) the speaker is stating that she thinks that men are after only one thing. In (34) the speaker is stating her opinion on the issue of men and love. And finally in (35) the speaker is stating her opinion/impression of men. Clearly these excerpts are all subjective and not objective facts. While obviously a more comprehensive search will turn up more instances, from this limited search we can see that the construction is used more frequently with a subjective opinion compared to an objective fact—as expected.

An interesting comparison that can be made is that sentence (31b), repeated below as (36a), where a DP initial quantifier, as in (36b), instead of the floated quantifier is fine.

(36)   a.   ??Men are **all** mortal.

         b.   **All** men are mortal.

(36b) is not at all degraded in comparison to its subjective opinion counterpart (36) with a non-floated quantifier. This comparison is particularly enlightening because the predicate here is still an objective fact, but here the FQ is not identifying the predicate as the focus. Since this is the only change in the sentence we have to assume the difference in the level of acceptability of the sentence is a result of this change.

The difference in acceptability between (31a) and (b) when viewed in f-structure terms corresponds with what is being argued in this paper, namely that FQs float in order to mark the focus. The acceptability of the sentence is affected by the plausibility of the resulting information structure.

---

[16] Strings of the following type were searched for 'X are all adj'. where X is one of the following nouns: *men, women, boys, girls, people, kids,* and *children.*

5.6 FQ and sentential stress

A connection has been found between the location of nuclear stress and focus-sensitive elements. In this section the relationship between FQs and intonational prominence is examined. In particular the location of the nuclear accent is used as a diagnostic for focus and this in turn is used to show that FQ do indeed precede foci.

Focus particles have an intonationally prominent element in their c-command domain. For example, *only* can associate with nearly any focused phrase as long as this phrase is c-commanded by *only* (Jackendoff 1972). The focus is identified by the presence of the nuclear accent.

(37) a.   Peter only gave Mary$_F$ a book.

 b.   Peter only gave Mary a book$_F$.   (Jaeger and Wagner 2003)

In both sentences the focus particle associates with the focus although there is no change in the word order; in (a) the focus is the direct object while in (b) it is the indirect object. Beaver and Clark (2003) show that if an element is not marked by intonational prominence then the element cannot associate with *only*. They argue that context cannot completely override intonational focus effects.

The presence of an intonationally prominent element has been used as evidence that an element is a focus marker, for example *either* (Hendriks 2004). This same line of inquiry can be used when looking at FQs, the question being the relationship between the location of the FQ and the location of the nuclear accent. An example of a prosodically prominent constituent following the FQ can be seen in the following example. In Figure 5.1, not only is there a prosodically prominent constituent, *Indiana*, but the constituent bears the nuclear accent and is marked by the pitch accent that has been (albeit controversially) associated with contrast (Pierrehumbert and Hirshberg 1990).

(38)   Lajuna: I won't go to Indiana, see I don't have any family in Wisconsin
 My family's **all** in Indiana.   (SBC 044)

In these examples the nuclear accent is located on material following the FQ. In Figure 1 the most prominent constituent is *Indiana*. From the context as well as the location of the nuclear accent we can determine that the focus follows the FQ.

In question now is the consistency of this finding. While natural speech would be the obvious place to turn in order to investigate the relationship

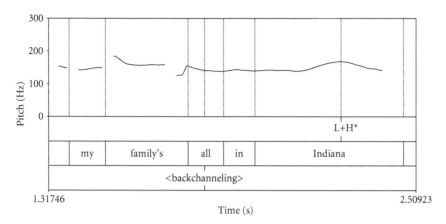

FIGURE 5.1 Pitch tracking.

Note: Only relevant accents are included in the figure

between FQs and nuclear accent, as mentioned there are very few instances of FQ floated from full DP, thus providing limited natural data for analysis.[17] Looking at sentences with pronominal subjects is less telling since by nature the pronoun is the topic and the predicate is the focus and thus the nuclear accent will occur in the predicate. What we can note about cases with pronouns and FQs is that in cases where there is a contrastive focus in the predicate, the pitch accent on the contrastive focus is not always as high and marked as one might expect.

One explanation for the difference in accent height on the contrastively focused element could be a result of the presence of the FQ. If the FQ identifies the following material as contrastively focused then the use of a higher pitch accent is not needed.[18] A contrastive accent would be redundant.[19] It may be the case that the presence of the accent on the FQ can be construed as marking the entire focus, the idea being that the contrastive focus needs to be marked either prosodically or syntactically but not both.

---

[17] In the cases of FQs floated from pronouns, the focus has to follow the FQ since pronouns are by nature topics (unless they are contrastive but I leave that aside for now).

[18] The lowered scale of the contrastive pitch accent following a pronoun could be thought to be a result of having less accents in the sentence. If pitch accent height is relative (see Féry, this volume), then if a pitch accent is the only accent, the accent won't be as high because it does not need to be high in comparison to any other accents. But in the case of sentences with FQs there is an accent on the FQ as well as the contrastively focused element.

[19] Whether or not there are specific accents that convey different meanings like contrast etc. is a controversial point.

Further investigation of spoken utterances in context needs to be examined in order to determine if syntactic marking and prosodic marking are both used in these cases and if they are used in simultaneously. Nevertheless, the lower-scaled contrastive accents do imply that phonology is aware of the syntactic choice to use a floating quantifier.

Returning to the issue at hand, in the absence of natural speech examples we turn to sentences with an embedded clause and FQ which are of use to examine from an intonational prospective.

(39)   I saw the men **all** wearing red **all** at the cafe.

In this sentence each FQ starts a new phonological phrase, as in (40).[20]

(40)   I saw the men [ALL wearing RED] [ALL at the CAFE].

In each phrase there is a pitch-accented constituent following the FQ, *red, same time.* An alternative prosodic rendition which places the nuclear stress on *men* (and thus no further pitch accents follow) is felt to be marked.

(41)   #I saw the MEN$_F$ all wearing red all at the cafe.

In contrast, with the removal of the FQs from the sentence, focal stress can be placed on *men* without the markedness.

(42)   I saw the MEN$_F$ wearing red at the cafe.

What about regular transitive sentences with an FQ, as in (43), compared to its FQ-less counterpart?

(43)   Who has seen the movie?
    a.   (THE CHILDREN have seen the movie)IP
    b.   (THE CHILDREN have **all** seen the movie)IP

In order to have the focus on the subject it must be marked by the nuclear accent, which in English is the last accent of the phrase, meaning there can be no further accents following it. The (a) version is preferred over the (b) version.[21] Sentences in which the FQ itself is not focused and which do not have an intonationally marked focus in their scope are degraded even when the context forces the reading where the subject is the focus.

Looking at FQs and intonation shows a tendency for the nuclear accent to follow the FQ. No cases were found where the nuclear accent preceded the

---

[20] Alternatively, the FQ itself can be emphatically stressed.
[21] If *all* is stressed the interpretation changes as do the judgments.

FQ. Moreover by looking at sentences with multiple FQs we find that each FQ obligatorily starts a new phonological phrase with, of course, a pitch-accented constituent. Dephrasing or having no pitch accents following the FQ are not possible prosodies.

5.7 FQs as focus markers

In this section I discuss FQs' adverbial nature and further explore the idea that FQs are a type of focus marker. The material that follows FQs is focused, frequently contrastively, implying that FQs are a type of focus marker, perhaps a focus particle. In this section the role of the FQ in the sentence is discussed and then the problem of how to classify FQs is approached. I conclude that while FQs are adverbial and mark foci they are not true focus particles like *only* and *even*. FQ usage is shown to be determined by f-structure.

In order to establish what FQs are we turn to Bobaljik's (1995) proposal that FQs are a type of adverb. A full account of Bobaljik's approach and arguments is beyond the scope of this paper but I highlight some of the main points as acceptance of this approach is crucial to the central claims of this paper. Bobaljik's claim is supported by ordering restrictions and the placement of FQs. Bobaljik (1995) and Fitzpatrick (2006) show that *all* patterns like adverbs, in particular the adverb *easily* (in its modal reading, not its manner reading) with respect to its distribution.[22]

(44)   The veggies (easily) will (easily) have (easily) been (*? easily) being (*easily) roasted . . . (Fitzpatrick 2006: table 2.1)

(45)   The veggies (all) will (all) have (all) been (*?all) being (*all) roasted . . .

Fitzpatrick (2006) also notes that FQs, like adverbs, can appear iteratively within a sentence, (46)–(48).

(46)   John **probably easily completely** finished that huge bowl of ice cream **yesterday.**   (Fitzpatrick 2006: 47, #28)

(47)   What the boys **all** did was **all** cheat.

(48)   a.   The students will **both** have **each** received their degree by the summer.

---

[22] Fitzpatrick proposes that FQs have adverbial distribution. He does not propose that FQs share semantic traits with adverbs.

b. The students will **all** have **each** received their degree by the summer.

c. The students will **each** have **all** received their degree by the summer. (Fitzpatrick 2006: 48)

I concur with the proposal that FQs are adverbial. What I add to this is that FQs are not just adverbial but also focus-sensitive, but not focus particles, like *only* or *even*, as FQs have a different type of relationship with the focus. Focus particles lexically encode a dependency on the focus. Adverbs like *always* and, as we will see, FQs do not encode a lexical dependency on the focus.

Müller (1998: 7) explains that focus particles 'imply alternatives (values) to their relational elements and they include or exclude these alternatives in a larger context'. Focus-sensitive elements can be broken down into true focus particles and faux focus particles (Beaver and Clark 2002).[23] Even within the class of focus particles all the members do not display the same behaviors as focus particles themselves do not form a homogenous class in terms of their behavior (Beaver and Clark 2003). Some adverbs (e.g., *always*) are sensitive to focus but not in the same way that true focus particles are. Beaver and Clark (2003) state that focus particles have a much tighter semantic relationship with the focus of the sentence than focus-sensitive adverbs do (Beaver and Clark 2003: 348ff.). FQs exclude the possible alternatives to the focus but do not have a tight semantic dependency on the focus that true focus particles have.

FQs have a much looser semantic and syntactic tie to the focus than true focus particles. Also in terms of their placement, focus-sensitive particles frequently are adjacent to the constituent that is the focus; the preferred readings of the sentences below have the focus particle identifying the adjacent constituent as the focus.

(49)   Only [John]$_F$ plays basketball

(50)   John only [plays basketball]$_F$

(51)   John plays only [basketball]$_F$.

(50) can have the reading where the focus is either on the verb or on the VP, depending upon where the accent is located. While FQs precede the focus,

---

[23] There are several basic traits used to identify focus particles. To name a few: focus particles have to c-command the focus, they engender scopal effects, they are limited to certain attachment sites (only to certain maximal projections), and finally displaced sentence-initial focus markers are ruled out (Johannessen 2005; 425–7).

their placement is much more limited by syntax and their relationship with the non-focal subject cannot be sidelined. FQs have a relationship with the topical subject and they have a relationship with the following focus. Additionally complicating the picture is the fact that FQs themselves are sometimes contrastively focused, not a possibility with true focus particles.

While FQs usually precede foci, in other cases they themselves are perceived as being contrastively focused. This is the result of the pitch accent on the quantifier which evokes a scale ranging from *all* to *none*. Bader and Frazier (2005) raise the possibility that the determiner quantifier may have a grammatically given contrast set which distinguishes each from other members of this small closed set of grammatical function words. This scale then, would always be available when *all* is used.[24] From this set scale, *all* is selected.

(52)   [The boys]$_{TOP}$ have [$\begin{bmatrix} [all]_{FOC} \\ some \\ \dots \\ none \end{bmatrix}$ $_{TOP}$ seen the movie]$_{FOC}$.

In (52) following Erteschik-Shir (1997), the focus marked on the FQ is a subordinate focus. A subordinate focus is a focused constituent embedded within a topic. This topic defines a contrast set, which includes *all, some, none* plus other relevant members of the scale. The set is topical since it is always available with *all*. From this set *all* is selected and thereby the other members of the set are removed as possible answers. This forces a subordinate focus on *all* and explains the presence of the pitch accent and contrastive interpretation of the quantifier.

While FQs are found before all types of foci, they are predominantly found before foci that are members of a set, what Erteschik-Shir terms contrastive foci. This is seen in (53)–(55) which are from natural speech.

(53)   …when you start pumping if your well has a large enough diameter, the water's **all** coming from the well, it's not coming from the aquifer.   (MICASE)

(54)   …the cytochromes are **all** different, A B and C?   (MICASE)

(55)   but like the kids are **all** into pokemon right now and it uh they have these fads that go through.   (Buckeye)

---

[24] Bader and Frazier (2005) are discussing the determiner quantifier use of *all*. They are in fact contrasting it with adverb quantifiers. Nevertheless, their idea of the permanently available contrast set seems to hold for the floating quantifier *all* as well as the determiner quantifier.

In (53) there is a contrastive focus. The contrast is between water coming from the aquifer and water coming from the well. What is interesting is that the contrast set is made explicit after a member of the set has already been selected. In (54), the speaker is setting up a contrast set between A, B, and C. Again in this case the members of the contrast set are specified later. And finally, in (55) the contrast set is specified after a selection of one member. The set is *Pokemon* versus *other fads* and *Pokemon* is selected.

It is striking that the contrast set is made explicit after a member of the set has been selected; usually one first introduces the members of the set and then selects one member. In these cases the member is selected before the set is introduced. This indicates that perhaps participants of the discourse are attuned to expect contrast after the FQ and take the presence of a contrast set as a given.

(56)   [The boys]$_{TOP}$ have all $\begin{bmatrix} \lfloor seen\ the\ movie \rfloor _{TOP} \\ -\ -alternative-\ - \end{bmatrix}_{FOC}$.

The presence of the FQ may serve to indicate that the relevant member of the contrast set is the focus and any other members are not possible. Pitch accents are found on the FQ as well as the focus. This correlates with the proposal that contrastive accents following FQs are lower than in sentences without the FQs because the listener is made aware of the contrast by the use of the FQ, rendering additional means superfluous.

The quantifier comes with a contrast scale whenever it is used. A particular discourse though, may not support a contrastive interpretation of the quantifier. In these cases the contrast on the quantifier is then extended and the interpretation is of a contrastive quantifier and predicate. The interpretation then is that there is contrast on the focus and not specifically the quantifier.

(57)   [The boys]$_{TOP}$ have $\begin{bmatrix} \lfloor all\ seen\ the\ movie \rfloor _{TOP} \\ -\ -alternatives-- \end{bmatrix}_{FOC}$.

In these cases, there is a contrastive focus. When the quantifier itself is contrastive, but the predicate is not, the non-floating version is more frequently used than the floating version. In these cases the quantifier is still pitch-accented and evokes the same scale and as a contrastive focus it still removes the other members as possible answers. Speakers might opt for the non-floating quantifier when they want to convey contrast on the quantifier as a way to aid processing. Since in the floated position there are two possible interpretations (contrast on the quantifier and/or contrast of the predicate), use of the non-floating quantifier removes possible ambiguity. The quantifier is no longer marking the predicate as contrastive. Furthermore, since the quantifier itself is a focus, its role as a focus marker is not needed in this type of sentence.

Looking more in depth at the discourse surrounding the utterance from Figure 1 illuminates the information structure more clearly.

(58)   LAJUAN: I won't go home when he's here.
        CAM: Are you serious?
        LAJUAN: I won't go to Indiana, see I don't have any family in Wisconsin.
        My family's all in Indiana.   (SBC 044)

In this sentence while *all* may invoke a scale, a contrast set is not supported by the discourse and *all* is not contrastive. What is contrastive is the focus *Indiana*. This is contrasted with Wisconsin. The contrast set here is {Wisconsin, Indiana}. *All* removes the alternatives to the focus *Indiana*. *All* reduces the tolerance to alternatives. Note the following continuation is odd sounding.

(59)   I won't go to Indiana, see I don't have any family in Wisconsin
        #My family's **all** in Indiana except for a few relatives in Wisconsin.

We have clearly seen that the use of FQs is influence by f-structure. In addition to the FQ's relationship to the focus, it is also related to the DP, subject or object depending on where it occurs, and to this I turn now.

FQs are argued to be adverbial and not nominal markers (Bobaljik 1995, among others). Nevertheless FQ cannot be classified as modifying only the VP or the DP since they can have a relationship with both the DP and the VP. FQs display some similarities with some nominal modifiers (as in split topics in languages like German; see Nakanishi forthcoming) in that both the subject and the predicate provide restrictions on the FQ.

The relationship that the FQ and the subject have is such that the FQ provides a 'totality' effect. It makes it clear that the entire subject (or all the members that make up the subject) are involved.[25] Bobaljik gives the following examples:

(60)   a.   The reporters **all** harangued the candidate.

        b.   The reporters harangued the candidate.   (Bobaljik 1995: 198, #7)

If even one reporter did not participate in the haranguing, (60a) is not true, while in (60b) not all reporters need to participate for the sentence to be true (see Dowty 1987 for more on this).

---

[25] See Bobaljik (1995) and references therein for more on this.

Yet the maximizing effect can be seen as redundant in many cases. Take the following sentence:

(61)   Larry Darrel and Darrel came into the café all at the same time.

(Bobaljik 1995: 213)

The presence of *all* is redundant here. Listing the proper names assumes that they all went or else the speaker would not list them. It has been proposed that *all* does not add any meaning to the sentence. For example Aldridge (1982), cites Quine as proposing that 'all' is 'logically redundant' (see Estling Vannestål 2004: 61). Huddleston (1982: 253 as citied in Estling Vannestål 2004) argues that in cases where you have *all the* 'all' serves to emphasize the totality already present in the DP but does not itself introduce it. These researchers discuss the DP-initial (non-floated) *all*. Nevertheless it raises an interesting question, if DP-initial *all* contributes no new meaning to the sentence, what can the floated 'all' be doing? (60) showed that the contribution is not always redundant, (61) shows that it frequently can be viewed as such.

Evidence presented in this paper argues that in fact *all* is not redundant in these sentences. The FQ introduces alternatives to itself and the focus. In this sense it creates a contrastive effect. These alternatives, crucially, are not alternatives to the subject. The subject is the topic, the alternatives are for the focus.

5.8 Conclusion

In this paper the role of the FQ in the sentence has been explored. The FQ indicates that what follows it is the focus, frequently a contrastive focus. The choice between the use of a floated versus non-floated quantifier is neither random nor stylistic, but in fact determined by the information-structure status of the material following the quantifier. FQs shed light on the syntax–phonology interface because we derive evidence that the phonology is sensitive to the contrastive focus-marking property of the floated quantifier. Also the phonology must be sensitive to the f-structure constraints of the language. If it weren't then we should have found FQs sentence-finally in natural speech.

6

Prosodic prominence: A syntactic matter?

JOÃO COSTA

6.1 Introduction

Recent literature on the behavior of focus marking across languages reveals that a complete account of this phenomenon cannot overlook that focus involves—or at least may involve—prosodic marking and word-order effects. For instance, in Romance languages like Spanish or European Portuguese, most descriptions converge in showing that focused constituents appear at the right edge of the sentences, where nuclear stress falls (e.g. Zubizarreta 1998, among others).

Less consensus is found in the literature on focus on the exact interpretation of the interplay between syntax and prosody. Most authors coincide in acknowledging that focus is marked syntactically and prosodically, but there is little agreement on the nature of the relation between the two components. Summarizing a long debate, one can say that the point of disagreement is the locus of focus encoding. For some authors, focus is a syntactic primitive, realized either as a feature (Jackendoff 1972) or as a functional category (Brody 1990; Rizzi 1997). According to this view, prosodic effects are coincidental. More articulated views on the syntax–prosody interface propose an interplay between these two components. Accordingly, syntactic movement may be triggered by the need to create legitimate prosodic objects. In a specific implementation of these ideas, Zubizarreta (1998) proposes that p-movement is a last-resort syntactic operation triggered by the need to resolve a conflict generated when adjacent nodes have prosodic contradictory properties. Such a conflict would arise, for instance, when the Nuclear Stress Rule (assigning prominence to the most embedded constituent) and a Focus Prominence Rule (assigning prominence to the focus of the sentence) assign equal prominence to two sister nodes. According to

Zubizarreta (1998), there are two strategies to solve this type of problem: either to treat some material as metrically invisible and assign the prominence to the rightmost constituent (in other words, do stress shift), or to perform a prosodically motivated movement operation (p-movement) and undo the prosodic ambiguity. Zubizarreta proposes that metrical invisibility is the option in a language like English, which explains that there may be prominence on a preverbal subject, in a context like (1):

(1)   A: Who smiled?
      B: JOHN smiled.

On the contrary, in a language like Spanish, all material must be metrically visible, which makes it impossible to assign focus to a preverbal subject, since it would be prominent under the Focus Prominence Rule, but adjacent to a verb assigned prominence by the Nuclear Stress Rule. This conflict is solved if the subject stays in the rightmost position and p-movement applies to the remaining material (which can be achieved under several syntactic mechanisms: VP-fronting to the left of the subject or stranding the subject in its base-generated position), as in (2):

(2)   A: Quién sonrió?
      B: Sonrió JUAN.

As clearly explained by Zubizarreta, this movement operation must be considered syntactic, since it obeys syntactic requirements, and because it interacts with the Nuclear Stress Rule, which, according to this author, must apply at the end of the syntactic derivation, because, at least in some languages, it is sensitive to selectional constraints (Gussenhoven 1984).

Other approaches differ in the implementation, but share the idea that prosodic requirements may act as a trigger for syntactic movement or for word-order rearrangements. Analyses of this type can be found, for instances, in Neeleman and Reinhart (1999), according to whom scrambling in Germanic is triggered by the need to place an object in a position where it escapes the Nuclear Stress Rule, or in Costa (1998), where it is proposed that focused subjects stay in situ in order to be at the position where nuclear stress is assigned.

When this type of approach is considered, two questions necessarily come up:

a. If prosody may act as a syntactic trigger, can the idea that syntax is autonomous be maintained?
b. Since the prosodic reflex of focus differs crosslinguistically, what is the source for variation?

In this paper, I will address these questions, revisiting some data from European Portuguese. It will be argued that a model of syntax incorporating some of the ideas of early Minimalism (Chomsky 1993) and of Optimality Theory (Prince and Smolensky 1993), according to which global comparisons between derivations are allowed can account for the focus data presented, without running into the problems of incorporating prosodic factors as syntactic primitives or triggers.

The paper is organized as follows: in section 6.2, Zubizarreta's proposal on the way different languages solve prosodic conflicts in prominence assignment is presented; in section 6.3, empirical argumentation against the idea that there is prosodically motivated movement, and in favor of the idea of stress shift as last resort is developed; section 6.4 spells out an alternative analysis for the relation between prosody and syntax, maintaining the idea that syntax is prosody-free and dispensing with prosodically motivated movement; in section 6.5, some conclusions are presented.

6.2 Prosodic triggers for syntactic movement

Zubizarreta (1998) offers an interesting proposal for the crosslinguistic differences in the encoding of focus. According to the analysis defended, in languages like Spanish and Italian, all constituents are metrically visible, which makes p-movement the only available resource for solving prosodic conflicts. In languages like English and French, the same type of conflict may be solved in a different way, since constituents may be metrically invisible. Accordingly, a prominence on a non-final constituent is explained by the assumption that the remaining material is metrically invisible. Zubizarreta addresses the question of whether p-movement is unavailable in languages like English and French. In other words, one would wonder whether there is some type of parametric split in how prosodic conflicts are solved. The author convincingly shows that word-order rearrangements in specific discourse settings also emerge in French, although optionally, as illustrated in (3):

(3)   (What did you put on the table?)   (from Zubizarreta 1998: 147)
      Nous avons mis sur la   table <u>trois livres.</u>
      We   have   put on   the   table three books

On the contrary, in English, only metrical invisibility applies, and not p-movement. This option is not available in this language. The proposal made may be summarized in the following terms: languages split in the way they solve prosodic conflicts of the type described in Zubizarreta (1998). Either the conflicts are solved by p-movement (Spanish/Italian), or by metrical invisibility (English), or by both (French). Interestingly, p-movement in French is always optional and freely varies with metrical invisibility.

European Portuguese clearly functions as a language in which p-movement would apply, as illustrated in (4), since a focused subject cannot be marked in preverbal position with stress only:

(4)   (Who smiled?)

    a.   #O JOÃO sorriu.

    b.   Sorriu <u>o João</u>.

As such, it can be assumed that, like in Spanish and in Italian, metrical invisibility does not apply in this language either.

This approach makes several claims:

    a. p-movement and metrical invisibility (i.e. stress shift) are two instances of operations applying in syntax;

    b. p-movement and stress shift are equal last-resort strategies picked by different languages, or operating optionally within the same language;

    c. as it is defined, p-movement is a prosodically triggered syntactic operation.

These claims make interesting predictions:

    i. if a p-movement language displays stress shift, the two strategies should apply in free variation;

    ii. if p-movement is prosodically triggered, its prosodic and interpretive effects are constant;

    iii. p-movement should not take priority over stress shift, since they are two surface manifestations of the same operation;[1]

    iv. if p-movement is syntactic movement, when it conflicts with other syntactic requirements, ineffability should be expected.

In what follows, I will show that these predictions are not met, and that maybe the idea that there is prosodically motivated syntactic movement should be dispensed with.

---

[1] An anonymous reviewer points out that the predictions presented here follow from a conception of p-movement according to which this operation is not sensitive to other language-specific considerations. Note that, since in Zubizarreta's proposal, p-movement is a last-resort syntactic operation, it must be sensitive to syntactic effects, but there is no reason for stress shift to override its effects.

6.3 Prosodically motivated syntactic operations and the syntactic nature of stress shift: Empirical counter-arguments

As shown in Costa (1998, 2004), there are several constructions in which an information focus does not surface at the rightmost position in European Portuguese. In all such cases, focus is marked with the assignment of prominence to the focused constituent, in a similar way to what happens in French or English. Likewise, there are several contexts in which it can be shown that stress shift applies whenever the syntactic component is not able to place a constituent at the rightmost position. These two situations cast doubt on the idea that stress shift is an operation applying in the syntactic component. Let us go through the empirical arguments.

6.3.1 *DP-internal focus on possessives*

As shown in Castro and Costa (2003), a focused possessive in definite contexts must surface in prenominal position, bearing a heavy stress:[2]

(5) A: Que   livro compraste?
         Which book bought-2sg
         'Which book did you buy?'

     B: a. Comprei   o   TEU livro.
             Bought-1sg the your book

         b. *Comprei o livro teu.
             'I bought your book.'

Note that this heavy stress is a way to solve a prosodic conflict of the type discussed in Zubizarreta (1998). The Focus Prominence Rule would place the most prominent stress on the possessive, but the Nuclear Stress Rule would place prominence on the rightmost noun *livro* (book). Accordingly, two sister nodes have equal prominence. If p-movement were to apply DP-internally in order to leave the possessive at the rightmost position, where it would be assigned the sentence nuclear stress, the ungrammatical word order illustrated in (5Bb) would be generated. Following Castro and Costa (2003), the problem with the ungrammatical word order is to be found in the categorial status of the possessive. There is evidence to claim that it behaves as a head in European

---

[2] The question–answer pair in (5) illustrates that this is an instance of information focus. Additional contrastive effects may arise (as in any other information-focus context), but they are not necessary for the relevant stress pattern to emerge.

Portuguese, and that it is generated as the head of a functional projection in the language. As such, there is no position to the right of the noun where it could be base-generated. However, nothing precludes a derivation in which the NP constituent containing the noun would move to the left of the possessive. The fact that this does not occur casts some doubt on the idea that leftward movement of constituents applies across the board to solve prosodic conflicts.

There is, therefore, a preliminary conclusion that can be drawn from this behavior of possessives: evidence for metrical invisibility can be found even in a language in which the effects of p-movement can be seen.[3] Interestingly, the picture obtained is different from what was described above for French. Unlike in this language, there is no optionality for the possessive in European Portuguese: the derivation in which the possessive is placed at the position where it is assigned sentence nuclear stress is just ungrammatical.

6.3.2 *Relative order between adverb and direct object*

Let us revisit some well-known facts concerning the relative order between direct objects and VP-modifiers. As shown in (6), a VP-modifier may either precede or follow a direct object:

(6) a. O   João fala   francês bem.
         The João speaks French well

     b. O João fala bem francês.
         'João speaks French well.'

The two word orders are not equivalent in what concerns felicity in different discourse settings. As shown in Costa (1998), (6a), in which the adverb surfaces at the rightmost position is a legitimate answer to a question like *How does João speak French?*, with focus on the adverb, whereas (6b) is felicitous as a reply to *Which language does João speak well?*, with focus on the direct object. The word order in (6a) has been analyzed in Costa (1998) as

---

[3] As noted by an anonymous reviewer, in related languages, the pattern is different. For instance, in Spanish, the pronominal possessive is necessarily contrastive whenever it is stressed. As noted in the literature (e.g. Castro 2006), Spanish and Portuguese prenominal possessives are different in other respects (co-occurrence with determiners, gender marking, etc.). For this reason, no clear prediction can be made for one of the languages on the basis of the other. However, this crosslinguistic difference shows that different types of deaccenting may serve different discourse purposes. Clearly, the fact that Spanish possessives are necessarily contrastive shows that they are not a good test ground for the interaction between movement and stress in the context of information focus.

a case of DP-scrambling, yielding a configuration in which the DP left-adjoins to VP:

(7)   [$_{IP}$ fala$_v$ [$_{VP}$ francês$_i$ [$_{VP}$ bem [$_{VP}$ t$_v$ t$_i$

Still in Costa (1998), it is claimed that this movement is a kind of defocusing strategy for the DP. In order to leave the adverb in the rightmost position, where it can be assigned sentence nuclear stress, the object scrambles to the left.[4] As such, this type of movement could be thought of as an instance of p-movement.

There is, however, a problem: in an out-of-the-blue context, both word orders are felicitous, as shown in (8):

(8)   A: O que aconteceu? Porque é que estás tão contente?
               'What happened? Why are you so happy?'

        B: a.   O João comeu depressa a   salada.
                      João   ate   quickly the salad

               b.   O João comeu a salada   depressa.
                      João   ate   the salad quickly.
                      'João ate the salad quickly.'

The problem illustrated by (8) comes about when we consider the order V-DP-Adv (8Bb). If this word order is generated as a case of DP-scrambling, which, in turn, is a case of p-movement, this word order is unexpected, since in this context there is no motivation for the movement to occur.

A different interpretation is, therefore, needed for the data in (7) and (8). Keeping the idea that the relevant word order is obtained via scrambling, and that scrambling is the result of adjunction, one can think that, adjunction being an optional operation, whenever its effects have no import, such as in out-of-the-blue environments, scrambling will be purely optional in the sense of Saito (1989). In other words, the data in (8) weaken the idea that there is a prosodic motivation for direct-object scrambling, since this operation applies even in the absence of the prosodic context requiring it.

The conclusion to be drawn from this second set of data is, then, the following: the same syntactic configuration may obtain with or without interpretive and prosodic effects associated. In other words, the fact that a certain movement or configuration is often associated with a certain prosodic effect does not mean that prosody is a trigger for that movement.

---

[4] For the sake of the present discussion, it is irrelevant to know whether this is an instance of DP-scrambling or VP-remnant movement. For arguments against a remnant-movement analysis of sentences of this type, see Costa (2002).

6.3.3 *DP-internal focus on nouns or adjectives*

Bearing in mind the data just presented in 6.3.2, we have seen that, in different contexts, similar word orders may obtain, as long as the syntactic configuration is available. Let us now consider the relative order between noun and adjectives in the following set of examples. As shown in (9), and as it is well known for Romance languages (e.g. Cinque 1994), with certain adjectives both Adj-N and N-Adj orders are possible:

(9)　a.　Comprei　uma bola óptima.
　　　　Bought-1sg a　　ball great

　　b.　Comprei　uma óptima bola.
　　　　Bought-1sg a　　great　　ball
　　　　'I bought a great ball.'

As shown in (10), if the adjective is focused the word order in which the adjective is rightmost is preferred:

(10)　A:　Que bola compraste?
　　　　　Which ball did you buy?

　　　B:　a.　Comprei uma bola óptima.
　　　　　　　Bought　a　　ball　great

　　　　　b.　#Comprei　uma óptima bola.
　　　　　　　Bought-1sg a　　great　　ball
　　　　　　　'I bought a great ball.'

Not all adjectives permit the two word orders. Color adjectives occur post-nominally only, whereas numeral adjectives only occur prenominally, which follows from syntactic constraints on the DP-internal structure (see e.g. Cinque 1994 or Alexiadou 2001):

(11)　a.　Vi　　uma bola azul.
　　　　Saw-1sg a　　ball blue

　　b.　*Vi uma azul bola.
　　　　'I saw a blue ball.'

(12)　a.　Li　　o　primeiro livro.
　　　　Read-1sg the first　　book

　　b.　*Li o livro primeiro.
　　　　'I read the first book.'

Interestingly, even if the noun is focused in an information-focus context, it cannot follow a color adjective, as shown in (13). Likewise, even if the numeral adjective is focused, it cannot follow the noun, as shown in (14). In both contexts, stress shift applies, in a way similar to what happens in English or in languages in which metrical invisibility applies:

(13)   A: Que   coisa azul é que viste?
             Which thing blue saw-2sg
             'Which blue thing did you see?'

    B: a.   Vi   uma BOLA azul.
                  Saw-1sg a   ball   blue
         b.   *Vi uma azul bola.
                  'I saw a blue ball.'

(14)   A: Que   livro é que leste?
             Which book read-2sg
             'Which book did you read?'

    B: a.   Li   o   PRIMEIRO livro.
                  Read-1sg the first   book
         b.   *Li o livro primeiro.
                  'I read the first book.'

This set of data is interesting, since it completes the data shown in 6.3.3 above. In 6.3.3, it was shown that prosodic (and discourse) effects may be obtained when a configuration independently exists in the language. In the data involving DP-internal focus on nouns and adjectives, one can see that word-order rearrangements for the sake of prosodic well-formedness do not come up if its output is independently ruled out. In other words, whenever a position for an adjective is independently ruled out by syntactic constraints, p-movement cannot act, yielding configurations in which adjectives appear in unexpected positions. Instead, when syntactic constraints rule out a given configuration in which a focused constituent is placed rightmost, deaccenting and stress shift emerge as the strategy to encode focus.

6.3.4 *Focus on the verb*

Consider now the following example, in which the verb is the focus of the sentence:

(15)   A: O que é que o João fez ao Luís?
             'What did João do to Luís?'

    B: Ele MATOU o Luís.
         He killed   the Luís
         'He killed Luís.'

As shown in (15B), if the direct object is uttered in the answer to A, the verb is not at the rightmost position. In fact, there are valid options in the language in which the verb is final in this context: one can either use a null object or a clitic pronoun instead of the DP. However, if the DP is uttered, the best option is to leave it in situ, as in (15B). Importantly, topicalizing the DP is not a very good option in this context, since, as argued in Duarte (1987), displaced topics tend to be interpreted contrastively. Thus, we face a context in which syntactic movement of the material to the right of the focus is not a good option for solving the prosodic conflict created by the alleged inter-action between the Focus Prominence Rule and the Nuclear Stress Rule. As such, as in some of the contexts illustrated above, the non-final focus bears a heavy stress, and the material to its right is deaccented, as if it were metrically invisible.

6.3.5 *Focus in binding contexts*[5]

In ditransitive contexts, as expected, the rightmost constituent is the focus of the sentence:

(16) A: A quem é que   deste o livro?
          to whom did you give the book

      B: Dei   o livro   [F ao Paulo]
          (I) gave the book to Paulo.
          #Dei ao Paulo o livro.

(17) A: O que é que deste ao Paulo?
          what did you give to Paulo

      B: Dei   ao Paulo [F o livro].
          (I) gave to Paulo   the book
          #Dei o livro ao Paulo.

If one wants to assume a base-generated order in which the direct object precedes the indirect object, the case in (17B), in which this word order is reversed might be interpreted as an instance of p-movement. However, the data turn out to be slightly more complicated. As shown in (18) and (19), if the focused argument must bind an anaphor contained within the non-focused argument, the former cannot be rightmost:

(18) A: A quem   é que deste   os livros?
          to whom did you give the books?

---

[5] In Costa (2008), the same argument is used to evaluate the cartographic approach to focus.

B: Dei [F A CADA AUTOR] o seu livro.
       (I) gave to each author his book.

       *Dei   o seu livro a cada autor.
       (I) gave his book   to each author

(19)   A: O que é que deste aos autores?
              what did you give to the authors

       B: Dei   [F CADA LIVRO] ao seu autor.
              (I) gave   each book   to its author
              *Dei   ao seu autor cada livro.
              (I) gave   to its author each book

Note that focus is still marked in sentences (18B) and (19B), since the focused constituent bears a heavier stress and the non-focused constituent undergoes deaccenting. This piece of data is relevant, since it sheds light on the status of the stress rules. Zubizarreta (1998) contends that the Nuclear Stress Rule applies at the end of the syntactic derivation. From this proposal, it follows that p-movement must be syntactic. As such, one would expect that the competition between two syntactic requirements—anaphoric binding and p-movement—should yield a fatal contradiction and consequent ineffability. However, what we see in the data from (16) through (19) is that binding takes preference over placing a constituent at the rightmost position. In other words, it appears that focus is rightmost only if the configuration created does not violate any syntactic requirement. Otherwise, stress shift applies as in English: in (18B) and in (19B), the material to the right of the focused constituent is deaccented and acts as if it were metrically invisible.

The important conclusion to be drawn from this set of data is that rightmost position is available for focused constituents only if no syntactic requirement is violated by such a configuration.

6.3.6 *Acquisition facts*

Reinhart (1999) offers an approach to some language acquisition facts according to which the application of post-syntactic last-resort operations create processing difficulties for children. Assuming that stress shift is a last-resort operation, Reinhart hypothesizes that the computation of a sentence with stress shift implies a comparison with a derivation in which stress shift did not apply. Bearing the multiple derivations in mind imposes a computational overload for the acquiring child and a working memory problem. Szendrői (2004) and Costa and Szendrői (2006) show that this hypothesis is on the right track, testing the comprehension of focused sentences with and without stress shift. According to their results, children performed significantly worse when they had to deal with the interpretive effects of stress shift. Crucially, they had no problems with word-order rearrangements related to prosody and discourse.

This asymmetry in performance by children when exposed to two different strategies for focus marking can be interpreted as evidence favoring the idea that only stress shift is post-syntactic. As such, these facts favor a view according to which discourse-related word-order changes and stress shift are not acting in the same component. In other words, they cannot be seen as two alternative facets of a single phenomenon.

The conclusion to be drawn from the acquisition facts reported is, thus, that there is evidence to claim that stress shift is a last-resort operation, but the same does not hold for p-movement.

6.3.7 *Parenthetical insertion*

As spelled out in the introduction, the idea that p-movement and the Nuclear Stress Rule apply within the syntactic component implies that syntax is sensitive to prosodic constraints. The idea of a syntax-free phonology has been subject to a long debate and is often challenged by the observation that certain syntactic operations appear to be constrained by prosodic requirements. One such example comes from the work of Frota and Vigário (2002), who argue that parenthetical clauses can only be inserted whenever the constituent following them forms an Intonational Phrase. This is illustrated in (20):

(20) a. As alunas,   até onde sabemos,   andam a estudar muito.
          The students   until where know-1pl are-3pl studying much
          'The students, as far as we know, are studying a lot.'

      b. *??As alunas,   até onde sabemos,   estudam.
          The students   until where know-1pl study-3pl
          'The students, as far as we know, study.'

Frota and Vigário (2002) explain contrasts of the type given in (20) along the following lines: the parenthetical clause forms an independent Intonational Phrase. This is known in European Portuguese, since Intonational Phrase boundaries block the assimilation of word-final /s/ (Frota 1999), and such assimilation is indeed blocked at the edges of the parenthetical clause. The insertion of the parenthetical in (20b) is ruled out, since the material to its right is not sufficient to form a legitimate Intonational Phrase. On the contrary, in (20a), there is enough material to the right of the parenthetical, and an independent Intonational Phrase can be construed. Based on evidence of this type, these authors conclude that the insertion of parenthetical clauses is prosodically constrained, and that these facts—together with other weight effects—act as evidence for weakening the idea that the syntactic component of the grammar is phonology-free. The idea that the syntax may be constrained by prosodic effects may be tested, if one keeps the prosodic environment constant and changes the syntactic context. This task was done for the insertion of parentheticals in Martins and Mascarenhas (2004). These authors created a context in which the prosodic environment for the insertion of a parenthetical clause is ensured: a context in which there is an intonational phrase. This is illustrated in (21):

(21)   Os   meus primos, a   quem escrevo   regularmente, vivem   em
       The my   cousins, to whom write-1sg regularly,   live-3pl in
       França.
       France
       'My cousins, to whom I regularly write, live in France.'

As shown in Martins and Mascarenhas (2004), the appositive relative clause in (21) forms an Intonational Phrase, which can be confirmed because there may be no assimilation of the final fricative of the noun preceding it. Yet, although the relevant prosodic environment is available, insertion of a parenthetical is blocked in this context, as shown in (22):

(22)   Os   meus primos, (*até onde sabemos,)   a   quem   escrevo
       The my   cousins, (until where know-1pl,) to whom   write-1sg
       regularmente, vivem   em France
       regularly,   live-3pl in França.
       'As far as we know, my cousins, to whom I regularly write, live in France.'

The contrast between (22) and the sentences in (20) leads to an important conclusion: the distribution of parenthetical clauses is primarily syntactically constrained. The insertion of parentheticals is possible in places independently made available for adjunction. As it is well known, DP-internal positions are not legitimate adjunction sites for sentence modifiers. As such, and although the relevant prosodic context is available, the insertion of a parenthetical in the wrong syntactic environment is ruled out. This argues in favor of maintaining the idea that syntax is prosody-free. These data lead to the conclusion that the distribution of syntactic objects is primarily cons by syntactic notions. Prosodic effects may affect syntactic outputs, but only after elementary convergence requirements have been met. In other words, there is a preference for placing parenthetical clauses in adjunction sites where they are followed by an intonational phrase, but this is not a prerequisite for the licensing of the clause itself.

6.3.8 *Summary and questions*

The data listed in this section lead to the following conclusions:

i. The effects of metrical invisibility come up in p-movement languages (e.g. possessives, verb focus, adjectival focus, and focus on binders).
ii. The configuration obtained by p-movement is not necessarily linked to a prosodic effect (e.g. scrambling in out-of-the-blue contexts).
iii. p-movement only applies if the configuration it yields is independently legitimate. Otherwise, metrical invisibility applies (e.g. focus on different types of adjectives).
iv. Syntactic licensing requirements may preclude the application of p-movement, and force metrical invisibility (e.g. ban on rightmost position for focused binders).
v. There is evidence to claim that stress shift is a last-resort strategy, whereas word-order rearrangements are not (e.g. acquisition facts).
vi. There is evidence to claim that syntax is phonology-free, even in contexts in which, *prima facie*, the distribution of constituents is constrained by prosodic requirements (e.g. the insertion of parenthetical clauses).

These conclusions lead to the formulation of a new set of problems:

a. The conclusion that syntax is phonology-free is highly problematic for the idea that the Nuclear Stress Rule and p-movement apply in the syntactic component as proposed in Zubizarreta (1998).
b. The conclusion that the configuration obtained by p-movement may not involve discourse and prosodic effects seriously compromises the idea that there is some type of 'prosodic motivation' for this type of word-order rearrangements.
c. The conclusion that metrical invisibility (or stress shift) is more last resort than p-movement, and acts only when there is no legitimate syntactic output placing constituents at the rightmost position seriously compromises the idea that stress shift and p-movement are two instances of the same phenomenon.

In short, the arguments listed in this section seriously weaken the idea of prosodically motivated movement, since it was shown that what could be taken as instances of this movement may occur in the absence of a prosodic trigger, is always syntactically constrained, and is not a last-resort operation.

Given these considerations, an alternative explanation to the word-order effects associated with focus and prosody is needed.

6.4 Multiple outputs and filters

In the previous section, it was shown that incorporating prosodic constraints into the syntactic component yields some undesirable problems. Nevertheless, word-order variation associated with prosody and discourse is well attested. For this reason, it is necessary to know how to account for this type of data in a prosody-free syntactic model. The idea to be explored in this section follows the claims put forward in radical different terms in Chomsky (1993) and Prince and Smolensky (1993) that the grammar may generate multiple outputs. In Optimality Theory, this is clear and is one of the premises of the theory. A function *Gen(erator)* creates outputs that are filtered out by a set of ranked universal constraints. In early minimalism, the notion of economy is introduced, acting as a global filter comparing converging derivations. In most recent minimalist literature, the idea of global filters is abandoned, but whenever economy is considered, comparison between derivations (or stages of derivations) must be entertained. Keeping with the idea that the grammar may generate multiple outputs, it is important to know when this may happen. I contend that there are two privileged contexts for the generation of multiple outputs: (i) when a constituent may be licensed in two different ways; (ii) when an optional operation applies. An example of (i) is subject-licensing in null subject languages. According to several authors (e.g. Rizzi 1986), the subject can be licensed in Spec,IP or under government (or Agree) in a postverbal position. Under the view advocated here, this optional licensing creates a context in which the grammar can generate two word orders. An example of (ii) is adjunction. Adjunction is an optional operation, both in terms of ordering and in terms of directionality. As such, an adjunct can be licensed in multiple configurations, which yields optionality.

If nothing else happens, one of the multiple outputs generated by the syntactic component may be used. This is the case in situations in which there is optionality. However, in most cases, post-syntactic filters select one of the outputs generated. Let us consider an example: suppose one wants to generate a sentence in which the subject is focused in European Portuguese. Syntax generates two outputs—SV and VS. In both configurations, the subject is licensed. When this information is sent to the PF wing of the grammar, the two outputs are mapped onto prosodic constituents and the Nuclear Stress Rule applies, assigning prominence to the rightmost constituent. Prominence is not only relevant for prosodic purposes, but also for discourse purposes. Let us assume, following Reinhart (1995), that, at the level at which information structure is encoded, information focus must be marked with some type of prominence. At the interface with discourse, the SV output is ruled out, since the focused constituent is not the most prominent. Now, suppose that the same would happen in a language in which the subject is not licensed post-verbally. Then, a single output (SV) would be created, and mapped onto prosodic constituents. After the application of the Nuclear Stress Rule, deac-centing and stress shift must apply since there is no other output available. In this sense, stress shift is a last-resort strategy 'undoing' the effects of the Nuclear Stress Rule.[6]

This approach straightforwardly derives all the data discussed:

i. Since possessives and pre-nominal adjectives cannot be generated to the right of the noun, there is no legitimate syntactic output placing them rightmost. Since there is no p-movement, no movement operation will 'rescue' these word orders. The only repair strategy available is stress shift.

ii. The same reasoning applies to verb focus. V-to-I movement is cat-egoric, and applies obligatorily, in the sense that a verb can never be stranded in situ in a V-to-I language. As such, the verb has a fixed position, and if the object is pronounced, the verb cannot be rightmost. Since there is no p-movement, the only way to assign prominence to the verb is resorting to stress shift.

iii. Since scrambling is an adjunction configuration, and adjunction is cost-less and free, whenever there are no focus requirements on the constitu-ents affected by scrambling, it is predicted that it applies optionally.

iv. Binding is established at the syntactic component. There is no legitim-ate syntactic output in which an anaphor is not licensed. Hence, in the binding contexts, if the binder is the focus, it must be marked via stress shift, acting as last resort.

v. Since stress shift is a last-resort repair strategy, it is expected to yield processing problems that free adjunction and movement operations do not yield.

vi. Since, according to this proposal, syntax is phonology-free, it is expected that there are no prosodic constraints on syntactic operations.

---

[6] A reviewer correctly points out that this approach to the interaction between prosody, word order, and focus appears to take the focus information out of the syntactic structure. Indeed, under the view advocated here focus is not seen as a syntactic primitive, and it is taken as a discourse matter. The same reviewer points out that, according to this view, semantic effects of focus are unexpected. This is only true, however, if the discourse component of the grammar does not communicate with the semantic compon-ent. If a model such as Vallduvi's (1992) or Erteschik-Shir's (1997) is adopted, the information-structure component of the grammar communicates both with the prosodic and the semantic components.

Let us now check the merits of this proposal in dealing with the problems listed above. First, since the notion of p-movement is totally dispensed with, all the problems raised by its syntactic status and by the idea that there are prosodic triggers for syntactic movement disappear. Second, the idea that stress shift is the real last-resort repair strategy is consistent with the data collected, and solves the problems of having movement as a repair strategy for syntactic outputs and of having the stress rules applying in the syntactic component. Finally, this proposal predicts that metrical invisibility will possibly apply in all languages, since metrical invisibility is just the reflex of stress shift. Note, however, that this type of operation will only be at stake when the outputs generated by syntax and the application of the Nuclear Stress Rules do not comply with the prominence requirements imposed by discourse. A remaining problem for which I have no clear solution is the following: in out-of-the-blue contexts, in which any word order is equally good for focus purposes, in a language like European Portuguese, both SV and VS are legitimate outputs. As such, optionality is predicted. However, SV is preferred. The only way to account for this preference, as noted by an anonymous reviewer, is to propose that movement is preferred over non-movement, which is surprising if movement is considered a costly operation. I will leave this issue open, but I would like to suggest that it may be the case that movement is not necessarily more costly than other types of licensing. Consider, for instance, the crosslinguistic variation in the acquisition of wh-movement reported in Soares (2003). This author shows that in European Portuguese, in which there is optionality in wh-movement like in French, children start with wh-movement and only perform wh-in-situ at a much later stage, differing from French children. This observation makes it legitimate to suppose that the costly status of movement is subject to variation and that, in European Portuguese, there is independent evidence for a more unmarked status of movement when it freely varies with non-movement. However, this is an issue deserving further research.

6.5 Conclusion

The argumentation developed in this paper supports the classical view according to which syntax is phonology-free. The alternative proposal developed suggests that word-order effects related to discourse and prosody can be explained when the syntactic primitives enabling the generation of multiple outputs are taken into consideration. From the ideas developed here, it follows that there may be much more crosslinguistic variation, since it is necessary to know for each subconstruction whether syntax allows for a single output or for more than one output.

7

On the mechanics of Spell-Out

STEVEN FRANKS

7.1 Introduction and overview

This paper considers evidence from various Slavic languages bearing on the mechanics of Spell-Out. Spell-Out is typically described as a 'rule' (cf. e.g., Hornstein et al. 2005: 46–7) which applies to a syntactic representation, separating structure relevant for phonetic interpretation from structure relevant for semantic interpretation and sending that information off to the Phonetic Form (PF) and Logical Form (LF) interfaces, respectively. Concentrating on the PF-side, this paper shows that, once one begins to probe how Spell-Out actually works, one quickly discovers that Spell-Out in fact masks a confusing array of interacting processes needed to convert the abstract hierarchical arrangement of feature bundles we take to be syntax into the linearized sequence of articulatory instructions we take to be phonetics. Within minimalism's highly derivational architecture, Spell-Out processes run the gamut from those which are primarily syntactic in nature, and presumably apply very early in the mapping from syntax to PF, to those which are primarily phonological in nature, and presumably apply very late. The paper argues that Spell-Out subsumes a complex of operations, including at least deletion, linearization, and prosodification, and examines how these three processes interact. My primary window into the specific derivational steps which serve to map syntactic structures into those manipulable by the morphology and/or phonology will be South Slavic clitics, whose special properties lie at the nexus of syntax, morphology, and phonology.

Much which has traditionally been regarded as part of the syntax proper can be seen as a response to PF demands, decisions imposed on syntactic structures by the need for pronunciation. This new role for PF is manifested in several ways. For one thing, the syntax creates structure through the concatenation operation of 'merge', but leaves unspecified the linear order of the concatenated elements. In the spirit of Bobaljik (2002), Erteschik-Shir

(2005), and much other recent work, syntactic representations are seen as only containing hierarchical information. PF considerations thus become fundamental in determining word order. Linearization in this view is a property imposed on language by virtue of the temporal exigencies of articulation, an essential aspect of 'Spell-Out'. It will be argued that linearization must be done 'online' (i.e., cyclically, via 'Multiple Spell-Out') and that it reapplies at different points in the derivation, making use of different kinds of information. I will claim that initial linearization exploits c-command along the lines of Kayne's (1994) 'Linear Correspondence Axiom' (LCA), but that later relinearization exploits prosodic properties of specific lexical items. Ontologically prior to linearization, it seems to me, should however be the decision of what in fact needs to be linearized. For example, if, as has become standard since Chomsky (1995), movement is analyzed as remerger of a copy of the moving constituent, then it seems reasonable to imagine that the determination of which copy is ultimately going to be pronounced should be left unspecified by the syntax. That is, copy selection can be regarded as a property imposed not by the syntax *per se* but rather by the needs of the morphological and phonological components with which syntax interfaces.

The paper is organized as follows. Section 7.2 reviews several ideas in the literature about copy pronunciation. I will conclude that decisions about copy pronunciation must, like linearization, be made derivationally, although the interactions are complex: copy deletion can depend on linear adjacency but linearization requires a prior decision about which copy is being pronounced, ellipsis sometimes depends on specific morphology, prosody requires morphological material to host it but prosodic considerations might also impact on choice of copy, and so forth. Section 7.3 examines linearization. It is shown that the positioning of the Bulgarian interrogative clitic *li* requires linearization to apply cyclically. Section 7.4 then examines different kinds of ellipsis. It will be argued that that there are (at least) two kinds of PF ellipsis, an early one that saves certain derivations by deleting structure containing offending features and a much later one that ignores syntactic constituency altogether.[1] Finally, section 7.5 considers how pieces of the derivation that have been sent separately to Spell-Out are reassembled. It is suggested that this is done directly within the lexical 'subarrays' defined by each of the phase heads in the Numeration: subarrays are built derivationally, such that the product of merging all the members of one subarray in effect becomes (through Spell-Out)

---

[1] See also Merchant (2001, 2007) for discussion of types of ellipsis.

a lexical item, which can then literally serve as a member of another subarray within the same Numeration.

7.2 Aspects of copy pronunciation

I now turn to some aspects of copy pronunciation that any adequate model of the syntax–PF interface ought to accommodate. I begin by reviewing two fairly well-established accounts of lower copy pronunciation.

7.2.1 *Delayed clitic placement*

The first phenomenon is 'delayed clitic placement': lower copies of clitics are pronounced just in case the highest copy is *not* prosodically viable.[2] Consider second-position clitics in Bosnian/Croatian/Serbian (henceforth, BCS), which arguably move, in an iterated head-to-head fashion, to the highest head position in the clause. These elements are enclitic, which means that they require a hosting prosodic word to their left. The highest copy is ordinarily pronounced, but if there is no available host, then the next highest copy is sent to PF. Consequently, whenever BCS clitics are left by the syntax at the beginning of their Intonational phrase (I-phrase), we encounter them in lower than second position.[3] For example, as opposed to (1a) with overt subject *ja* 'I', in null subject variant (1b) the highest copy of the enclitics *sam ti* has no potential prosodic host to its left. This causes the next copy down to be pronounced:[4]

(1) a. #[[Ja]_ω **sam ti**]   obećala sam ti   (BCS)
          I   aux.1SG you.DAT promised aux.1SG you.DAT
          igračku#.
          toy.ACC
          'I promised you a toy.'

     b. *pro* sam ti #[[Obećala]_ω **sam ti**] igračku#.
          '(I) promised you a toy.'

Similarly, in the minimal pair in (2) the delayed clitic placement effect arises if the topicalized constituent *tvome prijatelju* 'your friend' happens to be

---

[2] I put this idea forward in Franks (1998, 2000) and it has since been adopted more broadly; cf., e.g., Bošković 2001.

[3] This paper only considers the role of prosodic boundaries in inducing pronunciation of a lower copy, but Lambova (2004) argues that potential intonation clash (resulting from the attempt to impose both topic and focus intonations on the same material) can have a similar effect.

[4] Here and elsewhere, pronounced copies are in boldface and non-pronounced ones are in outline font. Prosodic words are indicated by a subscripted 'ω' and I-phrase boundaries are demarcated with '#'.

pronounced as a separate I-phrase, as indicated in (2a), but not otherwise, as in (2b):

(2) a. #Tvome   [prijatelju]$_\omega$ #   #su   [[prodali]$_\omega$ su]   (BCS)
        your.DAT   frend.DAT   aux.3PL   gave   aux.3PL
        knjigu.#
        book.ACC
        'To your friend, they sold the book.'

    b. #Tvome prijatelju su prodali su knjigu.#

In (2a), since the 3rd plural auxiliary clitic *su* cannot find prosodic support when immediately preceded by an intonational break, the lower copy must be pronounced instead.

This system correctly predicts that, when there is no way for the highest copy of the clitics to avoid being initial in its I-phrase, then the lower copy *must* be pronounced. Thus, since parentheticals are necessarily flanked by I-phrase boundaries, these induce obligatory pronunciation of lower copies. Compare (3) with (1a), where *tvoja mama* 'your mother' is an appositive:

(3) #Ja#, #tvoja [mama]$_\omega$ #, #sam   ti   [[obećala]$_\omega$ sam   (BCS)
     I   your   mother   aux.1SG you.DAT   promised aux.1SG
     ti]   igračku#.
     you.DAT   toy.ACC
     'I, your mother, promised you a toy.'

Further evidence in support of this kind of account of BCS is based on closely related Slovenian. In this language, the clitics are not necessarily dependent on a prosodic word to their left to be pronounced; cf. Franks and King (2000: 31–48) or Bošković (2001: 151–68). Hence, in the Slovenian translation of (3), cited by Golden and Milojević Sheppard (2000), the highest copy of the clitics can be retained. This is shown in (4).

(4) Jaz#, #tvoja mama#, [sem ti [obljubila]$_\omega$] sem ti igračko.   (Slovenian)
     'I, your mother, promised you a toy.'

Since it is possible to pronounce the highest copy of *sem ti* in Slovenian (4), this copy rather than the lower one must be the one which is ultimately shipped off for Spell-Out.

It is tempting to think of these facts in Optimality Theoretic terms: Spell-Out seeks to target the highest copy but compromises when that copy lacks prosodic viability. Moreover, while these desiderata prevail in BCS, Slovenian brooks no such compromise, pronouncing the highest copy regardless. One might argue that the clitics in BCS are subject to a prohibition against being initial in their I-phrase. This is in fact a standard optimality approach to clitics, as presented for example in Legendre (2003), who exploits the idea of a competition between EDGEMOST and NONINITIAL constraints.[5] Under such a view, these clitics in BCS prefer being non-initial over being edgemost, whereas their Slovenian counterparts have the opposite preference. Note however that this conception of the facts characterizes clitic properties purely in terms of linear order. It does not treat them as syntactic entities within a hierarchical structure, but instead as 'phrasal morphology', as articulated in Anderson (2005 and elsewhere). However, this purely PF linear account loses all of the many structural aspects of clitic placement (cf., e.g., Bošković (2004b) for a summary of reasons why South Slavic clitics should be analyzed as independent syntactic entities). Indeed, the mere fact that it is the *left* rather than right edge which is targeted (that is, EDGEMOST (X, *LEFT*) and NON*INITIAL*) becomes an accident rather than a principled consequence of the assumption that clitics move in the syntax (since movement is upwards and leftwards).

An alternative perspective, which I develop in Franks (2000), is that syntax is generative but optimality-like considerations police the interfaces. The clitics move in the syntax, but the syntax leaves unspecified which copy is pronounced. It is up to Spell-Out to resolve this, selecting from what the syntax offers the optimal PF instantiation. Spell-Out thus picks the highest prosodically viable copy. In this way, the syntax provides the correct structure, but the phonology filters out the illicit copies. Prosodic considerations are irrelevant to the syntax, but in the mapping to PF these play a critical role. In such a PF-filtering system, the syntax 'proposes' and the phonology 'disposes.' Under this view, rather than 'ranking' an I-phrase non-initiality constraint lower in Slovenian than in BCS, there would simply be no reason to posit a prohibition against I-phrase initiality in Slovenian at all. This prohibition, moreover, is just a property of specific lexical items; it is not part of the syntax *per se* of the languages to which these items belong. That is, different lexical items can be subject to different prosodic requirements, and PF seeks to meet those requirements in spelling out what has been generated by the syntax.

7.2.2 *Avoiding homophonous sequences*

Prosodic requirements are in fact not the only kind imposed on Spell-Out. A second phenomenon that invokes lower pronunciation of copies to consider

---

[5] Legendre (2003) states that EDGEMOST (X, LEFT) = E(X) means 'a feature [X] is left-aligned with the edge of a projection of the head [X] is associated with' and NONINITIAL (X) means '[X] is not realized in Intonational phrase-initial position.'

involves multiple *wh*-fronting. As observed in Billings and Rudin (1996), there is a PF constraint against consecutive homophonous *wh*-phrases in multiple *wh*-fronting languages such as Bulgarian.[6] Given this prohibition, in a multiple *wh*-question in Bulgarian, although ordinarily the highest copy is pronounced, when the two *wh*-words are identical, it is the lower copy of the second one which must be pronounced. Consider the minimal pair in (5) and (6):

(5) a. Koj   kakvo kupi?   (Bulgarian)
         who   what   bought
         'Who bought what?'

     b. *Koj kupi kakvo?

(6) a. Kakvo obuslavja kakvo?
         'What conditions what?'

     b. *Kakvo kakvo obuslavja?

Since pronunciation of the higher copy is blocked, (6) looks roughly like (7) in PF:

(7) **Kakvo ~~kakvo~~ obuslavja [~~kakvo obuslavja~~ kakvo]?**

This gives the order in (6a) rather than (6b).

   Notice that, according to this account, (6a) crucially involves *overt wh-movement*, despite appearances to the contrary. Bošković (2001, 2002b, 2004b) adduces some striking evidence from another multiple *wh*-fronting language, Romanian, that this is indeed correct. In Romanian there is a similar PF constraint, as shown in (8) with a structure as in (9).

(8) a. Ce precede ce?   (Romanian)
         'What precedes what?'

     b. *Ce ce precede?

(9) **Ce$_i$ ce$_j$ precede [~~ce$_i$ precede ce$_j$~~]?**

Interestingly, Romanian (8a) behaves as if the direct object *ce* had indeed moved in the syntax. Bošković points out that it can license a parasitic gap, a fact which indicates overt *wh*-movement:

(10) Ce ce precede ce fără să influenţeze *pg*?   (Romanian)
      '*What precedes what without influencing?'

---

[6] The constraint is part of a larger family of familiar PF constraints against sequences of homophonous elements, such as the double *-ing* filter in English, the double infinitive filter in Italian, the prohibition against sequences of identical clitics in many Slavic and Romance languages, or the ban on homophonous sequences of articles in ancient Greek.

This discovery, which is compelling enough to have entered the canon of textbooks such as Hornstein, Nunes, and Grohmann (2005), provides novel empirical support for the kind of model in which lower copy pronuncation is purely a PF matter.

Returning to Slavic, consider some further evidence for the strong PF adjacency nature of this constraint. First, as shown in BCS (11a), from Bošković (2002b), the intervening adverb *neprestano* 'constantly' obviates the effect:

(11) a. Šta neprestano **šta** uslovljava **šta**?   (BCS)
          'What constantly conditions what?'

      b. ?*Šta neprestano šta uslovljava **šta**?

As (11b) reiterates, pronunciation of a lower copy is only possible where required. These facts are also highlighted by the ungrammaticality of the order **na kogo kogo* 'to whom whom' in Bulgarian (12):

(12) a. *Koj na kogo kogo   e   pokazal?   (Bg)
          who to whom whom   aux.3SG pointed-out
          'Who pointed out who to whom?'

      b. Koj na kogo e pokazal kogo?

      c. Koj na koj kogo e pokazal?

In (12a), the first *kogo* is part of the dative phrase *na kogo* 'to whom', whereas the second *kogo* is accusative. To avoid adjacent occurrences of *kogo*, a lower copy of the second *kogo* is pronounced, as in (12b). Interestingly, as noted in Billings and Rudin (1996), replacing *na kogo* by the colloquial form *na koj*, as in (12c), resolves the homophony, so that the dative > accusative sequence once again becomes felicitous.

7.2.3 On Spell-Out

What do facts such as these suggest about Spell-Out? For one thing, since linear adjacency is crucial in deciding which copy of the *wh*-word to pronounce, linearization should precede copy deletion (linearization > copy deletion). Also, since prosodic information is needed to determine that the highest copy of the clitics cannot be pronounced, (at least some) prosodic phrasing must precede copy deletion as well (prosodification > copy deletion). Finally, it makes little sense to impose prosodic structure until linear order has been established among the elements being prosodified (linearization > prosodification).

On the other hand, Moro (2000) and others argue that copy deletion is needed to render c-command unambiguously asymmetric, as required in order to implement the Linear Correspondence Axiom. Copy deletion must therefore be a prerequisite to linearization, if the LCA has anything to do with determining linear order.[7] Consequently, copy deletion must also *precede* linearization (copy deletion > linearization), since otherwise the grammar would not know which copy to linearize. An obvious solution to this ordering paradox is cyclicity of application of the relevant processes. Under minimalism, with no unique S-Structure level to serve as the input to PF, Spell-Out can apply multiple times. The relevant information is thus sent to the articulatory interface iteratively in the course of the derivation. In Chomsky's system, the chunks of structure that are sent to Spell-Out piecemeal are the complements of 'phase' heads, e.g., C^0 or v^0, which define privileged domains. Assuming, then, some version of Multiple Spell-Out, one can understand these processes to operate in a bottom-up fashion, perhaps as in (13):[8]

(13)   copy deletion > linearization > prosodification

Notice, however, that the ordering of these processes is extrinsically determined, since the structure cannot be linearized until multiple copies have been resolved, nor can it be prosodified until linear order is determined, and copies cannot be deleted until adjacency to a preceding prosodic impasse or phonologically identical form has been established. The characterization in (13) thus raises serious questions and may be problematic for a strictly phase-based approach. For one thing, it seems likely that the infelicitous adjacencies that force copy deletion can be *local* in the sense of involving only a single phase. This suggests that deletion can apply at any time, i.e., both before *and* after prosodification and/or linearization. On the other hand, as explored in section 7.3, there are clear and much needed effects of making Spell-Out decisions derivationally. Perhaps, then, a better solution would exploit the system proposed in Franks (2000) and suggested above, whereby interface conditions are regarded as constraints rather than rules *per se*. This would preserve the derivational nature of the mapping embodied in Multiple Spell-Out but allow the particular 'processes' in (13) to interact more flexibly at each phase. Under this view, it would make no sense to order them, since they are not really processes applying to transform one representation into another, but rather criteria for the comparison of candidates generated by the syntax. Spell-Out would then mean that selection of copy, imposition of linear order, and appropriate prosodic structure are all evaluated simultaneously, with

---

[7] Chomsky (1995: 337) has also suggested that the 'LCA is an operation that applies after morphology,' so that the fusing of two heads into one lexical item (as, for example, under cliticization) might offer a way of circumventing the LCA applied independently to its subparts.

[8] On the lowest cycle, of course, copy deletion will be vacuous if remerge has not applied.

convergence on the maximally efficient choice. However, unlike in standard completely non-derivational Optimality Theory, in some cases no viable choice may exist, resulting in ineffability. This leads to an alternative conception, namely that these processes are 'anywhere rules', in the sense that there is no intrinsic ordering among them, but they still apply in a cyclic fashion, to progressively larger Spell-Out domains.

Another puzzle is that, for the clitics, when the highest copy cannot be pronounced for PF reasons it is the *next* highest prosodically viable copy that is retained, whereas with *wh*-phrases only copies in the original clause can be pronounced. Consider for example Bulgarian (14).[9]

(14) Kakvo (*kakvo) misli (*kakvo) Ivan (*kakvo) če   (??kakvo) (Bg)
      what   what   thinks what   Ivan what   that   what
      obuslavja   (kakvo)?
      conditions what
      'What does Ivan think conditions what?'

The highest copy of *kakvo* is, as before, blocked by adjacency to the preceding homophonous *kakvo*, but it is not obvious why any of the intermediate copies should not be viable.[10] Presumably, though, they are not, because otherwise the next highest copy would have to be the one pronounced, just as with the clitics. This suggests that sometimes the entire structure needs to be evaluated simultaneously. It will be argued in section 7.4 that PF ellipsis might require this (although presumably for very different reasons).

7.2.4 *Getting clitics higher*

I take clitics to be exhaustive instantiations of formal features (henceforth, FF), devoid of all but purely grammatical features. In this sense, clitics can be regarded as the Spell-Out of functional heads. One view of second-position clitics is that they move to the highest head position in some appropriate

---

[9] Bošković (2002b) cites (14) as follows, but all Bulgarian speakers I have asked find *kakvo* 'what' before *če* 'that' absolutely impossible and before the verb *obuslavja* 'conditions' very awkward:

(i)   Kakvo (*kakvo) misli (*kakvo) Ivan (%kakvo) če (kakvo) obuslavja (kakvo)?   (Bg)
       'What does Ivan think conditions what?'

The Bulgarian data are thus presumably similar to Romanian, for which Bošković provides (ii):

(ii)   Ce (*ce) crede (*ce) Ion (*ce) că (%ce) a (*ce) determinat (ce)?   (Rom)
       'What does Ion think determined what?'

[10] I address the PF and LF status of *wh*-phrases in intermediate SpecCP in Franks (2006a), suggesting some technical solutions to this classic problem. See also Bošković (2007).

functional domain; it is this movement which is the source of the EDGEMOST (X, LEFT) effect. If so, a reasonable question is 'How do they get there?' A reasonable answer—given that verbs are canonical hosts for special clitics—is that they somehow piggyback on the verb.

A compelling reason for the verb to move up through its extended projection is that its FF need to match those of all associated functional heads. In principle, it is just the verb's FF which need to move. In a verb-second language, such as German, the semantic features of the particular verb are pied-piped, whereas in other languages there is just FF movement.[11] There are various technical scenarios one could imagine to make this all work (cf. Franks 2000), but the basic claim is that the FF of the verb are copied up the tree in a stepwise fashion, with successive FF adjunctions, so that at the end there is a copy, situated high, of the verb's FF plus those of all the clitics. Now for the problem this raises: How can we take advantage of the insight that the verb provides a syntactic 'host' for the clitics even when the clitics are not actually pronounced adjacent to the verb? In Slavic languages like Bulgarian and Macedonian most clitics are positioned with respect to the verb, but in second-position languages like Bosnian/Croatian/Serbian and Slovenian the surface position of the verb is irrelevant. Consider for example the following variants:

(15) a. Sestra   ih   rado <u>poklanja</u> školskoj   (Croatian)
        sister.NOM them.ACC gladly gives   school.DAT
        knjižnici.
        library.DAT
        'Sister gladly gives them to the school library.'

   b. Sestra ih školskoj knjižnici rado <u>poklanja</u>.

   c. Školskoj knjižnici ih rado <u>poklanja</u> sestra.

   d. Rado ih sestra <u>poklanja</u> školskoj knjižnici.

The key lies in moving the verb overtly in some way that does not require it to be pronounced in its target position. The verb moves to second position, taking the clitics along with it, but for some reason the clitics are realized in that position while the verb is realized lower down. What exactly differentiates the clitics from the verb? My answer is that clitics are pure FF bundles whereas the verb contains substantive semantic features as well. Thus, if only FF are copied, and if there is a desideratum that the highest copy that can be sent to Spell-Out must be, then the clitics are going to be pronounced high but the

---

[11] Pied-piping is presumably what the diacritic feature 'strong' means—an instruction to PF to pronounce an element in that position.

verb cannot be. The verb is, instead, pronounced in the highest position to which a copy of its semantic features has been pied-piped.[12]

The scenario of pronouncing elements that are exhaustively FF bundles higher than their fully lexical counterparts is in fact widespread. A hallmark of clitics themselves is that they typically appear higher than full Noun Phrases (NPs). The reason is simple: although FF movement applies equally to clitics and lexical NPs, this 'scatters' the various features of lexical NPs (unless their semantic features are pied-piped along with the FF) but leaves clitics, as pure FF bundles, whole and intact.[13]

7.3 Aspects of linearization

At this point I offer some specific proposals about linearization, taking linear order to be introduced only on the PF-side as part of the Spell-Out process.

7.3.1 *Clitics and linearization*

Because pronunciation of verbs and clitics is divorced for second-position clitics as in (15), we cannot tell what the order between them and the verb really is. But when we look at verb-adjacent clitics, as are typical in Bulgarian and Macedonian, we find that the clitics *precede* the verb if they can. Within a clause, such clitics ordinarily appear immediately before the verb, regardless of how much material precedes them, as in Bulgarian (16):

(16) Včera   v gradinata   Mila sigurno **mu**   <u>dade</u>   (Bg)
      yesterday in garden.DEF Mila surely him.DAT gave
      knigite.
      books.DEF
      'Yesterday, in the garden, Mila surely gave him the books.'

---

[12] This view of movement is akin to that put forward in Zwart (1997), for whom overt movement involves both FF and semantic features (his 'Lexico-Categorial'), whereas movement traditionally analyzed as 'covert' is in fact overt but only involves FF. Although the idea is hardly new that second positions for clitics and verbs are intimately related—stemming as it does from Wackernagel (1892) and recently exploited in non-derivational frameworks such as Anderson (2005)—the reason why clitics are pronounced higher than the verb finds a conceptually well-grounded explanation only in the context of a model which treats FF as the driving force behind movement.

[13] Roberts's (1998) account of why English auxiliaries raise to T⁰ whereas main verbs do not expresses the same kind of idea—and indeed, he comments that 'another obvious place to look... is the area of clitics'. For Roberts too, FF movement is 'always and only overt'; strong features in addition cause the entire category to be pied-piped. Taking verb features in English to be weak, lexical verbs are as expected pronounced *in situ*. Auxiliaries, however, only have FF, so that when 'Move F moves all features of the element it moves... checking the weak feature of the V node causes the entire auxiliary to move' (Roberts 1998: 119).

The exception is what in the Romance linguistics tradition is known as the 'Tobler-Mussafia' effect, according to which, if the clitics would end up in absolute initial position, they must then follow the verb instead, as in (17):

(17)   <u>Dade</u> **mu**   knigite   včera.   (Bg)
       gave him.DAT books.DEF yesterday
       'She/he/you gave him the books yesterday.'
       (***Mu** dade knigite včera.)

These Bulgarian clitics are subject to a PF prohibition against being initial; cf. Franks (2006b, 2008). However, the domain of this non-initiality restriction is not the I-phrase, as is claimed for second-position clitics, but rather something larger. I proposed that the relevant prosodic domain is Nespor and Vogel's (1986 [2008]) 'Utterance', indicated by 'υ'. This can be seen in (18), where the clitics *mi go* are oblivious to the I-phrase boundary necessarily introduced by the parenthetical *edna moja prijatelka* 'a friend of mine':

(18)   υ # Mila# #edna moja prijatelka# #[mi   **go**   [dade]_ω]# υ (Bg)
       Mila one   my   friend   me.DAT it.ACC gave
       'Mila, a friend of mine, gave it to me.'

In sum, since the generalization is that the clitics are preverbal unless this would leave them in absolute initial position within the clause, linearization first makes them preverbal, but then this ordering is adjusted as needed. Further indication that linearization should abstract away from the Tobler-Mussafia effect is the fact that Macedonian, although syntactically very similar to Bulgarian, does not display this PF restriction: its clitics can be initial in the Utterance. Hence the Macedonian judgments are the opposite from Bulgarian here: the starred order in (17) is perfectly good in Macedonian, no Tobler-Mussafia effects obtain. I would thus argue that the correct way to understand (17) is to derive the Tobler-Mussafia effect on the PF-side of the grammar: the syntax produces an output in which the clitics precede the verb and this order is adjusted on the PF–side to comply with the prohibition in Bulgarian (but not Macedonian) against Utterance initial clitics.

   To handle this I endorse an approach, due originally to Bošković (2002a), that is compatible with the LCA. As discussed in Kayne (1994), the LCA has the effect of left-adjunction: when a head A moves to another head B, it adjoins to B's left, producing '[[A + B] ... A].' Taking this to be a principle of linearization means, however, that the clitics must move to adjoin to the verb, and not vice versa, since, everything else being equal, the clitics precede the verb.[14] Taking furthermore the clitics to be instantiations of functional heads *above* the verb, this means that the verb moves *past* the clitics, thereby providing a target to which the clitics can then adjoin (and linearize to the left, as per the LCA). In Bošković's system the syntax provides something like (19) for the clitic-verb order in (18). First, *dade* moves past *go*, as in (19a). Next, *go* adjoins to *dade*, as in (19b). Then, *mi* is merged and the '*go + dade*' complex later moves past that, as in (19c). Finally, *mi* adjoins to '*go + dade*' producing the order in (19d), with copies pronounced as indicated.

(19)   a.   [[dade] go...dade...] ⇒

      b.   [[go + dade] go...dade...] ⇒

      c.   [[go + dade] [mi [[go + dade] go]...dade...]] ⇒

      d.   [[**mi** + [**go + dade**]] [~~mi~~ [[~~go + dade~~] ~~go~~]...~~dade~~...]]

In sum, once the verb *dade* 'gave' has moved past the clitic *go*, *go* can adjoin to it. Then once the '*go + dade*' complex head moves past the clitic *mi*, *mi* can adjoin to that. The result is iterated left-adjunction, with clitics preceding the verb.

7.3.2 *Some guiding principles*

If the syntax *per se* makes no statements whatsoever about linear order, how are hierarchical syntactic structures ultimately mapped into flat ones?

7.3.2.1 *Making use of the linear correspondence axiom*   This happens, I believe, cyclically and in several different steps. Linearization is an ongoing process—not the compilation of a set of immutable statements about precedence—and linear order can be manipulated by resubjecting syntactic material to it as needed.[15] In all likelihood, however, the first and most potent linearization principle is the LCA, Kayne's widely accepted idea that asymmetric c-command maps into precedence. This applies cyclically, online, with the effect that heads precede their complements and adjunction is linearized to the left. Under this view, as just described, the Slavic special clitics precede their host. This is because these are syntactically distinct functional heads, reflecting paradigmatic features of case, tense, and agreement. They thus move in the syntax (or, more technically, their formal

---

[14] The caveat 'everything else being equal' means unless linearization to precede the verb would violate some other PF requirement, such as non-initiality. Also, the effects of left-adjunction are not visible in languages like BCS and Slovenian, where the clitics and verb need not be pronounced contiguously. Thus, Macedonian is the best indicator of what is really going on, since it involves minimal confounding effects.

[15] Thus, contra the system of Fox and Pesetsky (2005), I explicitly reject 'order preservation'.

features are copied). LCA-induced precedence is the straightforward consequence of this movement.

7.3.2.2 *Invoking prosodic considerations* In many of the Slavic languages there is, however, one simple clitic that displays very different behavior. This is the particle *li*, the syntax and semantics of which has received considerable attention in recent years; cf. e.g. Franks and King (2000: 349–57), Rudnickaya (2000), Bošković (2001: 197–253), or Franks (2006b). This lexical item is always unequivocally enclitic and has Yes/No interrogative and contrastive focus functions of various types in languages such as Russian, BCS, Czech, Macedonian, and Bulgarian. Here I concentrate on *li* in Bulgarian, which exhibits some of the more spectacular linearization effects.

The clitic *li* instantiates Yes/No polarity and focus features in a high head position, which for present purposes can be taken to be C⁰. As a clitic, *li* projects no prosodic structure itself and, as an enclitic, *li* is always pronounced at the right edge of an adjacent host prosodic word. When preceded by a possible host, *li* is linearized to that host's right. In Bulgarian (20), for example, *v tozi grad* 'to this city' moves in the syntax to the specifier of the Complementizer Phrase (SpecCP), directly in front of *li* in C⁰. This then encliticizes to *grad* 'city' (and the auxiliary clitic *si*, since it is not Utterance initial, remains in front of and eventually procliticizes to *xodil* 'went').

(20)   [V tozi]$_\omega$ [[grad]$_\omega$ li] [si   [xodil]$_\omega$]?   (Bg)
       in   this   city   Q   aux.2SG   went
       'Was it to this city that you went?'

Very often, however, SpecCP is empty so that there is nothing higher than *li*. When this happens, *li* must be linearized at the *right* edge of the prosodic word to its right.[16] Thus, *li* differs from the special clitics (which precede the verb if at all possible) in that if often follows the verb. In (21a) the conjunction *i* 'and', although not a prosodic word or viable host by itself, is sufficient to render the clitics *mu gi* not Utterance initial; in (21b) the future proclitic *šte* does this; and in (21c) the proclitic sentential negation element *ne* does.[17]

---

[16] This phenomenon is generally known as 'prosodic inversion'. For discussion, see Bošković (2001: 11–36), who offers a summary of reasons for not adopting prosodic inversion as a movement rule applying in PF, and Franks (2006b), where I develop the approach to *li* placement not as literal PF-*movement* but rather as an artifact of linearization.

[17] Note that in standard Bulgarian *ne* is post-stressing, so that the dative clitic *mu* in (21c) actually bears stress and hosts *ne*.

(21) a. [I   **mu**   **gi**   DAde]$_\omega$ včera.   (Bg)
          and him.DAT them.ACC gave   yesterday
          'And she/he/you gave them to him yesterday.'

      b. [Šte **mu**   **gi**   predaDEŠ]$_\omega$.
          will him.DAT them.ACC hand-over.2SG
          'You will hand them over to him.'

      c. [Ne MU]$_\omega$ [DAde]$_\omega$ knigite.
          neg him.DAT gave   books.DEF
          'She/he/you didn't give him the books.'

Under the exact same conditions, however, *li* necessarily follows the verb:

(22) a. [[I   [DAde]$_\omega$ **li**]] knigite   včera   na Ivan?
          and gave   Q   books.DEF yesterday to Ivan
          'And did she/he/you give the books to Ivan yesterday?'

      b. [[Šte predaDEŠ]$_\omega$ **li**] knigite   na Ivan?
          will hand-over.2SG Q   books.DEF to Ivan
          'Will you hand the books over to Ivan?'

      c. [[Ne DAde]$_\omega$ **li**] knigite   na Ivan?
          neg gave   Q   books.DEF to Ivan
          'Didn't she/he/you give the books to Ivan?'

That is because, unlike the special clitics, which as we have seen move to the verb, *li* is merged higher, above the verbal complex. Its enclitic nature then causes it to be linearized *after* the adjacent prosodic word, which, in (22), is (*i*) *dade*, *šte predadeš*, and *ne dade*.[18]

With post-stressing *ne*, *li* appears between the clitic *mu* and the verb, as in (23). While this is what one expects if *ne mu* in (21c) is indeed an independent prosodic word, it is interesting that *li* separates *mu* from *dade*, since under Bošković's analysis presented above these constitute a complex head in the syntax:

(23) [[Ne MU]$_\omega$ **li**] [DAde]$_\omega$ knigite.
      neg him.DAT Q   gave   books.DEF
      'Didn't she/he/you give him the books?'

Even more striking, however is what happens if there is a second special clitic, such as accusative *gi* 'them'. As seen in (24a), *gi* is most naturally proclitic on the verb following it, with *ne mu* independently a viable prosodic word.

---

[18] As revealed by (30d) below, *li* must be linearized to follow *dade* 'gave' earlier than the conjunction *i* is merged, above CP.

Consequently, merging interrogative C[0] *li* above the clause in (24a) causes it still to be prosodified after adjacent *ne mu*, except that now *li* appears *between* the two pronominal clitics. This is shown in (24b):

(24) a. [[Ne **MU**]$_\omega$ [**gi**   [DAde]$_\omega$] [Ana]$_\omega$.
           neg him.DAT them.ACC gave   Ana
           'Ana didn't give them to him.'

      b. [[Ne **MU**]$_\omega$ **li**] [**gi**   [DAde]$_\omega$] [Ana]$_\omega$?
           neg him.DAT Q   them.ACC gave   Ana
           'Didn't Ana give them to him?'

In short, *li*—which the syntax leaves in C[0], i.e., higher than and asymmetrically c-commanding IP/TP, so that, everything else being equal, it would be initially linearized by the LCA to precede—is prosodically adjoined to the right edge of the adjacent minimal prosodic word, which in (24b) is *ne mu*. Schematically, this is shown in (25):

(25) a. [ne **MU**]$_\omega$ [**gi** [DAde]$_\omega$] ... (merger of *li*) ⇒

      b. [[ne **MU**]$_\omega$ **li**] [**gi** [DAde]$_\omega$] ...

Assuming Multiple Spell-Out, LCA-driven linearization produces the order in (25a), which is prosodified as indicated. Next, *li* is merged in C[0]. If SpecCP is filled, as in (20), *li* can be linearized to satisfy both the LCA and its prosodic requirement of seeking support to its left. However, if nothing is in SpecCP, *li* as an enclitic cannot be initial in its prosodic word, hence must be prosodified at the right edge of its minimal host, i.e., *ne mu*, as in (25b).[19]

7.3.3 *An argument for cyclic linearization*

This section presents an argument for why the linearization process must be cyclic.

Recall the Tobler-Mussafia effect, which in Bulgarian (but not very similar Macedonian) adjusts clitics left in Utterance-initial position. Taking as always asymmetric c-command to map into precedence, compare the initial Spell-Out orders in (26):

(26) a. **Si**   **mu**   **gi**   pokazvala. (√ in Macedonian;
           aux.2SG him.DAT them.ACC shown.FEM * in Bulgarian)
           'You have shown them to him.'

---

[19] Splitting of *mu + gi* by *li* is particularly striking since nothing else can *ever* interrupt such a sequence of two pronominal clitics. As discussed in Franks (2005, 2006b, 2008), Bulgarian tolerates some intervention by various aspectual adverbials and destressed emotive particles, but these can never split the pronominal subcluster; only *li* can do this.

b. I   si   mu   gi   pokazvala. ($\checkmark$ in Macedonian
    and aux.2SG him.DAT them.ACC shown.FEM   *and* Bulgarian)
    'And you have shown them to him.'

Sentence (26a) reflects a stage before an order consistent with the Tobler-Mussafia effect has been imposed, hence it is good in Macedonian but not in Bulgarian. In (26b), on the other hand, the presence of *i* means that no Tobler-Mussafia relinearization is needed in either language.[20] In other words, once Utterance-level prosodic structure is imposed, the clitics in (26a) but not those in (26b) end up being initial. Hence, in (26a)—but not in (26b) because *i* 'and' there prevents the clitic group from being Utterance-initial—the clitic group *si mu gi* must be relinearized in Bulgarian (but not Macedonian). This is shown in (27):

(27) υ #[[si mu gi]$_{CG}$ [pokazvala]$_{\omega}$]# υ $\Rightarrow$ (Bulgarian only)
       υ # [[pokazvala]$_{\omega}$ [si mu gi]$_{CG}$]# υ

This process erases the precedence relation between the clitic group and its adjacent prosodic word and resubmits it to linearization, redefining precedence in a way consistent with the Utterance non-initiality restriction.

Given this, one might ask how *li* linearization, which is sensitive to the prosodic word, interacts with Tobler-Mussafia linearization, which is sensitive to the Utterance. The interrogative version of Bulgarian (26a) eventually emerges as in (28):

(28)   Pokazvala   li   si   mu   gi?
       shown.FEM   Q   aux.2SG him.DAT them.ACC
       'Have you shown them to him?'

---

[20] The fact that atonic *i* 'and' is sufficient to render these clitics in Bulgarian no longer Utterance-initial is significant, because it means that they are in fact not 'enclitic', in the standard technical sense of looking for a prosodic host only to their left. Interestingly, *i* does not similarly save I-phrase-initial clitics in BCS. Thus, starting with *i* in BCS (ib) would not cause the higher copy of the clitics to be pronounced:

(i)   a.   I obećala **sam ti** igračku.
           'And (I) promised you a toy.'

      b.   *I **sam ti** obećala igračku.

This implies that merely invoking a constraint such as NONINITIAL is inadequate; directionality of prosodic support must also be stipulated. I am not sure how to implement this, but clearly the problem in (ib) is that *i* projects no prosodic structure of its own, hence *i* is unable to host *sam ti*. (Possibly the clitics in (i) are linearized to the right of *obećala* 'promised' *before* merger of *i*, just as in (30d) below, where 'Utterance-initial' is determined at the CP level; alternatively, a lower copy of them is pronounced or they might undergo relinearization themselves.) Bošković's (2004b: 42) characterization that these BCS 'clitics must encliticize to a constituent that is right-adjacent to an I-phrase boundary' does correctly rule out (ib), but is to my mind unwieldy in requiring reference to the edge property of its host and misses the insight that these elements are prosodically enclitic.

How is the word order in (28) derived? I propose a derivational scenario which roughly proceeds through the steps sketched out in (29):

(29) a. [[si mu gi]$_{CG}$ [pokazvala]$_\omega$] (merger of *li*) ⇒

      b. [[[si mu gi]$_{CG}$ [pokazvala]$_\omega$] li] (Spell-Out as Utterance) ⇒

      c. ʋ #[[[si mu gi]$_{CG}$ [pokazvala]$_\omega$] li]# ʋ (√ in Macedonian; * in Bulgarian) →

      d. ʋ #[[[pokazvala]$_\omega$ li] [si mu gi]$_{CG}$]# ʋ   (Bulgarian only)

All heads are first linearized to the left, following the LCA, as in (29a). However, unlike in the case of (26), the special clitics are not considered Utterance-initial until after the C⁰ *li* has been merged and is itself linearized to its host's right, as shown in (29b). The entire CP is then sent to Spell-Out and prosodified as an Utterance, indicated in (29c). At this point—if these are Bulgarian clitics—the clitic group violates the prosodic prohibition against Utterance-initiality. Hence its linearization with respect to its host is erased and reevaluated to follow *pokazvala li*, with the effect in (29d). It is this kind of 'double right wrap' derivation that gives rise to the appearance of *li* splitting the verbal participle *pokazvala* 'shown' from the clitics *si mu gi* in Bulgarian (28b). Macedonian, on the other hand, lacks the Utterance-initial constraint, so step (29d) is never invoked and the final output remains as in (29c).

What happens when the conjunction *i* 'and' is thrown into the mix? Recall that this element is sufficient to render the special clitics not Utterance-initial, although it is not itself tonic and so cannot host enclitics, such as *li* (or any of the BCS clitics). Interestingly, although *i* saves the clitics in (26b), it fails to do so when added to (28).[21] When 'protected' by *li*, addition of *i* has no ameliorating effect whatsoever. The relevant Bulgarian paradigm is summarized in (30):

(30) a. Pokazvala **si mu gi**.
          'You have shown them to him.'

      b. I **si mu gi** pokazvala.
          'And you have shown them to him.'

      c. Pokazvala **li si mu gi**?
          'Have you shown them to him?'

      d. I pokazvala **li si mu gi**?
          'And have you shown them to him?'

---

[21] I have reported this observation in a number of places, most accessibly Franks and Bošković (2001).

Sentence (30d) is the crucial one, demonstrating the need for cyclic linearization. It reveals that the determination that the clitics are Utterance-initial—hence the resolution of this problem that gives rise to the Tobler-Mussafia effect in Bulgarian—must *precede* merger of the conjunction *i* above the interrogative C⁰ head *li*. But this is exactly what we should expect if *i* here is a higher head, outside of CP. The CP phase is sent to Spell-Out, it is necessarily prosodified as an Utterance, and linearization must be reevaluated to respect the clitics' non-initiality requirement. By the time *i* is merged, above CP, it is too late to render the clitics non-initial. The result is (30d), which is just (30c) with *i* tacked in front; unlike in (30b), in which *i* crucially counts, *i* in (30d) is irrelevant.

Note a crucial assumption: in the derivation of (30b) the string *si mu gi pokazvala* cannot be prosodified as an Utterance, it *must* wait until *i* has been merged, otherwise the wrong order would obtain. In the derivation of (30d), on the other hand, waiting is impossible: *li* defines a CP and this must be prosodified as an Utterance. In Franks and Bošković (2001), we took this Tobler-Mussafia paradigm as evidence for Chomsky's phase theory, in which CP is a phase but its complement, IP/TP, is not. However, in Chomsky's system it is actually the *complement* to a phase head that is sent to Spell-Out, not the phase itself. Clearly, this does not work for the Bulgarian data, which require that CP be an Utterance and Inflection Phrase/Tense Phrase (IP/TP) not be one: if *li*, as the head of the CP phase, were not included in the material shipped off to Spell-Out, then Tobler-Mussafia would of course apply.[22]

One should finally ask why *li* does not have the same effect as *i*, rendering *si mu gi* non-initial. The answer is that it never does count as initial, since, when CP is sent to Spell-Out, *li* in (30c) and (30d) is linearized at the *right* edge of *si mu gi pokazvala*.[23] Because there is no literal prosodic inversion, *li* never actually precedes the special clitics. Thus, *si mu go pokazvala li* is sent to Spell-Out prosodified as an Utterance, which then undergoes Tobler-Mussafia as in Bulgarian (29d) but not in Macedonian (29c).

7.4 Aspects of ellipsis

This section considers those aspects of ellipsis which a successful model of the Spell-Out process should accommodate. The questions addressed here concern

---

[22] Chomsky's reason for sending the *complement* of the phase head to Spell-Out was to keep the specifier of the phase syntactically active; in section 7.5 below, I suggest a model which achieves this and in which it only makes sense for phases themselves to be sent to Spell-Out.

[23] Of course, if SpecCP is occupied, as in (20), *li* has a host to its left and, when CP is sent to Spell-Out, no Tobler-Mussafia is necessitated.

what kinds of constituents can be targeted and where ellipsis can occur in the process of mapping syntactic representations into ultimately phonetic ones.

7.4.1 *Ellipsis and resolution of PF offense*

The most familiar type of ellipsis specifically targets syntactic constituents to remain unpronounced. Indeed, ellipsis is generally taken as a textbook standard for diagnosing constituency. Since it must apply to representations which preserve syntactic constituency, such ellipsis presumably applies very early in the Spell-Out process. Another argument leading to this conclusion can be made on the basis of the observation that ellipsis can actually save certain derivations by deleting structure containing syntactic features that would, had they not been deleted, offend PF; see among others Lasnik (1999) or Merchant (2001). Lasnik, for example, has argued widely and persuasively that direct objects even in English undergo object shift, but that the verb also undergoes short movement to a head position preceding the shifted object. This is shown in (31), using the system for representing copies adopted earlier:

(31)   You will **believe Bob** [$_{VP}$ ~~believe Bob~~].

This allows Lasnik (1999) to treat pseudogapping as VP-ellipsis. In his structure (32), *Bob* moves to a Specifier position outside VP, but the verb *believe* does not. Hence, the object is preserved under pseudogapping but the verb is elided along with the Verb Phrase (VP) containing it:

(32)   You might not believe me but you will Bob$_i$ [$_{VP}$ ~~believe t_i~~].

A similar problem is posed by matrix sluicing, analyzed by Lasnik as IP-ellipsis, as in his (33):

(33)   A: Mary will see someone.

   B: Who$_i$ [$_{IP}$ ~~Mary will see t_i~~]?

Lasnik (1999) then asks the question of why the verb fails to raise in (32) or why I-to-C movement of *will* fails in (33). Lasnik's crucial insight is that ellipsis somehow serves to save the derivation. He considers various ways of implementing this failure to move just in case ellipsis is going to occur, depending on how feature strength is construed. The last and most appealing formalization offered in Lasnik (1999) exploits formal feature movement and appeals to the idea that ellipsis provides an additional way of circumventing the PF crash that is caused by leaving a strong feature visible to PF (unchecked and unerased). Movement, leading to checking, can eliminate the offending strong feature, but ellipsis can also do that—provided it does not move. In this way, ellipsis saves (32) and (33). But this kind of ellipsis must be early in the Spell-Out process, since it crucially targets syntactic constituents complete with their feature specifications.

7.4.2 *Ellipsis and focus*

The role of functional sentence perspective in determining surface word order is well studied in the Slavic tradition. This section shows how word-order effects motivated by functional sentence perspective considerations can be achieved through the PF-side deletion of designated material rather than through literal PF-movement.

7.4.2.1 *Free word order*   The idea that focus can lead to PF-side movement has been recently applied to Russian scrambling by Erteschik-Shir and Strahov (2004). An alternative PF-filtering approach exploits copy deletion.[24] Consider how functional sentence perspective desiderata might feed copy deletion. Sentences can be partitioned into *Theme* (Topic) and *Rheme* (Comment), with the focus the most prominent part of the Rheme. In Slavic 'free'-word-order languages, I propose, this partition is usually accomplished by mapping *v*P into the Rheme. This means that the first pronounced element within *v*P demarcates the beginning of the Rheme. Compare the neutral word orders in Russian (34) and (35), where '$_T|_R$' indicates the division into Theme and Rheme and '$_{T=\emptyset}|_R$' means the sentence is entirely rhematic:

(34) a. A: What did Vanya do?
         B: Vanja $_T|_R$ prišel. (Russian)
             'Vanya arrived.'

      b. [$_{TP}$ **Vanja** <RHEME [$_{vP}$ **prišel** [$_{VP}$ ~~prišel Vanja~~]]>]

      c. A: What happened?
         B: $_{T=\emptyset}|_R$ Prišel Vanja.
             'Vanya arrived.'

      d. [$_{TP}$ ~~Vanja~~ <RHEME [$_{vP}$ **prišel** [$_{VP}$ ~~prišel~~ **Vanja**]]>]

(35) a. A: What did Vanya do?
         B: Vanja $_T|_R$ umer.
             'Vanya died.'

      b. [$_{TP}$ **Vanja** <RHEME [$_{vP}$ ~~Vanja~~ **umer** [$_{VP}$ ~~umer~~]]>]

---

[24] See also Stjepanović's (2007) analysis of free word order in BCS.

    c.   A: What happened?

         B: $_{T=\emptyset|R}$ Vanja umer.

           'Vanya died.'

    d.   [$_{TP}$ ~~Vanja~~ <RHEME [$_{vP}$ **Vanja umer** [$_{VP}$ ~~umer~~]]>]

First consider unaccusative (34), with the subject *Vanja* generated as a complement to the verb *prišel* 'arrived'. In sentence (34a), divided into Theme and Rheme, the higher copy of *Vanja* in SpecTP is pronounced, as shown in (34b), but in wholly rhematic (34c) the lower copy of *Vanja* must be pronounced. The Verb–Subject word order thus derives from the structure in (34d). With unergative (35), on the other hand, the Subject–Verb order emerges even in the 'out-of-the-blue' wholly rhematic sentence (35c). This is arguably because *Vanja* here is an external argument, hence there is no copy of *Vanja* within VP. The subject is instead introduced in Spec*v*P position, as indicated in (35d), where it ends up being pronounced even when included in the Rheme.

7.4.2.2 *String discontinuities*   Although this kind of ellipsis involves deletion of entire copies, there is also evidence for 'scattered' deletion of pieces of copies, the clearest examples of which are focus-driven. Consider for example, Bulgarian (20), repeated in (36), where the question could be about going to *this* CITY or to THIS CITY:

(36)   V   tozi [[grad]$_\omega$ li] [si   [xodil]$_\omega$]?   (Bg)

       in this   city   Q   aux.2SG went

       'Was it to this city that you went?'

It is however also possible just to place the focus on *tozi* 'this', as in (37):

(37)   [[V tozi]$_\omega$ li] grad [si [xodil]$_\omega$]?

       'Was it to THIS city that you went?'

How is this splitting achieved? In Franks (2006b) I argue that (37) requires copies of *v tozi grad* 'to this city' immediately above and below *li*, with splitting forced by the property of *li* as demarcating the focus. This is schematized in (38):[25]

(38)   [$_{CP}$ [V̲ [t̲o̲z̲i̲ ~~grad~~]] li [[v̶ [~~tozi~~ g̲r̲a̲d̲]] si xodil]]?

            [+Foc]

A similar example splitting a *wh*–phrase is given in (39):

(39)   a.   Koja   li   kniga šte mi   podariš?!   (Bg)

           which Q book will me.DAT give.2SG

           'Which(ever) book will you give me?!'

---

[25] For clarity, I use strikethrough for the ellipsis and underline the pronounced pieces of the split.

b.   [CP [Koja [~~kniga~~]] **li** [[~~koja~~ kniga] **šte mi** podariš]]?
         [+Foc]

These splits are striking because Bulgarian, as a DP language, does not otherwise permit left-branch extraction out of NPs. Instead, the generalization is
that no non-focus material can follow the element with the focus feature in
SpecCP. In this way, *li* induces scattered deletion and superficial splitting.[26]

7.4.2.3 *Just linear strings*   A different and far more superficial type of ellipsis
does not appear to recognize syntactic constituency at all. The relevant data,
having to do with focus-driven ellipsis, are from colloquial Croatian and
sometimes lead to dramatic surface splits. The basic problem is that
splitting can leave non-constituents on both sides of the splitter, thereby
precluding any of the various available purely syntactic approaches to
discontinuity. Consider BCS (40):

(40)   U izuzetno   sam   veliku sobu ušao.   (BCS)
        in exceptionally aux.1SG large   room entered
        'It was into an EXCEPTIONALLY large room that I entered.'

As before, this splitting can be effected through ellipsis of string-adjacent
material, as in (41):

(41)   [PP U [NP [AP izuzetno ~~veliku~~] ~~sobu~~]] sam [PP ~~u~~ [NP [AP ~~izuzetno~~
          [+Foc]
        veliku] sobu]] ušao...

The operative principle, as just observed for focus *li*, is that there can be no
material within the fronted phrase that is to the right of the element bearing
the [+Foc] feature. All material following the [+Foc] element is therefore
elided, regardless of its syntactic constituency. This results in the pronunciation of the next highest copy of that material, as shown schematically in (42).

(42)

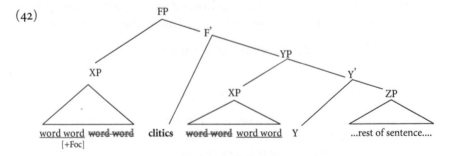

---

[26] This phenomenon is I believe different from the kind of *li* splitting displayed by Russian, since, as
discussed by Rudnickaya (2000) among others, in Russian splitting is more or less obligatory: the

Crucially, in this system material on neither side of the [+ Foc] element is required to be a constituent; instead, all that matters is that the deleted material within XP be contiguous.[27]

For some Croatian speakers,[28] this mechanism gives rise to a striking range of possibilities, where the word immediately in front of future auxiliary clitic *ću* is the likely focus:[29]

(43) a. Svakog ću   lijepog dana putovati vlakom svojoj (Croatian)
       every   fut.1SG nice   day   travel   train   self's
       kući.
       house.
       'EVERY nice day I will go to my house by train.' OR
       'Every nice day I will go to my house by train.'

    b. Svakog lijepog ću dana putovati vlakom svojoj kući.
       'Every NICE day I will go to my house by train.'

    c. Svakog lijepog dana ću putovati vlakom svojoj kući.
       'Every nice DAY I will go to my house by train.' OR
       'Every nice day I will go to my house by train.'

    d. Svakog lijepog dana putovat ću vlakom svojoj kući.[30]
       'Every nice day I will GO to my house by train.'

    e. Svakog lijepog dana putovati vlakom ću svojoj kući.
       'Every nice day I will go to my house by TRAIN.'

    f. Svakog lijepog dana putovati vlakom svojoj ću kući.
       'Every nice day I will go to MY house by train.'

It is not easy to know how to derive such unlikely strings. Particularly problematic are (43e) and (43f), in which the clitic is lower than immediately after the verb, since this is otherwise impossible. Given the analysis of clitics as functional heads, there cannot even be a copy of future

Russian version of (37) requires splitting—*v ètot li gorod* and not **v ètot gorod li*—regardless of which part of the PP is focused. The reason, I believe, is because in Russian there is simply no copy above *li* for scattered ellipsis to exploit, hence the only option ever for Russian *li* is to be pronounced at the right edge of the prosodic word to its right.

[27] Non-clitics can also intervene, a possibility which gives rise to more complex structures involving scattered deletion of pieces of scrambled phrases. Similar facts have been described for Russian (Pereltsvaig 2007) and Ukrainian (Féry this volume; Féry et al. 2007).

[28] Peti-Stantić (2007) offers these examples in examining whether spoken Croatian really adheres to second position for clitics; cf. also Franks (2007).

[29] The order in (43c), and also (43a) in literary registers, can be neutral as well, since these can be derived through the standard clitic placement rule in addition to focus-driven ellipsis.

[30] This order can also be neutral, but only if there is a prosodic break after *svakog lijepog dana*.

clitic *ću* that low. These data hence reveal that what is pronounced in front of the clitics in colloquial Croatian must actually be higher. I therefore conclude that the splits in (43) derive from a syntactic structure as in (44):

(44)   [Svakog dana putovati vlakom svojoj kući] *ću* [svakog dana putovati vlakom svojoj kući].

Essentially, there is a copy of the entire clause both above and below *ću*; ellipsis along the lines of (41)/(42) then applies to produce the various possibilities in (43), depending upon the locus of focus in the fronted phrase.

7.4.2.4 *Prepositional phrase splits and lexical non-distinctness*   PP-internal splitting in Croatian provides another interesting illustration of the same general principles. Consider the split in (45b):

(45)   a.   Od   jučer   **ga**   prodaje za velike novce.   (Croatian)
             from yesterday it.ACC sells   for large   money
             'Since yesterday (s)he's selling it for big bucks.'

       b.   Od jučer prodaje za velike **ga** novce.

       c.   *Od jučer prodaje za **ga** velike novce.

This split, judgments again due to University of Zagreb Professor Anita Peti-Stantić, is quite unexpected under familiar models of clitic placement. However, if the entire clause is fronted past *ga*, (45b) can be derived as in (46):

(46)   [Od jučer prodaje za velike ~~novce~~] **ga** [~~od jučer prodaje za velike~~ novce]
                                            [+ Foc]

As before, all material in the fronted phrase that follows the actual focused element is elided. In this way, apparent PP splits can be derived without moving non-constituents, providing an alternative to the kind of PF-side movement argued for in, e.g., Erteschik-Shir and Strahov (2004).

What then about (45c), in which the clitic cannot go immediately after the preposition? While it is possible that this is merely a reflection of the difficulty in focusing *za* 'for', there seems to be more to the story. The Slavic splitting data reveal a general PF requirement that a preposition needs to be directly followed by some piece of its complement; compare the grammatical split in (40). If so, (45c) can be rejected out of PF considerations. Some support for this conclusion is to be found in the interesting fact that accidental properties of the particular lexical item can sometimes rescue splittings: when such splittings involve a preposition that has an intransitive (i.e., adverbial) variant, then the splitting is not in fact filtered out by PF. Two such Janus-faced prepositions in BCS are genitive governing *ispred* 'in front of' and *pored* 'alongside', as in (47) and (48):

(47)   a.   <u>Ispred</u>   ga   je   <u>ulaza</u>   dočekala policija.
                in-front-of him.ACC aux.3SG entrance.GEN waited   police
                'The police were waiting for him in front of the entrance.'

         b.   <u>Pored</u>   je   <u>tog</u>   <u>čovjeka</u>   sjela.
                alongside aux.3SG that.GEN man.GEN sat
                'She sat alongside that man.'

(48)   a.   On je   sjedio <u>ispred/pored</u>.
                he   aux.3SG sat   in-front/alongside
                'He was sitting in front/alongside.'

         b.   <u>Ispred/Pored</u> je sjedio.
                '(He) was sitting in front/alongside.'

However, prepositions such as *prema* 'towards' that do not admit intransitive usage, as shown in (49a), invariably block this kind of splitting. Compare (49b) with (47b):

(49)   a.   *Išao je   <u>prema</u>.
                went aux.3SG towards
                [Intended: 'He was going towards.']

         b.   *<u>Prema</u> je   <u>tom</u>   <u>čovjeku</u>   došao.
                towards aux.3SG that.DAT man.DAT came
                [cf. √<u>Prema tom čovjeku</u> je došao. OR √<u>Prema tom</u> je <u>čovjeku</u> došao.]
                'He was coming towards that person.'

Both deletions in (50) are valid operations, for example if *pored* or *prema* were contrastively focused, but the sequence *prema je* in (50b) is subsequently filtered out as deviant whereas *pored je* in (50a) is not:

(50)   a.   √[<u>Pored</u> ~~tog čovjeka~~] je [~~pored~~ <u>tog čovjeka</u>] . . .

         b.   *[<u>Prema</u> ~~tom čovjeku~~] je [~~prema~~ <u>tom čovjeku</u>] . . .

The reason (50a) survives is because, once the lexical item *pored* has been inserted, the adverbial and prepositional variants are non-distinct, hence *pored* can function as a genitive assigning preposition for morphosyntactic case-checking purposes but as an intransitive adverbial for PF purposes. We thus expect that the kind of splitting in (45c) should be marginally possible with a preposition like *ispred* and indeed, according to A. Peti-Stantić (p. c.), it is: *Policija dočekala ispred ga je ulaza* (. . . *a ne pored*) 'The police were waiting for him IN FRONT OF the entrance (. . . and not alongside)'.

In sum, although prepositions need some piece of their complement to follow them, the existence of an intransitive variant somehow allows such prepositions to dodge this requirement. It is as if PF cannot tell whether any particular instance of *pored* 'alongside' has a case-assigning feature or not, nor can it remember that, before ellipsis in (50a), the case-governing variant had been invoked to make *tog čovjeka* 'that man' genitive. This indicates that case valuation, however implemented, necessarily precedes the sort of focus-driven ellipsis at work here. This makes it very different from the more familiar type of ellipsis. Traditional ellipsis is the failure to send syntactic structure to Spell-Out, hence it is constrained by constituency and, as we saw in Lasnik's (32) and (33), applies early enough to delete features that must be checked and erased before PF (i.e., strong ones). The kind of ellipsis that allows (47) to slip through, on the other hand, can occur only after lexical insertion under non-distinctness has taken place.

An informal survey of BCS prepositions shows that they fall into two classes along precisely these lines: splittability is enabled by potential intransitivity. This correlation supports the superficiality of this kind of ellipsis, but raises the far from trivial question of how to exploit the correlation. The general structure of the solution however is clear: at one point in the derivation a lexical item satisfies some requirement and then, at a later point, when a contradictory requirement is imposed on it, that item can also satisfy the second requirement. This is because of non-distinctness: lexical insertion requires that the form selected from the lexicon for Spell-Out of some morphosyntactic feature set be featurally non-distinct and lexical syncretism is expressed in the lexicon in terms of non-distinctness (i.e., underspecification) of features.

The general phenomenon of syncretic morphological forms managing to satisfy the contradictory requirements of two different structures is widespread. Here are three relevant constructions, albeit quite different from the PP-split phenomenon just discussed. In the across-the-board *wh*-movement construction in Russian (51), the feminine relative pronoun *kotoroj* 'which' is syncretic instrumental and dative, whereas the masculine forms *kotorym/kotoromu* are distinct:

(51) devuška, kotoroj   [ja byl uvlečen t_{INST} i   (Russian)
      girl   which.INST/DAT I was carried-away   and
      često daval t_{DAT} dengi]
      often gave   money
      'the girl who I was carried away with and often gave money to...'
      [cf. mal'čik, *kotorym/*kotoromu... '(the) boy *who.INST/*who.DAT...']

In German free relatives, as in (52), inanimate *was* is syncretic nominative and accusative, whereas the animate forms *wer* and *wen* are distinct:

(52) Ich werde was   da   steht mitbringen.   (German)
      I   will   what.NOM/ACC there stands with-bring
      'I will bring along what is standing there.'
      [cf. Ich werde ??wer/*wen da steht mitbringen. 'I will ??who.NOM/
        *who.ACC...']

In Hungarian, which distinguishes verb conjugations for definite and indefinite direct objects, coordination of objects of different types creates a problem for lexical insertion, but syncretism evades it. As shown in (53), the past-tense first singular *láttam* 'saw' is syncretic definite and indefinite conjugation, whereas the present-tense first singular forms *látom/látok* are distinct:

(53) Láttam   a   két szép   kutyát és   egy
      saw.1SG-DEF/INDEF the two beautiful dogs   and one
      csunya cicát.   (Hungarian)
      ugly   cat
      'I saw the two beautiful dogs and one ugly cat.'
      [cf. *Látom /*Látok... '(I) *see.1SG-DEF/*see.1SG-INDEF...']

In each of these, the various structures are created in the syntax and evaluated from two independent perspectives. When one phase is spelled out, an item is selected for lexical insertion, and that item remains active and available for feature checking when a different phase is spelled out. If the particular morphological form did not happen to be syncretic, then there would be no appropriate lexical item available and the conflict would result in ineffability. In the course of Spell-Out to PF, however, the syncretism of particular morphological entries allows those feature conflicts to survive.

7.5 A technical speculation about multiple Spell-Out

I want finally to offer a theoretical digression, speculating about the mechanics of phase theory and specifically addressing the following question: How are pieces of the derivation which have been separately sent to Spell-Out later reassembled? My approach to this question builds on Chomsky's (2001b) notion of lexical 'subarrays.' Chomsky observed that, in order for economy considerations such as 'merge over move' to be effective, only convergent derivations starting from the same Numeration can be compared. However, to avoid competition involving lexical items from distinct functional complexes within a single sentence, Chomsky needed to adopt subarrays. These are autonomous sets of lexical resources defined by each of the phase heads in the Numeration. However, the problem of how these subarrays are reassembled for the purposes of spelling out the entire sentence was left unresolved. My solution is to build subarrays derivationally, such that the product of merging all the members of one subarray into a phase in effect becomes (through Spell-Out) a lexical item which can then serve as a member of another subarray within the same Numeration.[31] Merge collapses the subarray into a spelled-out unit, which is then literally added into the subarray associated with some other phase head. This is how the various clausal and nominal arguments can be derivationally assembled and deployed in the same phase.

This formalization of Multiple Spell-Out implies that the output of each phase, if it is to merge successfully as an argument, must remain active by preserving some unvalued feature. Moreover, in order to be visible to some higher probe, that unvalued feature must be at the top (=left edge) of the phase, analogous to the accessible outermost layer of a morphological word. From this perspective, when an element with an unvalued feature moves (i.e., a copy remerges) at the top of its phase, this enables the phase to function as an active lexical item within some other subarray. In Franks (2006a) I call this 'agnostic' movement: by moving and saving itself, the element also preserves the phase to which it belongs. The result is a system in which everything inside of a sentence, as the pieces are shipped off to Spell-Out, becomes a word, so that even the sentence itself is ultimately just one big word. We now see why it is phases rather than phase-head complements which are sent to Spell-Out: a spelled out CP or Determiner Phrase (DP), if it is to be an argument, will have some unvalued feature(s) at its left edge. Edge visibility is an intrinsic property of words. The CP or DP can thus be inserted into the subarray defined by some other phase head, of which it then functions as an argument.

7.6 Conclusion

In this paper I have deployed Slavic facts to identify a variety of likely PF effects on the output of syntax, considering how factors such as linear order, prosodic structure, and copy deletion might interact. It was proposed that these cooperate to mediate the mapping from hierarchical syntactic

---

[31] See also Uriagereka (1999).

representations to linearized PF ones. While initial linearization was argued to be LCA-inspired, attention was drawn also to subsequent processes which can reevaluate precedence relations for prosodic reasons. Examples were the realization of simple enclitics like *li* and the relinearization of Bulgarian special clitics to conform to the Tobler-Mussafia non-initiality requirement. Different kinds of ellipsis—defined in general as PF non-expression of syntactically fully structured material, rather than LF copying into syntactically vacuous phrases—were also examined. It was argued that, beyond copy deletion and silent phrases, there are late ellipsis processes which ignore the internal constituency of the units targeted. Lastly, a derivational model of Multiple Spell-Out was adopted, applying cyclically to larger and larger chunks of structure, and a particular view was suggested of how independently spelled-out phases are combined.

This paper has admittedly been in many ways programmatic. The potential relevance of data to the workings of Spell-Out was noted, but the derivational details and the resolution of various conceptual alternatives was left for future research. We are left, in addition, with the complicated but promising exercise of reexamining the various proposals made in sections 7.2–7.4 from the 'derivational subarray' perspective laid out in section 7.5.

I conclude by reiterating a theme which inspired the workshop from which the papers in this volume are drawn: the division of labor between syntax and PF. The analyses presented in this paper, I believe, help to demonstrate that the burden has now decidedly shifted towards PF: linearization, copy selection, ellipsis, and possibly even movement are defined in the effort to pronounce. Of course, all this may just amount to saying PF is a lot more abstract than we thought.

8

Semantic and discourse interpretation of the Japanese left periphery*

MAMORU SAITO

8.1 Introduction

Japanese scrambling often makes no contribution to interpretation and seems purely stylistic. Yet, it can have semantic and discourse effects. The purpose of this paper is to examine the interpretive mechanism for movement chains by investigating this peculiar property of scrambling. In the course of the discussion, I will also present a hypothesis on the structure of the Japanese left periphery.

The basic idea pursued in this paper is that Japanese scrambling is stylistic but can nevertheless affect interpretation because of the general mechanism of movement and its interpretation. Let us consider the example of *wh*-movement in (1) to illustrate this mechanism first.

(1) a. What$_i$ did John buy t_i

  b. [For which x: x a thing] John bought x

(1a) is interpreted as in (1b), which indicates that the *wh*-phrase is construed as an operator *[for which x: x a thing]* at the landing site and as a variable *x* at

* This is a revised and shortened version of the paper presented at the Sound Patterns of Syntax Workshop held at Ben-Gurion University on June 11–13, 2007. A still earlier version of this paper was presented in syntax seminars at Nanzan University and the University of Connecticut in the spring of 2007, and also at the Siena-Nanzan Workshop on Comparative Syntax and Language Acquisition held at the University of Siena on May 4–5, 2007. I would like to thank the audiences at these places, especially Jonathan Bobaljik, Steve Franks, Idan Landau, Luigi Rizzi, Ian Roberts, Masaki Sano, Koji Sugisaki, and Kensuke Takita, and also an anonymous reviewer for helpful comments and suggestions. The research leading to the final revision was supported in part by the Nanzan University Pache Research Grant I-A-2 (2008).

the initial site. This in turn suggests that the *wh*-phrase is composed of a feature, say [wh], which yields its interpretation as a *wh*-operator, and a feature, say [arg(ument)], which is responsible for its interpretation as a variable, in addition to the phonetic features [phon] and the categorial features [cat]. Then, extending Chomsky's (1993) copy and deletion analysis of movement, it can be hypothesized that movement copies the *wh*-phrase at the landing site as in (2a), and the chain is interpreted as in (2b) with the appropriate deletion of features.

(2)   a.   What$_{\{wh, arg, phon, cat\}}$ [did John buy what$_{\{wh, arg, phon, cat\}}$]

    b.   What$_{\{wh, \cancel{arg}, phon, cat\}}$ [did John buy what$_{\{\cancel{wh}, arg, \cancel{phon}, cat\}}$]

[phon] is retained at the landing site as the movement is overt, and I assume that [cat] is retained at all positions of the chain. The specific syntactic features [wh] and [arg], on the other hand, are retained at the positions where they are licensed and properly interpreted. The [arg] feature satisfies the selectional requirement of the verb at the object position, and the [wh] feature is attracted to the CP Spec position by the question C.

Given this mechanism for movement and its interpretation, the simple example of scrambling in (3a) is analyzed as in (3b).

(3)   a.   Hon -o$_i$ [Taroo-ga t_i katta]
            book-ACC   -NOM   bought
            'Taroo bought a book'

    b.   Hon-o$_{\{arg, phon, cat\}}$ [Taroo-ga hon-o$_{\{arg, \cancel{phon}, cat\}}$ katta]

As the scrambled phrase *hon-o* 'book-ACC' is not an operator, it consists only of [arg], [phon], and [cat]. The [arg] feature should be retained at the object position because *hon-o* is interpreted as an argument at that position. Hence, the scrambling chain is interpreted as in (3b). This makes scrambling purely stylistic or semantically vacuous as no substantial feature is retained at the landing site. But note that the [arg] feature is copied at the landing site although the copy is eventually deleted. I will argue in this paper that this enables the [arg] feature to interact with higher functional heads, and that scrambling can have semantic effects because of this. Further, a scrambled phrase may contain features such as [top(ic)] in addition to [arg]. This, I will argue, is the source of the discourse effects of scrambling.

In the following section, I will first present examples of the Japanese *wh*-construction and demonstrate that scrambling can indeed be semantically vacuous as illustrated in (3b). Then, I will show how the mechanism of chain interpretation captures the A/A′ properties of scrambling discussed in detail by Mahajan (1990) and Tada (1993), among others. In section 8.3, I will turn to the effects of scrambling on the scope interaction between the subject and sentential negation. Modifying Miyagawa's (2001, 2003) analysis of the phenomenon, I will argue that there is a functional head, *Pred(ication)*, above TP, and that the [arg] feature preposed by scrambling can be attracted by this head. Then, in section 8.4, I will consider Kuno's (1973) observation that only a matrix-initial topic can receive thematic (as opposed to contrastive) interpretation, and also some exceptions to this generalization pointed out in Kuroda (1988). I will argue that only those topics in the specifier position of the Pred projection can be interpreted as thematic, and that scrambling of topics interacts with this in an intricate way. Section 8.5 concludes the paper with a brief discussion of the Japanese left periphery from a crosslinguistic perspective.

8.2 The basic properties of Japanese scrambling

In section 8.2.1, I will review two well-known properties of Japanese scrambling. I will first consider scrambling of *wh*-phrases and show that it need not have any effect on interpretation. Then, I will discuss Mahajan's (1990) generalization that only clause-internal scrambling exhibits properties of A-movement. In section 8.2.2, I will argue that the chain interpretation mechanism alluded to above successfully accounts for the relevant facts.

8.2.1 *Radical reconstruction and the A/A′ distinction*

Let us first consider the examples of *wh*-questions in (4).[1]

(4)   a.   [$_{TP}$ Taroo-ga   [$_{CP}$[$_{TP}$ dare-ga   sono hon -o   katta]
                    -NOM   who-NOM that book-ACC bought
             ka] siritagatteiru] (koto)
             Q   know-want   fact
             '[Taroo wants to know [Q [who bought that book]]]'

      b.   *[$_{TP}$ Dare-ga   [$_{CP}$[$_{TP}$ Taroo-ga   sono hon -o   katta]
                    -NOM   -NOM that book-ACC bought
             ka] siritagatteiru] (koto)
             Q   know-want   fact
             '[Who wants to know [Q [John bought that book]]]'

---

[1] In these examples and some others to follow, I show the rough structure of the sentence in single quotes instead of English translation. Also, *koto* 'the fact that' is added at the end of some examples in order to avoid the unnaturalness resulting from the lack of topic in a matrix clause. I ignore this in the rough structure or translation in single quotes.

In both (4a) and (4b), the embedded CP is a question, as indicated by the question marker *ka* in C. In the former, the *wh*-phrase *dare* 'who' is contained within this CP and takes scope at this CP. The example is interpreted as in (5).

(5)   Taroo wants to know [for which x: x a person] x bought that book

In (4b), on the other hand, *dare* is the matrix subject and is not contained within the question CP. As the example is totally ungrammatical, the contrast in (4) suggests the simple generalization in (6).

(6)   A *wh*-phrase must be contained within the question CP where it takes scope.

   This generalization, first discussed by Harada (1972), extends to the English examples in (7).

(7)   a.   [$_{CP}$ Who$_i$ [$_{TP}$ t_i asked whom to find out [$_{CP}$ what$_j$ [$_{TP}$ Bill bought t_j]]]]

      b.   [$_{CP}$ Who$_i$ [$_{TP}$ t_i wonders [$_{CP}$ [which picture of whom]$_j$ [$_{TP}$ Bill saw t_j]]]]

      c.   ??[$_{CP}$ [Which picture of whom]$_j$ does [$_{TP}$ Bill wonder [$_{CP}$ who$_i$ [$_{TP}$ t_i saw t_j]]]]

Since *wh*-movement places *wh*-phrases in their scope positions, *who* takes matrix scope and *what* takes embedded scope in (7a). The third *wh*-phrase, *whom*, is in the matrix object position. As it is contained in the matrix question but not in the embedded question, it must take scope at the matrix CP in accordance with (6). Thus, the example only has the interpretation as a matrix multiple *wh*-question. (7b), on the other hand, is ambiguous as pointed out by van Riemsdijk and Williams (1981). *Wh*-movement places *who* at the matrix CP Spec and *which (picture)* at the embedded CP Spec. The third *wh*-phrase, *whom*, is pied-piped to the embedded CP Spec, and is contained in the matrix CP as well as the embedded CP. Accordingly, it can take either matrix or embedded scope, again as correctly predicted by (6). Finally, *whom* in (7c) is pied-piped out of the embedded question CP, and hence, can only take matrix scope. Although the example is degraded because of the *wh*-island effect, its interpretation clearly conforms to the generalization in (6).

   Having seen that (6) is well motivated, let us now turn to an example of *wh*-scrambling. (8a) is a straightforward example with an embedded *wh*-question.

(8) a. [$_{TP}$ Taroo-ga   [$_{CP}$ [$_{TP}$ Hanako-ga   dono hon -o   yonda]
            -NOM   -NOM which book-ACC read
         ka] siritagatteiru] (koto)
         Q   know-want   fact
         '[Taroo wants to know [Q [Hanako read which book]]]'

     b. [$_{TP}$ Dono hon -o$_i$ [Taroo-ga   [$_{CP}$[$_{TP}$ Hanako-ga t_i
              which book-ACC   -NOM   -NOM
         yonda] ka] siritagatteiru]] (koto)
         read   Q   know-want   fact
         '[Which book$_i$, Taroo wants to know [Q [Hanako read t_i]]]'

In (8b), the *wh*-phrase, *dono hon* 'which book', is scrambled out of the embedded question all the way to the initial position of the matrix clause. Given (6), we would expect the example to be ungrammatical like (4b) because the *wh*-phrase is not contained within the CP where it takes scope. Yet, (8b) is grammatical and receives the same interpretation as (8a).

Based on examples of this kind, I proposed in Saito (1989) that scrambling can be 'semantically vacuous' in the sense that a scrambled phrase can be radically (totally) reconstructed at LF. Then, the scrambled object in (8b) can be placed back in its initial position at LF, and the example can be interpreted in a way that is consistent with (6), that is, exactly like (8a). This amounts to saying that scrambling can be merely stylistic and need not have any effect on interpretation. However, it is known that scrambling can affect interpretation. In the remainder of this section, I will discuss one such case, namely, the interaction of scrambling with anaphor binding.

It was observed by Mahajan (1990), who examined Hindi scrambling, that a phrase preposed by clause-internal scrambling can serve as the antecedent of an anaphor. For example, (9b) contrasts sharply with (9a).

(9) a. ?*[Otagai   -no   sensei] -ga   [Taroo-to   Hanako]-o
           each other-GEN teacher-NOM   -and   -ACC
         suisensita   (koto)
         recommended fact
         '*Lit.* Each other's teachers recommended Taroo and Hanako'

     b. [Taroo-to   Hanako]-o$_i$ [[otagai   -no   sensei] -ga t_i
              -and   -ACC   each other-GEN teacher-NOM
         suisensita]   (koto)
         recommended   fact
         '[Taroo and Hanako]$_i$, each other's teachers recommended t_i'

(9a) is out because the anaphor *otagai* 'each other' is not bound. This is remedied in (9b) as the potential antecedent *Taroo-to Hanako* is scrambled to a position c-commanding the anaphor. This indicates that scrambling can affect binding relations. Interestingly, it is only clause-internal scrambling that exhibits this effect. Thus, long scrambling out of a finite clause does not extend the binding possibility as (10) shows.

(10) a. *[Otagai -no sensei] -ga [$_{CP}$ Ziroo-ga [Taroo-to
          each other-GEN teacher-NOM   -NOM   -and
          Hanako]-o suisensita to] itta (koto)
          -ACC recommended that said fact
          '*Lit.* Each other's teachers said that Ziroo recommended Taroo
          and Hanako'

      b. *[Taroo-to Hanako]-o$_i$ [[otagai -no sensei]-ga
                  -and   -ACC each other-GEN teacher-NOM
          [$_{CP}$ Ziroo-ga t_i suisensita to] itta] (koto)
                  -NOM recommended that said fact
          '[Taroo and Hanako]$_i$, each other's teachers said that Ziroo
          recommended t_i'

(10b) is ungrammatical despite the fact that long scrambling places *Taroo-to Hanako* in a position that c-commands *otagai*.

Mahajan concludes then that clause-internal scrambling can be A-movement while long scrambling out of a finite clause is necessarily A'-movement. More specifically, he hypothesizes that there are two kinds of scrambling: A-scrambling to TP Spec and A'-scrambling that involves adjunction to TP.[2] The former is clause-bound because it is A-movement. The latter, on the other hand, can take place across a CP boundary. Given this hypothesis, nothing prevents a clause-internal application of A'-scrambling. The prediction is borne out by the following example:

(11) Zibunzisin-o$_i$ [Taroo-ga t_i suisensita] (koto)
      self   -ACC   -NOM recommended fact
      'Himself$_i$, Taroo recommended t_i'

---

[2] More accurately, Mahajan (1990) proposes that the landing site of A-scrambling is AGR Spec. It was Miyagawa (2001, 2003) who updated this analysis and proposed that A-scrambling is movement to TP Spec. See also Kuroda (1988), which presents a TP Spec analysis from a different perspective.

If clause-internal scrambling is necessarily A-movement, *zibunzisin* 'self'
A-binds its antecedent *Taroo* and the example should be in violation of
Condition (C) of the Binding Theory. Its grammaticality, thus, constitutes
evidence that clause-internal scrambling can be A'-movement.

In the following subsection, I will briefly go over the unified analysis of A
and A' scramblings proposed in Saito (2003, 2005). It relies crucially on the
chain interpretation mechanism mentioned in section 8.1 and forms a basis,
together with Mahajan's (1990) analysis, for the discussion in the subsequent
sections.

8.2.2 *A unified analysis of A and A' scramblings*

Although Mahajan's analysis successfully accounts for the A/A' properties of
scrambling, it is tempting not to postulate two distinct kinds of scrambling
and to pursue a uniform analysis. The radical reconstruction property of
scrambling also remains to be explained. In this section, I will briefly discuss
an attempt at a uniform analysis presented in Saito (2003, 2005).

Recall first the chain interpretation mechanism introduced in section 8.1.
According to it, the example of clause-internal scrambling in (12a) is analyzed
as in (12b).[3]

(12)   a.   [$_{TP}$ [Taroo-to   Hanako]-o$_i$ [[otagai   -no   sensei]-ga
                     -and   -ACC   each other-GEN teacher-NOM
           t_i suisensita]]   (koto)
                   recommended   fact
           '[Taroo and Hanako]$_i$, each other's teachers recommended t_i'

       b.   [$_{TP}$ [T.-to H.]-o$_{\{arg, phon\}}$ [[otagai-no ...]-ga [T.-to H.]-o$_{\{arg, phon\}}$
           suisensita]]

All features of *Taroo-to Hanako* are first copied at the landing site.[4] Then,
[arg] is deleted at the landing site and [phon] is deleted at the initial site. As a

---

[3] I will henceforth omit the categorical features [cat] as they play no role in the discussion in this
paper.

[4] Given that *v*P constitutes a derivational phase, the movement must proceed though its edge.
However, I will ignore *v*P phase and assume that only CP constitutes a phase in this paper for ease of
exposition. The simplification is justified in part because short scrambling to the *v*P edge is known to
have properties quite distinct from scrambling across the subject. For example, as pointed out by
Mahajan (1990), Tada (1993), and Nemoto (1993), among others, it exhibits strict A-properties with
respect to binding. I will assume that it is more like object shift and in particular, that the [arg] feature
copied at the *v*P edge by short scrambling is retained at that position. This means that real scrambling,
as analyzed in this paper, originates at the *v*P edge. See Saito (2003) for more detailed discussion on
this point.

result, only [phon] is in a position that c-commands *otagai* 'each other'. Then how can this scrambling license the anaphor? We would expect the [arg] feature to be responsible for anaphor binding. I argued in Saito (2003) that the derivational application of Condition (A) provides an answer. It is proposed by Belletti and Rizzi (1988), among others, that Condition (A) is an anywhere condition. They present examples of psych-verb construction such as (13) as evidence.

(13)   [$_{TP}$ [Pictures of himself]$_i$ [$_{VP}$[$_{V'}$ worry t_i] John]]

The reflexive *himself* is not bound by its antecedent *John* in this sentence. However, the subject is a theme argument and hence, it is plausible that it originates in a position lower than the experiencer *John*. Belletti and Rizzi argue then that the reflexive can be licensed prior to the movement of *pictures of himself* to the subject position. This analysis implies that Condition (A) can be satisfied at any point of a derivation. Given this conception of Condition (A), *otagai* in (12b) is licensed when its antecedent is copied at the sentence-initial position, that is, prior to the deletion of [arg] from this position.

The failure of long scrambling to license anaphors follows from this analysis, given that CPs constitute phases in the sense of Chomsky (2000). Let us first consider how the chain interpretation mechanism applies to the long-distance *wh*-movement in (14).

(14)   Which book$_i$ does John think that Mary read t_i

Given that the embedded CP is a phase, the *wh*-phrase *which book* must first move to its edge as in (15a).

(15)   a.   [$_{CP}$ Which book$_{\{wh, arg, phon\}}$ [$_{C'}$ that [$_{TP}$ Mary read which book$_{\{wh, arg, phon\}}$]]]

       b.   [$_{CP}$ Which book$_{\{wh, ~~arg~~, phon\}}$ [$_{C'}$ that [$_{TP}$ Mary read which book$_{\{~~wh~~, arg, ~~phon~~\}}$]]]

Upon the completion of this phase, the complement TP is transferred to the interpretive components before the derivation continues to construct the matrix clause. This implies that chain interpretation by feature deletion must apply at this point as in (15b) because [wh] and [phon] are not interpreted at the object position. (15b) indicates properly that *which book* is not pronounced and is interpreted as a variable at this position. Then, the matrix part is constructed as in (16a) and construed as in (16b).

(16)   a.   [$_{CP}$ Which book$_{\{wh, phon\}}$ [$_{C'}$ does [$_{TP}$ John think [$_{CP}$ which book$_{\{wh, ~~arg~~, phon\}}$ [$_{C'}$ ···

b.   [$_{CP}$ Which book$_{\{wh, phon\}}$ [$_{C'}$ does [$_{TP}$ John think [$_{CP}$ which book$_{\{wh, \text{arg}, \text{phon}\}}$ [$_{C'}$ ...

Which book is copied at the matrix CP Spec with two sets of features, [wh] and [phon], because [arg] is already deleted at the embedded CP Spec. The *wh*-phrase is pronounced there and is interpreted there as a *wh*-operator.

Long scrambling out of a CP should apply in basically the same way. Let us consider (10b), the example that shows that a phrase preposed by long scrambling cannot serve as the antecedent of an anaphor. In this example, *Taroo-to Hanako* should first move to the edge of the embedded CP as in (17a).

(17)   a.   [$_{CP}$ T.-to H.-o$_{\{arg, phon\}}$ [$_{TP}$ Ziroo-ga T.-to H.-o$_{\{arg, phon\}}$ suisensita]]

       b.   [$_{CP}$ T.-to H.-o$_{\{\text{arg}, phon\}}$ [$_{TP}$ Ziroo-ga T.-to H.-o$_{\{arg, \text{phon}\}}$ suisensita]]

Then, chain interpretation by feature deletion should apply as in (17b) before the complement TP is transferred to the interpretive components. Next, the matrix clause is constructed as in (18a) and the derivation is completed with the deletion of [phon] at the embedded CP Spec as in (18b).

(18)   a.   [$_{TP}$ T.-to H.-o$_{\{phon\}}$ [[otagai-no...]-ga [$_{CP}$ T.-to H.-o$_{\{\text{arg}, phon\}}$ [$_{TP}$ Ziroo-ga...

       b.   [$_{TP}$ T.-to H.-o$_{\{phon\}}$ [[otagai-no...]-ga [$_{CP}$ T.-to H.-o$_{\{\text{arg}, \text{phon}\}}$ [$_{TP}$ Ziroo-ga...

Note here that [arg] is not copied at the matrix-initial position because it was deleted at the embedded CP Spec. Hence, the [arg] feature of *Taroo-to Hanako* does not c-command the anaphor *otagai* at any point of the derivation. The ungrammaticality of (10b) is thus accounted for.

According to the analysis illustrated above, the landing site of scrambling can always be a position from which anaphor licensing is possible. Long scrambling out of a CP fails to license an anaphor not because the landing site is an A′-position but because the [arg] feature of the scrambled phrase is not copied at the landing site. The analysis crucially relies on the hypothesis that Condition (A) is an anywhere condition. This is consistent with (11), repeated below as (19).

(19)   Zibunzisin-o$_i$ [Taroo-ga t_i suisensita]   (koto)
       self   -ACC   -NOM   recommended   fact
       'Himself$_i$, Taroo recommended t_i'

As the (subject-oriented) anaphor *zibunzisin* can be licensed prior to the application of scrambling, the example is correctly predicted to be grammatical.[5]

Let us finally return to the example of radical reconstruction in (8b), repeated below as (20).

(20)   [$_{TP}$ Dono hon -o$_i$ [Taroo-ga   [$_{CP}$[$_{TP}$ Hanako-ga t_i
         which book-ACC   -NOM   -NOM
         yonda] ka] siritagatteiru]] (koto)
         read   Q   want-to-know   fact
         '[Which book$_i$, Taroo wants to know [Q [Hanako read t_i]]]'

The problem was that the *wh*-phrase *dono hon* 'which book' is not contained within the question CP where it takes scope. The *wh*-phrase first moves to the edge of the embedded CP as in (21).

(21)   [$_{CP}$ Dono hon-o$_{\{wh, arg, phon\}}$ [$_{TP}$ Hanako-ga dono hon-o$_{\{wh, arg, phon\}}$
         yonda] ka]

As Japanese lacks syntactic *wh*-movement, two hypotheses have been entertained for *wh*-licensing in this language. Huang (1982) proposes that *wh*-phrases are raised covertly to CP Spec and are interpreted there. If this is the case, the [wh] feature can be retained at the landing site as in (22a) and the matrix clause can be derived as in (22b).

(22)   a.   [$_{CP}$ Dono hon-o$_{\{wh, \text{arg}, phon\}}$ [$_{TP}$ Hanako-ga dono
                hon-o$_{\{wh, arg, \text{phon}\}}$ yonda] ka]

         b.   [$_{TP}$ Dono hon-o$_{\{\text{wh}, phon\}}$ [Taroo-ga ... [$_{CP}$ dono
                hon-o$_{\{wh, \text{arg}, phon\}}$ [$_{TP}$ ...

In (22b), [wh] is retained at the embedded CP Spec as it is licensed and interpreted there, and is deleted at the final landing site. On the other hand, Nishigauchi (1990) argues that *wh*-phrases in Japanese are licensed through unselective binding from [+Q] C. In this case, the first step of the movement is interpreted as in (23), and the [wh] feature is retained at the embedded object position.

---

[5] This analysis of (19) is inconsistent with Lebeaux's (1988) conception of Condition (C) as an everywhere condition, and provides an additional piece of evidence for Chomsky's (1993) proposal that the condition applies to the output of the derivation. This is so because the [arg] feature of *zibunzisin* is copied at the sentence-initial position as shown in (i).

(i)   Zibunzisin-o$_{\{\text{arg}, phon\}}$ [Taroo-ga zibunzisin-o$_{\{arg, \text{phon}\}}$ suisensita]

Thus, if Condition (C) is an everywhere condition, the example is predicted to be ungrammatical, contrary to the fact.

(23)   [$_{CP}$ Dono hon-o$_{\{wh, \text{arg}, phon\}}$ [$_{TP}$ Hanako-ga dono hon-o$_{\{wh, arg, \text{phon}\}}$
       yonda] ka]

In either case, the radical reconstruction property of scrambling is captured
by the proposed mechanism of chain interpretation.

In this section, I presented a uniform analysis of scrambling, clause-internal and long-distance, with a feature-based interpretive mechanism of
movement chains. In the following section, I will extend the analysis to data
on subject-negation scope interaction discussed in detail in Miyagawa (2001,
2003). I will argue that the [arg] feature that is copied at the landing site of the
initial step of scrambling can be attracted by a higher functional head Pred.
This provides further support for the analysis of scrambling just presented,
and interestingly, resurrects part of Mahajan's (1990) hypothesis that there are
two distinct kinds of scrambling.

8.3 Pred phrase above TP

In section 8.3.1, I will review Miyagawa's analysis of subject-negation scope
interaction. Then, in 8.3.2, I will present a revision of his analysis, proposing
that a functional projection above TP plays a crucial role in the account for
the phenomenon.

8.3.1 *Miyagawa on subject-neg scope interaction*

Miyagawa (2001, 2003) makes an important observation about the effects of
scrambling on the scope of subject in relation to sentential negation. First, a
subject tends to take scope over negation, as (24a) shows.[6]

(24)   a.   Zen'in-ga   sono tesuto-o   uke -na -katta (yo /to
            all   -NOM that test -ACC take-Neg-Past   Part that
            omo -u)
            think-Pres
            'All did not take that exam' (All > Not, *Not > All)

       b.   Sono tesuto-o$_i$ zen'in-ga t_i uke -na -katta (yo /to
            that test -ACC all   -NOM   take-Neg-Past   Part that
            omo -u)
            think-Pres
            'That exam$_i$, all did not take t_i' (All > Not, Not > All)

---

[6] I will show the morphological make-ups of the verbal complexes in the examples in this section
because the position of negation is important for the discussion.

However, once the object is scrambled to the sentence-initial position, the narrow-scope reading of the subject becomes readily available as in (24b).[7] This effect is observed only with clause-internal scrambling. (25) indicates that long scrambling out of a CP does not make the narrow-scope construal of the subject possible.

(25)   Syukudai -o$_i$ zenn'in-ga   [$_{CP}$ sensei -ga t_i das   -u
       homework-ACC all   -NOM   teacher-NOM   assign-Pres
       to] omow-ana -katta (yo)
       that think -Neg-Past   Part
       'Homework$_i$, all did not think that the teacher would assign t_i'
       (All > Not, *Not > All)

The difference between clause-internal scrambling in (24b) and long scrambling out of a CP in (25) is reminiscent of the binding paradigm discussed in the preceding section. In both cases, only clause-internal scrambling can affect interpretation. Miyagawa in fact argues that it provides supporting evidence for Mahajan's non-uniform analysis of scrambling, which he himself has developed over the years. Let us first consider the structure of (24a), shown in (26).

(26)   [$_{TP}$ Zen'in-ga$_i$ [$_{T'}$ [$_{NegP}$ [$_{vP}$ t_i [$_{v'}$ [$_{VP}$ sono tesuto-o [$_V$ uke-]] v]]
       [$_{Neg}$ -na-]] [$_T$ -katta]]]

The subject *zen'in-ga* 'all-NOM' is raised to TP Spec in order to satisfy the EPP requirement of T. Consequently, it is in a position higher than the Neg head and takes wide scope. According to Miyagawa's version of the non-uniform analysis of scrambling, the object may move to TP Spec and check the EPP-feature of T instead of the subject, or it may adjoin to TP after the subject moves into TP Spec. The two cases are shown schematically in (27).

---

[7] The wide-scope construal of the subject in examples without scrambling is a tendency and is not without exceptions. As Miyagawa notes, the facts are relatively clear with specific quantifiers (such as *zen'in* 'all members'), specific verbs (native Japanese as opposed to Sino-Japanese), and specific sentence endings (such as the assertive particle *yo* or embedding by *to omo-u* 'I think that'). But even then, exceptions can be found. For example, suppose that an instructor for a course gives the students a choice between taking the final exam and submitting a term paper. If she utters (i) in this context while trying to guess how many copies of the exam she should prepare, the narrow-scope reading of the subject is quite natural.

(i)   Zen'in-ga   siken-o   erab -ana -i   to   omo -u
      all   -NOM   exam-ACC   choose-Neg-Pres   that   think-Pres
      'I think that all will not choose an exam (over a term paper)' (All > Not, Not > All)

Nevertheless, the contrast between (24a) and (24b) is clear, and I agree with Miyagawa that it represents a phenomenon that needs to be explained.

(27)   a.   [$_{TP}$ Object$_i$ [$_{T'}$ [$_{vP}$ Subject [$_{v'}$ [$_{VP}$ t_i V] v]] T]]

    b.   [$_{TP}$ Object$_i$ [$_{TP}$ Subject$_j$ [$_{T'}$ [$_{vP}$ t_j [$_{v'}$ [$_{VP}$ t_i V] v]] T]]]

In the former case, the object is in an A-position and can license an anaphor contained within the subject as in (9b). The latter accounts for A'-scrambling that is observed in examples like (11).

Given this analysis of scrambling, (24b) has two possible structures, depending on whether the object moves to TP Spec or adjoins to TP. These structures are shown in (28).

(28)   a.   [$_{TP}$ Sono tesuto-o$_i$ [$_{T'}$ [$_{NegP}$ [$_{vP}$ zen'in-ga [$_{v'}$ [$_{VP}$ t_i [$_V$ uke-]] v]] [$_{Neg}$ -na-]] [$_T$ -katta]]]

    b.   [$_{TP}$ Sono tesuto-o$_i$ [$_{TP}$ zen'in-ga$_j$ [$_{T'}$ [$_{NegP}$ [$_{vP}$ t_j [$_{v'}$ [$_{VP}$ t_i [$_V$ uke-]] v]] [$_{Neg}$ -na-]] [$_T$ -katta]]]]

In (28a), the object NP moves to TP Spec and checks the EPP-feature of T. This allows the subject to remain in vP Spec. The subject is then asymmetrically c-commanded by the Neg head, and takes narrow scope. This is how scrambling makes the narrow-scope construal of the subject possible, according to Miyagawa. In (28b), on the other hand, the structure is identical to (26), except that the object is adjoined to TP. In particular, the subject moves to TP Spec to check the EPP-feature of T. Hence, it takes wide scope over negation. The scope ambiguity of (24b) is thus accounted for. This analysis also predicts correctly that long scrambling out of a CP has no effect on the scope of the matrix subject. It is known that A-movement to TP Spec cannot take place across a CP boundary. Hence, long scrambling must involve TP-adjunction. The structure of the matrix part of (25) is then as in (29).

(29)   [$_{TP}$ Syukudai-o$_i$ [$_{TP}$ zen'in-ga$_j$ [$_{T'}$ [$_{NegP}$ [$_{vP}$ t_j [$_{v'}$ [$_{VP}$ [$_{CP}$.. t_i ..] [$_V$ omow-]] v]] [$_{Neg}$ -ana-]] [$_T$ -katta]]]]

Here, the matrix subject must raise to TP Spec to check the EPP-feature of T. Therefore, it must take wide scope over negation.

Although Miyagawa's account for the contrasts in (24)–(25) is quite elegant, a couple of questions arise. First, the English counterpart of (24a), shown in (30), exhibits scope ambiguity.

(30)   Everyone didn't take that exam (Every > Not, Not > Every)

This suggests that negation can take sentential scope, and if so, the non-ambiguity of (24a) cannot be attributed to the fact that the subject is in TP Spec. Secondly, and more importantly, the contrast in (24) seems to obtain even when the object is an anaphor bound by the subject. This is illustrated by (31) and (32).

(31) a. Zen'in-ga   zibun-zisin-ni   toohyoosi-na -katta (to
        all   -NOM self -self -DAT vote   -Neg-Past   that
        omo -u)
        think-Pres
        'Everyone did not vote for herself/himself' (All > Not, *Not > All)

   b. Zibun-zisin-ni$_i$ zen'in-ga t_i toohyoosi-na -katta (to
        self -self -DAT all   -NOM   vote   -Neg-Past   that
        omo -u)
        think-Pres
        'For herself/himself, everyone did not vote' (All > Not, Not > All)

(32) a. Zen'in-ga   zibun-zisin-o   seme -na -katta (to
        all   -NOM self -self -ACC blame-Neg-Past   that
        omo -u)
        think-Pres
        'Everyone did not blame herself/himself' (All > Not, *Not > All)

   b. Zibun-zisin -o$_i$ zen'in-ga t_i seme -na -katta (to
        self -self -ACC all   -NOM   blame-Neg-Past   that
        omo -u)
        think-Pres
        'Herself/himself, everyone did not blame' (All > Not, Not > All)

To my ear, there is no substantial difference whether the object is a regular NP as in (24) or it is an anaphor as in (31) and (32). And Miyagawa's account does not extend to the latter case.

When the scrambled object is *zibunzisin* 'self', it cannot be in TP Spec because that would cause a Condition (C) violation. The illicit structure for (31b) is shown in (33).

(33)   [$_{TP}$ Zibun-zisin-ni$_i$ [$_{T'}$ [$_{NegP}$ [$_{vP}$ zen'in-ga [$_{v'}$ [$_{VP}$ t_i [$_v$ toohyoosi-]] v]]
       [$_{Neg}$ -na-]] [$_T$ -katta]]]

The structure is ruled out as *zibunzisin* in TP Spec A-binds its antecedent *zen'in* 'all'. Then, the scrambled object must be adjoined to TP as in (34).

(34)   [$_{TP}$ Zibunzisin-ni$_i$ [$_{TP}$ zen'in-ga$_j$ [$_{T'}$ [$_{NegP}$ [$_{vP}$ t_j [$_{v'}$ [$_{VP}$ t_i [$_v$ toohyoosi-]]
       v]] [$_{Neg}$ -na-]] [$_T$ -katta]]]]

But in this case, *zen'in* must move to TP Spec in order to check the EPP-feature of T. It is then predicted incorrectly that *zen'in* must take wide scope over negation in (31b) exactly as in (31a). The examples in (31) and (32), thus, suggest that Miyagawa's account cannot be maintained as such. In the following subsection, I will propose a revision based on a functional projection PredP, above TP, together with the chain interpretation mechanism discussed in the preceding section.

8.3.2 *Pred phrase and scrambling*

The generalizations that emerge from the discussion in the preceding subsection are as follows. First, when the subject is sentence-initial, it takes scope over negation, as in (24a), (31a), and (32a). Second, when the object is placed before the subject by clause-internal scrambling and the subject is no longer sentence-initial, the subject need not take wide scope over negation even if it is in TP Spec. This is shown by (31b) and (32b). The initial conclusion that can be drawn from these facts is that the sentence-initial element must take scope over negation but a phrase in TP Spec need not. Then, what is the position of the sentence-initial element? If negation can scope over TP Spec, it must be higher in the structure than TP Spec. This leads to the hypothesis that the sentence-initial element is in the Spec of a higher functional head, which I call *Pred* here.[8] The structure of (24a) will then be as in (35).

(35) $[_{\text{PredP}}$ Zen'in-ga$_i$ $[_{\text{Pred'}}$ $[_{\text{TP}}$ t_i' $[_{\text{T'}}$ $[_{\text{NegP}}$ $[_{vP}$ t_i $[_{v'}$ $[_{\text{VP}}$ sono tesuto-o $[_{\text{V}}$ uke-$]]$ v $]]$ $[_{\text{Neg}}$ -na-$]]$ T$]]$ Pred$]]$

The scope of negation extends to TP, as suggested also by the English example (30). But the subject *zen'in* 'all' in (35) is in PredP Spec, and hence, takes wide scope over negation. In (31b), on the other hand, the scrambled object *zibunzisin* 'self' occupies the PredP Spec position, being sentence-initial. The structure of the example is then as in (36).

(36) $[_{\text{PredP}}$ Zibunzisin-ni$_i$ $[_{\text{Pred'}}$ $[_{\text{TP}}$ zen'in-ga$_j$ $[_{\text{T'}}$ $[_{\text{NegP}}$ $[_{vP}$ t_j $[_{v'}$ $[_{\text{VP}}$ t_i $[_{\text{V}}$ too-hyoosi-$]]$ v $]]$ $[_{\text{Neg}}$ -na-$]]$ T$]]$ Pred$]]$

In this case, *zen'in* can take narrow scope because it remains in TP Spec. (36) suggests that the Spec of PredP is an A'-position as the example is not a Condition (C) violation.

---

[8] The Pred projection is proposed in Bowers (1993), where Pred roughly corresponds to *v* of Chomsky (1995). Its role is quite different in the present context: it is higher than TP and is intended intuitively to capture the theme-rheme relation in traditional terms.

This accounts for the effect of clause-internal scrambling on the scope of the subject. The analysis entertained here is in fact quite similar to Miyagawa's. It just employs a higher functional projection PredP instead of his TP. The remaining problem is the contrast between (24b) and (25), that is, the fact that long scrambling out of a CP has no effect on the scope interaction between the subject and negation. (24b) and (25) are repeated below as (37a-b).

(37) a.   Sono tesuto-o$_i$ zen'in-ga t_i uke -na -katta (yo   /to
           that   test   -ACC all   -NOM   take-Neg-Past   Part   that
           omo -u)
           think-Pres
           'That exam$_i$, all did not take t_i' (All > Not, Not > All)

     b.   Syukudai -o$_i$ zenn'in-ga   [$_{CP}$ sensei-ga t_i das -u
           homework-ACC all   -NOM   teacher-NOM   assign-Pres
           to]   omow-ana -katta (yo)
           that think -Neg-Past   Part
           'Homework$_i$, all did not think that the teacher would assign t_i'
           (All > Not, *Not > All)

Given the mechanism for the formation and interpretation of movement chains discussed in the preceding section, the contrast suggests that the Pred head attracts an [arg] feature. Recall that the interpretation of clause-internal scrambling proceeds as follows:

(38) [$_{TP}$ $\alpha_{\{arg, phon\}}$ [Subject [$_{T'}$ [$_{vP}$ ... $\alpha_{\{arg, phon\}}$ ...] T]]]

Suppose, as seems reasonable, that chain interpretation by the deletion of features need not take place as soon as a chain is formed, but only needs to apply before a phase is completed and its complement is transferred to the interpretive components. Then, the [arg] feature of the scrambled phrase can be attracted by the Pred head before it is deleted at the landing site of scrambling. In this case, the scrambled phrase moves into PredP Spec as in (39).

(39) [$_{PredP}$ $\alpha_{\{arg, phon\}}$ [$_{Pred'}$ [$_{TP}$ $\alpha_{\{arg, phon\}}$ [Subject [$_{T'}$ [$_{vP}$ ... $\alpha_{\{arg, phon\}}$ ...]
       T]]] Pred]]

As the [arg] feature is attracted by Pred, it is retained at the PredP Spec position as well as the initial site. On the other hand, long scrambling out of a CP proceeds as in (40).

(40) a.   [$_{CP}$ $\alpha_{\{arg, phon\}}$ [$_{TP}$ Subject [$_{T'}$ [$_{vP}$ ... $\alpha_{\{arg, phon\}}$ ...] T]]]

     b.   [$_{TP}$ $\alpha_{\{phon\}}$ [Subject [$_{T'}$ [$_{vP}$ ... [$_{CP}$ $\alpha_{\{arg, phon\}}$ [$_{C'}$ ...]] ...] T]]]

The scrambled phrase first moves to the embedded CP Spec as in (40a), and chain interpretation must apply at this point because the complement TP is transferred to the interpretive components upon the completion of the CP phase. In the matrix clause, only [phon] is copied at the sentence-initial position as in (40b). As a result, the Pred head in the matrix clause cannot attract [arg] of the scrambled phrase and attracts that of the subject instead. Consequently, the matrix subject takes wide scope over negation in (37b).

It was shown above that Miyagawa's (2001, 2003) paradigm can be success-fully accounted for by postulation of the Pred head that attracts an [arg] feature. Before concluding this section, I would like to briefly discuss the implications of this proposal for the analysis of scrambling. First, scrambling is distinct from the movement to PredP Spec illustrated above, but it feeds this movement. Since Pred attracts an [arg] feature, it must attract the [arg] feature of the subject if scrambling does not take place, as illustrated in (41).

(41) $[_{\text{PredP}} \alpha_{\{\text{arg, phon}\}} [_{\text{Pred'}} [_{\text{TP}} \alpha_{\{\text{arg, } \text{phon}}\}} [_{\text{T'}} [_{vP} \ldots \text{object V} \ldots] \text{T}]] \text{Pred}]]$

This is so because the closest [arg] feature to the Pred head is that of the subject. Then, how can the [arg] feature of the object be attracted by the Pred head in (37a)? Here, scrambling plays a crucial role. That is, scrambling places the object in a position closer to Pred than the subject, and consequently allows Pred to attract the object. This derivation was shown in (39). (39) in fact illustrates the peculiar role that scrambling plays for the interpretation of a sentence. The [arg] feature is deleted at the landing site of scrambling because it is not licensed there. Thus, scrambling itself is 'semantically vacu-ous'. But it allows the [arg] feature of the scrambled phrase to be attracted to PredP Spec. As a result, it allows the subject to remain in TP Spec and fall within the scope of negation.

Secondly, the edge of PredP should be allowed as a landing site of scram-bling in addition to the edge of TP. This can be best illustrated with long scrambling out of a CP. Recall that only [phon] of the scrambled phrase is copied at the sentence-initial position in this case, as was shown in (40b). I just argued that Pred then cannot attract the scrambled phrase as it lacks [arg] and must attract the subject as in (42).

(42) $[_{\text{PredP}} \text{Subject}_{\{\text{arg, phon}\}} [_{\text{Pred'}} [_{\text{TP}} \text{Object}_{\{\text{phon}\}} [\text{Subject}_{\{\text{arg, } \text{phon}}\}} [_{\text{T'}} \ldots$

But this results in a wrong word order: the matrix subject precedes the scrambled object.[9] The sentence, then, should be derived instead by first

---

[9] In addition, this derivation is arguably ruled out as an instance of Chomsky's (2000) defective intervention effect, since the scrambled object intervenes between the Pred head and the subject.

moving the subject to PredP Spec and then scrambling the object to a position preceding it as in (43).

(43) $[_{\text{PredP}}$ Object$_{\{\text{phon}\}}$ [Subject$_{\{\text{arg, phon}\}}$ $[_{\text{Pred'}}$ $[_{\text{TP}}$ Subject$_{\{\text{arg, }\sout{\text{phon}}\}}$ $[_{\text{T'}}\cdots$

This implies that there are two kinds of scrambling across the subject. One is to the left edge of TP and the other is to the left edge of PredP. As far as I can tell, there is no need to suppose that they are different except for the landing site. In particular, both are optional and are not triggered by a specific feature such as the EPP. So this does not undermine the uniform analysis of scrambling. But descriptively, scrambling to the edge of TP corresponds to Mahajan and Miyagawa's A-scrambling and scrambling to the edge of PredP to their A'-scrambling. In this sense, the analysis of scrambling we arrived at incorporates the insights of both the uniform and the non-uniform approaches.

8.4 Discourse effects of scrambling

In this section, I will extend the analysis proposed above to the 'first-position effects' in Japanese. It has been known since Kuroda (1965) and Kuno (1973) that matrix-initial phrases receive unique interpretations. For example, a matrix-initial nominative phrase is interpreted as an 'exhaustive listing focus' when the predicate is individual level. Further, only a matrix-initial topic, Kuno argues, can be construed as a 'thematic topic', as opposed to a 'contrastive topic'. In section 8.4.1, I will present an analysis of these facts in terms of the Pred projection and discuss the effects of scrambling on the thematic interpretation of topic. Then, in section 8.4.2, I will examine the predictions that the feature-based chain interpretation mechanism makes and show that they are indeed borne out.

8.4.1 *The first-position effects: Exhaustive listing focus and thematic topic*

As discussed in detail in Kuno (1973) and Heycock (1994, 2008), Japanese exhibits 'first-position effects'.[10] First, a matrix-initial nominative phrase is interpreted obligatorily as an 'exhaustive listing focus' when the predicate is individual level in the sense of Carlson (1977). Thus, while (44a) can be a

---

[10] Kuno (1973) presents the basic facts while Heycock (1994, 2008) proposes that the effects arise in the mapping from syntax to information structure. As far as I can see, the discussion that follows is consistent with Heycock's proposal.

neutral description of an event, (44b) must be interpreted with focus on
Hanako.[11]

(44) a. Hanako-ga   kooen-o   aruiteita
          -NOM park -ACC walking-was
          'Hanako was walking in the park'

      b. Hanako-ga   heburaigo-ga   hanaseru
          -NOM Hebrew -NOM speak-can
          'It is Hanako that can speak Hebrew'

It is only the sentence-initial nominative phrase that obligatorily receives
focus. (45a) means that monkeys are the creatures that are smart.

(45) a. Saru   -ga   kasikoi
          monkey-NOM smart
          'It is monkeys that are smart'

      b. Nihon-ga   saru   -ga   kasikoi
          Japan -NOM monkey-NOM smart
          'It is Japan where monkeys are smart'

(45b), on the other hand, means that Japan is the place where monkeys
are smart, with focus on Japan but not necessarily on monkeys. In other
words, it is interpreted as 'It is Japan where monkeys are smart' but not
necessarily as 'It is Japan where it is monkeys that are smart'. It does not
exclude the possibility that creatures other than monkeys are smart in
Japan. The phenomenon is restricted to the matrix clause. Thus, when
(44b) is embedded as in (46), *Hanako* need not be interpreted with
focus.

(46) Taroo-wa   [CP Hanako-ga   heburaigo-ga   hanaseru   to]
          -TOP   -NOM Hebrew -NOM speak-can that
      omotteiru
      think
      'Taroo thinks that Hanako can speak Hebrew'

The Pred projection proposed in the preceding section provides a means to
represent exhaustive listing focus in structural terms. As the Pred head attracts

---

[11] What is important here is the fact that *Hanako* in (44b) *must* be construed as focus. Any phrase
can be focused, for example, with stress. A 'neutral' way to express the propositional content of (44b)
would be with the topic marker *-wa* on *Hanako*. The sentence would then mean 'speaking of Hanako,
she can speak Hebrew' or 'Hanako can speak Hebrew' without focus on *Hanako*.

[arg], the sentence-initial nominative phrase must be in its Spec position. The structure of (45a), for example, should be as in (47).

(47)   [$_{PredP}$ saru-ga$_{\{arg, phon\}}$ [$_{Pred'}$ [$_{TP}$ saru-ga$_{\{arg, \text{phon}\}}$ [$_{T'}$ ...]] Pred]]

Then, the generalization can be stated as in (48).

(48)   A nominative phrase in matrix PredP Spec is obligatorily interpreted as focus when the predicate of the sentence is individual level.

Similarly, Kuno (1973) argues that a phrase marked by *-wa* can be interpreted as a thematic topic only when it is matrix-initial. The particle *-wa* can attach to any phrase and induce a contrastive topic interpretation. But the thematic topic interpretation seems possible only when the *wa*-phrase is in the initial position of a matrix clause, as the examples in (49) illustrate.[12]

(49)   a.   <u>Taroo-wa</u>   (kyonen) sono hon -o   katta
             -TOP   last year that   book-ACC bought
        A. '<u>Speaking of Taroo</u>, he bought that book' (*thematic*)
        B. '<u>Taroo</u> bought that book, but I don't know about <u>other people</u>' (*contrastive*)

      b.   Taroo-ga   (kyonen) <u>sono</u> hon -wa   katta
             -NOM   last year that   book -TOP bought
        'Taroo bought <u>that book</u>, but I don't know about <u>other books</u>' (*contrastive*)

      c.   Taroo-ga   [$_{NP}$ [$_{TP}$ <u>Hanako-wa</u>   sukina] hon] -o   katta
             -NOM   -TOP   like   book -ACC bought
        'Taroo bought a book that <u>Hanako</u> likes, but I don't know if <u>other people</u> like the book' (*contrastive*)

In all of these examples, the *wa*-phrase can receive contrastive topic interpretation. But *Taroo-wa* in (49a) can in addition be construed as a thematic topic because it is in the initial position of a matrix clause.

The Pred projection accommodates this generalization as well. The matrix-initial topic in (49a) is in the Spec of PredP as the structure in (50) shows.

---

[12] What counts as 'matrix' is less clear in this case. For example, a sentence-initial *wa*-phrase in a CP complement of a verb can be construed as a thematic topic as in (i), in contrast to (49c), where a *wa*-phrase appears within a relative clause.

(i)   Taroo-ga   [Hanago-wa   sono hon -ga   sukida to]   omotteiru (koto)
       -NOM   -TOP   that book-NOM like   that think   fact
      'Taroo thinks that speaking of Hanako, she likes that book'

(50)   [PredP Taroo-wa{top, arg, phon} [Pred' [TP Taroo-wa{~~top~~, arg, ~~phon~~} [T' . . .]]
       Pred]]

Thus, Kuno's generalization can be restated as in (51).[13]

(51)   Only those topics in matrix PredP Spec can receive thematic
       interpretation.

In (50), I assumed that a topic carries the feature [top], and that this
feature is retained and interpreted at PredP Spec when the topic receives
thematic interpretation. I will discuss this in more detail in the following
subsection.

The thematic interpretation of topics is particularly interesting because it
interacts with the 'free-word-order phenomenon' in an intricate way. *Sono
hon-wa* 'that book-TOP' in (49b) cannot be a thematic topic, but it can be
when it is placed at the sentence-initial position as in (52).

(52)   <u>Sono hon -wa</u>   Taroo-ga   (kyonen) katta
       that book-TOP   -NOM   last year bought
       A. '<u>Speaking of that book</u>, Taroo bought it' (*thematic*)

       B. 'Taroo bought <u>that book</u>, but I don't know about <u>other books</u>'
          (*contrastive*)

The same is true for PP topics, as shown in (53).

(53)   a.   Taroo-ga   (kyonen) <u>Teruabibu-e -wa</u>   itta
                 -NOM   last year Tel Aviv -to-TOP   went
            'Taroo went to <u>Tel Aviv</u>, but I don't know about <u>other places</u>'
            (*contrastive*)

       b.   <u>Teruabibu-e -wa</u>   Taroo-ga   (kyonen) itta
            Tel Aviv -to-TOP   -NOM   last year went
            A. '<u>Speaking of Tel Aviv</u>, Taroo went there' (*thematic*)
            B. 'Taroo went to <u>Tel Aviv</u>, but I don't know about <u>other places</u>'
               (*contrastive*)

In the remainder of this subsection, I will argue that the thematic interpretation of the PP topic in (53b) is made possible by scrambling.

First, it has been shown convincingly that sentence-initial NP topics
can be generated directly at that position. One piece of evidence comes

---

[13] It has been proposed in the literature that thematic topics occupy the Spec position of a
functional head. For example, Kuroda (1988) argues that *wa*-phrases are interpreted thematically
when they are in CP Spec.

from examples such as the following, discussed first also by Kuno (1973):[14]

(54) Sono e_i -wa   Taroo-ga   [$_{NP}$[$_{TP}$ e_i kaita] hito] -o
     that painting-TOP   -NOM   drew person-ACC
     (yoku) sitteiru
     well know
     'Speaking of that painting, Taroo knows the person who drew it'

In this example, the sentence-initial topic relates to a gap inside a complex NP. Hence, the example should be a Subjacency violation if it is derived by movement. Yet, it is perfectly grammatical. Kuno concludes then that the topic can be licensed by some sort of 'aboutness relation' at the sentence-initial position and can be generated there directly. Perlmutter (1972) completes this analysis based on the fact that Japanese allows *pro* in any argument position. More specifically, he points out that the gap need not be produced by movement because it can be *pro*. Then, (54) is an equivalent not of topicalization as in (55a) but of left-dislocation as in (55b).

(55)   a.   ?*That painting$_i$, John knows [$_{NP}$ the person [$_{CP}$ who owns t_i]]

        b.   That painting$_i$, John knows [$_{NP}$ the person [$_{CP}$ who owns it$_i$]]

The analysis is confirmed by the fact that (54) remains grammatical when an overt pronoun appears in the position of the gap as in (56).

(56) Sono e_i -wa   Taroo-ga   [$_{NP}$ [$_{TP}$ sore$_i$-o   kaita]
     that painting-TOP   -NOM   it -ACC drew
     hito] -o   (yoku) sitteiru
     person-ACC well know
     'Speaking of that painting, Taroo knows the person who drew it'

This analysis of sentence-initial NP topics implies that they need not move to PredP Spec but can be merged directly at that position. However, I argued in Saito (1985) that the situation is different with PP topics. First, PP topics, in distinction with NP topics, cannot correspond to a position within a complex NP, as (57) shows.

(57) ?*Osuro-de$_i$-wa   Taroo-ga   [$_{NP}$ [$_{TP}$ (yonenkan)
      Oslo -in -TOP   -NOM   for four years

---

[14] The NP topics in (54) and (56) below can be construed contrastively as well. This is not indicated in the translations just because it is not important for the discussion here.

e_i benkyoosita] hito] -o   sitteiru
    studied   person -ACC know
'Speaking of Oslo, Taroo knows a person who studied there'

The contrast between this example and (58a–b), which contain no islands, already suggests that a PP topic cannot be generated directly at the sentence-initial position but must be moved to that position.

(58) a. Osuro-de$_i$-wa [$_{TP}$ Taroo-ga   (yonenkan) e_i benkyoosita]
      Oslo -in -TOP   -NOM   for four years   studied
      'Speaking of Oslo, Taroo studied there'

    b. Osuro-de$_i$-wa Hanako-ga   [$_{CP}$ Taroo-ga   (yonenkan)
      Oslo -in -TOP   -NOM   -NOM   for four years
      e_i benkyoosita to]   itteita
      studied   that said
      'Speaking of Oslo, Hanako said that Taroo studied there'

Secondly, PP topics, as opposed to NP topics, do not allow overt resumptive pronouns. For example, (59) contrasts sharply with (56).

(59) *Osuro-de$_i$-wa   Taroo-ga   [$_{NP}$ [$_{TP}$ (yonenkan)   soko -de$_i$
    Oslo -in -TOP   -NOM   for four years   there -in
    benkyoosita] hito] -o   sitteiru
    studied   person-ACC know
    'Speaking of Oslo, Taroo knows a person who studied there'

This indicates that the 'gap' in PP topic sentences cannot be *pro*. This is so because if it can be *pro*, we would expect an overt pronoun to be also possible. (59), then, confirms that examples with sentence-initial PP topics must be derived by movement, and that (57), in particular, must be derived by movement of the PP topic from within the complex NP.[15]

    This analysis implies that scrambling of PP topics can affect interpretation in an interesting way. Let us consider the examples in (60).

(60) a. Kanemoti -ga   Nyuuyooku-e kaimono -ni iku
      rich people-NOM New York -to shopping-for go
      'It is rich people that go to New York for shopping'

---

[15] It is speculated in Saito (1985) that (59) is ungrammatical and (57) must involve movement because a PP topic, as opposed to an NP topic, cannot be licensed at the sentence-initial position by the 'aboutness' relation with the rest of the sentence. (59) is in fact much improved if an NP topic is substituted for the PP topic, as (i) shows.
(i) Osuro$_i$ -wa   Taroo-ga   [$_{NP}$ [$_{TP}$ (yonenkan)   (soko$_i$-de) benkyoosita] hito] -o   sitteiru
   Oslo -TOP   -NOM   for four years there-in studied   person-ACC know
   'Speaking of Oslo, Taroo knows a person who studied there (for four years)'

b. <u>Nyuuyooku-e -wa</u>   kanemoti -ga   kaimono -ni iku
New York -to-TOP rich people-NOM shopping-for go

A. '<u>Speaking of New York</u>, rich people go there for shopping' (*thematic*)

B. 'Rich people go to <u>New York</u> for shopping, but I don't know about <u>other places</u>' (*contrastive*)

(60a) is actually ambiguous. It can be a description of some rich people heading toward New York for shopping. In this case, the predicate is stage level. But it can also express a property of rich people with the construal of the predicate as individual level. It is this interpretation that is important for the purpose here. Since the predicate is individual level, the sentence-initial *kanemoti-ga* 'rich people-NOM' is interpreted obligatorily with exhaustive listing focus. This is expected as this sentence-initial phrase must be in PredP Spec.

In (60b), the PP *Nyuuyooku-e* 'New York-to' is turned into a topic and placed at the sentence-initial position. The topic can receive thematic interpretation, which indicates that it can be in PredP Spec. And interestingly, *kanamoti-ga* 'rich people-NOM' no longer needs to be construed as an exhaustive listing focus. This in turn shows that it need not be in PredP Spec because the position is occupied by the PP topic. Then, (61) is a possible representation for (60b).

(61) $[_{PredP}$ Nyuuyooku-e-wa$_{\{top, arg, phon\}}$ $[_{Pred'}$ $[_{TP}$ kanemoti-ga$_{\{arg, phon\}}$ $[_{T'} \ldots]]$ Pred$]]$

This situation is a familiar one. In the preceding section, a case was discussed where a scrambled object moves into PredP Spec, allowing the subject to stay at TP Spec. It was noted then that this movement of the object is possible only when it is mediated by scrambling. The Pred head attracts the closest [arg] feature, which should be that of the subject. But when the object is scrambled over the subject, Pred can attract its [arg] feature and it can move into PredP Spec. In (61) as well, the Pred head cannot ignore the subject and attract the PP topic from within T'. This implies that the PP topic can move to PredP Spec only if it first undergoes scrambling to the edge of TP as in (62).

(62) $[_{PredP}$ PP-wa$_{\{top, arg, phon\}}$ $[_{Pred'}$ $[_{TP}$ PP-wa$_{\{top, arg, phon\}}$ $[$subject$_{\{arg, phon\}}$ $[_{T'} \ldots$

Again, scrambling is semantically vacuous as all features are deleted from its landing site. But it enables the scrambled PP topic to move into PredP Spec and be interpreted thematically.

Two phenomena have been analyzed so far. First, scrambling makes it possible for the object to move into PredP Spec, and as a result, allows the subject to stay in TP Spec and take narrow scope with respect to sentential negation. Secondly, it allows PP topics to move into PredP Spec and receive thematic interpretation. Although these two phenomena look quite different, the analysis is basically the same. Scrambling can have semantic and discourse effects because it makes it possible for non-subjects to be attracted by the Pred head. The instances of scrambling that were important in this discussion all had the edge of TP as the landing site. However, it was noted at the end of the preceding section that scrambling can also move a phrase to the edge of PredP. In the following subsection, I will consider the discourse effects of this kind of scrambling.

8.4.2 *Scrambling as topicalization*

In this subsection, I will examine how scrambling to the edge of PredP affects the thematic interpretation of topics. The crucial examples to be discussed are those presented in Kuroda (1988) as exceptions to Kuno's (1973) generalization that only sentence-initial *wa*-phrases can be interpreted thematically. The first part concerns cases where an object is scrambled over a thematic topic. In the second part, I will discuss cases that are more involved and interesting, that is, those in which a topic is scrambled to the edge of PredP. In both parts, I will argue that the analysis developed in the preceding sections makes the correct predictions.

A brief discussion on the [top] feature is in order before I start examining examples with scrambling to the edge of PredP. It was assumed above, for example in (62), that topics carry this feature and that this feature can end up in PredP Spec. When the feature is in PredP Spec, the topic can be construed as a thematic topic. At the same time, as noted above, topics can appear in any position and receive contrastive interpretation. In (49b), for example, the topic is in the object position. It seems then that the [top] feature can be licensed at any position and yield the contrastive interpretation. Given this, it should be possible to retain the [top] feature at any position of the chain when a topic is moved. This is illustrated in (63).

(63) a. $XP_{\{top,\ldots\}}$ [.... $XP_{\{\text{top},\ldots\}}$ ...]
      b. $XP_{\{\text{top},\ldots\}}$ [.... $XP_{\{top,\ldots\}}$ ...]

Again, the contrastive interpretation is always possible, and the thematic interpretation obtains only when the feature is retained at PredP Spec.

Let us now consider cases of scrambling to the PredP edge. It was argued in the preceding section that scrambling can place an object to the edge of PredP after the subject moves into PredP Spec. The relevant structure in (43) is repeated in (64).[16]

(64) [$_\text{PredP}$ Object$_{\{(arg), phon\}}$ [Subject$_{\{arg, phon\}}$ [$_\text{Pred'}$ [$_\text{TP}$ Subject$_{\{arg, \text{phon}\}}$ [$_\text{T'}$ ...

In the examples discussed there, the subject was in nominative. But what if it is a topic marked by -*wa*? Kuno's (1973) generalization predicts that it cannot receive thematic interpretation because it is not sentence-initial. On the other hand, the analysis presented above predicts that it can because it is in PredP Spec. And the latter prediction is borne out by examples of the following kind from Kuroda (1988):

(65) Sono hon -o$_i$ Taroo-wa   (kyonen) t_i katta
        that   book-ACC   -TOP   last year   bought

   A. 'Speaking of Taroo, he bought that book' (*thematic*)

   B. 'Taroo bought that book, but I don't know about other people' (*contrastive*)

In this example, the subject *Taroo-wa* can be interpreted either as a thematic topic or as a contrastive topic. In the former case, the representation is as in (66).

(66) [$_\text{PredP}$ Object$_{\{arg, phon\}}$ [Subject$_{\{top, arg, phon\}}$ [$_\text{Pred'}$ [$_\text{TP}$ Subject$_{\{\text{top}, arg, \text{phon}\}}$ [$_\text{T'}$ ...

First, the subject is attracted to PredP Spec and its [top] feature is interpreted thematically. Then, the object is scrambled to the edge of PredP. As the [arg] feature is deleted at the landing site, this movement is semantically vacuous. This demonstrates that the distribution of thematic topics cannot be characterized in purely linear terms but must be explained in terms of a structural position in the sentence.

   The second case to be examined is scrambling of PP topics to the edge of PredP. For this, let us directly consider the relevant examples in (67).

(67) a. Hanako-wa   (kyonen) Teruabibu-e -wa   itta
              -TOP   last year Tel Aviv -to -TOP   went

      A. 'Speaking of Hanako, she went to Tel Aviv, but I don't know
          about other places' (Hanako-*thematic*, Tel Aviv-*contrastive*)

      B. 'Hanako went to Tel Aviv, but I don't know about other people
          and other places' (Hanako-*contrastive*, Tel Aviv-*contrastive*)

---

[16] The [arg] feature is copied and deleted at the landing site if the scrambling is clause-internal. Otherwise, it is not copied at all, as discussed above.

b. <u>Teruabibu-e -wa</u>$_i$ [<u>Hanako-wa</u>   (kyonen) t_i itta]
Tel Aviv   -to-TOP   -TOP   last year   went

A. 'Speaking of Tel Aviv, <u>Hanako</u> went there, but I don't know
about <u>other people</u>' (Tel Aviv-*thematic*, Hanako-*contrastive*)

B. 'Speaking of Hanako, she went to <u>Tel Aviv</u>, but I don't know
about <u>other places</u>' (Tel Aviv-*contrastive*, Hanako-*thematic*)

C. 'Speaking of Tel Aviv and speaking of Hanako, she went there'
(Tel Aviv-*thematic*, Hanako-*thematic*)

D. '<u>Hanako</u> went to <u>Tel Aviv</u>, but I don't know about <u>other places</u>
and <u>other people</u>' (Tel Aviv-*contrastive*, Hanako-*contrastive*)

In these examples, both the subject *Hanako* and the PP *Teruabibu-e* 'Tel Aviv-
to' accompany the topic marker *-wa*. The possible interpretations for (67a)
are as expected. Only the sentence-initial subject can receive thematic interpretation. In (67b), the PP topic *Teruabibu-e-wa* 'Tel Aviv-to-TOP' is placed
at the sentence-initial position and interestingly, the sentence is four-ways
ambiguous, as indicated. The most striking is the interpretation in C: As
pointed out in Kuroda (1988), when a PP topic precedes a *wa*-marked subject,
both can receive thematic interpretation.[17] Let us examine the interpretation
in B first and then this case.

The interpretation in B obtains when the PP topic is scrambled to the edge
of PredP as in (68).

(68)   [$_{PredP}$ PP-wa$_{\{top, arg, phon\}}$ [NP-wa$_{\{top, arg, phon\}}$ [$_{Pred'}$ [$_{TP}$ [NP-wa$_{\{top,}$
arg, phon}$ [$_{T'}$ $\cdots$

The subject *Hanako-wa* is attracted to PredP Spec and receives thematic
interpretation. Then, the PP topic is scrambled to the edge of PredP. This
interpretation provides further evidence for scrambling to the edge of PredP.
(68) is in fact identical to (66) except that a PP topic is scrambled instead of
an object. There is another slightly different representation that also yields the
interpretation in B. In (68), the [top] feature of the scrambled PP topic is
deleted at the landing site. But as noted above, the [top] feature can be
retained at any position of a chain. Thus, it should be possible to retain the
feature at the landing site as in (69).

(69)   [$_{PredP}$ PP-wa$_{\{top, arg, phon\}}$ [NP-wa$_{\{top, arg, phon\}}$ [$_{Pred'}$ [$_{TP}$ [NP-wa$_{\{top,}$
arg, phon}$ [$_{T'}$ $\cdots$

---

[17] It is, unfortunately, difficult to provide a precise definition for 'thematic topic'. What is clear is
that (67b) has an interpretation in which neither topic is contrastive. I assume with Kuroda (1988)
that this means that both topics can be thematic at the same time.

This representation also leads to the interpretation in B because the [top] feature of the PP topic can still be interpreted contrastively.

And interestingly, (69) yields the interpretation in C as well. The [top] feature of the PP topic is at the edge, that is, at the outer Spec of PredP. Hence, if a [top] feature can be interpreted thematically when it is in a Spec position of PredP, it should be possible to interpret both the PP topic and the NP topic as thematic topics on the basis of (69). Thus, the interpretation in C is correctly predicted by the analysis proposed in this paper. This is another case in which a non-sentence-initial topic receives thematic interpretation, and provides further evidence for the analysis of thematic topics in terms of hierarchical structure over that in terms of linear order.[18]

It was shown above that the effects of clause-internal scrambling on the thematic interpretation of topics can be captured properly with the analysis of scrambling proposed in the preceding section. The analysis for the scrambling of topics to the edge of PredP, in particular, makes interesting predictions for long scrambling out of CP. I will examine these in the remainder of this section.

Recall that only clause-internal scrambling has effects on anaphor binding and the scope interaction between the subject and sentential negation. This was so because the relevant feature was [arg]. Clause-internal scrambling takes place as in (70) while long scrambling proceeds as in (71).

(70) $[_{TP}\ \alpha_{\{arg,\ phon\}}\ [\ldots \alpha_{\{arg,\ \underline{phon}\}}\ldots]]$

(71)   a. $[_{CP}\ \alpha_{\{\underline{arg},\ phon\}}\ [_{C'}\ldots \alpha_{\{arg,\ \underline{phon}\}}\ldots]]$

     b. $[_{TP}\ \alpha_{\{phon\}}\ [\ldots [_{CP}\ \alpha_{\{\underline{arg},\ phon\}}\ [_{C'}\ldots]]\ldots]]$

In (70), the [arg] feature of the scrambled phrase is copied at the landing site. This makes it possible for α to bind an anaphor and to be attracted to PredP Spec. The feature is deleted at the landing site prior to interpretation because it is licensed only at the initial site. In the case of long scrambling, the initial step of movement is to the embedded CP Spec, and the resulting chain is interpreted with the deletion of features as in (71a). In the matrix clause, only [phon] is copied at the landing site as in (71b). Thus, α can neither serve as the binder of an anaphor nor be attracted to PredP Spec.

But the situation is different with the [top] feature: The hypothesis that was entertained above is that [top] can be licensed and retained at any

---

[18] As was noted in n. 13, Kuroda (1988) indeed presents an analysis in structural terms. For him, *wa*-phrases receive thematic interpretation when they are in CP Spec. He argues that the interpretation C of (67b) is in accord with his hypothesis that Japanese is not a forced 1-1 agreement language, because multiple topics occupy the CP Spec position without agreeing with the C head.

position of a chain. Then, long scrambling of a topic out of a CP can proceed as in (72).

(72)   a. $[_{CP}\ \alpha_{\{top,\ \text{arg},\ phon\}}\ [_{C'} \cdots \alpha_{\{top,\ arg,\ \text{phon}\}} \cdots]]$

     b. $[\alpha_{\{top,\ phon\}}\ [\cdots [_{CP}\ \alpha_{\{top,\ \text{arg},\ \text{phon}\}}\ [_{C'} \cdots]] \cdots]]$

The [top] feature of the scrambled topic is retained at the embedded CP Spec after the initial movement in (72a). Then it is copied and retained at the matrix-initial position in (72b). This predicts that a topic preposed to the matrix-initial position by long scrambling can be interpreted thematically. The prediction is indeed borne out by (73).

(73)   <u>Teruabibu-e -wa</u>ᵢ   [_TP Hanako-ga   [_CP Taroo-ga   (kyonen)
    Tel Aviv -to-TOP   -TOP   -NOM   last year
    tᵢ itta   to] itteita]
     went that saying-was

    A.   '<u>Speaking of Tel Aviv</u>, Hanako was saying that Taroo went there'
       (*thematic*)

    B.   'Hanako was saying that Taroo went to <u>Tel Aviv</u>, but I don't know about <u>other places</u>' (*contrastive*)

As indicated, the preposed PP *Teruabibu-e-wa* 'Tel Aviv-to-TOP' can be construed as a thematic topic. The relevant derivation is shown in (74).

(74)   a. $[_{CP}\ \text{PP-wa}_{\{top,\ \text{arg},\ phon\}}\ [_{C'} \cdots \text{PP-wa}_{\{top,\ arg,\ \text{phon}\}} \cdots]]$

     b. $[_{PredP}\ \text{PP-wa}_{\{top,\ phon\}}\ [\text{NP-ga}_{\{arg,\ phon\}}\ [_{Pred'} \cdots [_{CP}\ \text{PP-wa}_{\{top,\ \text{arg},\ \text{phon}\}} \cdots] \cdots \text{Pred}]]]$

The PP topic first scrambles to the edge of the embedded CP as in (74a). The [top] feature is retained and the [arg] feature is deleted at the landing site. In the matrix clause, the Pred head attracts the subject *Hanako-ga* to its Spec position as in (74b). Note that the PP topic cannot be attracted to this position as its [arg] feature is deleted at the embedded CP Spec. Finally, the PP topic scrambles to the edge of PredP and its [top] feature is interpreted thematically at the landing site.

(73) shows that it is not just clause-internal scrambling that can affect interpretation. It is then not correct to say that there are two kinds of scrambling, one with effects on interpretation and one without, and that only the latter can take place long-distance. Scrambling is scrambling, and how it affects interpretation depends on how the features of the scrambled phrase are interpreted in the scrambling chain. This analysis is confirmed when it is examined whether long scrambling of a PP topic affects the scope of

the matrix subject. Recall Miyagawa's (2001, 2003) observation that long scrambling out of a CP does not allow the matrix subject to take narrow scope with respect to negation. A relevant example is shown in (75).

(75) Teruabibu-e$_i$ zen'in-ga   [$_{CP}$ Hanako-ga t_i iku to]
      Tel Aviv -to all   -NOM   -NOM   go that
      omow-ana-katta (yo)
      think -not-Past   Part
      'To Tel Aviv$_i$, all did not think that Hanako would go t_i' (All > Not, *Not > All)

The proposed analysis was that long scrambling does not carry the [arg] feature of *Teruabibu-e* 'Tel Aviv-to' into the matrix clause, and consequently, the matrix Pred attracts the subject *zen'in-ga* 'all-NOM' to its Spec position.

   The situation remains the same when a PP topic is scrambled, but at the same time, the scrambled PP topic can be interpreted thematically. This is shown in (76).

(76) Teruabibu-e -wa$_i$ zen'in-ga   [$_{CP}$ Hanako-ga t_i iku to]
      Tel Aviv -to-TOP all   -NOM   -NOM   go that
      omow-ana-katta (yo)
      think -not-Past   Part

   A. '<u>Speaking of Tel Aviv$_i$</u>, all did not think that Hanako would go there' (*thematic*, All > Not, *Not > All)

   B. 'All did not think that Hanako would go to <u>Tel Aviv</u>, but I don't know about <u>other places</u>' (*contrastive*, All > Not, *Not > All)

This is exactly what is expected under the proposed analysis. The [arg] feature of the scrambled PP topic is deleted at the embedded CP Spec. Thus, the matrix Pred head attracts the subject *zen'in-ga* to its Spec exactly as in (75). As a result, the subject takes scope over negation. Then, the PP topic is scrambled to the edge of the matrix PredP. Its [top] feature can be retained at this final landing site, and if it is, it can be interpreted thematically as indicated by the reading in A. This example shows clearly that [top] and [arg] can function independently, and hence, provides further support for the feature-based interpretation of movement chains.

8.5 Conclusion and further issues

It was argued in this paper that the semantic and discourse effects of scrambling can be accounted for by the interpretive mechanism for movement chains. Scrambling itself is semantically vacuous in the sense that no substantial feature needs to be interpreted at the landing site. However, because scrambling, like any other movement, copies all features of the moved item at the landing site, it interacts with higher functional heads, in particular, Pred, and affects interpretation in intricate ways. Further, since [top], which can be licensed at any position, can take a 'free ride' on scrambling, a topic scrambled to the matrix-initial position can be interpreted thematically. The functional head, Pred, plays an important role also in this analysis of the distribution of thematic topics. Before concluding this paper, I would like to raise some issues regarding the precise nature of this functional head and make a few speculative remarks.

The main properties of Pred are summarized in (77).

(77)   a. It is always present above a finite TP, and attracts [arg] to its Spec.

     b. The phrase in PredP Spec takes scope over everything in the complement TP, including sentential negation.

     c. A nominative phrase in matrix PredP Spec is interpreted obligatorily as an exhaustive lising focus when the predicate of the sentence is individual level.

     d. A topic can be interpreted thematically when its [top] feature is in matrix PredP Spec.

I have entertained the hypothesis that there is a single Pred projection above TP, and it plays a role in all the phenomena in (77b–d). There is in fact suggestive evidence that PredP is not recursive. Let us consider (78), for example.

(78)   a. Nihon-ga   saru   -ga   kasikoi
          Japan -NOM monkey-NOM smart
          'It is Japan where monkeys are smart'

     b. <u>Nihon-wa</u>   saru   -ga   kasikoi
          Japan -TOP monkey-NOM smart
          A. '<u>Speaking of Japan</u>, monkeys are smart there' (*thematic*)
          B. 'Monkeys are smart in <u>Japan</u>, but I don't know about <u>other places</u>' (*contrastive*)

     c. Nihon-ga   <u>saru   -wa</u> kasikoi
          Japan -NOM monkey-TOP smart
          'It is Japan where I know <u>monkeys</u> are smart but don't know about <u>other creatures</u>' (*contrastive*)

(78a–b) show that only the sentence-initial nominative phrase is interpreted obligatorily as exhaustive listing focus. (78b), in particular, indicates that a nominative phrase need not have this interpretation when it is preceded by a topic. In this case, the nominative phrase need not be in PredP Spec because the position can be occupied by the topic. Finally, in (78c), the sentence-initial nominative phrase must be an exhaustive listing focus, and the topic must be interpreted contrastively. The latter fact suggests that PredP cannot occur recursively as in (79).

(79)   [$_{PredP}$ Focus [$_{Pred'}$ [$_{PredP}$ Topic [$_{Pred'}$ [$_{TP}$ ...] Pred]] Pred]]

If (79) were possible, the topic in (78c) should be able to receive thematic interpretation as it is in PredP Spec.

   (78c) suggests further that a Pred head cannot have multiple Specs occupied by a focus and a topic as in (80).

(80)   [$_{PredP}$ Focus [Topic [$_{Pred'}$ [$_{TP}$ ...] Pred]]]

This is particularly interesting because it was shown above that Pred can host multiple Specs when they are all topics. A relevant example in (67b) is repeated below in (81).

(81)   <u>Teruabibu-e -wa</u>$_i$ [<u>Hanako-wa</u>   (kyonen) t_i itta]
        Tel Aviv   -to-TOP   -TOP   last year   went

   C. '<u>Speaking of Tel Aviv</u> and <u>speaking of Hanako</u>, she went there'
       (Tel Aviv-*thematic*, Hanako-*thematic*)

Although I do not have an explanation for why (80) is impossible, I suspect that it receives an account in terms of the analysis based on the mapping from syntax to information structure as developed in Heycock (1994, 2008). Loosely speaking, a sentence with a thematic topic is construed as representing a *topic* and an *assertion*. In this case, PredP Spec is mapped to *topic* and the complement TP to *assertion*. Focus, then, must be contained in the TP so that it can be part of the *assertion*. When PredP Spec contains an exhaustive listing focus, it is mapped to *focus* and the complement TP to *presupposition*. As a thematic topic cannot be part of *focus*, it cannot be in PredP Spec in this case. A refinement along this line may shed some light on the precise nature of thematic topic and exhaustive listing focus.

   A question that is more directly relevant to comparative syntax concerns the identity of Pred. Since it hosts thematic topics and exhaustive listing focus, it is tempting to relate it to the Topic and Focus heads that Rizzi

(1997) postulates in the left periphery of CP. More precisely, he proposes to split the C-system as in (82).

(82)   Force - (Topic)* - (Focus) - (Topic)* - Finite

As topics and focused phrases move into the Spec positions of the relevant heads, this system accounts for Italian examples such as (83), where *questo* 'this' is in focus, and *a Gianni* 'to Gianni' and *domani* 'tomorrow' are topics.

(83)   a.   Credo   che   a   Gianni,   QUESTO,   domani,   gli   dovremmo
             I-believe that to Gianni this   tomorrow we should
             dire
             say
             'I believe that we should say this to Gianni tomorrow'

        b.   Credo che a Gianni, domani, QUESTO, gli dovremmo dire

        c.   Credo che QUESTO, a Gianni, domani, gli dovremmo dire

There are, however, clear differences between the Topic/Focus heads in Italian and what I called the Pred head in Japanese. The former is optional and recursive, which is not the case with the latter. The former attracts [top] and [focus], while the latter attracts [arg]. The Topic and Focus projections in Italian can occur in embedded clauses, as (83) shows. On the other hand, only those phrases in matrix PredP Spec are interpreted as thematic topics and obligatorily as exhaustive listing focus. This last fact suggests that topic and focus interpretation in Japanese is accomplished ultimately in the mapping to information structure, as Heycock argues. Yet, a close comparison between the two systems may uncover the possible forms of variation in the left periphery.

Another tempting comparison is between Pred and the head that hosts the sentence-initial verb in Celtic languages. Bobaljik and Carnie (1996) present the Irish example in (84) to show that the sentence-initial verb is located lower than C.

(84)   Ceapaim [go   bhfaca   sé   an   madra]
        I-think   that saw-Dep he the dog
        'I think that he saw the dog'

The verb *bhfaca* clearly follows the complementizer in this example. They also argue that the subject is raised to the Spec position of a functional head and the verb is raised to a still higher position. McCloskey (1996) argues for the same conclusion, providing examples such as (85) as evidence.

(85) Tá sé críochnaithe againnn
       is it finished   by-us
       'That has been finished by us'

Since this example is passive, the subject is raised from the object position to a position preceding the verb *críochnaithe*. The landing site of this movement is plausibly a Spec position of a functional head, and the example suggests that subjects in general are licensed at this position. The sentence-initial *tá* precedes this position, which indicates that it is in a fairly high position. Bobaljik and Carnie then hypothesize that the subject is in TP Spec while the verb raises to AGR. (See also Roberts (2005) for detailed discussion on this analysis.) The Japanese Pred is probably not AGR as the language lacks agreement altogether. However, if it is an equivalent of AGR in Celtic, an interesting variation can be observed. The relevant head in Celtic attracts a verbal head while that in Japanese attracts an [arg] feature to its Spec.

The discussion above on the crosslinguistic comparison is merely speculative. But it suggests that the postulation of Pred in Japanese opens up a way to compare the Japanese left periphery with other languages. The main purpose of this paper was to provide a precise analysis for the semantic and discourse effects of scrambling. But I hope it also serves to stimulate research leading to contributions from Japanese on the nature of the left periphery.

9

Rhythmic patterns cue word order[*]

MOHINISH SHUKLA AND MARINA NESPOR

9.1 Introduction

Human language can be construed as a system of rules that governs the organization of the words of a language to convey meaning. In most languages, the basic ordering of words in an overt linear sequence is determined by fundamental syntactic rules of organization (Baker 2001). The basic word order shows language-specific variations. For example, while in some languages, like English or Greek, direct objects (O) follow verbs (V), in others, like Hindi or Turkish, objects precede the verbs (Greenberg 1963; Comrie 1981). It has been observed that the basic VO or OV order of a language captures major generalizations about the ordering of other words and phrases in that language (Greenberg 1963; Dryer 1992).

However, the variation among OV and VO languages—in total about 86% of the languages of the world (Dryer 2005)[1]—presents a problem for acquisition. Given a pair of words X-Y, how is the young learner to determine whether this represents a VO or an OV case, before the knowledge of words? In this chapter, we consider the hypothesis that the different word orders are manifested as different rhythmic patterns in spoken languages.

Overt speech is more than just a linear sequence of words. It is organized into prosodic domains that link the fundamental units of spoken language to multi-word utterances (Selkirk 1984; Nespor and Vogel 1986 [2008]). In 9.2, we outline our proposal that relates a specific domain of the prosodic

* For interesting discussions on many issues related to the topic of the present paper, we thank Ricardo Bion, Ansgar Endress, Judit Gervain, Jacques Mehler, and Marcela Peña. The research described in this paper was funded by the ESF Eurocores OMLL grant, the Italian National Grants (COFIN) 2003–7, and the James S. McDonnell Foundation.

[1] Dryer (2005) reports ~14% of languages as lacking a dominant word order. The rest include all possible orders of S,V, and O. However, SOV and SVO are the most frequent of all languages, accounting for ~76% of his sample.

hierarchy, the phonological phrase, to the acquisition of word order. This proposal is based on the observation that different physical manifestations of phonological phrase prominence trigger either trochaic or iambic grouping—the so-called Iambic–Trochaic Law (ITL).

In 9.3, the phonological phrase is discussed in greater detail. We review linguistic evidence for the phonological phrase. We discuss (a) how prominence in phonological phrases reflects word order, and (b) acoustic cues that mark phonological phrases in languages with differing word orders. In 9.4, we review psycholinguistic evidence for the phonological phrase in speech processing by adults and infants. In 9.5, we discuss the acquisition of grammar by infants. We show how infants might acquire word order through the perception of language-specific prominence patterns of phonological phrases. Further, we suggest that general perceptual capacities, coupled with some elementary distributional computations, can account for the remarkable achievements of pre-linguistic infants in acquiring the grammar of their language. Concluding remarks are presented in 9.6.

9.2 The phonological phrase organization reflects word order

Word order is one of the first syntactic properties infants acquire, as evidenced by the fact that they do not make mistakes when they start uttering their first two-word sentences and by the fact that, long before then, they react differently to good and bad word order (Brown 1973; Meisel 1992; Clahsen and Eisenbeiss 1993). How can we account for this remarkable achievement? We propose that infants have the possibility of acquiring word order prelexically, that is, before the acquisition of the lexicon. Based on Nespor et al. (2008), in this chapter we propose that they do so on the basis of the rhythmic patterns of the language of exposure.

The VO or OV pattern in various languages reflects a general tendency to place heads either before or after their complements, and to place main clauses either before or after subordinate clauses. Thus, the VO or OV word order is related to the direction of branching: right-branching in head-complement (or VO) languages and left-branching in complement-head (or OV) languages (see Dryer 1992). In 9.3 we will see that the prosodic level that signals word order is the phonological phrase (PhPh). The location of prominence within a phonological phrase has been proposed to depend on whether it is mapped from a head-complement or complement-head language: rightmost in the former, leftmost in the latter (Nespor and Vogel 1982, 1986/2008). It has further been proposed that in a language with both orders of heads and complements, the location of prominence varies in a similar manner, according to the order within individual phrases (Nespor, Guasti, and Christophe 1996). In addition, the physical manifestation of prominence differs in the two cases: it is manifested mainly through duration in iambic PhPhs and mainly through pitch and intensity in trochaic PhPhs (Nespor et al. 2008). Since in a head-complement pair of words with unmarked prosody the complement bears phrasal stress (Nespor and Vogel 1982, 1986/2008; Cinque 1993; Féry and Herbst 2004), infants might be forced to identify the complement, and thus its order with respect to the head, because of a mechanism of general perception.

A uniform rhythmic pattern throughout the language will lead the infant to conclude that its language of exposure has a uniform order of heads and complements, and thus of subordinate clauses with respect to main clauses. The head-complement parameter could thus be set with a general perception mechanism.[2] Infants exposed to languages in which the order varies, a problem for parameter setting, will also identify word order, realizing that it is mixed. In these languages, there is usually a main pattern and some deviations from it. The same mechanism would thus allow the acquisition of word order both in a regular and in a mixed language, accounting for the fact that there is no delay in the acquisition of the latter with respect to the former.

9.3 The phonological phrase

Connected speech can be analyzed as a hierarchical organization of constituents ranging from the syllable and its constituent parts until the utterance (Selkirk 1984; Nespor and Vogel 1986/2008). The phonological phrase is one of the phrasal constituents of the phonological, or prosodic, hierarchy, crucial both in signaling syntactic constituency and in providing cues to word order.

As is the case for the other constituents of the prosodic hierarchy, PhPhs are signaled both by phenomena that apply throughout their domain and by edge phenomena. These different cues are used both in the processing of speech by adults, for example to disambiguate certain sentences with an identical sequence of words but different syntactic structures (Nespor and Vogel 1986 [2008]; Christophe et al. 2004, Millotte et al. 2007; Millotte et al. 2008), and in language acquisition by infants (Gout et al. 2004).

---

[2] In this chapter we use the term 'parameter setting' in its most general sense, as a shorthand to mean the acquisition of a certain language-specific property, like the relative order of heads and complements.

The domain of the phonological phrase extends from one edge of a syntactic phrase until, and including, its head. There are thus two possibilities; which one is chosen depends on syntactic structure. If the structure is right-branching, the phonological phrase starts from the left edge of a syntactic phrase (X") and it ends at the right edge of its head (X). If the structure is left-branching, the phonological phrase starts from the right edge of a syntactic phrase and it ends at the left edge of its head. These two possibilities are illustrated in (1a) and (1b), where the underlined parts indicate the domain of the phonological phrase in right-branching (or head-complement) and left-branching (or complement-head) structures, respectively.

(1)   a. $_{X"}[\underline{\ldots[\ ]_X\ldots\ldots}]$

     b. $[\underline{\ldots\ldots_X[\ ]\ldots}]_{X"}$

That is, the domain over which the phonological phrase extends depends on syntactic structure, in that it extends on opposite parts of the head, and thus varies depending on word order. The two possibilities are illustrated in (2) and (3), on the basis of adpositional phrases in Italian and Turkish, respectively. Notice that, though adpositions are heads syntactically, they behave as non-heads, as do all closed-class items, in phonology (Nespor and Vogel 1986/2008).

(2)   a.   per Luca
       'for Luca'

     b.   accanto al giardino
        'next to the garden'

     c.   dietro alla porta
        'behind the door'

(3)   a.   tren ile
       train—with
       'by train'

     b.   Aynura göre
        Aynur—according to
        'according to Aynur'

     c.   dakika gibi
        minutes—like
        'like minutes'

In addition to this basic PhPh domain, hypothesized to be universal, there is a possibility of restructuring: if non-branching, the first complement or modifier on the recursive side of the head can be restructured into the same PhPh of the head (Nespor and Vogel 1986/2008). The level at which the non-branching condition holds appears to present some cross-linguistic variation: it is the level of the word, e.g. in Italian, but the level of the clitic group, e.g. in English (Hayes 1989), as exemplified in (4) and (5), respectively.

(4) a.   [mangia]$_{PP}$ [frutta]$_{PP}$ → [mangia frutta]$_{PP}$
          '(s/he) eats fruit'
          [mangia]$_{PP}$ [la frutta]$_{PP}$ → *[mangia la frutta]$_{PP}$
          '(s/he) eats the fruit'

     b.   [scrive]$_{PP}$ [poesie]$_{PP}$ → [scrive poesie]$_{PP}$
          '(s/he) writes poems'
          [scrive]$_{PP}$ [delle poesie]$_{PP}$ → *[scrive delle poesie]$_{PP}$
          '(s/he) writes the poems'

(5) a.   [eat]$_{PP}$ [fruit]$_{PP}$ → [eat fruit]$_{PP}$
          [eat]$_{PP}$ [the fruit]$_{PP}$ → [eat the fruit]$_{PP}$

     b.   [he wrote]$_{PP}$ [poems]$_{PP}$ → [he wrote poems]$_{PP}$
          [he wrote]$_{PP}$ [the poems]$_{PP}$ → [he wrote the poems]$_{PP}$

9.3.1 *The relation of prominence in phonological phrases to word order*

Different phonological phenomena, that apply either throughout the constituent or at (one of) its edges, signal that the elements that constitute a phonological phrase have a certain level of cohesion. In addition to segmental phenomena, prominence marks one of the PhPh edges. As in all constituents of the phonological hierarchy, relative prominence in a PhPh is assigned to its daughter constituents: the constituent located at one of the edges is marked as strong and all the other constituents are marked as weak (Liberman and Prince 1977).

The location of the strong element of the phonological phrase—as well as the domain over which it extends—depends on the relative order of heads and complements (Nespor and Vogel 1986/2008). In head–complement structures the strongest element within a PhPh is rightmost, while in complement–head structures it is leftmost. Thus the element of a PhPh that bears the main prominence is either the rightmost or the leftmost depending on the recursive side of a given language: in right recursive languages, e.g., Greek, French, or Arabic, the strongest element is at the right edge; in left recursive languages, e.g., Turkish, Basque, or Japanese, the strongest element is at the left edge.

Some languages, like German or Dutch, do not have a uniform rhythmic pattern—either iambic or trochaic. While mainly iambic, these two languages have some trochaic phonological phrases. These different rhythmic patterns reflect word order in all cases. While both in German and in Dutch, in most phrases, heads precede their complements, in certain cases, verb phrases have the order complement–verb and adpositional phrases are postpositional, as exemplified in (6) and (7), respectively, on the basis of Dutch.

(6)   a.   Ik <u>koop land</u>
             'I buy land'

       b.   Paul weet dat ik <u>land koop</u>
             'Paul knows that I buy land'

(7)   a.   op de trap
             'on the stairs (state)'

       b.   de trap op
             'on the stairs (movement)'

These different orders of heads and complements do not reflect two values of the head—complement parameter: there are different syntactic reasons that determine the two orders (Koster 1975; Haider and Prinzhorn 1986, among others). Nevertheless, different rhythms mark the specific surface word orders.

9.3.2 Acoustic differences mark different prominence patterns

We saw, above, that different word orders are reflected in different prominence patterns. In this section, we will see that the different prominence patterns are accompanied by different acoustic cues.

Several authors have examined the physical, acoustic correlates of the various prosodic domains, which include intonation patterns, pausing, phrase-final lengthening and constituent-initial articulatory strengthening (e.g., Wightman et al. 1992; Fisher and Tokura 1996; Keating et al. 2003).

In recent work, it has been proposed that the physical manifestation of prominence within phonological phrases differs according to whether the strong element is in initial or in final position. Specifically, it has been hypothesized, in agreement with the Iambic–Trochaic Law, that it is realized more through pitch and intensity if initial and more through duration if final (Nespor et al. 2008). That initial prominence is mainly marked by intensity and final prominence by duration has been shown to be the case for music (Bolton 1894; Woodrow 1951; Cooper and Meyer 1960) as well as for stress at the foot level (Hayes 1995). The different physical manifestations of prominence depending on location thus appear to be, more generally, derived from acoustic perception. The Iambic–Trochaic law states that if the sounds in a sequence alternate in degrees of intensity, being identical in all other respects, humans perceive them as a sequence of binary trochaic (i.e. strong first) groups. If the sounds of a sequence alternate in duration, they are instead perceived as a sequence of binary iambic (i.e. strong last) groups. This is graphically represented in (8a) and (8b), respectively.

(8) a. H=High intensity, l = low intensity
         ...H l H l H l H l H l...→
         ...[H l] [H l] [H l] [H l] [H l]...

     b. L = Long duration, s = short duration
         ...L s L s L s L s L s...→
         ...[s L] [s L] [s L] [s L]...

Nespor et al. (2008) examined the acoustic characteristics of phonological phrases with differing word orders both crosslinguistically and within the same language. To look at crosslinguistic variation, Turkish phonological phrases were used to exemplify initial PhPh prominence and French PhPhs to exemplify final prominence. These specific languages were chosen because they both have word-final stress and a similar syllabic structure, so that it was possible to find quite well-matched phrases that crucially differ in the location of PhPh stress. The specific material used consisted of phonological phrases in which the words occupying the position of phrasal prominence were identical in the two languages: either French words borrowed into Turkish, like *cognac*, or Turkish words borrowed into French, like *kilim*. These authors demonstrated that, at the level of the phonological phrase, higher pitch and intensity characterize the initial position, while increased duration characterizes the final position.

In the same study, confirmation of the hypothesis that different acoustic correlates characterize either initial or final PhPh prominence came from German, a language in which, as we said, both orders are found. In PhPhs consisting of two words, either N(object)–V or V–N(object), phrasal prominence falls on the complement independent of its location. In addition, it was found that the prominence on the complement N was characterized more by intensity and pitch when preverbal and more by lengthening when postverbal (Nespor et al. 2008).

The conclusion may thus be drawn that specific (acoustic) types of phrasal stress signal whether a language is head–complement or complement–head, and, within one language, the order of head and complement for each phrase.

9.4 Detecting and using phonological phrases

It has been well established that prosody plays a key role in understanding spoken sentences (e.g., Lehiste 1973; Nespor and Vogel 1983; Warren 1996;

Cutler et al. 1997; Frazier et al. 2006). While in the previous section, we looked at linguistic reasons to motivate phonological phrases and the acoustic cues that mark phonological phrases, in this section we review psycholinguistic evidence that both infants and adults can both detect and utilize phonological phrases in speech processing.

9.4.1 *Adult data*

In adults, in general, prosodic effects have been observed in two kinds of studies: (a) disambiguating possible syntactic (and semantic) parses of a spoken sentence and (b) identifying word boundaries in speech.

Since larger prosodic groupings like the intonational phrase (IP) are more salient in speech, several researchers have examined the effects of IP-breaks in disambiguating garden-path sentences like *The workers considered the last offer from the management was a real insult*, where *the last offer from the management* might be initially construed as the object of the verb *consider* instead of a sentence complement *[that] the last offer* (Marslen-Wilson et al. 1992; see also, e.g., Nespor and Vogel 1983, Clifton et al. 2006, and also Snedeker and Yuan 2008, for data from 4–6 year olds). In addition, evidence has also been found that, under some conditions, smaller prosodic phrases, corresponding to the phonological phrase, can also be used to disambiguate syntax (example in (9) below; see also Kjelgaard and Speer 1999; Clifton et al. 2006).

More recently, Millotte and colleagues (Millotte et al. 2007; Millotte et al. 2008) have provided direct evidence that phonological phrase prosody can directly influence online syntactic analyses. For example, consider the phrases (9a) and (9b) (from Millotte et al. 2008; phonological phrases are marked):

(9)   a.   [[Le petit chien]PP [*mord* la laisse]PP [qui le retient]PP]IP
           The little dog   bites the leash   that holds it back.

      b.   [[Le petit chien *mort*]PP [sera enterré demain]PP]IP
           The little dead dog   will be buried tomorrow.

The word *mord/mort* (pronounced identically in the two cases, /mɔʀ/) is initially ambiguous as to it being an adjective or a verb. In a sentence-completion task, the authors found that when the prosody indicated a grouping as in (9a), participants were more likely to infer a verb continuation. Conversely, they were more likely to infer an adjective continuation for (9b).

Using the same sets of stimuli as in (9), Millotte et al. (2008) also found that the detection of a category-labeled word (/mɔʀ/ as noun or adjective) was influenced by prosody: if /mɔʀ/ came at the end of a phonological phrase, as in (9b), it was more quickly detected if the participant was instructed to respond to *mort*, rather than to *mord*.

Thus, the metalinguistic ability of adult participants to detect words in fluent speech is conditioned by the prosodic phrasing of the sentence. However, other studies have shown that even the online, implicit segmentation of fluent speech into words is influenced by prosody (e.g., Salverda et al. 2003; Christophe et al 2004).

In particular, Christophe et al (2004) asked French participants to monitor target words, e.g. *chat* /ʃa/ (cat) that occurred either in a locally ambiguous context (e.g., <u>chat grin</u>cheax /ʃagʀɛ̃ʃø/, where the chagrin /ʃagʀɛ̃/ is a French word, or an unambiguous context (e.g., <u>chat d</u>rogué /ʃadʀoɡe/; there's no French word beginning with /ʃad/). These authors found delayed lexical access when a local lexical ambiguity was included in one phonological phrase. In contrast when a phonological phrase boundary intervened between the two words of the lexical competitor, no delay was observed. From this study the conclusion was drawn that lexical access is constrained by phonological phrases.

9.4.2 *Infant data*

Although infants have been shown to be sensitive to prosodic groupings in speech (e.g., Hirsch-Pasek et al. 1987; Kemler et al. 1989; Jusczyk et al. 1992; Morgan 1994; Nazzi et al. 2000), their limited linguistic prowess makes it difficult to empirically investigate how they might use prosody to resolve syntactic ambiguities.

Nevertheless, newborns can discriminate bisyllables (e.g. *latí*) that come from within (e.g., ge*latí*na) or across (e.g., go*rí*la *tí*sico) prosodic phrases, suggesting that they are sensitive to and can utilize the acoustic cues that distinguish the two types of bisyllables (Christophe et al. 2001; Christophe et al. 2004).

Further, Soderstrom et al. (2003) showed that 6- and 9-month-old infants, when familiarized with a word sequence (e.g., *people b(u)y the (w)hole*), preferred passages where such sequences were well-formed phrases (. . . *people by the hole* . . .), as compared to passages where a (phonological) phrase boundary interrupted the sequence (. . . *people # buy the whole* . . .)

In addition, Gout et al. (2004) showed that 10 to 12.5-month-old American infants use phonological phrase boundaries to constrain online lexical access. Thus, when trained to turn their heads to isolated bisyllabic English words like 'paper', these infants were more likely to turn towards sentences in which 'paper' did not straddle a phonological phrase (e.g., [The scandalous **paper**]PP [sways him]_{PP} [to tell the truth]_{PP}) than to sentences in which 'paper' straddled a phonological phrase (e.g., [The outstanding **pay**]_{PP} [**persuades** him]_{PP} [to go to France]_{PP}). Similar results were found for French 16-month-old infants (Millotte 2005).

These observations underline the importance of phonological phrases not just within linguistic theory (previous section), but also in understanding the online processing of speech both in adults and in infants. With the phonological phrase motivated on both linguistic and psycholinguistic grounds, we can ask how these can be used in acquiring word order. Indeed, we can ask more generally, how grammar acquisition can be aided by perceptual mechanisms.

9.5 Perceptual mechanisms in grammar acquisition

One of the basic requirements of any theoretical proposal of grammar is that the structures proposed be acquirable by the infant. There is however a gap between the knowledge acquired and the richness of the input available to the infant, the so-called Plato's problem (Chomsky 1984). Any theory of first language acquisition must account, among other things, for the fact that some of the basic grammatical properties appear to be acquired at the prelexical stage. However, there are not many proposals as to the precise learning mechanisms that are responsible for the early acquisition of the major syntactic properties.

The problem of grammar acquisition is eased if infants have access to, and can utilize, cues in the input that robustly mark specific syntactic properties of the language. A first step would be to show that the grammatical rules to be acquired have distinct, perceptually accessible correlates in fluent speech. Therefore, understanding basic human perceptual capacities can contribute to understanding both the nature of the language competence and how it is acquired.

With this in mind, we can now understand how phonological phrases can be used to acquire word order.

9.5.1 *Using phonological phrases to acquire word order*

Given both inter-linguistic (Turkish and French) and intra-linguistic (German) evidence for different physical correlates of phonological phrase prominence depending on the relative order of head and complement, it is feasible that this may be exploited in first language acquisition.

Experimental evidence shows that 6–12-week-old infants discriminate French from Turkish exclusively on the basis of phonological phrase stress

(Christophe et al. 2003). The material for that experiment consisted of French and Turkish utterances containing two phonological phrases. The utterances were well matched as to the number of syllables and were resynthesized so that discrimination between the two languages could not be based on phonemic or phonetic segmental properties.

The results suggested that infants react to the difference between (10a) and (10b).

(10)   a.   ...#wsws...
        b.   ...#swsw...

Notice, however, that if there are no boundaries (#), it is impossible to know whether in a sequence...swswswsws...the strong node is initial or final in its phrase. Thus the signal must contain some cues to the location of the constituent edges.

The different manifestation of prominence based on the Iambic–Trochaic Law may be one such cue and thus account for infants' ability to discriminate the two languages. That is, even in the absence of knowledge of phrase boundaries, the acoustic nature of prominence—whether more intense and higher in pitch or not—can indicate whether the strong node is initial or final.

That is, to an infant, an utterance may appear as a series of weak syllables punctuated by perceptually prominent, strong syllables. Depending on the acoustic properties of such prominent syllables, the infant can infer the word-order properties of the language.

Not only are there such differing acoustic cues to the two kinds of prominence in phonological phrases that differ in word order, but it has also been shown that infants are sensitive to such cues. Several authors have shown that infants can discriminate relative pitch levels and can memorize the pitch and temporal characteristics of auditory material (e.g., Trehub 2003). Indeed, Krumhansl and Jusczyk (1990) and Jusczyk and Krumhansl (1993) found evidence that 4.5-month-old infants organize tone sequences such that tonal phrases start with a high pitch and end with a long duration.

Note that all this data is still correlational. That is, although existing evidence shows that (a) specific acoustic patterns mark specific word orders at the phonological phrase level, (b) that infants are sensitive to such acoustic cues, and (c) infants can parse phonological phrases in speech, it has not yet been established if infants indeed use such acoustic cues to determine word order.

What kinds of data would be required to support our claim? First, we are examining corpora of child-directed speech in different languages to see if the correlation between different types of acoustic cues and different word orders is indeed reliable in naturalistic input. The stimuli used in Nespor et al. (2008) are a small but carefully constructed set, to best reveal acoustic differences that mark phrases with different word orders. Through the analysis of corpora we will be able to establish the robustness of these findings in speech samples that more closely approximate the input to the infant.

In addition, we can ask experimentally if infants can use prosody in an online task to figure out word order. For example, if we show an unfamiliar transitive action performed by an unfamiliar character, and accompany such a video with a phrase like 'wug pilk', then depending on the prosody, this could be interpreted as either Verb–Object or Object–Verb. Consequently, while the input is ambiguous (two words and two novel referents—an object and an action), we predict that prosody will bias infants towards one interpretation or another. In particular, a trochaic phrasal stress will bias infants towards an Object–Verb reading, while an iambic phrasal stress will bias them towards a Verb–Object interpretation.

9.5.2 *The Iambic–Trochaic Law as a general perception mechanism*

The Iambic–Trochaic Law has been primarily expressed in music and other non-linguistic, acoustic stimuli. However, recent work suggests that this might be a more domain-general perceptual mechanism. Bion et al. (submitted) carried out experiments on sequences of syllables and Peña et al. (in progress) on visual stimuli. The auditory experiments were based on pitch and duration. Intensity was not investigated, since, at least for the acoustic modality, there is ample evidence that intense stimuli are perceived as group-initial (Hay and Diehl 2007). Bion et al. habituated adults with sequences of syllables alternating either in pitch or in duration, and subsequently tested them with pairs of acoustically flat syllables. Participants were found to significantly prefer pairs that in habituation had either higher pitch initially or longer duration finally. That is, the Iambic–Trochaic Law is responsible for segmentation and storage in memory.

9.5.3 *Other perceptual mechanisms for grammar acquisition*

Although we suggest that the Iambic–Trochaic Law can lead the infant to acquiring word order, it is plausible that there are other cues perceptually available in the speech stream that can aid in discovering word order. It is, in fact, desirable that multiple cues lead the infant to converge on the same structure. More generally, perceptual mechanisms might play a role in several aspects of grammar acquisition.

For example, it has been known for several years that infants are capable, at birth, of discriminating their native language from other languages, and also discriminating two foreign languages, when these come from different rhythmic classes (e.g., Moon, Cooper, and Fifer 1993; Nazzi, Bertoncini, and Mehler 1998; Ramus et al. 2000). These early discrimination capacities are well correlated with the amount of vocalic space per utterance (as a percentage of time of the total utterance occupied by vowels, %V) in languages from different rhythmic classes (Ramus, Nespor, and Mehler 1999). Given that differences in %V correspond to the complexity of syllable structures in a language, it has been proposed that a sensitivity to %V might bias infants towards different segmentation strategies (Mehler and Nespor 2003; Nespor et al. 2003).

More recently, it has been proposed that %V also provides an indirect cue to syntax—low %V languages tend to be head–complement, while high %V languages tend to be complement–head (Shukla, Nespor, and Mehler in preparation). Thus this cue, perceived already by newborns, could give a bias as to the order of words in the language of exposure.

Several researchers have explored other aspects of perception that are salient for infants (and adults). It has been proposed that perceptual primitives—specialized mechanisms that render certain kinds of stimuli highly salient—place strong constraints on the kinds of inferences that infants draw from a given stimulus (Endress, Scholl, and Mehler 2005; Endress, Dehaene-Lambertz, and Mehler 2007; Endress and Mehler under review). Such perceptual primitives allow participants to detect both immediate repetitions and configurations at the edges of constituents.

For example, both adults (Endress et al 2005; Shukla, Nespor, and Mehler 2007) and infants (Seidl and Johnson 2006) have been shown to be better at extracting word-like units or learning rules over syllables at the edges of phrases as compared to their middles. Further, Gervain, Macagno, et al. (2008) have shown that neonates can more quickly process 'words' that contain immediate syllable repetitions.

All these studies are thus aimed at investigating basic perceptual mechanisms that infants bring to the task of language acquisition. These mechanisms can then be invoked in order to build better models of grammar acquisition (see also, e.g., Slobin 1973; Morgan and Demuth 1996; Dupoux and Peperkamp 2002).

9.5.4 *Distributional cues and acquisition*

The proposal that different perception mechanisms contribute to make the identification of word order possible, does not exclude that cues of a different nature also contribute to signaling word order, independently of the knowledge of words. For example, several researchers have shown that young infants can track distributional properties of syllables in order to extract word-like units from fluent speech (Saffran et al. 1996; Aslin et al. 1998; Peña et al. 2002).

Further, on the basis of an artificial grammar experiment in which frequent items alternate with infrequent ones, it has, in fact, been shown that 7-month-old Japanese and Italian infants have opposite order preferences (Gervain, Nespor, et al. 2008). That is, infants appear to be able to keep track of the most frequent words in the input as well as their location with respect to the less frequent words. Interestingly, the preferred word order corresponds to that of their native language: frequent–infrequent for Italian and infrequent–frequent for Japanese.

Thus signals of different nature might reflect important properties of the syntax of a language. And infants at the prelexical stage may have at their disposal different learning mechanisms based on perception, on the ability to compute distributional regularities and other linguistic biases, that aid them into the acquisition of basic grammatical properties (see, e.g., Peperkamp et al. 2006).

9.6 Conclusions

Although generative theories of grammar provide a substantial understanding of the mature state of the human language faculty, *how* the rules of grammar are acquired has been a much harder question to answer. Since the discovery, on the one hand, that even newborns are very sensitive to the rhythmic properties of language (Mehler et al. 1987, 1988) and, on the other hand, that young, prelexical infants are capable of computing fairly sophisticated distributional properties of speech (e.g., Saffran et al. 1996), the precise mechanisms that are responsible for language acquisition have been at the center of attention. In fact, the notion that such rhythmic and distributional properties might aid in acquiring language—either grammatical or lexical properties—have played a large role in the latest theories of acquisition. In this chapter, we draw attention to another potential source of information that relies on basic perceptual capacities of infants.

Spoken language, that constitutes the primary linguistic evidence for the infant, comprises a set of hierarchically organized phonological constituents that are not in direct correspondence with syntactic units (Selkirk 1984; Nespor and Vogel 1986/2008). One level of the hierarchy, the phonological phrase, differs amongst languages in accordance with the underlying syntax.

In particular, the prominence pattern of phonological phrases reflects the direction of branching in the language—initial prominence for left-branching (or complement–head) languages, and final prominence for right-branching (head–complement) languages (Nespor and Vogel 1986/2008). Infants appear to be sensitive to the different rhythmic patterns at this level of the hierarchy (Christophe et al. 2003). In addition, we find that the acoustic correlates of the two kinds of prominence patterns differ systematically; if prominence is initial, it is marked primarily by higher pitch and intensity, if final, primarily by duration (Nespor et al. 2008).

Indeed, these differing patterns for initial and final elements of a 'phrase' are proposed to be a basic perceptual Gestalt—the Iambic–Trochaic Law. Therefore, innate perceptual capacities might well direct the infant exposed to a given language to the correct word order of that language without any recourse to lexical information. Thus, we may account for the empirical observation that the earliest productions of infants respect the word order of their language.

More generally, we suggest that early perceptual capacities of infants can provide substantial information that aids the infant in acquiring grammar. Such perceptual capacities, coupled with distributional learning, might place strong constraints on the possible grammars, thus substantially easing the problem of language acquisition.

10

Object clauses, movement, and phrasal stress[*]

HUBERT TRUCKENBRODT AND ISABELLE DARCY

10.1 Introduction

In this paper, we report the results of an experiment concerning the effect of object clauses on phrasal stress of the matrix verb. The presentation of the experiment is embedded in a discussion of the interaction of phrasal stress with movement in German.

Section 10.2 includes some background on stress assignment and an introduction to the interaction of syntactic movement with the assignment of phrasal stress. The experimental methods are laid out in Section 10.3, the results of the experiment in Section 10.4. The results are discussed in Section 10.5. Section 10.6 provides a summary.

10.2 Phrasal stress

10.2.1 *Our research question in the context of the two-level analysis of phrasal stress*

Narrow focus attracts stress in German. The cases of interest in this paper involve a wide focus, and the generalizations governing stress assignment within that.

Between a preverbal direct object and a following verb in clause-final position, nuclear stress in German (the strongest stress in the intonation phrase) is assigned to the object as in (1). This is the case as long as the object has not undergone syntactic scrambling. By contrast, nuclear stress is found

[*] We thank Marga Reis and Michael Wagner for helpful comments. All errors are of course our own. This work was funded by the German Science Foundation (DFG) as part of the project B15 in the SFB 441 in Tübingen.

on the verb if the verb is not preceded by a stressed argument. For example, the verb is stressed if it is preceded by a stressless pronominal object as in (2), or by an adjunct as in (3). See Krifka (1984) and Jacobs (1993) for discussion of the argument–adjunct distinction.

(1) [What happened?]
   a. <u>Peter</u> hat ein <u><u>Buch</u></u> verkauft.
       Peter has a   book sold
       'Peter has sold a book.'

   b. # <u>Peter</u> hat ein <u>Buch</u> <u><u>verkauft</u></u>.

(2) [What happened to the book?]
   a. <u>Peter</u> hat es <u><u>verkauft</u></u>.
       Peter has it sold
       'Peter has sold it.'

   b. # <u>Peter</u> hat <u><u>es</u></u> verkauft.

   c. # <u><u>Peter</u></u> hat es verkauft.

(3) [What happened?]
   a. <u>Peter</u> hat während eines <u>Seminars</u> <u><u>geschlafen</u></u>.
       Peter has during a   seminar   slept
       'Peter has slept during a seminar.'

   b. # <u>Peter</u> hat während eines <u><u>Seminars</u></u> geschlafen.

The literature contains different accounts of these stress-patterns.[1] The accounts that seem particularly revealing to us separate two phrasal prosodic levels, as indicated by single and double underlining in (1)–(3). The nuclear stress (doubly underlined) is merely the rightmost stress among beats of phrasal stress assigned at the lower level. This rightmost stress is strengthened by a rule (Gussenhoven 1983b; Selkirk 1995; Uhmann 1991). The crucial generalizations are therefore to be captured at the lower level (single or double underlining in (1)–(3)). The Sentence Accent Assignment Rule (SAAR) of Gussenhoven (1983b, 1992) assigns accents that pertain to that lower level: Within a focus, the SAAR assigns accent to each argument, modifier, and

---

[1] Accounts that concentrate on the search for primary sentence stress include Cinque (1993) and Zubizarreta (1998). The theory of focus feature percolation by Selkirk (1984, 1995) shares elements with the two-level accounts discussed in the text. A recent multi-level account is developed in Wagner (2005).

predicate *except for a predicate adjacent to an accented argument.*[2] The SAAR thus assigns accents to arguments inside of a larger focus, in particular to the subject and to the object in (1a), as well as to the subjects in (2a) and (3a). The SAAR further assigns accent to the adjunct (modifier) in (3a). The SAAR finally assigns accents to the verb (predicate) in (2a) and (3a), but, by the provision highlighted above, the SAAR does not assign accent to the verb in (1a), where it stands next to an accented argument. A more general formulation is offered as a reanalysis the SAAR in Truckenbrodt (2006a, 2007b):

(4)   Stress-XP: Each lexical XP requires phrasal stress.[3]

In a DP such as [$_{DP}$ ein [$_{NP}$ Buch]] in (1), Stress-XP requires phrasal stress in the lexical NP, thus [$_{DP}$ ein [$_{NP}$ <u>Buch</u>]]. Stress-XP does not require anything of the functional DP, and so correctly does not require phrasal stress on a pronoun like [$_{DP}$ sie]. In this fashion, Stress-XP correctly enforces phrasal stress on the subjects in (1a)–(3a), the object in (1a) and the adjunct in (3a). The account in terms of Stress-XP reduces the prosodic argument–adjunct distinction to the syntactic distinction between arguments and adjuncts. Arguments of a verb are syntactically sister to V and are fully contained in the VP: [$_{VP}$ [$_{DP}$ ein [$_{NP}$ <u>Buch</u>]] verkauft$_{V}$]. Stress-XP does not require stress on the verb in this case: For one thing, the verb itself is a head and not a phrase, and so does not require phrasal stress by Stress-XP. For another, the VP satisfies Stress-XP by way of stress on <u>Buch</u> in the VP (which is independently required by the application of Stress-XP to the NP). The structure with an adjunct preceding a verb is syntactically different on standard syntactic assumptions insofar as the adjunct is adjoined to VP: [$_{VP}$ [während eines <u>Seminars</u>] [$_{VP}$ <u>geschlafen</u>]]. Here the verb is itself a VP, and thus requires stress by Stress-XP.[4]

In our experiment, we investigate whether an object clause has the same effect on the stress pattern as a DP-object argument. In (5), the verb *darlegen* follows an adjunct which cannot exempt *darlegen* from being stressed. Will the object clause that follows the verb *darlegen* in (5) exempt this verb from being stressed, in the same way in which the preceding DP object exempts the verb from carrying stress in (1a)?

---

[2] The full formulation of the SAAR in Gussenhoven (1992) is: 'If focused, every predicate, argument, and modifier must be accented, with the exception of a predicate that, discounting unfocused constituents, is adjacent to an argument' (p. 84). We return to other aspects of the SAAR.

[3] This constraint is originally from Truckenbrodt (1995). It is also employed in Samek-Lodovici (2005) and Féry and Samek-Lodovici (2006).

[4] See Truckenbrodt (1999) for the details of the application of the mapping constraints to adjunction structures.

(5)   Der <u>Manager</u> will   auf der <u>Versammlung</u> *darlegen,*
    the manager wants at   the assembly   present
        dass der <u>Millionär</u> die <u>Firma</u>   verwalten soll.
        that the millionaire the company administer should.
    'The manager wants to suggest at the meeting that the millionaire administer the company.'

10.2.2 *Interaction of stress and movement*

On standard syntactic accounts,[5] the object clause is taken to be extraposed to the right by syntactic movement in a more or less obligatory process of extraposition. Thus, the object clause will also follow an auxiliary or modal after *glauben* as in (6).

(6)   ...dass die Maria glauben soll   [CP dass der Werner die
    that DET Maria believe should   that DET Werner DET
    Manu heiratet]
    Manu marries
    '...that Maria is supposed to believe that Werner is marrying Manu.'

This suggests that the object clause is also extraposed in (5). We therefore need to take the interaction of stress assignment and movement into account in assessing predictions about the case we are interested in.

    For English, Bresnan (1971, 1972) has made a case that stress can reflect underlying, rather than derived, syntactic structure. This argument has been criticized (Berman and Szamosi 1972; Lakoff 1972; Gussenhoven 1992) but is adopted in the analysis of Selkirk (1995) and we adopt it here. Since the issue directly concerns the stress on the verb, we review some cases here.

    To begin with, English has the argument–adjunct asymmetry discussed for German above, but in a more subtle fashion. The SAAR/Stress-XP, together with strengthening of the rightmost stress, are designed also to account for phrasal stress in English. The English verb, when preceding a stressed object as in (7a), does not require phrasal stress, while it requires phrasal stress when preceding an adjunct as in (7b) (the reality of this distinction was experimentally demonstrated by Gussenhoven 1983a).

(7)   a.   <u>John</u> was [VP teaching [NP <u>linguistics</u>]]

     b.   <u>John</u> was [VP [VP <u>teaching</u>] in [NP <u>Ghana</u>]]

This is the mirror image of the German contrast between (1a) and (3a), and it is predicted in the same way by the SAAR/Stress-XP. It is more subtle in

---

[5] See for example Sternefeld (2006: vol. 1, ch. III.8).

English for a variety of reasons. Among them: (i) The verb-final syntax of German lets the contrast come out as a contrast in regard to main stress, while the head-initial syntax of English lets the contrast emerge only as a contrast in non-nuclear phrasal stress. (ii) In English, German, and other languages, prenuclear lexical words that are not assigned phrasal stress by the SAAR/Stress-XP can optionally receive phrasal stress by what appears to be a process of gratuitous strengthening, so that the verb in (7a) can also receive gratuitous phrasal stress. This of course obscures the difference between (7a) and (7b). Gratuitous strengthening is not available in position following the predicted nuclear stress, so that the verb in (1a) cannot receive gratuitous stress, and the contrast to (3a) in German is more robust. To be sure, gratuitous strengthening also has the potential to obscure the stress pattern in (5).

We now turn to the interaction of movement and stress in English. The stresslessness of the verb in (7a), which is allowed due to the presence of the stressed object, can be retained if the stressed object is moved, as in the example in (8); see Bresnan (1971). Crucially, the verb *written* does not seem to require phrasal stress in (8a) even if it is new. This may be contrasted with an unstressed moved object as in (8b), which would not allow a stressless verb in its underived position, and, consequently, does not allow a stressless object after movement either.

(8)   a.   John asked [[what <u>books</u>]$_i$ she had written t$_i$]
      b.   John asked [[what]$_i$ she had <u>written</u> t$_i$]

We here recast Bresnan's account of this interaction in terms of *stress reconstruction*, using Stress-XP and a simple copy theory of movement and reconstruction, as in (9).

(9)   a.   John asked [[what <u>books</u>]$_i$ she had written [~~what books~~]$_i$]
      b.   John asked [[what]$_i$ she had <u>written</u> [~~what~~]$_i$]

If stress were calculated regardless of the silent copy, the VP [$_{VP}$ written t$_i$] would require stress on the verb in both (9a) and (9b) by Stress-XP. The stress difference between the two cases can be understood if stress assignment is reconstructed. In that case, the VP [$_{VP}$ written [~~what books~~]] in (9a) contains phrasal stress on the reconstructed object, and so does not require stress on the verb by Stress-XP. On the other hand, the reconstructed VP [$_{VP}$ <u>written</u> what] in (9b) would not be stressed on the pronominal object (cf. [<u>written</u> something]) so that stress falls on the verb here (with or without reconstruction). The argument, then, is that the stresslessness of the verb in (8a) is allowed due to stress reconstruction of a stressed argument.

In German, the interaction of movement and stress has not been studied, to the best of our knowledge. However, a range of standard observations, when confronted with the account in terms of Stress-XP, allow us to make some relevant remarks.

It seems that cases of displacement within the *Mittelfeld* do not reconstruct for stress. For example, certain objects of individual-level predicates are argued to be outside of VP for semantic reasons by Diesing (1992). These do not show stress reconstruction, as shown for an accusative-marked experiencer predicate in (10).

(10)   Das hat einen <u>Zuschauer</u> <u>gewundert.</u>
      that has a   spectator surprised
      'That has surprised a spectator.'

Scrambled constituents in the Mittelfeld, where they are stressed, never seem to reconstruct for stress: they never license a stressless verb; cf. (11).

(11)   [What about the books?]
      <u>Peter</u> hat <u>manche</u> Bücher schon <u>gelesen.</u>
      #<u>Peter</u> hat <u>manche</u> Bücher schon <u>gelesen.</u>
      Peter has some   books already read
      'Peter has already read some (of the) books.'

Thus, scrambling seems not to reconstruct for stress assignment.

On the other hand, V-to-C movement and movement of the subject to SPEC,CP do seem to reconstruct for stress assignment in German. By way of background, consider first the distinction between (12a) and (12b).[6] While different factors arguably play a role in the stressing of simple subject-verb clauses, it seems that one of them is unaccusativity, as argued by Uhmann (1991) (see den Besten 1983 for the syntactic analysis). This is plausibly relevant here: The nominative subject is a thematic object in object position in (12a), but not in (12b). With this, Stress-XP derives the stress patterns: The unaccusative VP [VP <u>Otto</u> kommt] contains stress on the argument in (12a), so that no stress is required on the verb by Stress-XP. On the other hand, the unergative verb is a VP [VP <u>geigt</u>] in (12b), so stress on the verb is here correctly forced by Stress-XP. If this analysis is correct, it is now important for the interaction of stress with movement that the intuitive difference between cases like (12a,b) is empirically retained under movement of the subject to SPEC,CP (Vorfeld) and fronting of the finite verb to C, as in (13a,b).

---

[6] The arguably related distinction between (13a) and (13b) is from von Stechow and Uhmann (1986: 308).

(12) a.   [$_{VP}$]   (13) a. [$_{CP}$ DP   C/V   t t]
      dass   Otto kommt   Otto   kommt
      that   Otto comes   Otto   comes
      'that Otto is coming'   'Otto is coming'

      b.   [$_{VP}$]   b. [$_{CP}$ DP C/V t t]
      dass   Otto geigt   Otto geigt
      that   Otto fiddles   Otto fiddles
      'that Otto is playing   'Otto is playing violin
      violin (right now)'   (right now)'

This suggests that both movement to SPEC,CP and movement to C reconstruct for stress. If they did not, the identical surface structural configuration
of the two cases in (13a,b) would wrongly lead to identical stress patterns.
Assuming stress reconstruction of both instances of movement as in (14), the
constituents correctly inherit the different stress patterns assigned to them
due to their different underlying syntactic configurations.[7]

(14) a.   Otto kommt   [$_{VP}$ ~~Otto kommt~~]
                comes

      b.   Otto geigt   ~~Otto~~ [$_{VP}$ ~~geigt~~]
                fiddles

It therefore seems that movement of the subject to SPEC,CP and movement
of the finite verb to C reconstruct for stress, while scrambling in the Mittelfeld
does not reconstruct for stress.

   In our experiment, the question whether the verb is stressed in (5) can be
understood as the question whether CP-extraposition reconstructs for stress.
If it does, we expect a stressless verb *darlegen* in (5) because the VP contains
stress in the reconstructed CP. Without stress reconstruction, the VP projection of this verb contains only the verb *darlegen*. This verb is then expected to
be stressed by Stress-XP.

10.2.3 *Background from previous experiments*

The predictions of SAAR/Stress-XP have entered into the experiments reported
in Truckenbrodt (2002, 2004, 2005, 2007a). The evidence from pitch accents
reported there showed that these predictions are borne out in experimental

---

[7] It would not be enough to postulate that one but not the other of these two movement processes
reconstructs for stress. If only movement of the subject to SPEC,CP reconstructed for stress, the verb in
C could not 'inherit' the consequence of stress assignment in the VP in a way that distinguishes (13a)
from (13b). If, on the other hand, only movement of the finite verb to C reconstructed for stress, there
would not be a reason why the verb ends up unstressed in (13a).

settings, for simple cases: In sentences read as answers to the question 'What's new?', arguments and adjuncts (with lexical NPs) carry a pitch accent, and a clause-final verb that follows the direct object does not carry a pitch accent.

These pitch accents are downstepped (i.e. their high peaks are successively lowered). Intonation phrase boundaries (here: 'i-boundaries') can be detected by the interruption of downstep by upstep and reset (see Truckenbrodt 2002, 2007a; for downstep delimitation by larger phonological domains in other languages, see Ladd 1988; Laniran and Clements 2003; Pierrehumbert and Beckman 1988; van den Berg et al. 1992). Simply put (cf. (15)), in this pattern a medial i-boundary is indicated by a return to the initial height just *before* the i-boundary ('upstep'). Further downstep then proceeds from this upstepped level.

Truckenbrodt (2005) investigates environments for i-boundaries with this criterion, drawing on a single speaker. In the results, i-boundaries consistently occur at the right edge of clauses: at the right edge of a subject clause in the Vorfeld as in (15a); at the right edge of a relative clause of a constituent in the Mittelfeld as in (15b); and at the right edge of the first conjunct of embedded coordinated clauses as in (15c). At the same time, continuing downstep (no i-boundary) was found across the left edges of clauses, such as the left edge of the relative clause in (15b). Here the object1 that precedes the relative clause is not upstepped.

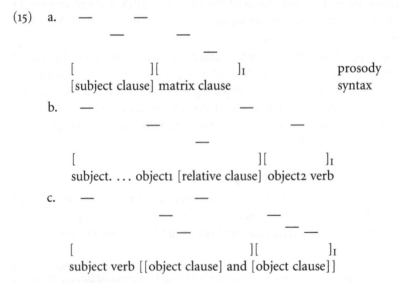

(15) a.

[   ][   ]ᵢ   prosody
[subject clause] matrix clause   syntax

      b.

[   ][   ]ᵢ
subject. ... object1 [relative clause] object2 verb

      c.

[   ][   ]ᵢ
subject verb [[object clause] and [object clause]]

The configuration of a single object clause, of particular interest here, was likewise tested. Here continuing downstep gave evidence for the absence of an intonation phase boundary between matrix and embedded clause. This was found both with shorter matrix clauses as in (16) and with longer matrix clauses as in (17).

(16) [

Der Werner hat dem Maler gesagt, dass er der Lola
DET Werner has the painter said that he DET Lola

]ᵢ

das Weben zeigen will.
the weaving show wants

'Werner has said to the painter that he wants to show Lola weaving.'

(17) [

Die Lena und die Hanne haben der Manu gesagt, dass sie
DET Lena and DET Hanne have DET Manu said that they

]ᵢ

dem Maurer ein Lama malen wollen.
the bricklayer a llama paint want

'Lena and Hanne have said to Manu that they want to paint a llama for the bricklayer.'

This conforms to the generalization that right, but not left edges of clauses trigger an i-boundary in this data. The sentences in (16) and (17) also contain something close to, but not quite like our test case: a matrix verb (here *sagen*, 'say') followed by a complement clause. This verb did not carry phrasal stress. However, in these cases the matrix verb is preceded by an indirect object which itself has the possibility of exempting the following verb from being stressed. We compare the cases in (16) and (17) with our results in the discussion section below.

10.3 The experiment: Method

10.3.1 *Stimuli*

We used four conditions with near-minimal contrasts. Each condition contained eight sentences. One sentence from each condition is shown in (18). A list of all stimuli can be found in the appendix of this paper.

The verb *darlegen* constitutes the test case in (18). Condition O ('object') is a control condition in which this verb is expected to be unstressed, since it is preceded by a stressed direct object. Condition A ('adjunct') is a control condition in which the verb is expected to be stressed, since it is not adjacent to a stressed argument; it is preceded by an adjunct; the pronominal, contextually given, object is naturally scrambled and unstressed here. Both of the control conditions O and A are followed by an adjunct clause (*auch wenn...*) so as to keep constant across all four conditions that there is continuation after the crucial verb. Conditions D and V are two test conditions. In both cases *darlegen* is preceded by an adjunct (in parallel to condition A), but in this case it is also followed by an object clause. The object clause is a *dass*-clause in condition D, and a V2 clause in condition V.

(18)   *Condition O: verb preceded by direct object*
Der <u>Manager</u> will   eine neue <u>Strategie</u> *darlegen,*
the manager wants a   new strategy present
     auch wenn er daran nicht so richtig   <u>glaubt.</u>
     also if   he in-it   not   so properly believes
'The manager wants to present a new strategy, even if he doesn't fully believe in it.'

Condition A: verb preceded by adjunct
Der Millionär soll   die Firma verwalten.
Der <u>Manager</u> soll   das auf der   <u>Versammlung</u> *darlegen,*
the manager should that at   the   assembly   present
     auch wenn er sich damit viele <u>Feinde</u> macht.
     also if   he REFL with-it many enemies makes
'The millionaire is supposed to administer the company. The manager is supposed to present that at the assembly, even if he makes many enemies with that.'

Condition D: verb followed by 'dass' object clause
Der <u>Manager</u> will   auf der <u>Versammlung</u> *darlegen,*
the manager wants at   the assembly   present
     dass der <u>Millionär</u> die <u>Firma</u>   verwalten soll.
     that the millionaire the company administer should.
'The manager wants to suggest at the meeting that the millionaire administer the company.'

Condition V: verb followed by V2 object clause
Der <u>Manager</u> will   auf der <u>Versammlung</u> *darlegen,*
the manager wants at   the assembly   present
     der <u>Millionär</u>   soll   die <u>Firma</u>   verwalten
     the millionaire should the company administer
'The manager wants to suggest at the meeting that the millionaire administer the company.'

The control conditions, then, should give points of comparison with an unstressed verb (condition O) and a stressed verb (condition A). In the test cases D and V, an unstressed verb (as in condition O) points towards stress reconstruction of extraposition; a stressed verb (as in condition A) points towards the absence of stress reconstruction.

10.3.2 *Production and perception tasks*

In order to ensure a neutral context, the stimuli of conditions O, D, and V were additionally preceded by a context sentence such as 'Imagine what I heard.' (see Appendix). In condition A the preceding sentence shown in (18) was assumed to sufficiently fulfill that function.

Six native speakers of German read the thirty-two stimuli in pseudo-randomized order, with ninety-seven filler sentences interspersed. They were given the instruction to read all sentences in a natural way, at a normal rate of speech. They read the whole set of 129 sentences twice.

The thirty-two test recordings were saved in separate files on a computer for a subsequent perception task to determine the stress, and for acoustic analysis.

In a perception task, twelve listeners (different from the speakers) judged the tokens that had been recorded as to the location of stress. They were paid for their participation. According to a short background questionnaire they were asked to fill out, none of them had any history of hearing disorder, and none of them grew up bilingually or spent a large amount of time (longer than two years) in a foreign language country. Each listener judged the recordings of first one speaker, then of a second speaker, then of a third speaker, in a listening session of about one hour total. This allowed the listeners to take into account speaker-specific phonetic strategies in realizing stress. The recordings of each speaker were pseudo-randomized in the presentation. Listeners A and B judged speakers 1, 2, and 3; listeners C and D judged speakers 2, 3, and 4; listeners E and F judged speakers 3, 4 and 5; etc. The order in which speakers were presented to each listener was rotated (1, 2, 3, or 2, 3, 1, etc.), so that the productions of each speaker were judged by six listeners, twice in first, twice in second, and twice in third position.

The complete sentences with their contexts were played to the listeners. The crucial words for the task were printed on a sheet of paper. For the cases in (18) (in their order above), this would be as shown in (19). The listeners had to decide, for each token they heard, what the relation in strength of stress is between Part 1 (argument or adjunct) and Part 2 (verb). The options were (i) Part 1 is stressed more than Part 2 (which we counted as an unstressed verb) and (ii) stress on Part 1 is smaller or equal to stress on Part 2 (which we counted as a stressed verb).

(19)

	Part 1	Part 2	Stress-relation: Part 1 > Part 2	Stress-relation: Part 1 ≤ Part 2
1.	neue Strategie	darlegen		
2.	Versammlung	darlegen		
3.	Versammlung	darlegen		
4.	Versammlung	darlegen		

new strategy   present
assembly

We evaluate stress in our recordings by summing over listener judgments for each condition O, A, D, and V. In each of these conditions, there are eight tokens from each of six speakers, recorded twice (N=96 in each condition). Each of these tokens was judged by six listeners. There is thus a total of 576 listener judgments for each of the four conditions.

In choosing this method, we allow that the grammatical effect of the object clause on the stress or absence of stress on the verb enters into the experiment in two ways. First, in the way the speakers pronounce the sentences in accord with their internal grammar. Second, in case the stress relations are not entirely clearly audible in the productions, there may be a listener effect as well: Since the listeners hear the entire sentence, they may be biased in their judgments by their own internal grammar in favor of judgments that conform to that grammar. Since we are interested in the internal grammar of German speakers, we see no harm in allowing this grammatical knowledge to enter into both the production and the perception. In the end, our results do not bear specifically on either production or perception, but on the grammar that underlies both, by assumption.

Responses were coded manually into an analysis file. We computed the response rate of 'verb stressed' for each listener and compared it against the mean across listeners in each condition, in order to ensure that all listeners performed the task correctly. If the rates for a given listener exceeded two standard deviations from the mean, this listener was excluded and an additional listener was recruited for the task. In total three listeners were replaced. After the replacements, the twelve listeners on whom the following results draw were well within this tolerance range of two standard deviations.

The productions were acoustically processed with Praat. Variation in choice of pitch accents and boundary marking makes it difficult to give a detailed account of the acoustic results. We aim instead at giving an overall impression of the course of Fo. Labels were applied to delimit the initial subject of the main clause ('SU'), the preverbal argument or adjunct XP ('XP'), the following final verb of the matrix clause ('V'), and the following clause ('F'). Fo-measurements were taken manually at the following points: The highest peak in SU, the highest peak in XP, the highest peak in F. In addition, it was visually determined whether V showed rising or falling intonation (ignoring interpolation from material preceding V); for falling intonation, the highest point preceding the fall and the lowest point following it were measured. For rising intonation, the lowest point preceding the rise and the highest point after the rise were measured.

10.4 The experiment: Results

10.4.1 *Main perception result*

Figure 10.1 shows our main result of the perception part. It shows, for each of the four conditions, percentages of judgments as 'verb stressed'.

The control conditions A and O are clearly separated in the expected direction. The verb is mostly stressed in the A(djunct) condition, and mostly unstressed in the O(bject) condition. The separation is not absolute (condition

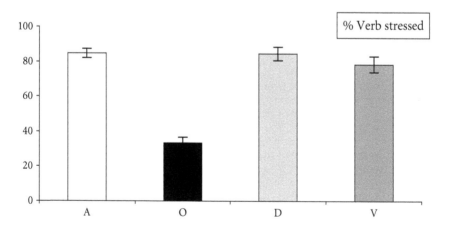

FIGURE 10.1 Percentage of 'verb stressed'-judgments for each condition (A: Adjunct; O: Object; D: dass-clause; V: V2-clause). Total number per condition out of 576 judgments: A: 488; O: 192; D: 487; V: 452.

O sentences are judged as 'verb stressed' in about 33 percent of cases, and condition A sentences are judged as 'verb stressed' in about 85 percent of cases).

Both test conditions D and V pattern with control condition A, and clearly differ from control condition O (condition D has 85 percent and condition V 78 percent judgments as 'verb stressed'). Thus, the verb is mostly stressed in the D and V conditions, in a way that resembles the verb next to an adjunct (condition A) and that differs from a verb next to an accented object (condition O).

10.4.2 *No effect of verb frequency*

It seemed possible to us that frequency might play a role in verb stress. Frequently occurring words like *sagen*, 'say', *glauben*, 'believe', might be more prone to being unstressed than rarer verbs like *murmeln*, 'murmur'. However, it turns out that there is no such correlation in our data.

Table 10.1 gives an overview of frequencies of the eight verbs used in our experiment. The frequencies are taken from the CELEX Database (Baayen et al. 1995). Figure 10.2 plots the responses from our experiment separately for these eight verbs. The plotting order in Figure 10.2 is from frequent to infrequent, following Table 10.1. (In some minor cases of discrepancies between written and spoken frequency, the written frequency was used for ordering the verbs.)

If frequency mattered, there would be a left-to-right trend in Figure 10.2. This does not seem to be the case for any of the columns in Figure 10.2. Verb frequency does not seem to affect verb stress in our experiment.

TABLE 10.1 CELEX-frequencies of the verbs of the experiment

	Written corpus	Spoken corpus	English translation
sagen	2043	6037	say
glauben	471	1832	believe
annehmen	136	60	assume
melden	125	80	report
vermuten	49	29	suspect
träumen	26	5	dream
murmeln	25	0	murmur
darlegen	22	5	present

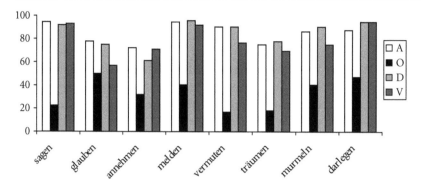

FIGURE 10.2 Response rate (%) as 'verb stressed' according to verb frequency (decreasing from left to right) and condition.

10.4.3 *Uniformity of listener judgments*

In this section we assess the uniformity of the listener judgments for the individual tokens. For each token, the number of listeners that gave the judgment that we call 'verb stressed' for that token (6/6, 5/6,..., 0/6) were computed. The results are plotted in Figure 10.3. If, for example, six out of six listeners gave the same judgment for one token, this token is counted towards the first category 6/6.

In Figure 10.3, unanimous listener judgments appear at the very left (6/6) and at the very right (0/6). The approximate overall 'U-shape' of the plotted values shows that, on the whole, listener judgments were relatively uniform. This suggests that there was a good number of tokens that were produced with relatively clear cues as to the presence or absence of stress on the verb.

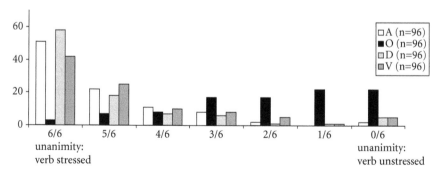

FIGURE 10.3 Homogeneity of judgments (as verb stressed) for six judgments per token. Absolute numbers are plotted for each condition.

Figure 10.3 also shows a 'left-right' asymmetry. The high columns of conditions A, D, and V under 6/6 are higher than the high column of condition O on the right. The higher values for condition O are more distributed across 3/6–0/6. We suspect that such a bias towards 'verb stressed' judgments resulted from our way of eliciting the listener judgments. As shown in (19), we asked the listeners to decide whether the preverbal part (in the following: 'XP') is stressed (a) more than the verb ('verb unstressed') or (b) less *or equal* to the verb ('verb stressed'). It seems possible that the inclusion of the 'equal' judgment with category (b) has led listeners to choose this category in cases of uncertainty. This would explain the asymmetry of the 'U' in Figure 10.3.

10.4.4 *Productions*

Figure 10.4 shows the production measurements. Each speaker is plotted separately. Recall that the main clause consists of SU XP V (ignoring un- accented elements), followed by a second clause (see (18)). The plots show measurements of the highest peaks of the main clause subject ('SU'), the main clause preverbal XP ('XP'), the verb ('L(H)', see below) and the highest peak of the following clause ('F'). Fo averages of the four experimental conditions are plotted. Each condition is based on sixteen tokens for each speaker, minus any missing values (see below). Variation in regard to an Fo fall or rise on the verb at the end of the main clause is handled as follows. The speakers plotted on the left showed a large majority of rises. For these speakers, only the utterances with such rises on the verb entered into the averages plotted. (Missing values due to this criterion: speaker BI: one utterance of condition A; speaker LU: four utterances of condition O; speaker PI: two utterances of condition A, five utterances of condition O.) The measurements of the rise are plotted as L and H. The speakers plotted on the right showed considerably greater variation between rises and falls. For these, only the L minimum of the verb is plotted, and the preceding or following H peak in the verb is not plotted. Note that the plots only partly approximate actual Fo contours insofar as there were typic- ally low points in the actual contours separating the peaks that are plotted.

The measurements provide evidence that the main clause and the following clause were separated by an intonation phrase break in all four conditions. (This accords with the intuitive impression when listening to the produc- tions.) There are three indications of this.

Consider first relative values for F, the highest peak in the second clause. Figure 10.5 on p. 206 shows two expectations about the scaling of the second clause. If, as in (a), there is no intonation phrase break preceding F, downstep between SU and XP is expected to be continued on the accented verb and on

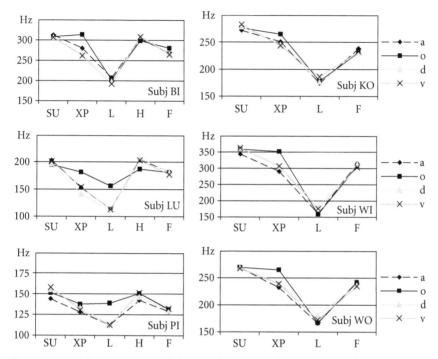

FIGURE 10.4 Measurements of the productions, plotted separately for the six speakers. SU: highest peak in the initial subject; XP: highest peak in the preverbal XP; LH: low and high extrema in case of a rise on the verb (plots on the left) otherwise L: minimum on the verb (plots on the right); F: highest peak in the following clause.

F in the second clause. Downstep across the left clause boundary was found in Truckenbrodt (2005). On the other hand, if, as in (b), the second clause is separated by an intonation phrase break, downstep on XP is not expected to be continued into the second clause. Instead, by the models of Ladd (1988), van den Berg et al. (1992), and Truckenbrodt (2007a) (see also Pierrehumbert and Beckman 1988), we expect that the second clause is itself lowered relative to the first clause by downstep. Estimating broadly, we may expect XP and F to be of comparable height in (b).

The plots in Figure 10.4 bear out the expectation of the intervening intonation phrase break. With the exception of speaker KO, the speakers do not show lowering between XP and F; rather, they show values of comparable height for XP and F.

The second indication for the presence of an intonation phrase break in all conditions can be seen in the value of H, plotted for the speakers in

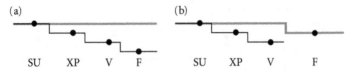

FIGURE 10.5 (a) Downstep within the same intonation phrase. (b) Downstep within a first intonation phrase, and partial reset of a second intonation phrase (i.e. downstep of the second intonation phrase relative to the first).

Figure 10.4 on the left. In condition O (with the verb unstressed), this is plausibly the value of a boundary tone at the end of a prosodic domain here. In conditions A, D, and V, this is either a boundary tone or the end of a rising pitch accent on the stressed verb. The high scaling of this point interrupts the pattern of downstep. In the model of scaling of Truckenbrodt (2007a), the scaling of such a boundary tone or accentual rise to the height of the initial peak is analyzed as upstep, and is direct evidence for its status as a boundary tone or nuclear accent of an intonation phrase (i.e. of a prosodic domain that includes the initial peak). The presence of such high tones at the end of the main clause verb in all conditions is thus evidence of the presence of an intonation phrase break at the end of the main clause.

The third indication of the medial intonation phrase breaks relates to the clearest systematic difference across the four conditions and is seen in point XP in Figure 10.4. In conditions A, D, and V, this point is lowered (downstepped) relative to the initial peak on SU. In condition O, on the other hand, the values of XP in Figure 10.4 are either not lowered relative to SU or lowered less than in the other conditions (with the partial exception of speaker PI). In conditions A, D, and V, the constituent XP is a PP adverbial followed by a verb that is (according to the perception results) mostly stressed; here the matrix clause is phrased (SU)(XP)(V). In condition O, the constituent XP is a preverbal object and the following verb is unstressed (by general expectations and by the perception results). The matrix clause is phrased (SU)(XP V). The greater height on XP in this condition O is expected if the matrix clause forms a separate intonation phrase: In that case, the preverbal object is the nuclear stress of an intonation phrase, and its pitch peak can be expected to receive a boost in height due to prominence (Pierrehumbert 1980). In the model of Truckenbrodt (2007a), it would be scaled as upstepped, i.e. as returning to the height of the initial peak.

Taking the evidence for stress from the perception results and the intonation phrase break from the production results together, the typical phrasing of the four conditions in our recordings is as shown in (20) (see (18) for the examples in full length and for glosses of these examples).

(20) O:

```
[                          x    ][                    x   ]
(    x   )(                 x    )(           ...      x   )
```

Der <u>Manager</u> will eine neue <u>Strategie</u> darlegen, auch wenn er daran nicht ... <u>glaubt</u>.

'The manager wants to present a new strategy, even if he doesn't fully believe in it.'

A:

```
[                              x    ][              x        ]
(    x    )(                    x    )( x   )(     ...   x    )
```

Der <u>Manager</u> soll das auf der <u>Versammlung</u> <u>darlegen</u>, auch wenn er ... <u>Feinde</u> macht.

'The manager is supposed to suggest that at the meeting, even if he makes enemies with that.'

D:

```
[                               x    ][           x           ]
(    x    )(                     x    )( x   )(    ...   x      )
```

Der <u>Manager</u> will auf der <u>Versammlung</u> <u>darlegen</u>, dass der <u>M</u>. die <u>Firma</u> verw. soll.

'The manager wants to suggest at the meeting that the millionaire administer the company.'

V:

```
[                               x    ][           x           ]
(    x    )(                     x    )( x   )(    ...   x      )
```

Der <u>Manager</u> will auf der <u>Versammlung</u> <u>darlegen</u>, der <u>M</u>. soll die <u>Firma</u> verwalten.

'The manager wants to suggest at the meeting that the millionaire administer the company.'

No prosodic differences between object *dass*-clauses ('that'-clauses) and object V2 clauses are evident in the results.

The medial i-boundary is not surprising in the conditions O and A, where the second clause is an adjunct clause that may be classified as 'unintegrated' in the sense of Reis (1997). The medial boundary is surprising in the test conditions D and V, where the second clause is an object clause.

10.5 Discussion

10.5.1 *Experimentally supported conclusions*

We found in the perception results that the verb is stressed in the test conditions D and V: the object clause does not seem to exempt the verb from receiving phrasal stress. We found in the production results that the object clause at issue is separated by an intonation phrase break.

The stress on the verbs from the perception results shows that CP extraposition did not reconstruct for stress in our data. However, the surprising i-boundary around the object clause makes it difficult to generalize this conclusion and to maintain that CP extraposition generally does not reconstruct for stress. It is possible (and we assume this to be the case) that one intonation phrase could not reconstruct for stress into another one. Thus, if stress reconstruction would include reconstruction of the strongest stress of an intonation phrase in its original strength, stress reconstruction from $[\ldots \underline{\underline{x}}]_I [\ldots \underline{x}]_I$ to $[\ldots [\ldots \underline{x}]_I \underline{\underline{x}}]_I$ would result in the illegitimate representation of an intonation phrase (the outer one) with two prosodic heads (nuclear stresses). Consequently, we cannot draw a general conclusion, directly supported by experimental evidence, about stress reconstruction of extraposition.

The surprising i-boundary is itself very interesting. We think it cannot be an artifact of our experimental design. In particular, the design was not such that the subjects were biased towards productions with two intonation phrases. In the list of 129 pseudo-randomized sentences that included the thirty-two productions of interest and ninety-seven fillers, the sixteen sentences with object clauses were elicited alternating with fifty biclausal sentences, two triclausal sentences, and sixty-one monoclausal sentences. Further, the production of these sentences was interrupted by preceding context sentences (monoclausal in all cases). We therefore believe that the i-boundary comes out of the sentences themselves.

Instead of a general answer to our test question, we have found something else that we think is interesting: the patterns of phrasing in (20) that include the i-boundary preceding the object clauses in conditions D and V.

We pursue our test question in a more tentative way in the following section, drawing on intuitive prosodic judgments together with the experimental results.

10.5.2 *Tentative account*

When setting up the experiment, we did not find either the rendition with the stressed verb (as found in our results) or the rendition with an unstressed verb as in (21) below unnatural. We still find this to be so, and we now include this as a stress judgment into our discussion. Further, in the subtle way in which such judgments are possible, we find there to be a preference concerning the interaction with intonation phrases. Given a stressless verb, there is a preference for the absence of a medial intonation phrase. This is indicated at the end of (21).

(21)   [Der <u>Werner</u> hat auf dem <u>Treffen</u>   gesagt, dass er der
      DET   Werner has at   the   meeting said   that he DET
      <u>Lola</u> das <u>Weben</u>   zeigen will]$_I$
      Lola the weaving show   wants
      'Werner has said at the meeting that he wants to show Lola weaving.'
          [<u>SU</u> <u>ADJ</u> V <u>CP</u>] > [<u>SU</u> <u>ADJ</u> V][<u>CP</u>]

When the verb is stressed, as in our experimental results and as in (22), there is an inverse preference: a medial intonation phrase is more natural than its absence, as in (22). This corresponds to our experimental results, with a stressed verb and a medial intonation phrase break.

(22)   [Der <u>Werner</u> hat auf dem <u>Treffen</u> <u>gesagt</u>,]$_I$ [dass er der
      'Werner has said at the meeting that he wants to show
      <u>Lola</u> das <u>Weben</u> zeigen will]$_I$
      Lola weaving.'
          [<u>SU</u> <u>ADJ</u> <u>V</u>][<u>CP</u>] > [<u>SU</u> <u>ADJ</u> V <u>CP</u>]

When we now replace the adjunct with an indirect object, as in (23), we have a sentence of the kind recorded in Truckenbrodt (2005). The verb was stressless there, which seems to be a natural rendition, and which comes with a preference for the absence of a medial i-boundary as shown. In the experimental results in Truckenbrodt (2005), there was likewise no medial i-boundary.

(23)   [Der <u>Werner</u> hat dem <u>Maler</u>   gesagt, dass er der
      DET   Werner has the   painter said   that he DET
      <u>Lola</u> das <u>Weben</u> zeigen will]$_I$
      Lola the weaving show wants
      'Werner has said to the painter that he wants to show Lola weaving.'
          [<u>SU</u> <u>IO</u> V <u>CP</u>] > [<u>SU</u> <u>IO</u> V][<u>CP</u>]

If we go by these judgments, the different experimental results of Truckenbrodt (2005) as in (23) and of the present experiment as in (22) would seem to be real differences in preferred phrasings, rather than differences that would stem from different experimental conditions or speaker-specific preferences.

   A possibility to address in the comparison between (22) and (23) is that the number of beats of phrasal stress could be the cause of their difference. With an additional beat of phrasal stress on the verb in (22), the prosodically longer structure might be more likely to fall apart into two intonation phrases than (23). However, prosodically longer versions of sentences like (23) were also among the stimuli in Truckenbrodt (2005), as shown in (17), and these also consistently showed the entire utterance in a single intonation phrase. Inversely, the intuitive preference shown in (22) persists when (22) is prosodically shortened (by pronominalizing the subject and having it given in the context, or by omitting the adjunct). Thus, prosodic length does not seem to be the decisive difference between the two cases.

Our impression, then, is that there is an 'integrated' pattern as in (21) and (23) that involves a stressless verb, i.e. stress reconstruction of extraposition, and that also involves the absence of a medial i-boundary. This seems to contrast with a 'non-integrated pattern' as in (22), which involves the absence of stress reconstruction and the presence of a medial i-boundary.

We think it is not impossible that these two patterns correspond to two different landing sites of extraposition, as schematically shown in (24).

(24)   a. adjunction to matrix CP   b. extraposition within matrix CP
     (non-integrated)   (integrated)

[x]$_I$ [x]$_I$ [x]$_I$
[[matrix cl.]$_{CP}$ [object cl.]]$_{CP}$ [matrix cl. [object cl.]]$_{CP}$
stress reconstruction blocked   stress reconstruction not blocked

If the extraposing object clause adjoins all the way at the top to the matrix clause CP, as in (24a), we would expect separate intonation phrasing because the object clause would, for the purpose of phrasing, follow the matrix clause (see Truckenbrodt (1999) for the role of adjunction; Truckenbrodt (2005) for constraints that would have that effect). The right edge of the matrix clause would introduce an i-boundary, preceding the object clause. Stress reconstruction of the object clause would be blocked by the intonation-phrase status of the object clause. If, on the other hand, the extraposing object clause adjoins any lower as in (24b), it would be contained in the matrix clause for the purpose of phrasing. It would then plausibly be phrased with the object clause. Stress reconstruction would not be blocked by a medial i-boundary and would then apply, leading to a stressless verb. Some support for this hypothesis can be seen in (25). When a negative quantifier in matrix subject position binds a pronoun in the object clause, the preference for separate phrasing seems to go away, even if a stressed verb is chosen. In this case, adjunction to the matrix clause CP would destroy the c-command relation between the quantifier and the pronoun. Choice of a lower adjunction site would allow the c-command relation, and lead to the integrated intonation phrasing.

(25)   [Niemand$_7$ hat auf dem <u>Treffen</u> <u>gesagt</u>, dass er$_7$
       Nobody   has at   the meeting said   that he
       der <u>Lola</u> das <u>Weben</u> zeigen will]$_1$
       DET Lola the weaving show wants

     'Nobody$_7$ has said at the meeting that he$_7$ wants to show Lola weaving.'
     [SU <u>ADJ</u> <u>V</u> <u>CP</u>] > [SU <u>ADJ</u> <u>V</u>][<u>CP</u>]

The comparison of the experimental results of Truckenbrodt (2005) (see (23)/(24b)) and our current results (see (22)/(24a)) still suggests a surprising difference in preference. Why would the integrating pattern be preferred when an indirect object precedes the verb, as in (23), but the non-integrating pattern when an adjunct precedes the verb, as in (22)? It is tempting to relate this to an independent prosodic difference between indirect object and adjunct. The adjunct, as was seen in (3), is normally followed by a stressed verb. An indirect object, on the other hand, at least optionally exempts a following verb from being stressed:

(26)   What happened with the book?
    a.   <u>Peter</u> hat es einem <u>Kind</u> geliehen. Or:
    b.   <u>Peter</u> hat es einem <u>Kind</u> <u>geliehen</u>.
       Peter has it a-DAT child lent

    'Peter has lent it to a child.'

To connect this to the difference between integrated and non-integrated intonation phrasing, we need to introduce a property of stress reconstruction we have not yet addressed: stress reconstruction of an element with phrasal stress must not cross another element with phrasal stress! Consider (27), an example from Bresnan (1971). In our terms, stress reconstruction of the wh-phrase into the VP satisfies Stress-XP and thereby allows the verb to remain stressless. Gussenhoven (1992: 82, 84) noted that this effect is observed only when the embedded subject *Helen* is contextually given, and correspondingly unaccented (and the remainder of the sentence new). If the embedded subject carries its expected phrasal stress (here: due to Stress-XP), only the stress pattern in (27b) is possible. Here the verb is stressed. Stress reconstruction of the wh-phrase seems to be blocked across an intervening element with phrasal stress, here *Helen*.

(27)   a.   John asked [what <u>books</u> Helen had written __]
    b.   John asked [what <u>books</u> <u>Helen</u> had <u>written</u> __]

Here then, is how the difference between a preverbal adjunct vs. preverbal indirect object might lead to different preferences in intonation phrasing. If stress reconstruction of extraposition is possible, it may still be hard to process, because it needs to be anticipated: the element to be reconstructed follows the verb. This is different from leftward movement, where the element to be reconstructed is encountered before the reconstruction site and before the verb in the VP. If stress reconstruction of extraposition is hard to anticipate, speakers pronouncing the sequence [. . . adjunct __$_i$ V CP$_i$] may prefer to stress the verb because of the difficulty of anticipating stress reconstruction. However, given that choice, i.e. given a stressed verb, stress reconstruction of the CP across the verb is blocked! It is blocked in parallel to (27b): stress reconstruction of phrasal stress may not cross another phrasal stress. If stress reconstruction is the incentive for low extraposition and for choice of the integrated pattern (24b), this incentive will have gone away with a stressed verb. If there is a weaker incentive for high extraposition, this will then be chosen instead.[8]

On the other hand, in the sequence [. . . indirect object __$_i$ V CP$_i$], the indirect object licenses a stressless verb regardless of stress reconstruction. The assumed problem of anticipating stress reconstruction will here not bias towards stressing the verb. If the incentive for low extraposition is stress reconstruction, this choice can still be made and stress can be reconstructed (though without an effect on the verb).

Thus, if an adjunct before a verb biases towards a stressed verb, and an indirect object before the verb biases towards an unstressed verb, stress reconstruction will be blocked in the first case but not in the second case. If the option of stress reconstruction guides preferences in adjunction sites and thereby intonation phrasing, this may be the cause of the difference found in the two experiments.

10.6 Summary

The presentation of our experiment and the discussion of its results gave us opportunities to discuss the interaction of movement and stress. We employed an account in which the SAAR of Gussenhoven (1983b) is analyzed in terms of Stress-XP plus the possibility of stress reconstruction. Stress-XP is from Truckenbrodt (1995), for the interaction of movement with stress we

---

[8] In the account of Truckenbrodt (2005), this incentive could be satisfaction of the otherwise suppressed constraint Align-CP,Left in position of adjunction to CP.

draw on Bresnan (1971). We argued that German movement of the finite verb to C and movement of the subject to SPEC,CP reconstruct for stress, while German scrambling does not reconstruct for stress. We also reviewed that stressed elements intervene in stress reconstruction.

Our experiment sought to determine whether extraposition of an object clause reconstructs for stress. The experiment led us to discover and document the prosodic pattern in (28) in German. The perception part of the experiment shows the stress on the matrix verb. The analysis of the productions brings out the unexpected medial i-boundary. The pattern is found for object clauses that are *dass*-clauses ('that'-clauses) as well as for object clauses that are V2 clauses. It is compared to two control conditions in our experiment.

(28)   [x][x   ]$_I$
        [Subject ... Adverb V [object clause]]

While extraposition did not reconstruct for stress in our material, the experimental results do not allow us to conclude that extraposition generally does not reconstruct. It seems possible that it does not reconstruct for stress in the presence of an i-boundary that separates the extraposed material.

In the more tentative part of our discussion, we also drew on intuitive judgments and compared the results to those of Truckenbrodt (2005). This somewhat larger (but more uncertain) picture was seen to suggest that extraposition does indeed reconstruct in the absence of a medial i-boundary. An integrated prosodic pattern (no i-boundary, stress reconstruction) and a non-integrated pattern (i-boundary, no stress reconstruction) may go back to different syntactic extraposition sites. We suggested that the preferences for a non-integrated pattern in our experiment may relate to a difficulty in anticipating stress reconstruction.

Appendix

Condition O: verb preceded by stressed object

01
Gestern ist mir Folgendes zu Ohren gekommen.
Die Maria soll eine Verleumdung glauben, auch wenn sie sie in der Boulevard-Presse gelesen hat.
02
Vor kurzem hab ich Folgendes mitgekriegt.
Die Lola soll wirres Zeug träumen, auch wenn sie schon Medikamente dagegen nimmt.

03
Ich habe vorhin Folgendes gehört.
Die Jana wird einen Unfall melden, auch wenn sie das sehr ungerne tut.

04
Stell dir das mal vor.
Der Leon hat eine Verschwörung angenommen, auch wenn er sich die Ereignisse anders erklären konnte.

05
Gestern hab ich Folgendes mitgekriegt.
Die Lola soll einen Mord vermuten, auch wenn das sehr unwahrscheinlich ist.

06
Heute morgen habe ich Folgendes gehört.
Der Mörder soll Zaubersprüche murmeln, auch wenn er sich damit nur lächerlich macht.

07
Letzte Woche hab ich Folgendes gehört.
Der Manager will eine neue Strategie darlegen, auch wenn er daran nicht so richtig glaubt.

08
Gestern hab ich Folgendes gehört.
Der Jonas soll Dummheiten sagen, auch wenn er damit nur Spott erntet.

Condition A: verb preceded by adjunct

a1
Der Werner heiratet die Manu.
Die Maria soll das seit Juli glauben, auch wenn er nichts davon gesagt hat.

a2
Die Lara organisiert die Gala.
Die Lola soll davon seit langem träumen, auch wenn es dafür wenig Anhaltspunkte gab.

a3
Der Jan hat eine Wohnung verwüstet.
Die Jana wird das auf der Versammlung melden, auch wenn sie das gar nicht gerne tut.

a4
Der Jonas wird nörgeln.
Der Leon hat das seit einer Weile angenommen, auch wenn er ihn noch nicht gut kennt.

a5
Die Maria gewinnt eine Reise.
Die Lola soll das in der Sendung vermuten, auch wenn sie sonst nicht so leichtgläubig ist.

a6
Die Heldin wird bald umkommen.

Der Mörder soll das in seiner Laube murmeln, auch wenn die Zuschauer das nicht hören können.

a7

Der Millionär soll die Firma verwalten.

Der Manager will das auf der Versammlung darlegen, auch wenn er sich damit viele Feinde macht.

a8

Der Leon hört laute Musik.

Der Jonas soll das seit dem Sommer sagen, auch wenn keiner ihm wirklich glaubt.

Condition D: verb followed by 'dass' object clause

d1

Gestern ist mir Folgendes zu Ohren gekommen.

Die Maria soll seit Juli glauben, dass der Werner die Manu heiratet.

d2

Vor kurzem hab ich Folgendes mitgekriegt.

Die Lola soll seit langem träumen, dass die Lara die Gala organisiert.

d3

Ich habe vorhin Folgendes gehört.

Die Jana wird auf der Versammlung melden, dass der Jan eine Wohnung verwüstet hat.

d4

Stell dir das mal vor.

Der Leon hat seit einer Weile angenommen, dass der Jonas nörgeln wird.

d5

Gestern hab ich Folgendes mitgekriegt.

Die Lola soll in der Sendung vermuten, dass die Maria eine Reise gewinnt.

d6

Heute morgen habe ich Folgendes gehört.

Der Mörder soll in seiner Laube murmeln, dass die Heldin bald umkommen wird.

d7

Letzte Woche hab ich Folgendes gehört.

Der Manager will auf der Versammlung darlegen, dass der Millionär die Firma verwalten soll.

d8

Gestern hab ich Folgendes gehört.

Der Jonas soll seit dem Sommer sagen, dass der Leon laute Musik hört.

Condition V: verb followed by V2 object clause

v1

Gestern ist mir Folgendes zu Ohren gekommen.

Die Maria soll seit Juli glauben, der Werner heiratet die Manu.

v2

Vor kurzem hab ich Folgendes mitgekriegt.

Die Lola soll seit langem träumen, die Lara organisiert die Gala.

v3

Ich habe vorhin Folgendes gehört.

Die Jana wird auf der Versammlung melden, der Jan hat eine Wohnung verwüstet.

v4

Stell dir das mal vor.

Der Leon hat seit einer Weile angenommen, der Jonas wird nörgeln.

v5

Gestern hab ich Folgendes mitgekriegt.

Die Lola soll in der Sendung vermuten, die Maria gewinnt eine Reise.

v6

Heute morgen habe ich Folgendes gehört.

Der Mörder soll in seiner Laube murmeln, die Heldin wird bald umkommen.

v7

Letzte Woche hab ich Folgendes gehört.

Der Manager will auf der Versammlung darlegen, der Millionär soll die Firma verwalten.

v8

Gestern hab ich Folgendes gehört.

Der Jonas soll seit dem Sommer sagen, der Leon hört laute Musik.

11

Optimality Theory and the theory of phonological phrasing: The Chimwiini evidence

CHARLES W. KISSEBERTH

11.1 Introduction

An important source of data on the interface of phonology and other aspects of linguistic structure (morphology, syntax, focus) is the Bantu language Chimwiini. This language is closely related to Swahili and has been spoken in the southern Somali town of Brava (=Mwiini) for several centuries. The historical evidence indicates that Swahili-like language forms were spoken as far north as Mogadisho in historical times, but the speakers in Brava were the only ones on the mainland to maintain their language in the course of the Somali expansion. Unfortunately, being a cultural and linguistic minority in Somalia, the people of Brava were targets during the Somali civil war in the 1990s and large numbers of speakers fled Brava and eventually formed diaspora communities in Kenya and Great Britain and the United States, though many remain in refugee camps in Kenya and there are still speakers remaining in Brava.

In 1974, Mohammad Abasheikh (a native speaker of Chimwiini who was doing a Ph.D. in linguistics at the University of Illinois at the time) and I presented a short account of various phonological phenomena in Chimwiini based on data we had collected in the preceding year (Kisseberth and Abasheikh, 1974, henceforth K&A). In this paper, we argued that vowel-length alternations in the language could only be understood on the assumption that the sentences of this language are organized into (phonological) phrases. This paper presented a laundry list of the situations under which long vowels had to shorten, but it clearly established that the domain in terms of which these rules of shortening apply is larger than the word but not necessarily as large as the clause or sentence. While successful in establishing this fact, the paper offered no theory of how the phonological phrases of the language were constructed. Despite this, it served to provide the stimulus for much further work in the area of the phonology–syntax interface and as such, achieved its basic goal.

In this paper we will review in section 11.2 the original problem (the alternation of long and short vowels) that led to the conclusion that it is necessary to organize sentences into a sequence of phonological phrases in order to explain these alternations. We will also review the solutions that have been proposed to account for the precise principles that determine the alternation of length as well as the prevailing theory as to how the phonological phrases are derived (the so-called 'indirect reference' model of Selkirk 1986). In section 11.3, we will argue that an independent phenomenon, pitch accent, also operates in exactly the same phrases. This new evidence about phrasing turns out to be even more robust than the vowel-length alternations in identifying phrases. In section 11.4, we demonstrate that the essential claim of the Selkirkian approach to the phonology–syntax interface—namely, that a phonological phrase is not itself a syntactic phrase—is abundantly supported by the facts of Chimwiini phrasing.

Section 11.5 highlights the manner in which the Optimality Theoretic point of view contrasts with the original derivational point of view of Selkirk (1986), and we then examine the ways in which Selkirk's original Align-XP Right principle is inadequate to a full account of phrasing in Chimwiini. Specifically, section 11.6 establishes the role of negative verbal forms, section 11.7 establishes the relevance of definiteness, section 11.8 demonstrates the importance of focus/emphasis.

Next, in section 11.9, we explore a question that has arisen in the literature: could Chimwiini provide evidence for a constraint known as Wrap-XP as well as Align-XP R? We argue that accentual facts are suggestive that this might be the case. And finally in section 11.10 we address the issue of the proper formulation of another constraint that has been proposed in the literature—namely, Align-Focus Right. Once again the accentual system of Chimwiini is critical to the resolution of this issue. Section 11.11 summarizes the results of this study.

11.2 Vowel length alternations in Chimwiini

Vowel length is contrastive in Chimwiini, as shown by the following examples. Long vowels are written with double vowels. The acute mark indicates 'accent', discussed below.

(1) [x-kúla] 'to grow'   [x-kúula] 'to extract'
     [sómo] 'namesake'   [sóomu] 'fasting'
     [x-téka] 'to fetch'   [x-téeka] 'to load an animal'
     [m-zígo] 'load'   [ku-zíika] 'to bury'

     [x-fanída] 'to pick better specimen'   [x-faanána] 'to resemble s.o.'
     [ku-baláma] 'to promise'   [ku-baaráma] 'to talk'
     [x-peléka] 'to send'   [x-peeléka] 'to be capable of
                                                being swept'

However, while vowel length is contrastive in Chimwiini and must be specified in underlying representations, vowel length is observable only in penult
or antepenult position in the word, but not both positions at the same time
(except in a few mostly Arabic loanwords).

(2) penult long: [x-shíinda] 'to defeat', [x-sóoma] 'to read', [ku-bóola]
     'to steal', [máashe] 'blind'
     antepenult long: [ku-miimína] 'to pour', [x-taambúla] 'to under-
     stand', [ku-liingána] 'to be equal'

     both penult and antepenult long: absent in native words, absent
     under morpheme concatenation,
     found only in loanwords: [taawúusi] 'peacock', [faanúusi] 'lamp',
     [faalúuta] 'a kind of gruel'

From the above observations it follows that long vowels are not found in
word-final position (we are speaking here only of words in isolation) and are
not found in any syllable that precedes the antepenult.

   When one examines morphologically complex words, long vowels are
freely distributed in underlying representation except there is no evidence
for word-final long vowels (since there is no evidence for stem-final long
vowels that contrast with short vowels). When an underlying long vowel
appears in a pre-antepenult syllable, it must be pronounced short.

(3) [mw-aalímu] 'teacher'   [mw-alimú=w-e] 'his/her teacher'
     [ku-waafíqa] 'to agree'   [ku-wafiqána] 'to agree with one another'
     [xaatíma] 'the end'   [xatimá=ye] 'its end'
     [joohári] 'jewel'   [joharí=ye] 'her jewel'
     [ku-leeléza] 'to loosen'   [ku-lelezéka] 'to be capable of being
                                      loosened'

     [x-sóoma] 'to read', [x-soomésha] 'to teach', BUT: [x-somesheléza]
     'to teach for'

[ku-réeba] 'to stop', [ku-reebéla] 'to stop for', BUT: [ku-rebelána] 'to stop for one another'

When an underlying long vowel appears in an antepenult syllable, it must be pronounced short only if the penult syllable is long. For example, in (4a) we see examples where a long vowel in a verb stem is shortened in front of the perfect ending /iil-e/:

(4a)   [x-súula] 'to want'   [suḷíile] '(s)he wanted'
       [x-sóoma] 'to read'   [soméele] '(s)he read'
       [ku-réeba] 'to stop, forbid' [rebéele] '(s)he stopped'
       [ku-masrúufa] 'to provide   [masrufiile] '(s)he provided'
          with food and other needs'

In (4b) we see a stem long vowel shortening in front of the passive suffix /oow/.

(4b)   [x-sóoma] 'to read'   [x-somóowa] 'to be read'
       [x-péenda] 'to love'   [x-pendóowa] 'to be loved'
       [x-shíika] 'to seize' [x-shikóowa] 'to be seized'

Up until this point we have focused on showing that long vowels shorten in specific environments. While these long vowels may be lexically long vowels, they also include vowels that are derived by phonological principles. There are a number of phonological contexts at the word level which derive long vowels. In each case, wherever one would expect a long vowel by virtue of one of these contexts, the vowel will not be long if it is (a) pre-antepenult or (b) pre-length. We have space only for a few examples to illustrate this point. In (5) we illustrate cases where sequences of vowels across morphemes lead (potentially) to long vowels either through coalescence or glide formation and compensatory lengthening.

(5)   ku + V yields: k-VV
       /ku + ala/: [k-áala] 'to plant'   /ku + iwa/: [k-íiwa] 'to know'
       /ku + uza/: [k-úuza] 'to sell'   /ku + iza/: [k-íiza] 'to refuse'
       /ku + uluka/: [k-uulúka] 'to fly'   /ku-eleza/: [k-eeléza] 'to explain'
       /ku + oloka/: [k-oolóka] 'to go'   /ku + epuka/: [k-eepúka] 'to avoid'
       but:
       /ku + uzoowa/: [k-uzóowa]   /ku + elezeka/: [k-elezéka]
       'to be sold'   'able to be explained'
       /ku + ash + iliz + a/: [k-ashilíza] /ku + uluka'uluka/: [k-uluka'ulúka]
       'to light for'   'to bounce'

si + V yields: s-VV

/si + eleze/: [s-eelezé]   /si + oloke/: [s-ooloké] 'don't go!'
'don't explain!'

/si + anike/: [s-aaniké]   /si + owe/: [s-oowé] 'don't bathe!'
'don't spread out!'

but:

/si + iz + oow + e/: [s-izoowé]   /si + oloke=:ni/:[s-olokée=ni]
'don't be refused/denied!'   'pl. don't go!'

In rule-ordering terms: all rules creating long vowels are ordered before rules defining where vowels must be short. In a constraint-based model, constraints on the distribution of long vowels are more highly ranked than constraints whose satisfaction will require long vowels.

In K&A (1974), vowel shortening in Chimwiini was analyzed in terms of a rule that shortened vowels in what amounts to a 'laundry list' of environments: in pre-antepenult position, in position before another long vowel, in word-final position. A much more insightful analysis of these alternations appeared in independent work by Bruce Hayes (1985) and Lisa Selkirk (1986). In essence, they noticed that if we assume (a) Chimwiini has the Latin stress rule, then (b) vowels can simply be said to shorten in unstressed position. The Latin Stress Rule says that stress falls on the penult, if the penult is long; otherwise stress falls on the antepenult (regardless of its length). Words that have just two syllables exhibit stress on the penult. It should be pointed out immediately, however, that there is no consistent phonetic correlate for the syllables that Hayes/Selkirk regard as 'stressed': it is an abstract stress. More on this point below.

The analysis works as illustrated in (6). The 'stressed' syllable is in caps. (We omit the indication of the location of accent in order to focus on the issue of abstract stress.)

(6)   [x-pIka] 'to cook'
      (there is no antepenult syllable, so stress falls on the penult, even though this syllable is short)

      [x-pIkisha] 'to cause to cook'
      (antepenult syllable 'stressed' since the penult is short; no underlying or derived long vowels)

      [x-sOOma] 'to read'
      (penult is 'stressed' since it is long in the UR, and since it is stressed it does not shorten)

      [x-sOOmesha] 'to teach'

(penult is short, so antepenult is 'stressed', and as a result the long vowel in the UR remains)

[x-someshEleza] 'to teach for'

(the penult is short, so the antepenult is 'stressed'; the long vowel in the root must shorten since it is in unstressed position)

[x-somOOwa] 'to be read'

(the penult has an underlying long vowel and thus is 'stressed'; the antepenult long vowel in the root must shorten since it is in unstressed position)

This analysis does not claim that the so-called 'stressed syllable' in Chimwiini has any particular phonetic characteristic. Hayes and Selkirk could not make such a claim since the primary source of their data (K&A) makes no reference to any such property. That source does mention the existence of an 'accentual' contrast in the language, but the relatively vague remarks made about this phenomenon were, not surprisingly, passed over by Hayes/Selkirk. We return later to this accentual system.

Why do we say that the 'stressed' syllable has no particular phonetic attribute? First of all, as we will show below, high pitch is the essential attribute of the accented syllable in Chimwiini, but 'stressed' syllables will sometimes bear high pitch and sometimes not, unstressed syllables will sometimes bear high pitch and sometimes not. High pitch is totally independent from 'stress'. The phonetic property that is much more linked to stress is vowel length. As we have said, only stressed vowels may be long. Still, not all stressed vowels are long. Thus vowel length is only possible under stress, but not a necessary property of a stressed syllable.

We are now in a position to turn to the crux of the problem regarding vowel-length alternations in Chimwiini. Specifically, the constraint on vowel length operates in a domain that is often larger than a word but usually smaller than a sentence. However, in order to properly evaluate the pronunciation of sentences, it is necessary to discuss a phenomenon that was not observed at the word level and is extremely significant for the interpretation of sentential pronunciation. A study of larger units reveals that while at the word level all final vowels are short, long final vowels do occur in medial position in a sentence.

The syllable structure of Chimwiini is such that every word ends in a vowel. Furthermore, as mentioned earlier, there is no evidence that would lead one to postulate a contrast between long and short vowels at the end of a word. Since in isolation every word ends in a short vowel, it is natural to assume that only short vowels occur underlyingly in word-final position. However, any word in the language *may* occur with a final long vowel at the sentence level. Examples:

(7) nominal word lengthened

[n-thí] 'land', [n-khávu] 'dry'   [n-thii n-khávu] 'dry land'

[múu-nthu] 'person', [mú-le] 'tall'   [mu-nthuu mú-le] 'tall person'

verbal word lengthened

[fíile] '[cl.1] died', [n-dála]   [filee n-dála] '[cl.1] died from
'hunger'   hunger'

[hu-péenda] '[cl.1] likes', [má-zu]   [hu-pendaa má-zu] '[cl.1] likes
'bananas'   bananas'

[x-sóoma] 'to read', [chúwo] 'book'   [x-somaa chúwo] 'to read a book'

[k-áasha] 'to light', n-thá 'candle'   [k-ashaa n-thá] 'to light a fire'

adjectival word lengthened

[mú-le] 'tall', [nthó] 'very'   [mu-lee nthó] 'very tall'

[n-khávu] 'dry', [nthó] 'very'   [n-khavuu nthó] 'very dry'

preposition lengthened

[káma] 'like'   [kamaa m-pháka] 'like a cat'

[ná] 'by'   [naa nóka] 'by a snake'

[kólko] 'than'   [kolkoo mí] 'than me'

particle

[ní] 'is'   [nii lúti] '(it) is a stick'

(Notice that whenever a word occurs with a final long vowel, it is never accented. The reason for this will emerge as we proceed.)

In a context where data tells us a word may end in a long vowel (e.g. the structures illustrated above), it will not in fact end in a long vowel if it is followed by a word that has three or more syllables or if it is followed by a word with a long syllable! In other words, the same restrictions on vowel length that we observed inside words also control the surfacing of a word-final long vowel. This immediately demonstrates that the constraint on long vowels works at the phrasal level.

(8) /ni/ 'is' can be lengthened:[nii mú-le] 'is tall'
but:
[ni chi-góbe] 'is short'—where /ni/ is followed by three syllables
[ni mu-lee nthó] 'is very tall'—where /ni/ is followed by three syllables, including one that is long
[ni súura] 'it is good, nice'—where /ni/ is followed by a penult long vowel

the final vowel of a verb can be long in front of a complement: [x-somaa ch-úwo] 'to read a book'

but:

[x-suka mi-sála] 'to plait, weave mats'—where the final vowel is followed by three syllables

[ku-na kaháwa] 'to drink coffee'—where the final vowel is followed by three syllables

[ku-biga bóoli] 'to rob'—where the final vowel is followed by a penult long syllable

the final vowel of a noun can be long in front of a modifier: [mu-nthuu mú-le] 'tall person'

but:

[chi-nthu chi-wóvu] 'something bad'—where final vowel is followed by three syllables

[chi-su chi-hábba] 'small knife'—where final vowel is followed by three syllables

[chi-buku ch-éepe] 'some/any book'—where final vowel is followed by a penult long vowel

We should note that there are some additional environments that are barriers to length on a final vowel: one cannot have a long vowel before a vowel, one cannot have a long vowel in a closed syllable, one cannot have a long vowel if the following syllable is closed. These additional complications may arise in examples later, but they do not contribute significantly to the discussion and will be ignored. Example: [mw-ana úyu] 'this child' (not *[mw-anaa uyu]); [ku-biga l̲-kópe] 'to blink' (not *[ku-bigaa l̲-kópe]), [ku-biga jársi] 'to ring a bell' (not *[ku-bigaa jársi]).

From the data above we can conclude that a word-final vowel lengthens just in case it is in a position where it can be 'stressed' (i.e. where the long vowel would be able to receive the stress by virtue of being in penult position or antepenult position followed by a short penult). We believe that the ultimate explanation for this word-final lengthening is that it occurs in response to the Optimality Theoretic constraint that a stressed vowel should be long, but a detailed discussion of this point is not relevant to the present paper. For our purposes, it is sufficient to note that in all cases where a word-final vowel is long, the next word either is CV or CVCV.

The confusing thing is, however, that a word-final vowel is not long before every following CV or CVCV word. For instance, it is not long in the examples below. (The slashes in the representation will be explained later.)

(9)   [Núuru/ tovelele m-túzi/ zí-jo] 'Nuru/ dipped in the sauce/ *zi-jo*'
       (*[Nuuru/ tovelele m-tuzii zí-jo])
       [mw-aalímu/ wa-somelele w-áana// chúwo] 'the teacher/ read to the
       children/ a book' (*[mw-aalímu/   wa-somelele w-anaa chúwo]
       [mw-áana/ jile róoti] 'the child/ ate the bread' (*[mw-anaa jile róoti])
       [m-phúunda/ chí-la] 'the donkey/ brayed'   (*[m-phundaa chí-la])

This superficially confusing variation between whether a word-final will
lengthen or not is mirrored in a similarly superficially confusing variation
between whether a word-internal long vowel will shorten when it appears
inside a sentence. Sometimes a long vowel that would be present in a word
when pronounced in isolation is retained when the word is inside a sentence,
but in other cases it is not.

(10)   cases where a word-internal long vowel shortens:
       [mw-ana úyu/ jilee náma] 'this child/ ate meat' (cf. [mw-áana] 'child',
       [jíile] '(s)he ate')
       [mw-na olosheló] 'the child who came' (cf. [mw-áana] 'child')

       cases where a word-internal long vowel fails to shorten:
       [m-somelele mw-áana/ chi-búuku] '(s)he read to the child/ a book'
       [mw-áana/ jiile] 'the child/ ate'
       [mw-áana/ ni-m-someléele] 'the child/ I read to him/her'

K&A suggest that the confusing data concerning word-final vowel alternation
and the confusing data concerning word-internal long vowel alternation can
be understood if (a) Chimwiini words in a sentence are grouped into phrases
and (b) the vowel-shortening principle operates inside a phrase but not across
phrases. (If we accept the Hayes/Selkirkian reinterpretation of length being
determined by the 'stressed'/'unstressed' contrast, then it is stress that would
operate inside a phrase and not across phrases.)

We can now rephrase the generalizations. If the final vowel of a word is
medial in a phrase, then it will be long if by being long it will receive 'stress'. If
it is final in the phrase, it cannot be long (since it is necessarily 'unstressed' in
that position). Furthermore, if a word in isolation has a long vowel, that
length surfaces when the word is final in a phrase. If another word follows,
then that long vowel will not be in 'stressed' position and will shorten. In the
examples above and subsequently, a slash will signal the end of a phrase.

If we accept the K&A argument about the determination of vowel length in
Chimwiini, then the central issue confronting the linguist is this: how are
phrases constructed? It is here that Selkirk (1986) provided a central insight.
In that paper, Selkirk argued that a phonological phrase in Chimwiini is

constructed by assigning a right phrase edge at the right edge of a (lexical) maximal projection. Although she cast this principle originally in a derivational model, we will refer to it as Align-XP R. Selkirk assumed that the phrasing of any sentence is exhaustive and that everything to the left of a right phrase edge up to a preceding right phrase edge (or up to the beginning of the sentence) is part of the phrase. The core claim of this characterization of the procedure for constructing phrases is that a phonological phrase is not itself necessarily a syntactic phrase but rather just the material that occurs between the right edge of one maximal projection and the right edge of the preceding maximal projection. The Chimwiini evidence available to Selkirk was not sufficient to support this basic claim in any totally convincing way, but we shall demonstrate its validity with abundant new data.

The Align-XPR principle proposed by Selkirk explains a great deal about the phrasing that is necessary in Chimwiini to explain the vowel-length alternations that can be observed. (11a) shows that a subject NP must be prosodically separated from its following verb phrase.

(11a)   subject noun phrase in a main clause
[mw-áana/ nii mú-le] 'the child/ is tall' (not: *[mw-ana nii mú-le], with one phrase)
[mw-áana/ mú-le] 'ibid., with deletion of the copular)
(not: *[mw-anaa mú-le], with one phrase)
(cf. [mw-anaa mú-le] 'a tall child')
[ch-áayi/ chi-leeséla] 'tea was brought'
[m-phúunda/ chí-la] 'the donkey brayed'
[niyaa n-jéema/ hu-tabíibu/ niyaa m-bóvu/ hu-xariba] 'intention good/ cures/ intention bad/ spoils'
[waawá=y-e/ chi-mw-aambíla] 'his father/ told him'

subject noun phrase in a non-finite clause
[Jáama/ tulubile Núuru/ k-oolóka 'Jaama/ asked for Nuuru/ to go'
(Note: In this example it is apparent that Nuuru is the subject of the infinitive phrase and not the object of the higher verb; if it were the object of the higher verb, then that verb would have to bear the object prefix *m* in agreement.)

[si-na-x-súula/ w-áana/ ku-barshowa adabdára] 'I do not want/ the children/ to be taught bad manners'
subject noun phrase in a complement clause
[mí/ k-éenda/ i-tulubila na Jáama] '(for) me/ to go/ was asked [wanted] by Jaama'

In (11b) we see that the first complement in a VP is separated prosodically from the second complement:

(11b)   [Núuru/ faramilile gáari/ chi-bumbu sh-píya] 'Nuuru/ ordered for the car/ a new horn'
    (Note: *Nuuru, gaari* keep their length, but *faramiliile, chi-buumbu* lose their length.)
    [mí/ n-thinzilee namá/ kaa chi-sú] 'I/ cut the meat/ with a knife'
    [m-somelele mw-áana/ ch-úwo] '(s)he read to the child/ a book'
    [chi-latiza ruuhú=y-e/ ilu y-aa chí-li] '(s)he threw self/ on the bed'
    [maliizo=pó/ sultani w-aa nóka/ chi-m-uza Hasíibu/ xabarí=z-e]
    'when he finished/ the king of the snakes./ asked Hasiibu/ his news'
    [m-phelee dáwa/ x-poléla] 'he gave me medicine/ to help (me) recover'
    [m-pholeze cháayi/ ka chi-jámu] 'he cooled down the tea/ with a saucer'
    [wa-m-pokeze m-géeni/ mi-zigó=y-e] 'they gave to the guest/ his luggage'
    [m-lungishize fúundi/ jaházi] 'he had a skilled worker build/ a boat'
    [Jáama/ tulubilee mí/ k-éenda] 'Jaama/ asked me/ to go'
    [shtuluba ka Yuusúfu/ ku-m-tafsirila n-dootó=z-e] 'he asked Joseph/ to explain to him his dreams'

    [(mí)/ n-somelela chi-buukú/ na Nuurú] 'I/ was read a book/ by Nuuru'
    [Hamádi/ mw-andikilile mw-áana/ xáti/ ka Núuru] 'Hamadi wrote for the child/ a letter/ to Nuuru'
    [m-pelekelele Áasha/ xáti/ postáani] '[cl.1] took for Aasha/ a letter/ to the post office'
    [fanya kooðí=z-o/ muxtasári] 'make your speech/ short'

The data in (11c) illustrate that non-subject XPs in preverbal position are prosodically separated from a following subject as well as one another:

(11c)   [báaba/ marádhi/ ya-chi-m-zíida/ chí-fa] 'father grew sicker and died—lit. father/ sickness/ increased with respect to him/ he died'
    [sku móoyi/ Hasíibu/ chi-m-uza maamá=y-e] 'one day/ Hasiibu/ asked his mother'
    [l-fuungúlo/ m-fungulile mw-aalímu/ m-láango] 'the key/ [cl.1] opened for the teacher/ the door (with it)'
    [l-kóombe/ mú-ke/ m-pakulile mw-áana/ zíjo] 'the spoon/ the woman/ dished out (with it) for the child/ *zijo*'
    [w-áana/ mú-ke/ wa-fulilee n-gúwo/ ka saabúni] 'the children/ the woman/ washed clothes (for them)/ with soap'
    [numbáa=ni/ i-waliko sandúuxu/ naa mí/ ni-'i-fungiilé] 'inside the house/ was a box/ and I/ I opened it'

[ináa=y-a/ ni Buluxíya/ na waawé/ waliko sul̲táani/ l̲akíini/ ísa/
file] 'my name/ is Buluxiya/ and my father/ was sultan/ but/ now/
he is dead'
[téena/ sku móoyi/ má-sku/ m-kulá=z-e/ wa-chi-weka majl̲ísi/
wa-chi-há̲da . . .] 'then/ one day/ at night/ his elder brothers/ held
a meeting/ (and) they said . . .
[Abú/ sh-kóopa/ chi-m-gafíile] 'Abu/ alcoholic drink/ missed (getting)'
(alternative: Abú/ gafile sh-kóopa 'Abu/ missed getting an
alcoholic drink')
[l̲-kóombe/ mú-ke/ m-pakul̲il̲e mw-áana/ zíjo] 'the spoon/ the
woman/ dished out (with it) for the child/ *zijo*'

On the assumption that the only phrases are those constructed by Align-XP R,
then it follows that there will not be phrasal separation between two elements
inside a minimal maximal projection (i.e. a maximal projection not itself
containing a maximal projection). This is very often true, as shown in the
examples below.

(12) shows instances where there is no phrasal break between a verb and a
following verb-phrase element. In each example, we see a verb or deverbal
noun that would have a long vowel in its isolation form, but lacks this long
vowel when followed by a complement.

(12)   verb followed by an argument
        [ni-sh-fungile chi-san̲duuxú/ na n-dani y-a chi-san̲duxu ichí/ chi-wali=
        moo ch-úwo] 'I opened the box/ and inside of box this/ was a book'
        (cf. [ni-sh-fungiilé] 'I opened it')
        [fanya koodhí=z-o/ muxt̲asári] 'make your speech/ short'
        (cf. [fá̲anya] 'make! do!')

        verb followed by a prepositional phrase
        [ch-oloka ka jiraani=y-e] 'he went to his neighbors' (cf. [ch-oolóka]
        'he went')
        [wáa-nthu/ wa-lungamene ka kul̲a chíi-nthu] 'people/ are united in
        each thing' (cf. [wa- lungam̲éene] 'they are united')

        verb followed by an infinitival phrase
        [w-ót̲te/ wa-sh-pokezanya ku-vula m-áayi] 'all/ took turns bailing
        water' (cf. [ku-vúula] 'to bail')

        verb followed by a headless adjective
        [m-weka chi-wít̲i/ hu-ja chi-vívu] 'the one who puts s.t. unripe
        aside/ eats s.t. ripe' (cf. [m-wéeka] 'one who puts s.t. aside')

The data in (13) show that there is no prosodic phrase break between a nominal and a modifier of that nominal in many cases.

(13) [chi-mera n-dilaa n-khúlu/ y-a múu-yi] 'he looked for the main street/ of the town' (Note: The long vowel at the end of [n-díla] 'street' shows that it is part of the same phrase as the adjective [n-khúlu].)
[kodhi muxtasári] 'a short speech' (cf. the case where the adjective does not stand in a modifier relationship with the same noun: [fanya koodhí=z-o/ muxtasári] 'make your speech/ short')

The example in (14) illustrates the absence of a prosodic break between an adjective and a modifier of that adjective:

(14) [sultani w-aa nóka/ chi-mw-aambila/ kuwa xisá=ze/ ni n-dee nthó] 'the king of the snakes/ told him/ that his story/ was very long' (Note: The long vowel at the end of [n-dé] 'long' shows that it is in the same phrase as the adverb [nthó] 'very'.)

while (15) illustrates the absence of a break between a preposition or complementizer or particle and a following word:

(15) [kamaa m-pháka/ naa m-phaná] 'like a cat/ and a rat' (cf. *na* 'and') [muxta núumba/ i-welo tayaarí] 'when the house/ was ready' (cf. [i-wéelo] 'it was')
[karkaa n-díla/ síimba/ chi-wa-'uza w-eenzí=w-e] 'on the way/ lion/ asked his companions' (cf. [karka] 'on, from, etc.')

Finally, the example in (16) illustrates the absence of a prosodic break between an auxiliary verb and the main verb.

(16) [chi-mw-ambila mw-aaná=w-e/ waliko chi-m-liindó] 'he told his son/ who (it was) waiting for him' (cf. [waalíko] 'he was')

Align-XP R is one of the critical principles of Chimwiini phrasing, but it is by no means the whole story. However, before turning to the other principles that are at work in Chimwiini phrasing it is important to present entirely independent evidence in favor of the phrasing that is required to account for the vowel-length alternations in Chimwiini. This new evidence has to do with a second prosodic system in Chimwiini that is separate from the 'abstract stress' system discussed up to this point.

11.3 Accent and phrasing in Chimwiini

In K&A, we recognized that accent (high pitch) regularly occurs on the penult syllable of a word in isolation (and in the case of monosyllables, the only syllable). We also identified a number of morphologically determined cases where accent is final. This contrast between penult and final accent was of course very easy to detect in words in isolation. However, due to our inexperience with systems where pitch alone is the manifestation of the presence of accent (and perhaps due to the significant downdrifting of high pitches across sentences in the default case), we had considerable trouble detecting accent locations at the sentential level. This was true of both penult and final accent as well (if not pre-pause).

One consequence of this inadequacy on our part was that we were unable to properly assess accent at the sentence level and thus we could not make extensive use of it in our research on phrasing. We were thus unable to transcribe the sentences that we elicited with accuracy on this matter, and thus our evidence for phrasing could only make use of vowel-length alternation evidence. It was not until the beginning of the present decade that we returned to examining our recordings of Chimwiini with the aid of pitch extraction software; using such software, the location of the accented syllables turned out to be easily detected. Furthermore, a tape recorded by Mohammad Imam Abasheikh that compared various sentences with differing focus in both statement and yes-no question form turned out to reveal the way that accent works at the sentential level.

The result of this research was both simple and powerful: accent is assigned to either the penult or the final syllable in a phonological phrase, and the phrases in question are exactly the same phrases as are required to account for the vowel-length alternations!

We begin our discussion of accent with the circumstances at the word level where final accent is assigned (remember, the default case is penult accent). We will discuss here only the most important cases. The first situation where final accent occurs will be referred to as *person-marking final accent*. Specifically, first- and second-person subject forms in the present and past tense in Chimwiini have final accent, while all third-person forms have penult accent. (Note: In the present and past tenses, both the second-person singular subject form and the [cl.1] (singular human) subject form are zero segmentally.)

(17) past tense
      [n-jiilé] 'I ate'   [jiilé] 'you (sg.) ate'

vs
[jíile] '(s)he ate'   [wa-jíile] 'they ate'

[n-someelé] 'I read'   [someelé] 'you read'
vs
[soméele] '(s)he read'   [wa-soméele] 'they read'

present tense
[n-naa-ku-já] 'I am eating'   [naa-ku-já] 'you are eating'
vs
[naa-kú-ja] '(s)he is eating'   [wa-naa-kú-ja] 'they are eating'

[n-na-x-soomá] 'I am reading'   [na-x-soomá] 'you (sg.) are reading'
vs
[na-x-sóoma] '(s)he is reading'   [wa-na-x-sóoma] 'they are reading'

All relative verb forms have final accent:

(18)   [oloshéle] '(s)he went'   but: [osheló] 'who went'
       [jíile] '(s)he ate'   [jiiló] 'who ate'
       [soméele] '(s)he read'   [someeló] 'who read'

Negative imperative verbs have final accent, while (most) affirmative impera-
tives have penult (and the ones that appear not to have penult accent can be
analyzed as still falling within the default pattern).

(19)   [píka] 'cook!'   but: [s-piké] 'don't cook!'
       [bóola] 'steal'   [si-boolé] 'don't steal!'
       [soomésha] 'teach!'   [si-soomeshé] 'don't teach!'

Nominals located after the conjunction *na* have final accent:

(20)   [m-pháka/ naa m-phaná] 'a cat/ and a rat' (cf. [m-phána/ naa
       mphaká] 'a rat/ and a cat')
       [Núuru/ na Jaamá] 'Nuuru/ and Jaama'
       [dhíbu/ na xasaará] 'trouble/ and misfortune'

The preceding data concern accent at the word level. Before looking at
the issue of phrasal accent, it is important to emphasize that accent and the
vowel-length-related notion of 'abstract stress' are entirely independent of one
another. The examples in (21) illustrate the independence of these notions.

(21)   [x-soomésha] 'to teach' (antepenult 'abstract stress' and penult accent)
       [si-soomeshé] 'don't teach!' (antepenult 'abstract stress' and final accent)

[someeló] 'who read' (penult 'abstract stress' and final accent)
[sóoma] 'read!' (penult 'abstract stress' and penult accent)

Let us turn now to the demonstration that accent is determined at the phrasal level and not the word level. This claim holds true both for penult accent and for final accent, but it will be simplest to begin by focusing on final accent. Take the case of person-marking final accent first. We have said that the verb is assigned final accent if the subject is either first or second person. However, when the verb is followed by a complement, then the accent is manifested not on the verb (which is without accent) but rather on the complement.

(22)   [n-jilee namá] 'I ate meat', [jilee namá] 'you ate meat'
        vs
        [jilee náma] '(s)he ate meat', [wa-jilee náma] 'they ate meat'
        [chi-jiilé] 'we ate', but: [chi-jile ma-tuundá] 'we ate fruit'
        [chi-neelé] 'we drank', but [chi-nele m-aayí] 'we drank water'

If there are multiple complements, the final accent appears at the end of each phonological phrase in the verb phrase. The data with regard to this point and the theoretical implications are taken up later.

The same essential point can be made with respect to the case of relative verb final accent. When the relative verb is followed by a complement, then the final accent is heard not on the relative verb itself but on the complement.

(23)   [sh-kombe chi-vunzila na Hamadí/ chi-waliko gháali] 'the cup that
        was broken by Hamadi/ was expensive'
        [muxta l-pépo/ l-anzizo ku-vuma ka w-iingí] 'when the wind/ began
        to blow hard'
        [báaba/ lazilo=po ka m-tanaa=ní] '(when) father/ came out of the room'
        [fijíri/ muxtaa yé/ ondoshelo ka u-sinzizii=ní] 'one morning/ when
        he/ woke up from sleep'
        [karka majlisi áyo/ ntháku/ jasirilo xkodhá] 'in that meeting/ there
        was no one/ who dared to talk'

Just as is the case with person-marking accent, if the relative verb has multiple complements, the final accent appears on each of the complements. These data and the implications of these data are dealt with later.

The conjunction-marking final accent is also phrasal. (Since the sentences are a bit complex, we have bolded the relevant phrases.)

(24)   [ni-sh-fungile chi-sanduuxú/ **na n-dani y-a chi-sanduxu ichí**/ chi-walimoo
        ch-úwo]

'I opened the box/ and inside of box this/ was a book'
[. . . k-éenda/ k-onyeza wáa-nthu/ n-ḏila ṯoosáni/ wa-na-pate ki-'i-ráasha/ **na ku-wa-'onyeza n-ḏila m-photoofú**/ wa-na-pate ki-y-eepúka] 'to go/ to show people the straight path/so that they get to follow it/ and to show them the crooked path/ so that they get to avoid it'

The bolded phrases in the above examples show a *na* phrase where the accent resides not on the immediately following noun but rather at the end of the entire phrase.

The above data show clearly that the final accent is phrasal. But each and every sentential example that we have cited in our discussion of the vowel-length alternation will attest to the phrasal nature of accent. In every phrase cited, non-final words never bear accent and there is no phrase that does not have the final word accented. In other words, every phrase required to explain the vowel-length alternations contains one and only one accent and it is on the last word in the phrase. Therefore, in order to account for accent, we must construct exactly the same phrases as are constructed to account for vowel length.

Having established that both vowel-length alternations and accent serve to identify the phrasing of Chimwiini sentences, and having provided evidence in support of Align-XP R, let us turn next to a critical aspect of Selkirk's analysis of the phonology–syntax interface: the claim that a phonological phrase is not necessarily a syntactic phrase.

11.4 Phonological phrases are not syntactic phrases

The only example contained in K&A that indicated that the phonological phrase must be different from a syntactic phrase was the example [kamaa m-pháka/ na m-phaná] 'like a cat/ and a rat', where the particle *kama* and the first member of the conjoined noun phrase group together separately from the second member of the conjunction. This example is perhaps not entirely conclusive since one could imagine claiming (as Selkirk noted) that *kama* forms a prosodic word with the following noun and thus [kamaa m-pháka] is simply the first of two conjoined words. This account is not viable because the accentual evidence demonstrates that *kama* does not form a prosodic word with the following noun. For example, one says [kamaa mí] 'if, as I' rather than *[kamáa mi], which is the expected pronunciation if *kama* formed a prosodic word with the following monosyllable. While this evidence is powerful, we are fortunate that there are many other examples that support the claim that the phonological phrase is not itself a syntactic unit of any sort.

The data in (25) again involve conjoined noun phrases, but this time the first member of the conjunct forms a phrase with a word that cannot plausibly be argued to be a proclitic to it—specifically, a verb.

(25)   [jilee n̲áma/ na root̲í] '(s)he ate meat /and bread'
    [wa-somel̲e̲l̲e w-áana/ naa wa-ké] '(s)he read to the children/ and
    the women'
    [yé/ pishilee nsí/ naa zi-jó/ yúuzi] 'he cooked fish/ and zi-jo /the day
    before yesterday'

In these examples we see that the verb is without accent in each case, clearly showing that the verb is not phrase-final. Furthermore, in the one case where the verb has a long vowel in its isolation form (cf. [wa-someléele] '(s)he read to them'), that vowel is shortened, again showing that the verb is not phrase-final. And in two cases, the final vowel of the verb is lengthened, a pronunciation that only occurs when the word is phrase-medial. The evidence unambiguously establishes that the verb forms a phonological phrase with the first conjunct.

A second case which shows that phonological phrases are not syntactic phrases involves the relative clause construction. If the head of a relative clause precedes the subject of the relative verb, then a particle –*a* links the two. The -*a* link agrees with the head. When the head immediately precedes the relative verb, there is no -*a* link. Both situations are shown in (26).

(26)   [w-ana w-aa yé/ wa-somel̲e̲e̲l̲ó] 'the children whom he/ read to'
    [mu-nthu wa Jáama/ had̲ilo kuwa ilé/ waliko Núuru] 'the person
    who Jaama/ said came/ was Nuuru'
    [mu-nthu m-pelo Jaamá/ chi-buukú...] 'the man who gave Jaama/ a
    book...'

In the case where the -*a* link is present, what we see is that the head and the subject of the relative verb are grouped into a single phrase. In other words, taking the first example for detailed discussion, [w-ana w-aa yé] 'the children whom he' forms a phonological phrase. The evidence for this is clear. The noun [w-áana] 'children' loses its vowel length and is unaccented, clearly showing that it is part of a phrase with the following word. The fact that we do not get *[w-anaa wa] shows that the phrase does not end at the -*a* link. The fact that we do get the -*a* link lengthened shows that this element forms a phonological phrase with the pronoun [yé]. There is no doubt that this phrase ([w-ana w-aa yé]) is not a syntactic unit of any kind.

When there is no -*a* link, then the head and the relative verb are in the same phrase. Thus we have a phrase like [mu-nthu m-pelo Jaamá] 'the man who gave Jaama'. The fact that [múu-nthu] 'man' loses its vowel length and also has no accent shows clearly that it forms a phrase with the following word(s). The fact that the relative verb [m-peeló] 'who gave him' loses its internal length and has no accent shows that this word forms a phrase with the following word. The fact that [Jáama] (personal name) retains its long vowel and bears accent shows that it stands at the end of a phrase. It is clear that [mu-nthu m-pelo Jaamá] does not constitute a syntactic phrase to the exclusion of [chi-búuku].

Chimwiini sentential complements provide another source of evidence that phrasing is a phonological construct and not a syntactic construct. Look at (27).

(27)   [n-na-x-ṯaraja kuwa Jaamá/ oloshelé] 'I hope that Jaama/ went'

In this sentence, the verb *–ṯaraja* takes a sentential complement that is introduced by the complementizer **kuwa**. Notice that the accentual facts indicate that [n-na-x-ṯaraja kuwa Jaamá] is a single phrase. If the verb and complementizer constituted a phrase, then we would expect a pronunciation *[n-na-x-ṯarajaa kuwá]. But this is unacceptable. The complementizer **kuwa** must be part of the same phrase as [Jáama]. The verb *oloshele* cannot be part of the same phrase; if it were, we would have to have the pronunciation *[n-na-x-ṯaraja kuwa Jama oloshelé]. Obviously, [n-na-x-ṯaraja kuwa Jaamá] 'I hope that Jaama' is not a syntactic phrase.

The evidence that phonological phrases are not the same as syntactic phrases is considerably more extensive than shown above. Many examples that demonstrate this fact have additional implications; specifically, they argue against any inference that might have been drawn that all phonological phrases end at the right edge of a (lexical) maximal projection. Before getting to the cases where Align-XP R does not account for the data, let us look at the way in which an Optimality Theoretic approach to phrasing differs from the original derivational approach of Selkirk (1986).

11.5 Optimality Theory and phrasing

The essential thrust of Selkirk (1986) was that at some point in a derivation, the surface syntactic structure of a sentence is mapped into a phonological representation where the words of a sentence are exhaustively parsed into a sequence of phonological phrases. In effect, a phonological phrase was one layer in a prosodic hierarchy that includes the prosodic word below it and the intonational phrase above it. From the examples presented, the implication existed that a single 'rule' (or parameter setting) defined a phrase.

An Optimality Theoretic perspective looks at matters differently (cf. Truck-enbrodt 1995, 1999; Selkirk 2000). The constraints on phrasing will of course be evaluating different possible surface phrasing choices to choose the optimal one. The various phrasing options are determined by a universal set of phrasing principles which are ranked for any given language both with respect to themselves and with respect to other phonological constraints in the language (i.e. it could be the case that a phrasing is chosen in order to optimize a given phonological demand). It is the business of the theoretical phonologist to identify what principles of phrasing are at work in the languages of the world and how they are ranked in particular languages.

Selkirk's edge-based account of phrasing was restricted to the role of syntax in phrasing and it suggested that the only pertinent syntactic aspect is X-bar phrase structure. It did not address the issue of whether phrasing in a language may reflect other aspects of linguistic structure besides syntax. Of course, the whole issue is confounded by the issue of which aspects of linguistic structure are properly 'syntax' and which are something else. We do not wish to become entangled in this issue, but only to emphasize that from an Optimality Theoretic point of view constraints on phrasing do not necessarily reflect a single module of grammar.

In Optimality Theory, some constraints are in conflict with one another (i.e. both may not be true at the same time). Other constraints may be compatible with one another. In the course of theoretical work since Selkirk (1986), various phrasing principles have been proposed in addition to the Align-XP Right (or its mirror image, Align-XP Left). One of the most important constraints conflicting with Align-XP R that has been proposed is Wrap-XP (cf. Truckenbrodt 1999). Wrap-XP demands that all the elements inside a (lexical) maximal projection be in the same phonological phrase. Thus given a VP of the shape V—NP—NP, Wrap-XP demands that the two NPs be in the same phrase along with the verb, while Align-XP R demands that the first NP be in a separate phrase from the second NP. We shall return later to the issue of whether Wrap-XP has any role in Chimwiini.

With this much theoretical background, we can return to the issue of whether phrasing in Chimwiini is entirely determined by Align-XP R.

11.6 The role of morphological negation in Chimwiini phrasing

As well supported as Align-XP R is in Chimwiini, it is immediately clear that it is not sufficient to account for all phrasing facts in the language. One striking case that it fails to explain is the phrasing of sentences that contain a negative verb form. In (28) we compare an affirmative sentence with its corresponding negative (the morphology is often quite different) and in (29) we provide some additional examples from our text collection.

(28) [marṭi w-íitu/ ile numbáa=ni] 'our guest/ went home' vs
      [marṭi w-íitu/ nth-aa-kú-ya/ numbáa=ni] 'our guest/ did not go/ home'
      [mu-kée=w-e/ shishile míimba] 'his wife/ became pregnant' vs
      [mu-kée=w-e/ nth-a-x-shíika/ míimba] 'his wife/ did not become/
      pregnant'
      [úyu/ ṭa-k-infa káazi] 'this one is suitable for the job' vs
      [úyu/ h-a-ṭa-k-íinfa/ káazi] 'this one is not suitable for the job'

(29) [uza gháali/ s-uuzé/ raxíisi] 'sell at a high price/ do not sell/ cheap'
      [n-khúku/ ha-m-úβli/ mw-a-n-khukú=w-e] 'a hen/ does not kill/ her
      chick'
      [mw-enye sh-tóka/ haa-ṭówi/ s-kúnyi] 'the one having a stick/ does
      not lack/ firewood'
      [mw-ana w-aa ṇóka/ nii ṇóka/ ha-ṭóowi/ ku-lúma] 'the child of a
      snake/ is a snake/ he never fails/to bite'
      [l-takí=l-a/ nii lí-le/ ḷaakíni/ ha-l-vaalíki/ shingóo=ni] 'my necklace/
      is long/ but/ it cannot be worn/ about the neck' [riddle]
      [h-alo n-ṭholokó/ haa-vúni/ m-púunga] 'the one who plants beans/
      does not harvest/ rice'

In each of the examples above we observe that a morphological negative verb form stands at the end of a phonological phrase even though no such phrase edge is predicted by Align-XP R and no such phrase edge (necessarily) exists in the corresponding affirmative sentence. We know that these negative verbs stand at the end of a phrase because (a) they bear an accent and (b) if they have internal vowel length in their isolation form, they retain this length in these examples.

What these examples show is not that Align-XP R demands a phrase edge where one does not exist, but rather that a phrase edge exists where Align-XP does not require one. In other words, a phrasing principle must exist that is complementary to Align-XP R, not one that leads to a structure that violates Align-XP R. We formulate this constraint as (30):

(30) Align-Neg R
      Align the R edge of a negative verbal form with the R edge of a
      phonological phrase.

An idiosyncratic role for negation has been observed before in the literature on phrasing in Bantu languages (cf. Hyman, Katamba, and Walusimbi 1987).

Obviously, a close comparison is warranted. However, further work on Chimwiini itself is needed. Although during hours of elicitation and in numerous narrative texts, negative verbs were with great regularity separated in phrasing from what follows, there do appear to be some environments where a morphological negative verb is *not* separated prosodically from its complement. One such case involves a relative negative verb.

(31)   [ha-fundowi na maamay-é/ hu-m-fundo l-mweengú] [proverb]
        'the one who is not taught by his mother/ is the one whom the world
        teaches'

        [ha-ta-x-fáanya/ ka:zi] 'he won't (do)/ work'
        vs
        [mu-nthu ha-ta-x-fanya kaazí] 'the man who won't work'

The failure of a negative relative verb to be separated prosodically from its complement appears to be part of a general absence of any sort of focus or emphasis inside a relative clause. In other words, it is only Align-XP R that serves to define phrasing in a relative clause.

Although we do not have a great deal of relevant material, we did identify another clear case where the assignment of a phrase edge to the end of the negative verb is blocked. Look at the following crucial sentences.

(32)   [nth-a-k-éenda/ numbáa=ni] 'he did not go/ home'
        vs
        [nth-a-k-enda numbáa=ni] 'he did not go *home* (i.e. he went somewhere
        else, not home)'
        [yé/ nth-a-m-letela Núuru/ chi-búuku, m-letelele Múusa] 'he did
        not bring Nuuru/ a book/ he brought Muusa (one)'
        [yé/ nth-a-m-letela chi-búuku/ Núuru/ m-letelele xalámu] 'he/ did
        not bring a book to/ Nuuru/ he brought him a pen'

These examples illustrate that if a postverbal element is being focused, then it is not possible to have the negative verb aligned with the right edge of a phonological phrase. Again we seem to be dealing with a conflict between focus and Align-Neg R.

The separation of the negative verb also does not occur within the scope of interrogatives:

(33)   [yé/ ha-ta-x-fáanya/ ka:zi] 'he/ won't (do)/work'
        vs
        [yé/ ha-ta-x-fanya káazi/ líini] 'he/ won't (do)work/ when?'

[ntha-ku-léeta/ chibuku chi-hába] 'he didn't bring/ the small book'
vs
[ntha-ku-leta chi-buku gáni] 'which book did he not bring?'

[yé/ ntha-m-leetéla/ Múusa// chi-búíuku] 'he/ didn't bring to/ Muusa/ a book'
vs
[yé/ ntha-m-letela náani/ chi-búuku] 'who didn't he bring a book to?—lit. he/ did not bring to whom/ book'

These examples, as well as the earlier examples, suggest a pervasive relationship between focus and phrasing. This connection will be explored in greater detail below.

11.7 Indefiniteness and phrasing in Chimwiini

Another example where Align-XP R can be seen to be insufficient to account for all the phrasing data in Chimwiini involves the definite/indefinite contrast in Chimwiini. We should point out, however, that work on this topic is rather preliminary.

The definite/indefinite contrast is not morphologically marked on a noun in Chimwiini. The contrast may be signaled in various ways, however, including word order, object marking on the verb, and most important for present purposes, phrasing. Specifically, when a noun is modified, phrasing serves to separate an indefinite from a definite interpretation. The following examples illustrate that when the noun is indefinite, the noun is in a separate phrase from the modifier.

(34) [Mwíini/ ni múu-yi/ chi-hába] 'Mwiini (=Brava)/ is a town/ small'
     [wé/ ta-ku-zala mw-áana/ mw-iimbíli] 'you/ will bear a child/ male'
     [numbáa=ni/ i-waliko bárza/ n-khúlu] 'in the house/ there was a reception room/ large'
     [barzáa=ni/ zi-walimoo zí-ti/ z-íingi] 'in the reception room/ there were chairs/ many'
     [ni-wa-wene waa-nthú/ w-íingi/ suxúu=ni] 'I saw people/ many/ in the market'

Phrasing may be the only way to distinguish an indefinite from a definite reference:

(35) [chi-wa-wene w-ana wa-wovú] 'we saw the bad children'
     vs
     [chi-wa-wene w-aaná/ wa-wóvu] 'we saw some children/ bad'

[n-uzile mezaa n-khulú] 'I saw the big table'

vs

[n-uzile meezá/ n-khúlu] 'I saw a table/ big'

It is as though the indefinite NP has an appositive structure 'a man, a rich one'. If so, then perhaps the Selkirkian algorithm can be maintained. (But our research on Shingazidja shows a different behavior: definite morphology plays a disruptive role in phrasing rather than indefiniteness.)

11.8 Focus (or more broadly: Emphasis) and phrasing in Chimwiini

Perhaps the single most important area where the Selkirkian algorithm fails (as a comprehensive account of phrasing) is in a range of cases which are doubtless not linguistically the same thing, but which seem to be manifested *phrasally speaking* in the same way. Sometimes what may be involved is focus, or sometimes, contrastive emphasis; or perhaps it may involve simply stylistic highlighting of some sort. We suspect that there are differences among these phenomena having to do with pitch height and loudness etc., but we have not observed differences in phrasing that might be connected to a distinction among these phenomena. For convenience, we shall simply refer to the phenomenon as 'Focus' or 'Emphasis'. We remain neutral as to what the linguistic representation of focus in a strict sense might be, and in any case the notion at issue here is a much looser one.

In Chimwiini, words that would normally be medial to a phrase may be emphasized, in which case they stand at the end of a phonological phrase. Typically, the accented syllable in that word will be raised in pitch such that it does not stand in the normal 'downdrift' intonation that otherwise exists (whereby each accented syllable is somewhat lower in pitch than a preceding accented syllable in the intonational phrase).

We illustrate below a range of examples. (36a) shows, for instance, that ordinarily the first postverbal XP in the VP groups into the same phrase as the verb, but (36b) shows the verb may also be at the end of a phonological phrase when emphasized.

(36a) [sh-funga safári] 'he set out on a journey (lit. tied a journey)'
       [ch-anza x-fanya káazi] 'he began to do work'
       [chi-biga hóo<u>di</u>] 'he asked for permission to enter (lit. beat *hoo<u>di</u>*)'
       [n-jilee <u>n</u>amá]'I ate the meat; I ate the MEAT'

(36b) [n-jiilé/ <u>n</u>áma] 'I ATE/ meat'
       [chi-lóota/ kuwaa yé/ wene ruuhú=y-e/ u-ko maha<u>l</u>a súura/ na
       na-ku-m-nesha moojé/ xámri]

'he DREAMED/ that he/ saw himself/ in a lovely place/ and he was
serving his master/liquor'
[(n)-na-x-suulá/ wé/ k-enda náa mi/ ku-ja úki] 'I WANT/ you/ to
go with me/ to eat honey'
[dhíbu/ ku-m-welela n-íingi/ mw-áana/ chi-'azíma/ k-ondoka ka ápo]
'difficulties/ being many to him/ the boy/ DECIDED/ to go
from there'
[wazíiri/ m-kúlu/ chi-mw-ambíla/ ku-m-letela m-phíingu/ na xpalá]
'minister/ chief/ TOLD HIM/ to bring to him a chain/ and a padlock'
[Hasíibu/ chi-m-jíiba/ kuwa ni wazíiri] 'Hasiibu/ ANSWERED
HIM/ that he (Hasiibu) was the minister'
[chi-láwa/ karka múu-yi/ óyo] 'he LEFT/ from town/ that'
[Yuusúfu/ waliko sh-pendóowa/ nthó/ na waawá=y-e] 'Joseph/ was
LOVED/ very much/ by his father'
[wótte/ báaba/ máama/ na mkulazé/ téena/ wa-ch-oondóka/ ka
nthi ízo/ wa-ch-éenda/ xkala na Yuusúfu] 'all/ father/ mother/ and his older
brothers/ then/ MOVED/from these lands/ (and) THEY WENT/ to live with
Joseph'

There are also examples of a postnominal element being set off from the
preceding word where it is not indefiniteness that is at issue. Some examples:

(37)   [mí/ m-phindi y-aa mí/ n-chhí-fa/ u-sultáani/ na-ta-walishowa
mw-áana/ úyu]
'I/ time of I/   when I die/   sultanship/ he will be installed on boy/
this= when I die, this boy will be made sultan'
[ba'ada y-a mi-yéezi/ hába] 'after months/ few'
[xabári/ **ízi**/ zi-m-komele sultáani] '[lit.] news/ these/ reached the
king' (it is being emphasized here that some definite news that was
the topic of discussion reached the king—the phrasing is not being
used here to indicate indefinite news)
[wazíiri/ m-kúlu/ chi-mw-ambíla/ ku-m-letela m-phíingu/ na xpalá]
'minister/ chief/ told him/ to bring to him a chain/ and a padlock'
[mí/ m-baliko sh-kála/ mu-yi úyu/ karka núumba/ íyi] 'I/ was residing
in/ this town/ in house/ this'
[má-sku/ z-ilee n-fúye/ níingi] 'at night/ came monkeys/ many'

(The noun *n-fuye* in the last example is of course indefinite here, but it is
obvious that there is not a contrast being made between a definite and
indefinite noun. Rather it would appear that there is some emphasis on the
monkeys being many.)

These data provide evidence for a constraint like (38):

(38) Align-Focus R
The Right edge of the focused element must be at the Right edge of
a phonological phrase.

Examples involving the alignment of a phonological phrase edge with the
right edge of a focused/ emphasized constituent will play a role in subsequent
discussion and we will return to the issue of the correct formulation of (38)
below.

11.9 Align-XP R and wrap-XP: Evidence from accent

Although the constraint Align-XP R is well motivated in Chimwiini as well as
other languages, Truckenbrodt (1999) has argued for the existence of another
constraint that makes reference to (lexical) maximal projections: Wrap-XP.
Essentially, Wrap-XP wants all the material in a maximal projection to be in
the same phonological phrase. In discussion in the literature (up to this point
in time) the only work this constraint does is to require all the elements in the
verb phrase to be in the same phonological phrase. As such, it conflicts with the
constraint Align-XP R, since that constraint wants the right edge of an XP to be
at the end of a phrase. Thus in a verb phrase of the structure V NP NP, for
example, the two constraints seem to be antagonistic to one another. Wrap-XP
demands the phrasing (V NP NP) while Align-XP R demands the phrasing (V
NP) (NP). Truckenbrodt argues, however, that if recursive phrasing is allowed,
one may satisfy both constraints: e.g. (V NP) NP) at the same time. Truckenbrodt notes that Chimwiini shows the need for the phrase edge after the first
NP, but does not show that there could NOT be recursive structure (i.e. that
Wrap-XP may still be satisfied). We will proceed now to an argument for
recursive structure and a role for Wrap-XP in Chimwiini.

Recall that we said that final accent occurs in Chimwiini as well as the default
penult accent. There are various situations where final accent is observed, but
in this section we will restrict ourselves to the environments which are most
useful for our present purposes. The first case involves person marking. Final
accent occurs in conjunction with the present and past tenses of the verb, but
only when the verb has a first-or second-person subject. To review briefly,
when the verb is the only element in the VP, then it bears the final accent:

(39) [n-jiilé] 'I ate', [jiilé] 'you ate', [chi-jiilé] 'we ate'
vs
[jíile] '(s)he ate', [wa-jíile] 'they ate' etc.

However, when the verb is not at the end of the phonological phrase, then the accent is manifested not on the verb but on whatever word ends the phonological phrase in which the verb appears:

(40)   [n-jilee namá] 'I ate meat', [jilee namá] 'you ate meat'
       vs
       [jilee náma] '(s)he ate meat', [wa-jilee náma] 'they ate meat'

Data of this sort could be characterized very simply: a first- or second-person past/present-tense verb form projects a final accent on the last word in the phrase that contains the verb.

   A problem with this generalization arises, however, when we look at cases where Align-XP right leads to verb phrases that are divided up into two or more phonological phrases.

(41)   [mí/ n-thinz-il-ee namá/ kaa chi-sú] 'I/ cut meat/ with a knife'
       [sh-pokele wa-geení/ mi-zigo ayó] 'we took from the guests / that luggage'
       [n-thovele maandá/ m-tuzii=ní] 'I dipped bread/ into the sauce'
       [ni-m-tovelele mw-aaná/ maandá/ m-tuzii=ní] I dipped for the child/ the bread/ into the sauce'
       [sí/ chi-m-bozele mw-aalimú/ chi-buku ch-a hisaabú] 'we/ stole from the teacher/ (his) arithmetic book'
       [ni-m-wadhihishilize Jaamá/ mas'alá] 'I explained to Jaama/ the problem'
       [n-na-ku-linda peesá/ ka mw-eenza=wá] 'I am expecting money/ from my friend'

What the data in (41) show is that the word at the end of *each* of the phonological phrases inside the VP exhibits a final accent when the verb has a first- or second-person subject. In other words, phrases that do not (seem to) contain the verb receive final accent.

   A similar set of facts holds for the final accent that derives from a relative verb. Most relative verbs are marked by a final *o* vowel, though passive forms do not follow this principle; all relative verbs however trigger the appearance of final accent, regardless of the subject of the relative verb.

(42)   (oloshéló) 'the one who came'
       (jiiló) 'the one who ate'
       (mu-nthu ikusiló) (ha-mw-íiwi) (mw-enyee n-dála)
       'the person who is satiated/ does not understand [lit. know]/ the hungry one'

But again, if the relative verb is not at the end of the phrase, then the final accent is heard not on the verb but on the word at the end of the phonological phrase that contains the relative verb.

(43) [yé/ suḽiḽe kumlola mwanáamke/ ḽazilo ka ahḽí] 'he/ wanted to marry a girl/ who came from his clan'
      [muxṯa ḽ-pépo/ ḽ-anzizo ku-vuma ka wiingí. . . .] 'when the wind began to blow hard . . .'

However, just as in the case of person-marking accent, when Align-XP R would produce multiple phrases inside a relative clause, final accent appears at the end of each of the phrases.

(44) [mu-nthu m-pelo Jaamá/ chi-buukú] 'the man who gave Jaama/ a book'
      [íyi/ ni raadíyo / i-sho w-ené=w-e/ hu-fafisho xabarí/ maraa n-thatú/ kiḽa muunthí]
      'this/ is radio / without owners/ which broadcasts news/ times three/ each day'

What we see then is that a final accent appears not only on the phrase that *obviously* contains the verb (in both the person-marking case and in the relative clause case), but also at the end of each XP in the verb phrase! If the phonological phrase structure is as predicted by Align-XP R, we do not predict that the verb would project final accent outside the immediate phonological phrase in which it occurs. If we hypothesize, however, that Wrap-XP and Align-XP R are both active in Chimwiini, and that the ban on recursive structure is ranked below these constraints, then it turns out that the phrase structure will in fact be just what is required: due to Wrap-XP, the verb will be contained in the same large phonological phrase as all of its complements. Due to Align-XP R, there will also be a right phrase edge at the end of every XP.

(45) (n-jilee namá) kaa chi-sú) 'I cut the meat/ with a knife'
      (ni-m-jiḽiḽe mw-aaná) namá) kaa chi-sú) 'I cut for the child/ the meat/ with a knife'
      (mu-nthu m-pelo Jaamá) chi-buukú) 'the man who gave Jaama/ a book'

Since there is no evidence against allowing both Wrap-XP and Align-XP R to be operative in Chimwiini, and since the resulting phrasing serves to permit a simple characterization of final accent (the verbs in question project final accent on each of the phonological phrases in which the verb occurs), we assume the appropriateness of this analysis. (See Truckenbrodt (1999) for discussion of the technical details of how violations of the ban on recursive structure are evaluated so that the phrasing in (44) is selected as the best way to satisfy both Align-XP R and Wrap-XP while minimally violating *Recursive Structure.)

11.10 Focus in Chimwiini revisited

It turns out that the above facts about final accent go a long ways to clarify the constraint on focus/emphasis in Chimwiini (and by implication for other languages as well). I suggested earlier that there is a constraint like (38), which we repeat below:

(38) Align-Foc R
The Right edge of the focused element must be at the Right edge of a phonological phrase.

This constraint, however, will not achieve the correct results in Chimwiini on the assumption of recursive phrasal structure that we argued for in the preceding section. To see this, we need to return to final accent. However, we will have to limit ourselves to final accent in connection with the present and past tenses. We cannot use relativization data because in all our data, we cannot find an example where a word internal to the relative clause receives emphasis or focus. We do not wish to claim that this is impossible since at the stage where we had the possibility of eliciting data, we did not understand the system sufficiently to study the matter.

Look at the example in (46) where the verb phrase has the structure V NP NP and focus/emphasis is placed on the verb and the verb form is one that projects final accent.

(46) (sí) (chi-m-boozelé) (mw-aalímu) (chi-buku ch-a hisáabu)
'we/ STOLE/ from the teacher/ the arithmetic book'
NOT: *(sí) (chi-m-boozelé) mw-aalimú) chi-buku ch-a hisaabú)
cf. the simple statement:
(sí) ((chi-m-bozele mw-aalímú) chi-buku ch-a hisaabú)

What we see from the above sentences is that if a word inside the VP is emphasized, then there is indeed a phrasal break at that point and the word has final accent as (45) would predict. But what is critical to our concerns is that the word at the end of the subsequent phrases does not have final accent, but rather the default accent! But why should this be so? The ill-formed sentence *(sí) (chi-m-boozelé) mw-aalimú) chi-buku ch-a hisaabú) satisfies

(45) and better satisfies Wrap-XP than does the correct sentence (sí) (chi-m-boozelé) (mw-aalímu) (chi-buku ch-a hisáabu). In other words, to account for the data, it must be the case that the latter pronunciation obeys the Align-Foc R constraint while the incorrect former pronunciation does not. (45) must be modified so that Wrap-XP cannot organize the VP into a single phonological phrase.

The following reformulation of (45) will, if ranked above Wrap-XP, make it impossible to satisfy both constraints at the same time.

(47)   Align-Foc R
        A focal/emphatic element must be rightmost in any phrase that
        contains it.

If Wrap-XP were satisfied in sentences like (46), then Align-Foc R would be violated since the verb would be inside a phrase but not rightmost in that phrase. Thus by ranking (47) above Wrap-XP, we will successfully prevent Wrap-XP from being involved in the optimal outcome.

11.11 Conclusion

Chimwiini is perhaps the ideal language to study for any student of phonological phrasing. Why? Because for the most part every phrase of every sentence in the language makes its existence clear, very often on the basis of two independent types of evidence (the presence of accent and the shortening, or lack of shortening, of long vowels). One does not have doubts about where the phrases are. The task is only to identify the principles that determine them. And every sentence in the language provides evidence as to the nature of these principles. It does not take any intricate conjunction of circumstances to find evidence for any given aspect of the system.

It was unfortunate that when we had abundant time to freely elicit data (1973–8), we failed to properly hear or understand the accentual evidence, and thus had to rely entirely on evidence from the vowel-length alternations. This was, of course, sufficient to make considerable headway. Fortunately, the role of accent was eventually established and it is possible to return to much tape-recorded data to delve more deeply into the system. Even more helpful for future research is that although Chimwiini is an endangered language, there are now refugee communities of speakers in a few cities in the United States and the possibility of new research exists. It is critical that these new sources of data be explored while it is still possible.

12

Functional complementarity is only skin-deep: Evidence from Egyptian Arabic for the autonomy of syntax and phonology in the expression of focus

SAM HELLMUTH

12.1 Introduction

Some degree of functional complementarity between syntax and phonology in the expression of information-structure categories is often assumed. For example, Gundel (1988) suggests that 'one would expect that in languages which [...] do not use sentence stress to code the topic-comment relation [...], syntactic structure would be used for coding topic-comment structure more frequently than in languages where sentence stress is relatively free'. The expectation seems to be that correlation between the use of phonological and syntactic strategies is such that we can predict availability of a strategy in one component of the grammar on the basis of the properties of the other component. This paper argues that the availability of a particular strategy for the expression of information structure (or not) can in fact be explained in terms of properties internal to that same component of the grammar, by testing for cases of apparent complementarity in the use of prosodic and syntactic strategies in a corpus of Egyptian Arabic (EA) speech data. EA is an interesting test case because it shares with Romance languages both the property of resisting deaccentuation of given items and plentiful availability of syntactic strategies for the expression of information structure, yet has been shown to display accentuation patterns, in all contexts, which are argued here to provide an independent explanation for patterns of accentuation in information-structure contexts.

The outline of the paper is as follows. Section 12.2 sets out some of the empirical evidence that might tempt one to assume complementarity between syntax and phonology in the expression of information structure, presenting data from Germanic and Romance languages. Section 12.3 introduces the facts of EA and demonstrates that it shares with Italian the key properties relevant to our discussion, namely availability of certain syntactic strategies (word-order shifts, argument elision, and clefting) and a lack of certain prosodic strategies (no deaccentuation of given items, no preference for accenting arguments over predicates). Section 12.4 takes two IS categories (focus and thetics) and explores whether there is any overlap in the use of prosodic vs syntactic strategies to express them in EA, on the basis of empirical evidence from a corpus of speech data. The key finding is that whilst there is overlap in the expression of focus, there appears to be no prosodic, but only syntactic, expression in thetics in EA. Section 12.5 argues that this apparent lack of overlap between syntax and phonology should not be taken as evidence of functional complementarity between the two, since in EA the lack of prosodic strategies in thetics correlates with the lack of deaccentuation of given items, and both can be explained from an independent property of the phonological grammar of the language (as evidenced by accent distribution in all contexts, Hellmuth 2007b). The paper concludes with a suggestion for the way ahead in the search for explanations in the investigation of the interaction of syntax and phonology in the expression of IS.

EA is defined here as the dialect of Arabic spoken in Cairo, Egypt, and by educated middle-class Egyptians throughout Egypt (often known as Cairene Arabic). The segmental and metrical phonology of EA are extremely well described, and have been much discussed in the phonological literature (see Watson 2002 for a comprehensive summary). Syntactically, EA has predominantly SVO word order (Benmamoun 2000).

12.2 The apparent division of labour in the expression of information structure

The notion information structure, or 'information packaging' (Vallduví 1992), denotes the way in which a particular proposition is conveyed, rather than its actual propositional or lexical content (Lambrecht 1994). Languages display a rich array of strategies for the expression of information structure, with elements of all and any area of the grammar—syntax, phonology, morphology—pressed into service. Examination of the interaction of different components of the grammar in the realization of IS contexts has been the subject of much research (see Féry et al. 2006 for a useful overview). The present paper treats only the interaction of syntax and phonology in the expression of IS.

Krifka (2006) suggests that there are three basic IS categories: focus, givenness, and topic. Only focus and givenness are relevant to our current purposes, and we adopt Krifka's definitions as below (paraphrased):

(1)   Focus indicates the presence of alternatives that are relevant for the interpretation of linguistic expressions.

(2)   Givenness indicates whether the denotation of an expression is present in the common ground or not, and/or the degree to which it is present in the immediate common ground.

The third IS category relevant to the present paper is thetics, described also as instances of 'sentence focus' (Lambrecht 1994), occurring in all-new contexts:

(3)   A thetic statement is one in which 'the domain of new information extends over the entire proposition, including the subject' (Lambrecht 1994: 14).

Importantly, adoption of these particular definitions of these IS categories, or indeed acceptance of their existence as distinct categories, is not crucial to the claim set out in this paper. The case regarding interaction in the expression of IS is made here on the basis of these categories and definitions, but could in principle be made on the basis of alternative definitions and/or alternative categories.

The focus of our attention here is the interesting fact that there appear to be clear groupings among languages according to which area of the grammar is engaged in the expression of a particular IS category. A classic example is use vs non-use of prosodic strategies in Germanic and Romance languages, treated in depth in Ladd (1996). As Ladd points out, in most Romance languages given items are not deaccented, as they would be in a Germanic language; the example here is from Italian (capitals denote primary accent) (Ladd 1996: 176):

(4)   [le inchieste]   servono a mettere a POSTO cose   andate
       [the investigations] serve   to put   to place   things done
       fuori   POSTO
       out-of place
       'The investigations are helping to put back in ORDER things that
        have got out of ORDER.'

Deaccenting of only part of a phrase is ungrammatical in Italian (Ladd 1996: 177):

(5) *Correre è come amminare in FRETTA, soltanto si deve andare molto PIU in fretta.
'Running is like walking in HASTE, only you have to go much MORE in haste.'

These facts have been confirmed by Swerts et al. (2002) who show from semi-spontaneous experimental speech data that there is no deaccenting within complex noun phrases (NPs) in Italian. Indeed Italian listeners are unable to reconstruct the context in which a complex NP occurred from prosody alone. In contrast, in Dutch, a given item within a complex NP will be deaccented, and Dutch listeners are able to reconstruct the context in which the complex NP was uttered with a high degree of accuracy (cf. also Swerts 2007).

Another IS context in which Germanic and Romance languages show very different realizations is thetics. In Germanic languages, in short thetic sentences, the main accent is usually on the subject argument rather than on the predicate, especially if the predicate is unaccusative or introduces the subject into the discourse for the first time (again, capitals denote primary accent) (after Ladd 1996: 188):

(6) The COFFEE MACHINE broke.
The SUN came out.
The BABY's crying.

In the same context, Italian and other Romance languages display non-canonical VS (verb–subject) word order (Ladd 1996: 191):

(7) S'è rotta   la CAFFETTIERA
has broken the coffee machine
'The coffee machine broke.'

Lambrecht (1994, 2001) has characterized the distinction between these strategies as a distinction between prosodic inversion (primary accent shift in English) and syntactic inversion (word-order shift in Italian). Given these two complementary strategies (syntactic vs prosodic), employed in the realization of an identical IS context (thetic statements), we might at this point be tempted to expect a strict division of labour between syntax and phonology (though Lambrecht expressly does not, as discussed in section 12.5 below).

For Vallduví (1991) complementarity between syntax and phonology is pivotal in explaining typological differences in the realization of IS categories. He points out a phonological distinction between two groups of languages, plastic and non-plastic: in non-plastic languages (such as Catalan, Italian, and French) the position of accents in a phrase is more or less fixed, whereas in plastic languages (such as German and English) the position of accents may vary. Vallduví thus argues that plastic languages will tend to have prosodic marking of IS whereas non-plastic languages will tend to have morphosyntactic marking of IS, such that changes in word order are instead used to shift constituents into sentence locations where they will appear with or without accent as needed.

In an example of this line of argument, Ladd (1996) suggests that a language like Italian, which resists deaccenting, may have other strategies for achieving similar effects, such as right-dislocation which results in a 'tag' pronunciation in a low-pitch range, as illustrated below. The utterance in (8) below is felicitous in a context in which 'your bath' is contrasted with someone else's bath which has already been run; in the same context a Germanic-style accentuation pattern, as in the Italian equivalent in (9), is unacceptable (Ladd 1996: 179):

(8)   Adesso faccio   scorrere il TUO,   di bagnetto.
       now   I make run   the yours, of bath.dim
       'Now I'll run YOUR bath.'

(9)   ??Adesso faccio scorrere il TUO bagnetto

Note that this is an instance of deaccenting of a given item ([bagnetto] 'bath') in a post-focus position. It could therefore in principle be the need to assign main prominence in non-phrase-final position to the focused item ([tuo] 'your') which conditions right-dislocation, rather than the need to express the given status of the item. I take Vallduví's concept of accent to indicate the position of main prominence in the sentence in a particular language (rather than the distribution of individual accents), thus Ladd's Italian example would be analyzed as an attempt to move [tuo] to phrase-final position where it can receive main prominence (cf. Zubizaretta 1998; Frascarelli 2000). Notwithstanding this reinterpretation, the example in (8) does appear to be an instance of use of a syntactic strategy in the absence of a suitable prosodic strategy.

One might thus be tempted to treat the case of prosodic vs syntactic inversion in thetics in a similar way, that is, to say that Italian doesn't use prosodic inversion because it has a syntactic strategy available (the shift to non-canonical word order). In this case however, Ladd himself points out that there is a basic prosodic difference between Germanic and Romance which arguably underlies the pattern of accentuation in thetics in Germanic but which is masked by the use of syntactic inversion in Italian. In fact, English displays a general preference for accenting arguments over predicates, observable independently in small clauses, and in short relative clauses containing no arguments, in which the main accent falls on the last noun rather than on the following verb (Ladd 1996: 191):

(10) a. infinitive small clauses   I have a BOOK to read
                                        They have given him a TUNE to play.

       b. short relative clause   I don't like the SHIRTS he wears.
           containing no nouns: It was caused by some FISH she ate.

In contrast, in Italian the phrase-final verb is accented in corresponding sentences, indicating that arguments and predicates are equally accentable in Italian (Ladd 1996: 191):

(11) a. Ho un libro da LEGGERE   'I have a book to read'
       b. Gli hanno dato una musica da   'They a gave him a piece to
           SUONARE   play'

Ladd here shows that an apparent division of labour between syntax and phonology, observable in thetics in English and Italian, is on reflection better explained by appeal to more general properties of the language (relative accentability of arguments and predicates in English). It is an approach of this kind that we seek to develop here.

The remainder of this paper seeks firstly to identify instances of apparent complementarity between syntax and phonology in the realization of IS in EA (in section 12.4), and secondly to argue that such instances are better explained by appeal to more general properties of the phonological grammar of EA (in section 12.5). If the hypothesis of complementarity between syntax and phonology is true we would expect either only syntactic strategies or only prosodic strategies to be used to express a given IS category. If there is any overlap (that is, if strategies of both kinds are observed) complementarity cannot be assumed in any case. As a precursor to this empirical investigation, the next section (section 12.3) establishes the position of EA in the typology of prosodic vs syntactic expression of IS, showing that EA is, in most respects, like Italian.

12.3 The syntactic and phonological reflexes of IS in Egyptian Arabic

This section sets out empirical evidence from the literature in favor of classification of EA as similar to Italian as regards realization of IS in two respects: EA has a range of syntactic strategies available for the expression of IS (changes in word order, clefting, and argument elision), but lacks certain key prosodic strategies (no deaccentuation of given items, no preference for accenting arguments over predicates).

12.3.1 *Syntactic strategies for the expression of IS in EA*

Starting with the IS category focus, this is reported by Gary and Gamal-Eldin (1981: 51) to be expressible in EA by means of syntactic clefts; both full clefts as in (12) and pseudo-clefts as in (13). According to Gary and Gamal-Eldin, these syntactic strategies are accompanied by prosodic effects: 'stronger stress' on the clefted item and 'reduced stress' on other items.

(12) [da muħammad illi   gi:h]   full cleft
      that Mohammad that came
      'It was Mohammad that came.'

(13) a. [muħammad huwwa illi   gi:h]   pseudo-cleft
        Mohammed he   that came
        'Mohaammed's the one who came.'

   b. [illi bi-jħibbi-ha   huwwa muni:b]
      that ASP-likes-her he   Muneeb
      'The one who likes her is Muneeb.'

Jelinek (2002: 94) points out that whenever a subject pronoun is realized overtly in EA this is to introduce a discourse element which is 'new or contrastive in the context', and is accompanied by prosodic effects in the form of 'added stress or a higher intonation peak'. According to Jelinek's data, reproduced in (14), in a sentence like (a) the pronoun [hijja] 'she' is optional, but for most EA speakers an overt pronoun here is infelicitous other than in a focus context (p. c. Ihab Shabana); in a focus sentence like (b), the pronoun is unambiguously obligatory (Jelinek 2002: 94) (bold type denotes added stress/ higher intonation).

(14) a. [(hijja) wasˤalit]
         (she)   arrive-perf.3fs
         'She arrived.'

   b. [**hijja** wasˤalit   muʃ huwwa]
      she   arrive-perf.3fs not he
      'It was SHE who arrived, not he.'[1]

---

[1] Jelinek translates this with a cleft in English, but there is no cleft or pseudo-cleft construction in the EA rendition.

The example in (14) illustrates that givenness may be expressed syntactically in EA, in that a given subject argument is most felicitously expressed as null (it is dropped); likewise, a given object argument is most felicitously realized by incorporation of an object pronoun onto the verb ('object cliticization'[2]).

In thetic contexts two (purely) syntactic strategies are observed (without accompanying prosodic effects), namely changes in word order and use of an existential construction. Although EA, along with other spoken Arabic dialects, is usually characterized as having SVO word order, a correlation has been observed between VS vs SV order and event-oriented vs action-oriented contexts respectively. This is noted for all modern Arabic dialects by Sasse (1987) and has been reported specifically for EA in a corpus study of spoken narratives (Brustad 2004: 342–4). The example in 15) shows a sentence from a spoken narrative in which a verb-initial word order is used to ensure that the indefinite (new) subject of the sentence appears in sentence-final position (example cited from Brustad 2004: 4):

(15) [ga:-li   s-sa:ʕa   tala:ta wagaʕ fi widni   fazi:ʕ]
       came-it-to-me the-hour three   pain   in ear-my   horrible
       'At three o'clock I got this horrible pain in my ear.'

Secondly, EA is also cited by Sasse (1987) as a language which makes extensive use of an existential construction [fi:h] in entity-oriented thetic sentences. All of his examples are from the rural Sharqiyya dialect (cited from Abu-Fadl 1961) but the use of [fi:h] in the Cairene dialect is also well documented, as in the example in (16) from Mughazy (2009):[3]

(16) [fi:h   ra:gil (#ir-ra:gil) mistanni:-k   barra]
       there-is man (#the-man)   waiting(m.s.)-for-you outside
       'There is a man (#the man) waiting for you outside.'

In sum then, the syntactic strategies available for the expression of IS in EA are clefts of various kinds (with accompanying prosodic effects), elision of arguments, word-order changes, and existential constructions.

12.3.2 Phonological strategies for the expression of IS in EA

The global prosodic contour of an EA declarative utterance containing no IS categories displays continuous declination throughout the sentence (Norlin

---

[2] Jelinek uses this description, but other authors argue that object pronouns in Arabic are not in fact clitics but are fully incorporated into the verbal complex (Shlonsky 1997).

[3] Mughazy's example here illustrates the general infelicity of definite subjects with [fi:h], but his paper also accounts for the non-trivial range of contexts in which [fi:h] occurs felicitously in EA with a definite subject.

1989; Rifaat 1991; Ibrahim et al. 2001), with a series of rising pitch movements (pitch accents), associated with the stressed syllable of each content word (Chahal and Hellmuth forthcoming). The start of the rising pitch gesture is stably aligned with the start of the stressed syllable and the end of the rise, the pitch peak, is aligned within the latter half of the stress foot, all else being equal (Hellmuth 2007a); after the peak the pitch contour falls across intervening unstressed syllables up until the beginning of the next rising pitch movement. There is no particular marking of the final (nuclear) accent in a broad focus declarative utterance, indeed the final pitch movement on the last lexical item is often realized within a compressed range (due to an effect of final lowering). These properties are illustrated in Figure 12.1 below (reproduced from Hellmuth 2006b: 71) which shows a broad-focus realization of the SVO sentence in (17).

(17) [maːma bititʕallim junaːni bi-l-leːl]
      mum   she-learns Greek at-the-night
      'Mum is learning Greek in the evenings.'

In focus contexts Gary and Gamal-Eldin (1981) report that in principle any syntactic constituent in an EA utterance can be highlighted by means of 'a combination of stronger stress and higher intonation'. Similarly, Mitchell (1993) notes that in EA the main prominence of the utterance (that is, the nucleus, as defined in the British school of intonation, e.g. O'Connor and Arnold 1961), can be located in different places in the sentence to indicate the

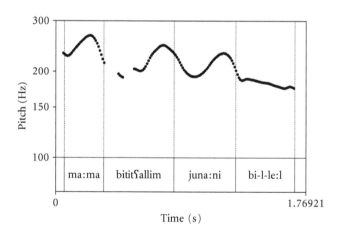

FIGURE 12.1 Sample pitch track of an EA neutral declarative utterance (read speech), showing declination and final lowering.

position of focus, without making changes in word order. Thus the example in (18) can be realized with main prominence on 'two' or on 'pounds' to create a contrast in amount or currency respectively (Mitchell 1993: 230):

(18)   [ʔitniːn giniːh masˤri]
         two   pounds Egyptian
         'Two Egyptian pounds.'

Instrumental studies have shown however that words appearing after a focus in EA are not deaccented (Norlin 1989; Hellmuth 2006a). A shift in the position of main prosodic prominence to a non-phrase-final position is thus possible in EA, as Mitchell and Gary and Gamal-Eldin describe, but does not condition full deaccentuation of postfocal arguments as it arguably does in Germanic. In EA main prominence shift is effected by means of realization of the focused item in an expanded pitch range together with realization of non-focused items in a compressed pitch range, a combination of effects also observed in Lebanese Arabic (Chahal 2003). The example in Figure 12.2 below illustrates a token of the SVO sentence in (17), but this time elicited in a frame paragraph such that the subject [maːma] 'Mum' was focused (contrasted with 'Dad') and the object [junaːni] 'Greek' was given (repeated from earlier in the discourse), as shown in (19). As can be seen, there is an accentual peak on the post-focal given object argument [junaːni], but it is realized in a compressed pitch range (bold type denotes main

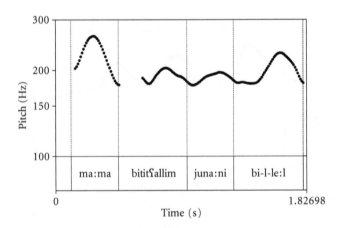

FIGURE 12.2 Sample pitch track of SVO-Adverbial sentence with contrastive focus on the subject and in which the object has given status (reproduced from Hellmuth 2006b: 279).

prominence in the utterance); the alignment of the start and end of the pitch
rise is unaffected by focus context (Hellmuth 2006a).[4]

(19) [ma:ma bititʕallim juna:ni bi-l-le:l]
      mum   she-learns Greek at-the-night
      'Mum is learning Greek in the evenings.'

Norlin (1989) investigated declaratives with focus in different positions in the
utterance, including on a sentence-medial lexical item, and found that focus-
induced pitch range compression was limited to post-focal contexts; pitch
peaks on an initial lexical item in such sentences were realized within a similar
pitch range to those in all new sentences.

The tokens illustrated in Figures 12.1 and 12.2 come from a corpus of 144 SVO
sentences, elicited in four different contexts such that the focus status of the
subject and the givenness status of the object were systematically varied (Hellmuth 2006a, 2006b). Close examination of the object nouns showed no cases of
deaccenting anywhere in the corpus, even when the object was given and
followed a focused subject. This matches the lack of deaccenting in EA observed
in a study of accentuation within complex NPs in EA (Hellmuth 2005) which
reproduced the methodology of Swerts et al's (2002) study of complex NPs in
Italian, and obtained directly parallel results for EA as were observed in Italian.

As well as displaying a lack of deaccenting, EA also shares with Italian the
property pointed out by Ladd (1996) of displaying no preference for accentuation of arguments over predicates. Evidence for this comes from accentuation patterns in small clauses and short utterance-final relative clauses (cf.
(10) in English and (11) in Italian above). Recall that in these predicate-final
cases, there is a difference in accentuation between English and Italian, with
English displaying a preference for accentuation of arguments over predicates,
not observed in Italian. In directly parallel examples to the English and Italian
examples, a clause-final verb in EA is accented as it is in Italian. (The examples
in (20) are realized with main prominence on the final lexical item).

(20) a. [hati:luh   manɡa:ya ʕasha:n jiduʔha]   small clause
          bring-to-him mango   in-order he-taste-it
          'Get him a mango to taste' (a special kind of mango).

      b. [mabaħibbiʃ   il-ʔomsˁaan illi bijilbisha]   short relative
          NEG-I-like-NEG the-shirts REL he-wears-them   clause
          'I don't like the shirts he wears'.

---

[4] The final adverbial is realized with a pitch boost due to influence from following material in the
frame paragraph.

However, the clause-final verb bears an obligatory resumptive pronoun in EA in these constructions, and it could be argued that the lexical argument is here embedded in the verb, thus attracting an accent. To obtain a strictly predicate-final utterance we need to look at sentences with a final intransitive verb, as in (21) below.[5] In such cases in EA main prominence is most naturally realized on the final lexical item and the phrase-final predicate (a finite verb) is thus accented; note however that even in a focus context, invoking, say, alternatives to 'Munir', and causing the main prominence of the utterance to be realized in non-final position, the final verb would still be accented (possibly within a compressed pitch range).

(21) [imba:reħ w-ana mrawwaħ   ʃufti mni:r bijitmaʃʃa]
      yesterday and-I going-home(m.s.) I-saw Munir he-walks
      'Yesterday while going home I saw Munir out walking.'

EA appears then to share with Italian the property of showing no preference for accentuation of arguments over predicates. Whilst other prosodic strategies for the expression of IS may be available in EA, such as variation in intensity (amplitude), these await formal investigation. In sum then, at present, we might expect to find use of gradient pitch range manipulation to realize focus via main prominence shift in EA, but we would not expect to find instances of deaccenting to realize givenness. Given that there is no preference for accentuation of arguments over predicates in EA we do not expect to find prosodic inversion in thetics.

12.3.3 *Summary: EA is like Italian*

In this section we have shown that, like Italian, EA displays a wide range of different syntactic strategies for the expression of IS: clefts of various kinds, elision of arguments, word-order changes, and existential constructions. Also like Italian, EA lacks deaccentuation as a phonological strategy for the realization of givenness. Note however that EA differs from Italian in that EA allows shift of main prominence to non-phrase-initial positions whereas Italian does not. In the next section, the complementarity hypothesis is tested by reviewing whether syntactic or prosodic strategies or both are used in the expression of IS in EA, in two IS contexts: focus and thetics.

---

[5] I am indebted to Mustafa Mughazy and Ihab Shabana for judgments on these sentences and to Mustafa Mughazy for suggesting the alternative predicate-final case explored here.

12.4 Testing the functional complementarity hypothesis in EA

In this section we explore new empirical evidence regarding the actual range of strategies observed in IS contexts in EA, in order to observe to what extent the use of syntactic and prosodic strategies does or does not overlap. Most of the data analyzed here are taken from a corpus of semi-spontaneous speech data, elicited in response to visual stimuli presented on a computer screen, collected by the author using a subset of the elicitation tasks provided in the Question-naire on Information Structure (QUIS) (Skopeteas et al. 2006). Digital recordings were made in Cairo on a Marantz PMD660 with a Shure headset condenser microphone at 44.1KHz 16bit, resampled to 22.05kHz; a broad phonetic and full prosodic transcription was made by the author with refer-ence to spectrogram and Fo contour extracted using Praat 4.5 (Boersma and Weenink 2006). Additional examples are also cited from the full QUIS corpus.[6]

12.4.1 *Focus*

The dataset described here comprises utterances elicited using a picture-based memory game from QUIS (Skopeteas et al. 2006). After seeing a picture of a transitive action, such as a man cutting a melon, the participant is asked a question of the type 'Is it a woman cutting the melon?' or 'Who is cutting the melon?'[7] These questions subdivide the IS concept of focus into two categor-ies, eliciting either contrastive focus or information focus on the subject of the sentence, respectively.[8] Parallel sets of questions elicited contrastive/informa-tion focus on the object of the sentence. There were eight picture stimuli in total, with responses elicited in two focus conditions (corrective/completion) from five speakers, yielding eighty tokens in total for analysis. Four tokens (two in each focus condition) were excluded because the speaker gave an infelicitous answer, leaving thirty-eight tokens in each focus condition for analysis. The range of realizations observed in the two types of focus context are summarized in Table 12.1.

The most common 'syntactic' strategy employed was ellipsis, whereby the speaker produced only the single wh-elicited argument in response to the question (e.g. 'The man'); ellipsis was especially common in response to a plain wh-question, that is, in information-focus contexts. Where the speaker

---

[6] For these additional examples, data collection/prosodic transcription was carried out by the author, and broad phonetic transcription by Dina El Zarka for SFB632.

[7] For the full task methodology and visual stimuli see task 'Anima' in QUIS (Skopeteas et al. 2006).

[8] These correspond to corrective focus and completion focus, respectively, in the typology of Dik et al. (1981); cf. Kiss (1998).

TABLE 12.1 Summary of strategies observed in focus contexts in the elicited dataset

	Ellipsis	Full cleft	Pseudo-cleft	Prosody only	Neutral syntax, neutral prosody	Total
Information focus	22	1	0	12	3	38
Contrastive focus	7	2	5	24	0	38
Total	29	3	5	36	3	76

produced a full sentence, a cleft construction was used in eight cases. More clefts were produced in contrastive focus contexts (N=7) than in information-focus contexts (N=1). There were three full clefts, as in (22), and five pseudo-clefts, introduced with [da] 'that', as in (23).

(22) [la la ar-**ra:gil** howa illi bijzuʔʔ   is-sitt...   ʔaw
     no no the-man he   REL he-pushes the-woman... or
     bijʃiddah]   full cleft
     he-pulls-her
     'No, it's the man who is pushing the woman.. or pulling her.'

(23) [laʔ da   **ra:gil** bijiʔtil ir-**ra:gil**]   pseudo-cleft
     no   that man   he-kills the-man
     'No, it's a man killing the man.'

In all but one of the cases in which a cleft was produced in a contrastive-focus context, the syntactic strategy was accompanied by prosodic effects. Most often, the clefted item was realized in an expanded pitch range, and following items in a compressed pitch range, as in the example in (23), illustrated in Figure 12.3 below. Other prosodic effects included insertion of a prosodic boundary after

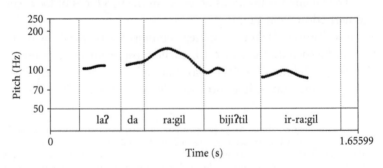

FIGURE 12.3 Sample pseudo-cleft [41ARZ-I04T-03M].

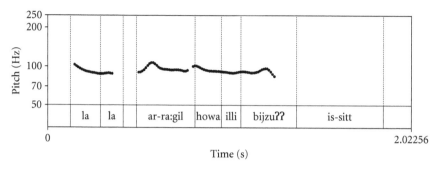

FIGURE 12.4 Sample full cleft [41ARZ-I02T-08M].

the clefted item, or compression of items in the subordinate clause only (without expansion of pitch range on the cleft itself). In the one instance of a cleft produced in an information-focus context (the token in (22), part of which is illustrated in Figure 12.4 above), the syntactic strategy did not appear to be accompanied by any prosodic effects (note that the final word was fully devoiced and thus no pitch trace is visible). [AU1]

Among the thirty-nine tokens in the remainder of the dataset, in which no syntactic strategy was used, all but three show some kind of prosodic effect. As expected these effects include gradient pitch range manipulation, but there were also an equal number of instances of insertion of a phrase boundary after the focused item. A prosodic effect was more likely to be used in a contrastive-focus context than in an information-focus context. The realizations are summarized in Table 12.2.

Pitch range manipulation was often accompanied by a parallel increase/reduction in intensity, as in the token in (24) which is illustrated in Figure 12.5 below.

(24) [la fiːh   raːgil bijaʔtaʕ batˤiːxa]
      no there-is man   he-cuts melon
      'No, there's a man cutting a melon.'

TABLE 12.2 Summary of prosodic strategies observed in the elicited dataset

	Pitch range manipulation	Inserted phrase boundary	Total
Info	4	8	12
Contr	14	10	24
Total	18	18	36

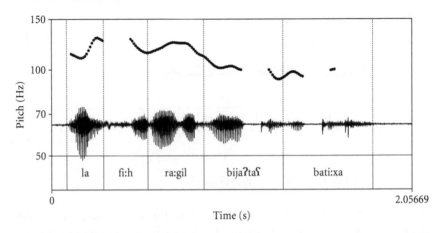

FIGURE 12.5 Sample pitch range compression and reduced intensity [41ARZ-K03–01M].

The count of inserted phrase boundaries included both major and minor prosodic junctures. A sample of a minor prosodic juncture, indicated by continued raised pitch after the end of the accented syllable (in the word ['raːgil] 'man'), is given in Figure 12.6 below which illustrates the token in (25) (recall that, after the pitch peak of each pitch accent, in phrase-medial position the f0 contour falls steadily after the peak; in Figure 12.6 we see sustained high pitch into the postaccentual syllable of the word

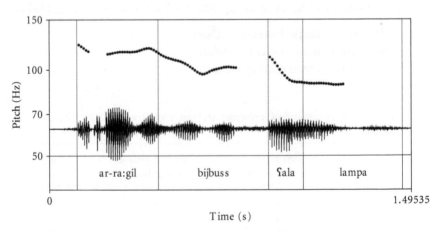

FIGURE 12.6 Sample minor juncture phrase boundary [41ARZ-O04–01M].

['raːgil], indicating a high phrase tone marking a minor prosodic juncture[9]).

(25)   [ar-**raːgil** bijbusˤsˤ ˤala lampa]
       the-man he-looks at   lamp
       'The man is looking at a lamp.'

In summary then, and contrary to the complementarity hypothesis, both syntactic and prosodic strategies are used in EA in the realization of focus. In some instances the strategies work in tandem, as in the instances of clefts accompanied by prosodic effects, but the strategies are also observed independently.

12.4.2 Thetics

The thetics dataset is made up of utterances elicited in 'all new' contexts. These include 128 descriptions elicited from eight speakers using single pictures each denoting a transitive or intransitive action (in response to the question 'What's happening?') (64 transitive + 64 intransitive utterances).[10] A further sixty-four tokens were extracted from the main QUIS corpus, being the opening utterance in other tasks such as descriptions of short animated films or picture sequences. The total corpus of potential thetics comprises 192 tokens. Among these 192 tokens, 161 (84 percent) are produced with an indefinite subject. In the other thirty-one tokens (16 percent), twenty eight are produced with a definite subject and three with a null subject; in these cases the speaker is deemed not to have interpreted the context as 'all new', thus they are excluded from analysis.

In the 161 tokens produced with an indefinite subject the following syntactic strategies are used:

(26)   10 existential construction [fiːh] 'there is'
       65 deictic presentational   [da]/[di]/[dul] 'this/those'
       86 monoclausal   indefinite subject is clause-initial

The expected construction in an eventive context, according to Sasse (1987), is the existential [fiːh]. In the current data set however it is used in only ten tokens (6 percent of felicitous tokens), and mostly only by one speaker, 04M, who produced five of the ten existential constructions observed. This speaker was incidentally the least computer-literate of the speakers, and the one who

---

[9] See El Zarka (2008) for an alternative analysis of sustained postaccentual pitch in EA.
[10] For sample methodology and visual stimuli see task 'Event Cards' in QUIS (Skopeteas et al. 2006).

most readily engaged with the event world of the pictures he saw (token [27ARZ-A11–04M]):

(27)   [illi bijaħsˁul   innu   fi:h   ra:gil   ...
       REL it-happens   that   there-is man   <uh>
       bijʕazzif ʕala ʔa:la   nuħa:sijja]
       he-plays   on   instrument   brass
       'What's happening is that there is a man playing a brass instrument.'

Although the number of existential [fi:h] constructions is relatively low, there are also a large number of what may be termed deictic presentationals (40 percent of felicitous tokens), whereby the subject is introduced with a deictic, arguably to avoid an utterance-initial indefinite subject (token [27ARZ-Y05T-03M]):

(28)   [da   ʕa:mil bijʃiddi ħa:ga   bi   silsila]
       this(m.) worker he-pulls something with chain
       'This is a worker pulling something with a chain.'

All of the remaining tokens are monoclausal utterances with a clause-initial indefinite subject (53 percent of felicitous tokens), and these include sentences with an overt verb (SV and SVO) as well as sentences containing no verb but only a subject and predicate (termed 'nominal sentences' in traditional Arabic grammar). There are no instances whatsoever of the use of syntactic inversion in EA in the current dataset; that is, utterances along the lines of *[bityanni sitt] (she-sings a-woman 'A woman sings') were not produced by any of the participants.

In order to look for potential instances of prosodic inversion, we need to find tokens in which the speaker chose to realize a picture description with an intransitive verb in a short utterance. Among the full dataset of 192 tokens, speakers used intransitive verbs in sixty-eight tokens, including:

(29)   [jiʕazzif] 'he plays' (of music)   [jurʕusˁ]   'he dances'
       [jiɣanni]   'he sings'   [jiʔajjatˁ] 'he cries' (of a baby)
       [jiʕu:m]   'he swims'   [jidˤħak]   'he laughs/smiles'
       [jigri]   'he runs'   [jisˤrux]   'he screams'

In thirty-four of these sixty-eight tokens the speaker nonetheless assigned an object to the verb ('He is playing the trombone.'/'He is running a marathon.'). The remaining thirty-four tokens—thetic sentences introducing a single agent argument to the discourse in an all-new context—were all produced with an accent on both agent and verb. Of these thirty-four tokens, just seventeen were produced as plain SV (with no other additional material in the utterance), and all of these plain argument + predicate utterances were realized with an accent on both subject and verb. An example of a thetic SV token is provided in (30) and illustrated in Figure 12.7 below, though the accent on the phrase-final verb is not readily visible due to the following rising phrase-boundary. In a parallel example, a thetic SV in which the speaker produced the subject with an adjectival modifier ('a small boy') as in (31), the accent on the phrase-final verb is somewhat clearer as illustrated in Figure 12.8. A deictic example, as in (32), is illustrated in Figure 12.9.

(30)   [sitti   bitɣanni]
        woman   she-sings
        'A woman is singing'

(31)   [walad sˤuɣajjar bijʔayyatˤ]
        boy   small   he-cries
        'A small boy is crying.'

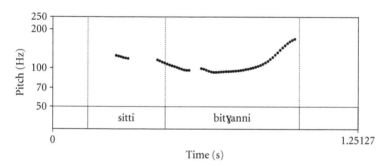

FIGURE 12.7 Sample intransitive thetic sentence with both words accented [27ARZ-Y09T-01M].

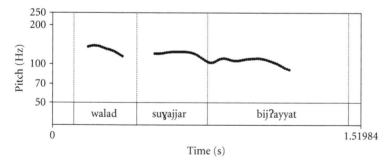

FIGURE 12.8 Sample intransitive thetic sentence with all words accented [27ARZ-Y15T-03M].

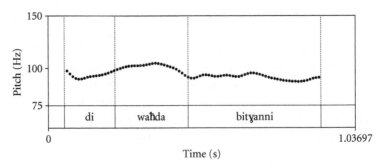

FIGURE 12.9 Deictic intransitive thetic sentence, with both arguments accented [27ARZ-Y09T-08M].

(32)   [di   waħda bityanni]
       this(f.) one   she-sings
       'This is someone singing.'

In the corpus of potential thetics examined here then, EA speakers employ a biclausal syntactic strategy (an existential construction or a deictic presentational) in just under half of felicitous tokens (46 percent). In the subset of the remaining cases in which we can readily test for instances of prosodic inversion (short sentences realized without an object argument) both argument and predicate are accented, suggesting that prosodic inversion is not employed in thetics in EA. Given the ban on deaccentuation of arguments in EA, and the availability of shifts of main prominence, it could be argued that we should instead be looking for instances of shift of main prominence to the initial argument in these cases. Nonetheless careful listening to the tokens in which a prosodic shift might be expected (the thirty-four short thetics realized without an object argument) reveals no cases in which main prominence is shifted away from the clause-final verb onto the clause-initial subject argument.

German and English are reported by Lambrecht (2001) to use prosodic shift in both focus and thetic contexts (to express both argument focus and sentence focus, in Lambrecht's terms), but it appears that prosodic shift (of main prominence) is used in EA only in the expression of focus (argument focus). This suggestion is supported by the observation in section 12.4.1 above that a shift of main prominence (realized by means of pitch range manipulation) is much more commonly observed in contrastive-focus contexts, than in information contexts. Although information-focus contexts arguably involve a choice among alternatives (among the set of entities about which the predication could hold), it appears that in EA shift of main prominence is restricted to contexts in which a choice is made among overt alternatives which are already present in the common ground. This matches a comment made by Gary and Gamal-Eldin (1981: 126) to the effect that use of contrastive stress in EA is 'limited to sequences where the contrasted elements are explicit'.

In summary then, and consistently with the complementarity hypothesis, syntactic strategies are observed in EA in the realization of thetics but no prosodic strategies (no deaccentuation of clause-final verbs and no main prominence shift onto clause-initial subjects).

12.4.3 *Summary*

The empirical survey reveals an overlap in the use of syntactic and prosodic strategies in EA in the expression of focus (section 12.4.1) but no such overlap in the expression of thetics (section 12.4.2). The former finding conflicts with the notion of functional complementarity between syntax and phonology in the expression of information structure, but the latter facts are just the type of scenario in which it might be tempting to make appeal to some form of functional complementarity between syntax and phonology in the expression of IS. One might for example wish to suggest that EA has syntactic strategies available for the expression of thetic status (biclausal existential and presentational constructions) and thus does not need to make use of prosodic shifts; or in the reverse logic, one might suggest that restriction of prosodic shifts to contexts involving overt alternatives is sustainable in EA because of the availability of alternative (syntactic) means of expression in thetic or information-focus contexts. The next section argues that this apparent lack of overlap in the division of labor between syntax and phonology should not be taken as evidence of functional complementarity, because the patterns of accentuation in thetics can be explained from independent properties of the phonological grammar of the language.

12.5 Discussion

The results of the empirical survey set out in section 12.4 are argued here to speak against functional complementarity between syntax and phonology in the expression of IS, for two reasons. The first and most obvious reason is that we see in EA an overlap in the use of syntactic and prosodic structures, within a single IS context (the focus context, described in section 12.4.1). This matches Lambrecht's careful comment that 'different focus-marking devices may to some extent coexist in the same language' Lambrecht (2001: 488). It may be that there are nuances of pragmatic function which distinguish the contexts in which a particular strategy (syntactic or prosodic) is employed but this is an empirical question which requires further investigation.

Perhaps the key problem with the notion of functional complementarity is not then the notion of mutual exclusivity (strictly either syntax or prosody) but rather the notion of a correlation between availability of strategies in one component and their necessary non-availability in the other. An example of this kind of notion is a suggestion by Engdahl and Vallduví (1994: 50) that 'the ability to exploit intonational structure for informational purposes makes syntactic marking less crucial'.

I propose that we should look for explanations for the non-availability of a particular strategy within its own component of the grammar in that language, rather than in some other component of the grammar. Thus the lack of a phonological strategy in language X will be due to some property of the phonology of language X, rather than due to a property of the syntax of language X. Any correlations among properties will be found within an individual component of the grammar, not across components of the grammar. In EA then, an explanation for the lack of prosodic shift in thetics must be found in the phonological, and not syntactic, grammar of EA.

The relevant correlating properties in EA are: (i) lack of deaccenting and (ii) equal accentuation of predicates and arguments (see section 12.3.2). I suggest that both can be explained by appeal to an independent phonological property of the language, namely that in EA every content word is routinely accented, as has been shown in a range of contexts and speech styles (Hellmuth 2006b). A formal phonological analysis of this phenomenon appeals to accent distribution at the level of the prosodic word in EA, instead of at some higher level of prosodic constituency such as the phonological phrase (Hellmuth 2007b). A typical EA utterance will be accented on every word, as already noted above. This is true even in naturally occurring spontaneous speech, as in the example from a corpus of spontaneous telephone conversations (Karins et al. 2002) shown in (33) and illustrated in Figure 12.10.

(33)   [w-eħna ʔaddimna l-aħmad   fi-l-madrasa   l-inglizijja
       and-we   applied   for-Ahmed in-the-school the-English
       illi   wara:na   it-tagribiyya]
       that behind-us the-experimental
       'We have applied for (a place for) Ahmed at the (experimental) English school behind us.'

How does a phonological requirement that every prosodic word bear an accent explain the examples of the prosodic reflexes of IS (focus and givenness)

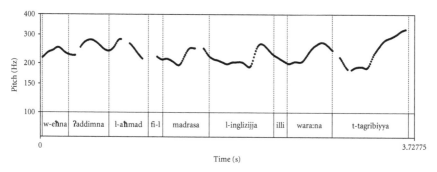

FIGURE 12.10 Pitch accent distribution in spontaneous speech in EA [4862B:330.53–334.27].

that we have see thus far? The argument goes like this: if every lexical word (whether argument or predicate) is routinely mapped to a prosodic word, and if in turn every prosodic word is routinely accented, then we have an explanation for the observed equal accentuation of predicates and arguments in EA. In a similar way, if a well-formed prosodic word in EA must obligatorily bear an accent then we have an explanation for the lack of deaccenting in EA, regardless of IS context (givenness or position relative to a focus). Interestingly, a similar pattern of rich accent distribution has been noted as a property of other languages including Spanish and Greek (Jun 2005), and most notably also of Italian (Grice et al. 2005). Thus rich accent distribution may also explain the lack of deaccenting and equal accentuation of predicates and arguments in Italian.

By way of analogy, I would like to suggest that attempts to classify languages as using mostly prosodic or mostly syntactic strategies for expression of IS are problematic in the same way that attempts to classify languages as being 'stress-timed' or 'syllable-timed' are. Whilst these rhythmic classifications are very useful, and indeed have some psychological reality,[11] it has been shown that they do not represent a genuine phonological distinction: when measured there is no actual isochrony of syllables or of stress groups (Roach 1982). Instead, the overall impression of being syllable-timed or stress-timed is now thought to be an epiphenomenon of other genuinely primitive properties of the segmental phonology of a particular language, such as the degree of complexity of consonant clusters or the degree of vowel reduction in unstressed syllables (Ramus 2002).

[11] Listeners are able to classify languages at extreme ends of the stress-timed vs syllable-timed continuum, but are not able to distinguish between languages which are close neighbors at some mid-point along the continuum.

In a parallel way then, I suggest that an apparent classification of a language as using mostly syntactic strategies or mostly prosodic strategies in the expression of IS should not be seen as a property of the language per se, but rather as the combined result of the independent properties of individual components of the grammar of that language (cf. Féry 2006). In essence, this equates to a claim that there is no IS module of grammar, but rather that surface IS expressions are due to the interaction of the other components of the grammar (including but not limited to syntax and phonology). The claim is testable in that it will stand or fail depending on whether explanations for observed tendencies in the expression of IS can (or cannot) always be found within the relevant component of the grammar. As investigation of the expression of IS in more and more languages continues, I expect that a continuum of variation in the division of labour between syntax and phonology will increasingly be revealed. There will likely be languages at either end of the continuum which display a strong preference for employing elements of the phonological grammar over elements of the syntactic grammar, or vice versa, but there will just as likely be languages in which the distinction is simply not clear-cut. The real determinant of what strategy is used in any IS context will be found within the individual components of the grammar.

Acknowledgments

Thanks to the participants of the BGU workshop and to Caroline Féry for comments, to the Egyptian speakers who participated in the data collection, to Mustafa Mughazy and Ihab Shabana for judgments, to Dina El Zarka for transcription of the main QUIS corpus, and to Project D2 of the SFB 632 Information Structure, Universität Potsdam (funded by the DFG) for use of the experimental stimuli and data.

13

Syntax, information structure, embedded prosodic phrasing, and the relational scaling of pitch accents*

CAROLINE FÉRY

13.1 Introduction

In an intonation language like German, pitch accents are heads of prosodic constituents, which are themselves mapped from the syntax. The pitch accents can be more or less 'strong', and be realized at different f0 values, depending on their position in the sentence and on the information structure they convey. This paper proposes that pitch scaling in an intonation language such as German is relational rather than absolute. In other words, the height of a pitch accent depends on the presence of other pitch accents in the same prosodic domain. A pitch accent is higher than it would be in a baseline all-new sentence if it is associated to a narrow focus, and it is lower if it is associated to a given constituent. But if there is no other pitch accent to which it can compare in the same prosodic domain, no adjustment of pitch takes place. This is illustrated with experimental data from German in section 13.3. Other languages may behave differently in this respect, but given our little knowledge of issues concerning phonological scaling of tones in intonation languages so far, it is too early to take a strong position on this issue. Pitch accent scaling is an important component of the relation between syntax and prosody. This paper presents a model in

* I would like to express our gratitude to Nomi Ertheschik-Shir and Lisa Rochman for their editorial work. Many thanks to my colleagues of the SFB 632 on Information Structure, as well as to an anonymous reviewer. Last but not least, Kirsten Brock owns my gratitude for a careful reading of this paper.

which information structures does not change prosodic phrasing, but only influences relative register of prosodic domains—it boosts narrowly focused constituents and lowers given ones. The prosodic phrasing is not touched when information structure changes. The next section introduces theoretical background information on prosodic phrasing and pitch accents, and section 13.3 reviews experiments relevant to the main issue of the paper. Section 13.4 concludes.

13.2 Background

13.2.1 *Prosodic domains and syntax*

A breakthrough in the long history of the theoretical approaches to how syntax shapes prosody was achieved by the emergence of prosodic hierarchies, as proposed by Selkirk (1984), Nespor and Vogel (1986), and many others after them. Prosodic hierarchies capture the insight that morphosyntactic units are mapped to prosodic units of different sizes, even if the mapping is not strictly isomorphic. A grammatical word, for instance, often forms a Prosodic Word, and some morphological operations, like reduplication or hypochoristic formation in many languages, can only be fully understood if their prosodic structure is taken into account (McCarthy and Prince 1990). At a high level of the prosodic hierarchy, sentences correspond to Intonation Phrases (Liberman 1975 [1978/9]; Pierrehumbert 1980; Liberman and Pierrehumbert 1984) and are assigned intonational patterns.

Phonologists largely agree on units like Prosodic Words and Intonation Phrases, but the intermediate prosodic domains have been a matter of debate. Most researchers assume two levels of prosodic phrasing between Prosodic Word and Intonation Phrase, and these have been given a variety of names, as for instance 'Minor Phrase' and 'Major Phrase' (Poser 1984; Selkirk 1986), 'Accent Phrase' and 'Intermediate Phrase' (Beckman and Pierrehumbert 1986; Gussenhoven 2004; Jun 2005), or 'Clitic Group' and 'Phonological Phrase' (Nespor and Vogel 1986 [2008]). Together with a restrictive view of what is allowed in the prosodic mapping from syntax to prosodic structure, like the Strict Layer Hypothesis (Selkirk 1984; Nespor and Vogel 1986 [2008]), which forbids recursive structure, the assumption of a maximum of two layers of phrasing can be interpreted as a prohibition on long sentences.

But of course, in the same way as syntax cannot restrict sentences to a certain length—there is no way of forcing a sentence to have, say, maximally five embedded clauses—there should also be no way of restricting the number of prosodic domains that a sentence may have. For this reason, the prosodic phrasing resulting from the syntax–prosody mapping should be recursive and unconstrained. As an answer to the contradiction between the few prosodic levels and the recursion prohibition, a few authors have proposed to eliminate the restriction imposed on the prosodic hierarchy, at least for those levels which are situated at the interface between syntax and prosody. Wagner (2005) proposes calling all levels of prosodic structure 'feet', and Ito and Mester (2007) call the levels higher than the metrical foot 'phonological phrase' or just 'phrase'. Ito and Mester distinguish between 'minimal phrase', 'phrases', and 'maximal phrase'. These three levels of phrasing may present different properties. Only the non-minimal and non-maximal phrases are recursive.

In this paper, the mapping between syntax and prosody results in prosodic domains that are called p-phrases (for prosodic phrases), and that can be embedded into each other. It assumes recursive phrasing at all levels of the prosodic hierarchy, starting at the Prosodic Word. In particular, it includes a recursive phrasing pattern of p-phrases and intonation phrases (called here i-phrases).

We will not be concerned too much about the details of how to construct prosodic phrasing from the syntactic structure. A number of competing theories have been proposed in the literature. To name just a few, consider 'relation-based' theories (Nespor and Vogel 1986 [2008]), 'edge-based' theories (Selkirk 1986), alignment in Optimality Theory (Truckenbrodt 1999; Selkirk 2000; Féry and Samek-Lodovici 2006), and minimalist phase and Spell-Out (Ishihara 2007; Kahnemuyipour 2004; Kratzer and Selkirk 2007). The main idea behind all accounts is that syntactic categories are mapped to prosodic phrases, either in considering syntactic constituents as the base of the mapping (relation-based and phase) or in taking syntactic edges as crucial (edge-based and alignment). Since the concern of this paper is not about how mapping arises, we simply assume the account formulated in Féry and Samek-Lodovici (2006), without entering into detail.

P-phrases have phonetic correlates, the most important ones being the presence of a main pitch accent per p-phrase, considered the 'head' of the p-phrase, and boundary tones. The presence of a pitch accent is often considered as definitional for a p-phrase, an idea that we use in the following discussion.

There are a few problems which are recurrent in all theoretical approaches to prosodic phrasing. These problems are related to the fact that prosodic phrases are projected from the surface syntactic structure, but that this syntactic level does not contain all the necessary information to explain the observed accent pattern.

First, consider German sentences with unergative intransitive verbs. In this kind of sentences, both the subject and the verb are accented.

In a conventional view of prosodic phrasing, which is adopted here for the default prosodic structure, every p-phrase is headed by a pitch accent. If this view is correct, as I assume for the default case, sentences like (1a) consist of two p-phrases. Sentences with unaccusative intransitive verbs have, in contrast, only one accent on the subject and none on the verb. This is illustrated in (1b). Accordingly, they form only one p-phrase.

(1) a. [Ein Junge]ₚ [tanzt]ₚ
         a   boy   dances
         'A boy dances.'

     b. [Die Diva ist gestorben]ₚ
         The diva is died
         'The diva has died.'

Since these sentences have the same surface syntactic structure, it has been assumed that deep syntactic properties are relevant for sentence accent assignment (Krifka 1984; Kratzer 1988; Diesing 1988). The subject is VP-internal in (1b), but VP-external in (1a).[1] In a minimalist model, in which each phase is a spell-out domain with its own pitch accent, it must be assumed that the verb plus subject are a single phase in the case of unaccusatives, but are spelled out in two phases in sentences with unergative verbs.

A second thorny aspect of the phrasing and subsequent accent pattern has to do with the distinction between argument and adjunct (see Gussenhoven 1992). Especially in locative prepositional phrases, but also in other types of prepositional or adverbial phrases, it is sometimes difficult to assess the argumental or adjunctive nature of phrases. Consider the German examples in (2). In (2a), the locative is an argument, but in (2b), it is an adjunct (see also Krifka 1984 for such pairs). The distinction is essential because, according to a large part of the literature (Gussenhoven 1992; Selkirk 1984; Cinque 1993) a verb is part of the p-phrase of an adjacent argument, and is consequently not accented, whereas the same is not true in case of an adjunct. In this latter configuration, both the adjunct and the verb are maximal projections and should be phrased separately (see below for experimental results on accent placement in this kind of sentences).

(2) a. [Moritz]ₚ [hat in Stuttgart übernachtet]ₚ
         Moritz   has in Stuttgart spent-the-night
         'Moritz spent the night in Stuttgart.'

---

[1] In an alternative model, the subject is a specifier in the VP, whereas the object is a complement in the VP.

b. [MORITZ]$_P$ [has in STUTTGART]$_P$ [GESUNGEN]$_P$
    Moritz   has in Stuttgart   sung
    'Moritz sang in Stuttgart.'

The third difficult case comes from aspects of information structure which change the pitch accent structure of a sentence. Some authors treat the effects of syntax and information structure on prosody in the same way in that information structure primarily changes the phrasing of sentences. The change in accent structure is then an indirect effect of the changed p-phrasing (Gussenhoven 1992; Truckenbrodt 1999). In a minimalist approach, this view of phrasing means that not only phases are mapped to prosodic phrases, but the information structure also projects phases and spell-out domains. The change in p-phrasing is illustrated in (3) with English examples. In (3a) the sentence is all-new and has two accents, one on the subject and another one on the object. In (3b), only the subject is focused. As a result, the phrasing has changed because there is a unique accent on the subject, and none on the object. All accounts of prosodic phrasing which assume that every p-phrase is obligatorily headed by a pitch accent, regardless of information structure, have to change prosodic phrasing when accent structure is modified.

(3) a. {What happened?}
         [MAX]$_P$ [stole a CHICKEN]$_P$
     b. {Who stole a chicken?}
         [MAX$_F$ stole a chicken]$_P$

In this paper, I propose separating the effects of syntax from those of information structure. Only syntax influences phrasing, and information structure determines the presence and the height of pitch accents. In some cases, pitch accents are just not realized, and a p-phrase can exist without a pitch accent. As a result, example (3) always has the phrasing shown in (3a), regardless of the information structure and pitch accents.

Some problems related to the phrasing of sentences with different information-structure patterns remain that have to do with the contextual framework of the sentences. For example, the same sentence can be thetic or categorical, depending on the context in which it is uttered. If the subject of a presentational sentence is a topic, as in (4a), both the subject and the verb are in separate p-phrases, and both have an accent. But if the whole sentence expresses a unique event, as in (4b), only the subject has an accent, because the subject and the verb are part of the same p-phrase. Since these sentences are both all-new, the difference in accent structure is truly due to a difference in phrasing. In other words, the deaccenting of the particle *durch* is not due to givenness, as in example (3), in which the chicken had already been mentioned in the context, and was deaccented for this reason. Similarly to (1), in which unergative and unaccusative verbs have different syntactic structures, thetic sentences must be syntactically distinct from categorical sentences. But the difference between thetic and categorical sentences is a discourse-structural one, and not necessarily anchored in the syntax.

(4) a. [Ein ZUG]ₚ [fährt   DURCH]ₚ (und ein Auto muss an der
         A   train is-passing through (and a car must wait at the
         Ampel warten.)
         traffic light.)

    b. (Achtung auf Gleis 1.)   [Ein ZUG fährt durch]ₚ
        Attention on platform 1.   A train is passing through

The theoretical status of pitch accents as heads of p-phrases has been instantiated in the form of a metrical structure which calculates the difference in strength of the metrical positions from their level of embedding in a tree or in a grid (Liberman 1975 [1978/9]; Liberman and Prince 1977; Selkirk 1984; Halle and Vergnaud 1987). In some of these approaches (see for instance Selkirk 2002), levels of the metrical structure may strictly correspond to prosodic domains, as shown in (5). The head of an Intonation Phrase (IP) has a stronger metrical position than the head of a p-phrase, which is itself higher than the head of a Prosodic Word (PW). If the number of levels in the prosodic structure is invariable, a one-to-one correspondence between metrical beats and prosodic domains can be established.

```
(5)  (                                          ×   )  IP
     (     ×  ) (          ×   ) (    ×   ) (      ×   )  p-phrase
     (     ×  ) ( × ) (          ×   ) (    ×   ) ( × )( × )  PW
```
    Ms Martin went to the market with a basket full of eggs

However, if p-phrasing is recursive, as assumed here, such a correspondence is not necessary. The height of metrical beats is related to the number of embeddings in the p-phrasing. This is illustrated in (6) with names grouped in different ways (see Wagner 2005 and Féry and Kentner 2008 for examples of this kind). In such a case, it is not possible to attribute a specific level of the prosodic hierarchy to a specific grouping. Doing so would inflate the number of prosodic domains in an uncontrollable way.

```
(6)                                                ×   p-phrase
                           ×                ×      ×   p-phrase
                    ×      ×                ×      ×   p-phrase
             ×      ×      ×      ×     ×      ×   p-phrase
```
    a. (((Lena and Arno)ₚ and Bill)ₚ ((and Tom and Anny)ₚ (and Sam)ₚ)ₚ)ₚ...

					×	p-phrase
×				×	×	p-phrase
×	×	×	×	×	×	p-phrase

b. (((Lena)$_P$ (and Arno and Bill and Tom)$_P$)$_P$ (and Anny and Sam) $_P$)$_P$...

To conclude this section, prosodic domains are mapped from syntactic phrases, but this mapping does not necessarily correlate with specific levels of prosody. Recursion of p-phrases is assumed, which allows a finer-grained scaling of pitch accents, as shown in the next section.

13.2.2 *The height (and strength) of pitch accents*

A problem which has only seldom been addressed in the relevant literature is how to calculate the fundamental frequency (fo) value of accents based on their prosodic and metrical positions (but see Pierrehumbert 1980; Liberman and Pierrehumbert 1984; Truckenbrodt 2004 for proposals involving simple structures). Consider nuclear stress. Since Chomsky and Halle (1968), phonologists and syntacticians regularly mention that the last accent in the sentence is the strongest one, and that it is the nuclear stress. This is certainly true for an accent standing for a narrow contrastive focus, especially if it is an early constituent in the sentence (see (3b)). In this case, the pitch accent is the last one, and postfocal material is flat and low, which gives an impression of extra prominence on the accent. But things are different when the sentence is all-new, that is when no constituent in the sentence is particularly emphasized, as in (3a) or (5). In this case, the nuclear stress is generally the pitch accent with the lowest frequency, the smaller pitch range, and the weakest acoustic energy.[2] The reason for this is to be found in the downstep pattern of pitch accents, which reduces each pitch accent relative to the preceding one (see Liberman and Pierrehumbert 1984 for English and Truckenbrodt 2004 for German).

To account for this effect, it is proposed here that p-phrases have an abstract range inside of which accents are scaled (see Bruce 1977; Clements 1981; Ladd 1990 for similar proposals for different languages). In the unmarked case, a sequence of p-phrases at the same level of prosodic phrasing has pitch registers organized in a downstepped pattern, as illustrated in Figure 13.1. Since the range of a p-phrase is narrower than the range of a preceding p-phrase in the same i-phrase, the pitch accent heading it is lower than the pitch accent preceding it. The reduced prominence of the last accent

---

[2] Gussenhoven (1992) and Selkirk (2000) deny the presence of nuclear stress in all-new sentences.

FIGURE 13.1 Downstep pattern of unembedded p-phrases.

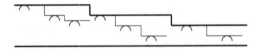

FIGURE 13.2 Downstep pattern of embedded p-phrases.

(the nuclear stress) in an all-new sentence is just a consequence of this pattern. Pitch accents are indicated with the help of a convex form.

Since the p-phrasing is recursive, every p-phrase can itself contain p-phrases, which are also in a downstep relationship to each other. The head pitch accents are thus scaled inside of these embedded p-phrases. A similar proposal of embedding downstepped regions has been made by a number of researchers (Ladd 1990; van den Berg, Gussenhoven, and Rietveld 1992; Truckenbrodt 2007; Féry and Truckenbrodt 2005). This is illustrated in Figure 13.2.

Information structure, like focus or givenness, enlarges or reduces the range of a prosodic phrase. A narrow focus has the effect of raising the top line of the corresponding p-phrase, and a given constituent has the effect of lowering it. This is illustrated in Figure 13.3 and Figure 13.4, respectively (see below, Féry and Ishihara 2009a,b).

As far as givenness is concerned, a difference is made between pre- and postnuclearity. If a given p-phrase appears before the nuclear accent, its range is narrowed, but a pitch accent can still be realized (see Figure 13.4). In the postnuclear region, however, the range is completely compressed, and no

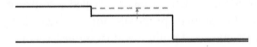

FIGURE 13.3 Raising of the top line of a p-phrase because of narrow focus.

FIGURE 13.4 Lowering of the top line of a p-phrase because of givenness.

pitch accent can be realized anymore.

This model of pitch accent scaling, based on register domains in downstep and upstep relationship with each other makes a number of predictions:

1. Downstep: An early pitch accent is higher than a later one in the same sentence, everything else being equal. Embedding of pitch ranges into each other accounts for finer differences.
2. Reset: A later accent can be higher than a preceding one if the preceding accent is the head of a more deeply embedded p-phrase.
3. Relative height: The scaling of pitch accents is relative. This means that a pitch accent height may only be raised or lowered as compared to pitch accents in the same intonational domain.

In the next section, some experimental data are discussed that confirm these predictions.

13.3 Experimental results

13.3.1 *Downstep occurs in all-new sentences*

The first prediction claims that pitch accents at the same level of prosodic phrasing are in a downstep relationship to each other, as illustrated in Figures 13.1 and 13.2. This has been shown a number of times for a sequence of arguments in simple syntactic structures or in lists, for English, German, and other languages (see, for example, Liberman and Pierrehumbert 1984 and Ladd 1990 for English; van den Berg, Gussenhoven, and Rietveld 1992 for Dutch; Truckenbrodt 2004 for Southern German).

Féry and Kügler (2008) show that in a German simple syntactic sentence, downstep is just one option of how to realize several accents in a sequence. Another one is that the last accent is upstepped and is thus much higher than it would be if downstep had happened regularly. We explain this result with an optional rule of H-raising (see, for instance, Laniran and Clements 2003 for H-raising in Yoruba, and Xu 1999 in Chinese). Notwithstanding the occurrence of H-raising in part of the data, downstep is considered the default realization of a Standard German all-new sentence.

13.3.2 *Reset at a p-phrase boundary*

The second prediction posits that the second of a sequence of two accents can be higher than the first one if they belong to different prosodic domains. This effect has been called 'reset' by Liberman and Pierrehumbert (1984). The constellation has been illustrated in Figure 13.2, and is also visible in

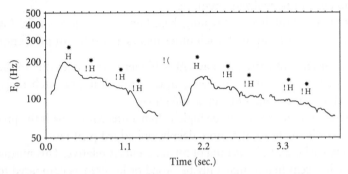

FIGURE 13.5 Partial reset and embedded downstep in the Dutch utterance (*Merel, Nora, Leo, Remy*), *en* (*Nelie, Mary, Leendert, Mona en Lorna*). From van den Berg, Gussenhoven, and Rietveld (1992).

Figure 13.5 from van den Berg, Gussenhoven, and Rietveld (1992). This figure shows that when a larger utterance is divided into two shorter i-phrases, each of them contains downstepped accents, and the first high tone of the second i-phrase is higher than the last tone of the first i-phrase, but lower than the first high tone of the first i-phrase.

Féry and Truckenbrodt (2005) reproduced for German an experiment by Ladd (1990), who showed that a sequence of three syntactically and semantically related English sentences are in a downstep and/or reset relationship, depending on how their internal syntactic and prosodic structure looks. In Féry and Truckenbrodt, two conditions were examined in a production experiment with the patterns in (7) and (8).

(7)   First condition: A while [B and C]
      {Why does Anna think that craftsmen have more expensive cars than musicians?}
      [Weil der <u>Maler</u> einen <u>Jaguar</u> hat]ₐ, [[während die <u>Sängerin</u> einen <u>Lada</u> besitzt]_B, und [der <u>Geiger</u> einen <u>Wartburg</u> fährt]_C]
      'Because the painter has a Jaguar, while the singer owns a Lada, and the violinist drives a Wartburg.'

(8)   Second condition: [A and B] while C
      {Why does Anna think that musicians have less expensive cars than craftsmen?}
      [[Weil die Sᴀ̈ɴɢᴇʀɪɴ einen Lᴀᴅᴀ besitzt]ₐ, [und der Gᴇɪɢᴇʀ einen Wᴀʀᴛʙᴜʀɢ fährt]_B], [während der Mᴀʟᴇʀ einen Jᴀɢᴜᴀʀ hat]_C

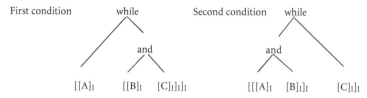

First condition   while   Second condition   while

and   and

[[A]₁   [[B]₁   [C]₁]₁]₁   [[[A]₁   [B]₁]₁   [C]₁]₁

FIGURE 13.6 Two conditions in the experiment reported in Féry and Truckenbrodt (2005).

'Because the singer owns a Lada, and the violinist drives a Wartburg, while the painter has a Jaguar.'

The difference between the prosodic structures of the two conditions is illustrated in Figure 13.6. In the first condition, B and C form a constituent together, and in the second condition, it is A and B which are grouped into a single constituent. In both conditions, the three sentences form a prosodic constituent together, so that the sentence standing alone is also in a relevant scaling relationship to the other two. I assume a recursive structure: all sentences are i-phrases, the grouping of two sentences is also an i-phrase, and the whole utterance is again an i-phrase.[3]

The tonal structure of a sentence of the first condition is shown in (9). Speakers were very consistent in their tonal realizations. Important for the pitch scaling is the value of the first H tone in each sentence.

(9)   {Why does Anna think that sportsmen have less expensive cars than craftsmen?}

$\quad\quad\quad$ L*H $\quad\quad\quad\quad$ L*H $\quad\quad$ H₁

[[Weil [der RINGER]ₚ [[einen LADA]ₚ besitzt]ₚ]₁ $\quad\quad$ A

$\quad\quad\quad\quad$ L*H $\quad\quad\quad\quad$ L*H $\quad\quad$ H₁

[[während [der MALER]ₚ [[einen JAGUAR]ₚ fährt]ₚ]₁ $\quad\quad$ B

$\quad\quad\quad\quad$ L*H $\quad\quad\quad$ H*L $\quad\quad$ L₁

[und [der WEBER]ₚ [[einen DAIMLER]ₚ hat]ₚ]₁]₁]₁ $\quad\quad$ C

'Because the wrestler owns a Lada, while the painter drives a Jaguar and the weaver has a Daimler.'

The production experiment was conducted at the University of Potsdam with five students, native speakers of Standard German, who uttered thirty-two experimental sentences each. The pattern which emerged from the experiment is that the first condition shows a downstep pattern throughout, as in

---

[3] This assumption differs from the pattern presented in Féry and Truckenbrodt, in which we were more traditional in avoiding recursion of intonation phrases.

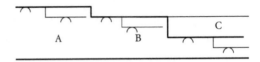

FIGURE 13.7 Result of the production experiment of Féry and Truckenbrodt (2005) for the first condition.

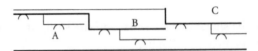

FIGURE 13.8. Result of the production experiment of Féry and Truckenbrodt (2005) for the second condition.

Figure 13.7, but the second condition elicited a reset on the C sentence, as shown in Figure 13.8. The first high tone of this sentence was slightly higher than the first high tone of sentence B. Moreover, this tone was much higher than it was in the first condition.

In short, downstep and reset both play a role in German, and in order to calculate the fo value of pitch accents in all-new sentences, it is necessary to take both into consideration. A model like the one illustrated in Figures 13.7 and 13.8 is helpful to understand the full pattern of tonal scaling.

13.3.3 *Relational scaling*

The third prediction has never been addressed in this form before, and the remainder of this chapter is dedicated to its empirical assessment. It posits that the scaling of the fo value of a pitch accent is essentially relational. Raising or lowering of pitch accents because of information structure only makes sense if it takes place relative to some other pitch accent. The reason for this is that pitch accents are adjusted to register domains which are downstepped relative to their predecessors, and embedded into each other, as shown above. If there is only one prosodic phrase, no downstep and no raising take place, because there is no other register domain relative to which this change can take place. This complex relationship cannot be expressed if pitch accents are addressed directly.

13.3.3.1 *Sentences with fronted objects*   In order to test this crucial prediction for the model presented, German sentences with object fronting, as illustrated in (10), are used. In this type of structure, an object is fronted in the sentence-initial,

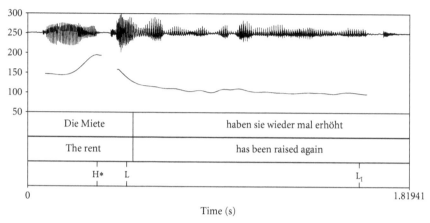

FIGURE 13.9 Pitch track of *Die* MIETE *haben sie wieder mal erhöht.*

preverbal position. Both a narrow focus on the fronted object and an all-new reading are available.

$$H^*L \qquad\qquad L_I$$

(10) [[Die MIETE haben sie   wieder   mal   erhöht]_F]_I
      the   rent   have   they   again   once raised
      'They have raised the rent again.'

Figure 13.9 shows a pitch track of this sentence. The only tonal excursion happens on the fronted object, and the remainder of the sentence has a low and flat intonational contour.[4]

Thirty students from the University of Potsdam were recorded. All participants were native speakers of German. Each of them read twelve experimental sentences aloud, as illustrated in (11), as answers to context questions. Additionally, they read 100 unrelated filler sentences presented in a pseudo-randomized order. The object of the target sentences was generic or specific, to check for possible effects of specificity.

(11) Wide focus: {Did you go out afterwards?}
      Narrow focus: {What did you drink?}
          Ein Bier haben wir getrunken./   Ein Jever haben wir getrunken.
          a beer/a Jever have we drunk   'We drank a beer/a Jever.'

---

[4] See Fanselow (2004) and Fanselow and Lenertová (2008) for syntactic accounts of these sentences.

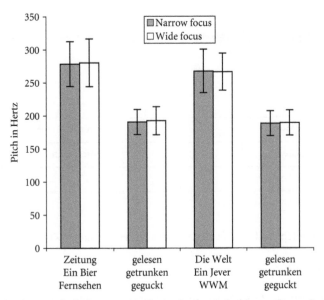

FIGURE 13.10 Averaged pitch accents in fo on the fronted objects of experiment 1. The first and third columns show the object (generic and specific) and the second and fourth columns stand for the verbs.

As predicted, in all sentences (altogether 360 realizations: 12 sentences x 30 subjects), a falling pitch accent was realized on the object and no other accent was present.

There was no difference in fo value between the narrow and the wide focus realization. All instances of the sentences were realized with a single accent on the object. There were some differences in the average fo of the objects and the verbs (see Figure 13.10). In the wide focus condition, the specific objects always had a lower pitch than the generic ones, but the difference is not significant[5] ($t = -0.543$, df $= 54.379$, $p = 0.5893$) and does not relate to the difference in focus context of interest here.[6] Thus no comparison regarding wide or narrow focus was significant ($t = -0.1571$, df $= 693.785$, $p = 0.8752$). No difference in height between an accent on the fronted object in a wide focus context and an accent on the same fronted object in a narrow focus

---

[5] I am grateful to Heiner Drenhaus for helping me with the statistical analysis of these data. A survey of additional experiments with similar sentences is reported in Féry and Drenhaus (2008).

[6] The remaining comparisons are not significant: verbs in the wide focus condition ($t = 1.0112$, df $= 170.951$, $p = 0.3134$), objects in the narrow focus condition ($t = 0.4405$, df $= 171.677$, $p = 0.6601$), and verbs in the narrow focus condition ($t = 0.9323$, df $= 171.772$, $p = 0.3525$).

context could be found. This result is compatible with the assumption that there is only one p-phrase, and that, in this case, the height of the top line of the p-phrase does not vary because there is no other register to which the unique p-phrase could adjust. For this reason, the pitch accents are scaled to a top line which is identical in the wide focus and in the narrow focus conditions.

13.3.3.2 *Subject + verb and object + verb*   In a second experiment, sentences consisting of subject + verb or of object + verb were tested. This experiment shows with another very simple syntactic structure that, if there is only one accent, and thus one p-phrase in the relevant VP, no change in fo value takes place in a narrow focus condition. But as soon as there are two accents in an all-new sentence corresponding to two p-phrases, the height of both accents is affected when a narrow focus is introduced. In such a case, the scaling of the accents is changed. These sentences were again tested in a production experiment, this time with fifteen female German students. The experimental sentences are illustrated in (12) to (15). They were inserted both in a wide focus (WF) and in a narrow focus (NF) conditions. There were four conditions, thus a 2 × 2 factorial design, and six sentences were constructed for each condition. Altogether 360 realizations were produced.[7]

(12)   Subject, WF:
    Q: {Why can't I find the ball?}
    A: Nun, wahrscheinlich haben ihn   [die Kinder mitgenommen]$_F$.
        well probably   have   it$_{ACC}$ the children taken-away
        'Well, probably the children took it away.'

(13)   Subject, NF:
    Q: {Who took the ball away?}
    A: Nun, wahrscheinlich haben ihn [die Kinder]$_F$ mitgenommen.

(14)   Object, WF:
    Q: {What did the children do?}
    A: Nun, wahrscheinlich haben sie [den Ball mitgenommen]$_F$.
        well probably   have   they the ball taken-away
        'Well, probably they took the ball away.'

(15)   Object, NF:
    Q: {What did the children take away?}
    A: Nun, wahrscheinlich haben sie [den Ball]$_F$ mitgenommen.

---

[7] Similar sentences in Hungarian and Japanese will be compared to German (see Ishihara and Féry, in prep).

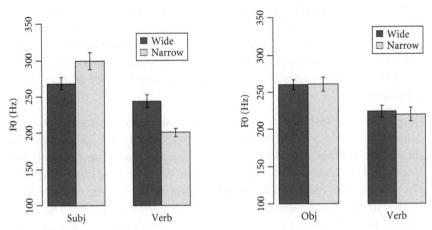

FIGURE 13.11 Mean fo-peak on the argument and on the verb (with 95% confidence interval).

The subject and the object sentences had a different accent pattern. An accent was always realized on the subject or on the object, but (16) shows that an accent was also sometimes realized on the verb in the subject sentences in the wide context condition (51 times in 90 utterances, 57 percent of the time). Otherwise no accent was produced on the verb, except for one case in an object sentence in the wide focus condition, which can be analyzed as a performance error.

(16)   Realized pitch accents on the verb
          Subject sentences in wide focus   51 (57%)
          Subject/Object sentences in narrow focus   0 (0%)
          Object sentences in wide focus   1 (1%)

Figure 13.11 shows the pitch height on the verb and on the subject/object in all conditions.

Because of the optional accent on the verb in the subject sentences, the verb was scaled significantly higher in the wide focus context than in the narrow focus context. This happened only in the subject sentences. The pitch accent on the verb in 57 percent of the cases had the effect of considerably raising the average fo of this constituent.

A secondary effect of the optional accent on the verb was a difference in the height of the pitch accent on the subject, which was higher in the narrow focus condition (when the verb was never accented) than in the wide focus condition (when the verb was sometimes accented).

Turning to the fo value of the unique accent in the object sentences, there was no significant difference between the pitch accent heights in the narrow and the wide contexts. This result confirms what was observed in the preceding experiment. The difference between the accent pattern and the concomitant fo value of the constituents is explained by phrasing. The object and the verb form only one p-phrase, both in the all-new and in the narrow focus contexts (Krifka 1984; Jacobs 1993), and, as a consequence, no change occurs in the scaling of the accents.

The subject, in contrast, optionally appears in a separate p-phrase. Following a suggestion by Gisbert Fanselow (p. c.), the subject can syntactically remain in situ in the VP, which leads to a unique p-phrase, as we saw above for the unaccusative sentences, or the subject may be fronted into the Spec IP position. In this latter case, the subject and the verb are separated in two p-phrases; see Fanselow (2004) and Frey (2004) for 'stylistic' or 'formal' fronting of one constituent in V2 sentences. The difference in phrasing between the object and the subject sentences is illustrated in (17). In (17a,b), the two options for the verb are shown for the subject sentences, and (17c) shows the unique phrasing in the object sentences.

(17)   Phrasing in subject and object sentences
      Subj: a. $[_{TP} \text{Aux } O_{pron} \quad S \text{ V}]_P$
              b. $[_{TP} \text{Aux } O_{pron} \quad S_i]_P [_{vP} t_i \quad \text{V}]_P$
      Obj: c. $[\text{Aux } S_{pron} O \quad \text{V}]_P$

The difference in phrasing correlates with a difference in metrical structure. Every p-phrase has a head, which means that the two phrasing options for the subject sentences in (17) correspond to different accent patterns, shown in (18) for the wide focus context. Both (18a) and (18c) have only one p-phrase, and thus one metrical head, but (18b) has two heads.

(18)   Metrical pattern in the subject and object sentences in the wide focus
      context

              ×
      a. (S   V)$_P$

              ×   ×
      b. (S) (V)$_P$

              ×
      c. (O   V)$_P$

The phrasing exemplified in (18) also corresponds to different register domains, as shown in Figure 13.12. (18a) and (18c) have only one p-phrase (Figure 13.12a). However (18b) has two p-phrases (Figure 13.12b).

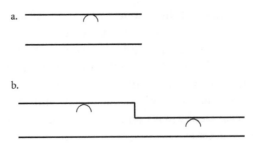

FIGURE 13.12 Difference in phrasing between the object and the subject sentences of experiment 2.

Consider next what happens in the narrow focus condition, as illustrated in Figure 13.13. In the conditions (18a) and (18c), shown in Figure 13.13a, nothing changes when the unique accent stands for a narrow focus. The register domain corresponding to the unique p-phrase has no other domain to which it can adjust. But in Figure 13.13b, narrow focus on the subject raises the top line of the first p-phrase, and lowers the top line of the second p-phrase, at least in those cases in which the subject is in a different p-phrase from the verb.

The pattern shown in Figure 13.13 provides an explanation for the last property of the results in Figure 13.11, namely the difference in height between the fo value of the subject and that of the object in the narrow focus condition. This value is higher on the subject than on the object. In the subject sentences with two p-phrases, a narrow focus has the effect of raising the corresponding top line, as shown in Figure 13.13b. Raising the top line is a purely relational effect, in which the register of one p-phrase is changed relative to the register of another p-phrase. In the object sentences and in the remaining cases of

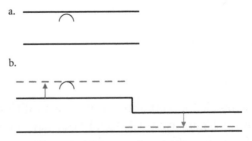

FIGURE 13.13 Pitch register change in the two p-phrases environment.

subject sentences, no readjustment is needed, since there is only one p-phrase. The verb has no accent in both cases, but the reason for the absence of accent is different. In the object sentences and in part of the subject sentence, this is due to the fact that only one p-phrase is formed on the entire sentence. In half of the subject sentences, the absence of pitch accent is due to compression of the post-nuclear register. These are the cases which relate to an increase of the height of the pitch accent on the subject, as shown in Figure 13.13b.

The metrical structure alone cannot account for this difference. It is sometimes assumed that a focus projects a pitch accent at a certain level of the prosodic structure (see, for instance, Selkirk 2002). Then both in (19a) and in (19b), an additional prominence is needed on the argument. Such a representation, however, leads to the expectation that the pitch height of a narrow focus does not depend on the presence of additional p-phrases. The pitch accents of the narrowly focused subject and object are expected to be identical, contrary to what we observe.

(19)   Metrical pattern in the subject and object sentences in the narrow focus context

$$
\begin{array}{llll}
\times & & \times & \\
\times & & \times & \times \\
\text{a.} \quad (S_F/O_F \ V)_P & & \text{b.} \quad (S_F)(V)_P &
\end{array}
$$

Also, if the metrical structure only reflects the relationship between accents, the difference between object and subject sentences just accounted for is unexpected. In both cases, a higher column of beats corresponds to a stronger pitch accent.

13.4 Discussion and conclusion

In short, the data presented in section 13.2 confirm that p-phrasing and metrical structure are not sufficient to account for all fo values observed in declarative sentences in German. A third component is needed which accounts for the relative scaling of accents. This component has been shown to be an abstract modeling of fo registers corresponding to p-phrases.

Traditionally it has been assumed that pitch accents can change their height on an individual basis: a narrowly focused word is higher than it would be in an all-new context. Similarly a given constituent has a lower fo value. In other words, accents are changed one by one.

The new perspective introduced in this paper is that the fo height of pitch accents is interpreted in relationship to neighboring accents. A change in one part of a sentence triggers changes in the other parts of the sentence.

Accents are purely relational. This explains why some narrowly focused accents increase their height while others do not. In particular, an accent as the head of a unique p-phrase does not change its value when its information structure is changed. This has been demonstrated with data involving object fronting, as well as with the object sentences of experiment 2. However when an accent standing for a narrow focus is in a sentence containing more than one p-phrase, the scaling of fo values is modified, and a narrow focus increases the fo height. This was illustrated with the subject sentences of experiment 2.

14

Deconstructing the Nuclear Stress Algorithm: Evidence from second language speech*

EMILY NAVA AND MARIA LUISA ZUBIZARRETA

14.1 Introduction

The relation between focus and prosody has long been recognized (Halliday 1967, 1970; Chomsky 1971; Jackendoff 1972), but it remains an issue of contention as to how this relation is established. On the one hand, focus has an effect on grammatical meaning. On the other hand, phrasal prominence plays an important role in determining which parts of the sentence can be interpreted as focused, i.e. as non-presupposed and under assertion. In some languages, focus affects the overt positioning of constituents in the syntactic structure (e.g. Hungarian), but not in others (e.g. English). Establishing the connection between phrasal prominence and focus-related meaning is particularly challenging in a model of grammar (such as the standard model in generative grammar), in which syntax mediates the relation between phonology and semantics.[1] One view has been to directly define the domain of focus in

* This research was funded by an NSF Grant BCS-0444088 (PI Maria Luisa Zubizarreta) and by a USC Undergraduate Research Grant. We would like to thank our Undergraduate Research Assistants Greg Madan and Monica Bennett for help with the coding of sound files, Sun-Ah Jun for very helpful discussions, as well as Julie Legate and Charles Yang for comments on an earlier version of this paper.

[1] There is a growing literature showing the impact of focus on the semantic interpretation of a sentence. While the effects of focus on truth-conditional meaning is generally observed in cases of contrastive focus and not in cases of informational focus, there is no reason to doubt that the two are one and the same semantic object. Furthermore, there is no reason to doubt that the semantics of focus in questions is any different from the semantics of focus in statements; the two only differ in the force conveyed by the sentence. Semantically, focus introduces a set of disjunctive propositions

terms of predicate-argument structure and pitch-accent distribution therein (the so-called 'Pitch-Accent First' theories put forth by Gussenhoven 1984 and Selkirk 1984). Another (more standard) view has been to introduce a feature *F(ocus)* to annotate the syntactic structure that feeds phonological interpretation (PF) and semantic interpretation (LF) (the so-called 'Stress-First' theories, put forth in Jackendoff 1972 and endorsed by many since then). At PF, it is required that the F-marked constituent of a phrase contain the rhythmically most prominent word in that phrase. At LF, an F-marked constituent is interpreted as the non-presupposed or asserted part of the sentence. Other approaches (also within the 'Stress-First' line of thought) attempt to directly relate main phrasal stress and interpretation (Neeleman and Reinhart 1998; Szendröi 2001, Vergnaud and Zubizarreta 2005; Reinhart 2006):

(1)   That part of the sentence that is *interpreted* as focused must contain the rhythmically most prominent word.

In the present work, we endorse the latter view, but will not discuss it further, except note that if (1) is indeed part of the grammar, then it must be the case that the PF and LF outputs are subject to congruency constraints beyond those imposed by narrow syntax.

In what follows we will only be concerned with the prosody of focus. Given space constraints, we cannot engage in a discussion of the different approaches on the focus-prosody connection, but see Truckenbrodt (2006a, 2007) for recent overviews of the literature. In this paper, we have two specific goals. We revisit the crosslinguistic analysis of NS for Germanic and Romance put forth in Zubizarreta 1998 and argue that the difference between the two types of languages can be traced back to a fundamental difference between them (already noted in Zubizarreta op.cit.), namely the fact that:

(2)   In Germanic, functional categories may be interpreted as metrically invisible, while in Romance functional categories are always metrically visible.

An important cue to the metrical invisibility of functional categories is that functional words (such as copulas, determiners, and prepositions) may be unstressed, which is indeed the case in Germanic but not in Romance. The metrical (in)visibility of functional categories has the following consequence (Zubizarreta and Vergnaud 2005):

(Hamblin 1973; Higginbotham1993). Contrastive focus may be analyzed as a case of exclusive disjunctions, while informational focus may be analyzed as a case of inclusive disjunctions (Vergnaud and Zubizarreta 2005).

(3)   In Germanic, a subset of the syntactic structure may be metrically interpreted, while in Romance the entire syntactic structure is always metrically interpreted (with the exception of traces which are never part of the metrical structure).

We will argue that (2)/(3) is the reason why we find non-phrase-final NS in wide focus contexts in Germanic in a variety of structural contexts, such as SV intransitives (*the <u>sun</u> is shining*), and reduced relatives (*there are <u>problems</u> to solve*). We will refer to these patterns, along with the transitive OV compounds (*they went <u>egg</u>-hunting*), as the Germanic NS pattern, which are inexistent in Romance in wide focus contexts. Indeed, any such pattern in Romance can only be associated with a narrow focus interpretation. We will provide evidence for an analysis that connects the Germanic NS patterns to the availability of unstressed functional words (in particular unstressed auxiliaries) based on the English speech of native Spanish speakers.

  Our second goal is to highlight the modular nature of the algorithms that generate NS placement. In fleshing out our analysis of the distribution of NS in Germanic, we will crucially separate two distinct components: the part that is grammatically encapsulated (i.e. the Nuclear Stress Rule or NSR) and that part that is discourse-related, namely Anaphoric Deaccenting or A-deacc (Ladd 1980, 1996; Selkirk 1984; Gussenhoven 1984).[2] Indeed, crosslinguistic data lends supports to such a view. While Romance languages lack the Germanic NS pattern, some of them (e.g. Italian and Spanish) also lack A-deacc (Ladd 1996; Zubizarreta 1998), yet there are others (e.g. French) that do have A-deacc (Ronat 1982; Zubizarreta op.cit.). We will present experimental data that supports such a modular view, based on the timing of acquisition of A-deacc and Germanic NSR by Spanish native speakers with English as the second language (L2).

14.2 The metrical (in)visibility of functional categories and the NSR

It has been widely recognized that main phrasal prominence tends to fall on the last word of the phrase in wide focus contexts—i.e. as an answer to a

---

[2] The term stress refers to the relative rhythmical prominence within some particular unit of speech. In stress languages like Germanic and Romance, (pitch) accent refers to one of the perceptual correlates of stress (based on the acoustics of an Fo event), the other correlates being loudness (based on the acoustics of intensity) and length (or duration) of segments. See n. 17 for related discussion.

question such as *What happened?* (The underlined word indicates the position of main phrasal prominence.)

(4)   a.   John read a <u>book.</u>

    b.   John worked on his <u>paper.</u>

(5)   a.   A glass suddenly <u>broke.</u>

    b.   A glass broke <u>suddenly.</u>

Yet, there is reason to believe that the NSR that computes main phrasal prominence in the English examples in (5) is sensitive to predicate-argument relations, while the NSR that computes main phrasal prominence in (4) is sensitive to constituent ordering. This is suggested, on the one hand, by the fact that in the counterparts to (4a) and (4b) in V-final Germanic languages, main phrasal prominence falls on the direct object and on the prepositional object respectively, even though these do not occupy the final position in their respective phrases. Cf. (4) and (6).

(6)   a.   Hans hat ein <u>Buch</u> gelesen.
        Hans has a book read

    b.   Peter hat an einem <u>Papier</u> gearbeitet.
        Peter has on a paper worked

Furthermore, even in English we find prosodic patterns that are not phrase-final, such as in intransitive SV structures, both unaccusatives (7) and unergatives (8) (Schmerling 1976; Selkirk 1984, 1995; Gussenhoven 1984), as well as in compound structures (9). (The examples in (7) and (8) are taken from our experimental protocol; the context questions are given in brackets.)

(7)   a.   My <u>friend</u> arrived. [Why are you so happy?]

    b.   My <u>bag</u> vanished.   [What's the matter?]

(8)   a.   A <u>student</u> ran. [What did they do to celebrate the new track at school?]

    b.   Because a <u>dog</u> is barking. [Why are those children screaming?]

(9)   a.   Peter is a <u>pasta</u> eater.

    b.   Every spring, Mary goes <u>bird</u>-watching.

It is also relevant to note that it is the presence of the adverb in examples such as (5) (either to the right or to the left of the verb) that pulls main prominence to the right. Cf. (5) with (10) (from our experimental protocol). This contrast, first noted by Gussenhoven (1984), suggests that an argument has a privileged status when it is a metrical sister of its selecting predicate.[3]

(10)   A <u>glass</u> broke. [What was that crashing sound?]

This conclusion is further reinforced by the minimal contrast (noted by Krifka 1984) between (6b), where the PP is an argument and attracts main prominence, and (11), where the PP is an adverb and main prominence falls on the verb.[4]

(11)   Peter   hat   an einem   kleinen   Tisch   <u>gearbeitet.</u>
       Peter   has   on a   small   table   worked
       'Peter worked on a small table.'

Given the above facts, it is reasonable to conclude that there are two algorithms at play for generating Nuclear Stress: one which is more specific and which is sensitive to the selectional relation that holds between a head and an argument (see n. 6 for definition of what counts as an argument), and another general algorithm that assigns main prominence to the rightmost constituent in the phrase. The latter applies when the former fails to apply. Following Zubizarreta (1998), we will refer to the former as the S-NSR and to the latter as the C-NSR (i.e. the 'elsewhere' case).[5]

---

[3] Note that appealing to a trace in object position to transmit main prominence to the subject in examples such as (7) and (10) will not work given that material such as an Adv between the subject and the verb consistently pulls the NS to the right; cf. examples such as (5a). Furthermore, NS on the subject is also found with unergatives.

[4] Truckenbrodt (2006a) accounts for the contrast between (6b) and (11) by exploiting the structural difference between complements (which are XP's sisters to a head) and adjuncts (which are XP's sisters to another XP). He proposes a two-tiered system, which consists of a rule 'Stress XP' that applies to the syntactic phrase, followed by a late rule that assigns main prominence to the last phrasal stress in the intonational phrase. Yet his proposed 'Stress XP' rule fails to account for stress patterns such as (7) and (8), essentially because it does not discriminate between subjects (of intransitives) and adjuncts. Yet, there are similarities between Truckenbrodt's two-tiered system and the system assumed here; see n. 6 for further discussion.

[5] Note that there is some similarity between Truckenbrodt's two-tiered system mentioned in n. 4 and the two-layered NSR in (12). More specifically, there is some degree of similarity between the S-NSR and 'Stress-XP', on the one hand, and between C-NSR and the intonation-level NSR. In both systems, the question arises as to why the former (i.e. S-NSR or Stress XP) does not apply in Romance. Our answer to that question is given in (2)/(3), which could easily be incorporated into Truckenbrodt's system as well.

(12)   Given two metrical sister nodes C_i and C_j, if one is a head and the other is its arg(ument), assign NS to the arg (S-NSR).[6] Otherwise, assign NS to the rightmost constituent node in the phrase (C-NSR).[7]

As mentioned earlier, the NSR applies to a metrical structure, which, in the case of Germanic, may be non-isomorphic to the syntactic structure; see (3). As mentioned earlier, traces are not metrically visible. Furthermore, we assume that *in the metrical structure a head is defined as a non-branching node and a non-head as a branching node.* A final caveat: while we adhere to the view that the NSR generates a metrical grid (as in Halle and Vergnaud 1987), which can be further affected by other rhythmic considerations, we will ignore this in the present work since it will not affect what we have to say here. Instead, we will adopt the more conspicuous notation introduced by Liberman (1975 [1978/97]), which applies directly to the metrical tree: a node that receives NS is labeled Strong (*S*) and its sister node is labeled Weak (*W*). The word dominated by an uninterrupted path of S nodes is interpreted as the locus of main phrasal stress.[8]

We illustrate how the NSR works by reviewing some of the core examples discussed above, as well as the much discussed variability of the NS position in intransitive structures (Sasse 1987; Ladd 1996) and in reduced relative clauses in Germanic (Bolinger 1972). Consider the metrical structure of the transitive (4a) and the transitive compound in (9a). In order to keep the syntax simple, we will omit those functional categories whose presence or absence does not ultimately affect the position of NS (such as Determiners). On the other hand, we do include T(ense), whose status as metrically (in)

---

[6] In fact, the relevant relation is not exactly between a head and its semantic argument, but between a head and its lexico-syntactic (l-s) argument, where a constituent is defined as an l-s argument of a head iff it is contained within the lexico-syntactic structure (in the sense of Hale and Keyser 2002) of the lexical head. This revision is important because it allows us to capture the fact that low manner adverbs, contained within the verbal projection of the head, seem to attract NS. E.g. *Hans hat ein Gedicht gut gelesen* 'Hans has a poem well read'; see Kahnemuyipour (2004: 117) on similar cases in Persian.

In English, the relevance of the l-s argument vs adjunct distinction can be appreciated in minimal contrasts such as *tree eater* (someone who eats trees) and *tree eater* (someone who eats while on a tree). Interestingly, manner modifiers within compounds also attract stress, e.g. *slow-roasting*, *fast-acting*, *quick-drying* (brought to our attention by Ed Holsinger). Other attributive modifiers do not, e.g. *ever-lasting*, *long-suffering*.

[7] Building on ideas put forth by Cinque (1993), Zubizarreta (1998) proposed an unification of the S-NSR and the C-NSR based on an abstract notion of 'most deeply embedded' constituent in the selectional ordering (S-NSR) and in the constituent ordering (C-NSR). More in-depth, crosslinguistic experimental research still needs to be done before we can evaluate the merits of such a proposal, but see Szendroi (2001) (on Hungarian) and Kahnemuyipour (2004) (on Persian) for relevant discussions.

[8] In the grid version, each node labeled S corresponds to a 'star'. The word with the highest number of stars is interpreted as the locus of main phrasal stress.

visible may affect the position of NS. In (13) and (14), V and N are metrical sisters and the S-NSR assigns NS to N. If T is metrically visible, the S-NSR fails to apply between T and its verbal sister *read a book* in (13) and between T and its nominal sister *pasta eater* in (14). Therefore, C-NSR applies assigning NS to the verbal predicate in (13) and to the nominal predicate in (14). When computing stress between the subject N and and its metrical sister T, again the S-NSR will fail to apply and C-NSR will assign NS to T. Thus, NS will ultimately fall on *book* and *pasta*, respectively. The same holds true if T is analyzed as metrically invisible. In such cases, the subject will be interpreted as the metrical sister of the verbal predicate *read a book* in (13) and of the nominal predicate *pasta eater* in (14), but the subject is not an argument of either; it is an argument of *read* and *eat*, respectively.[9]

(13)

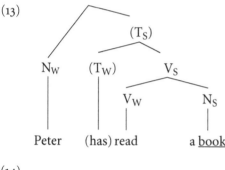

(14)

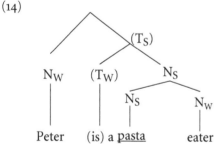

The same logic applies to the metrical structures of (5a) and (5b), shown in (15) and (16), respectively. Whether T is metrically invisible or not, the S-NSR will systematically fail to apply, given that the Adv is not an argument of V. The C-NSR applies instead, recursively assigning NS to the rightmost constituent.

---

[9] Or alternatively, the subject is an argument of the light verb 'v' to which the lexical verb is adjoined; see Hale and Keyser (2002) and references cited therein.

(15)

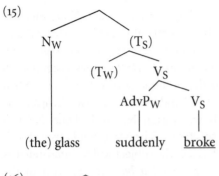

(16)

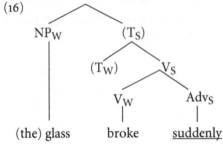

Similar analysis applies to intransitive SVPP structures (such as *A vampire appeared in the house; the girls swam in the pool*), where main phrasal prominence falls on the PP.

Where the metrical (in)visibility of Tense makes a difference is in intransitive structures and in reduced relative clauses. These are the cases where we indeed find variability of NS placement in Germanic. We discuss the intransitive structures first. While main phrasal stress on the subject in SV structures is both possible and frequent in wide focus contexts in Germanic (as in (7) and (8)), SV structures with main phrasal prominence on the verb are equally possible and frequent (although more so with unergatives than with unaccusatives; see section 14.4). The examples below are from our experimental protocol; patterns with NS on the subject with these tokens were also attested (see section 14.4 for further discussion.)

(17) a. The goalie <u>fell</u>.   [What happened at the game?]

      b. A boy <u>disappeared</u>.   [What happened at the playground?]

(18) a. An actress was <u>crying</u>.   [Why didn't they finish the play?]

      b. A patient <u>sneezed</u>.   [What was that noise?]

The variability of NS on such intransitive structures was extensively discussed by Sasse (1987), who showed that discourse/pragmatic considerations dictate which stress pattern the speaker chooses to utter. More precisely, Sasse argues that this distinction corresponds to the thetic vs categorical judgments described first by the philosophers Brentano and Marty and revived by Kuroda (1972). In the case where a simple event is asserted (thetic judgement), the pattern with NS on the subject is chosen. But not so in the case of complex events, in which the referent denoted by the subject is named and a property denoted by the predicate is predicated of that referent (categorical judgment); in that case NS falls on the verb. Halliday (1970), Gussenhoven (1983b), Ladd (1996), Kratzer and Selkirk (2007) also discuss this distinction, often referred to as eventive vs topic-comment structures.[10] Interestingly, in the presence of a modal the two stress patterns actually give rise to a difference in truth-conditional meaning (i.e. two distinct LFs), as in Halliday's often-cited example of a sign in the London Underground. The intended stress pattern is the one in (19b): 'If you are in the underground and have a dog, you must carry it.' The stress pattern in (19a) gives rise to the unintended reading: 'If you are in the underground, you must have a dog and carry it'.[11]

(19)   a.   <u>Dogs</u> must be carried.

       b.   Dogs must be <u>carried</u>.

Not all languages allow such variability in NS placement in out-of-the blue contexts. In particular, the Romance languages do not allow the stress pattern with NS on the subject. Sasse suggests that different languages use different strategies to encode the thetic/categorical distinction; e.g. Spanish uses word order, French uses the *il y a* or *voici* construction. That might very well be the case, but it still begs the question as to why some languages, but not others, may use variable stress patterns to encode such distinctions. French is particularly noteworthy in this respect because it is rather rigid in its word order, like English; yet, unlike English, it does not exploit variable stress patterns to mark such distinction. As in Italian and Spanish, French intransitive structures require phrase-final NS (irrespective of word-order considerations).

Our view is that Germanic languages can encode the thetic vs categorical distinction via stress because their grammar can generate both stress patterns in (19), but Romance cannot, and this typological distinction is to be related to the difference stated in (2)/(3). It is precisely in the case of (N (T V))

---

[10] Kratzer and Selkirk (2007) argue that an (overt or covert) spatio/temporal element functions as the 'topic' in the case of thetic statements, while the subject itself functions as the 'topic' in the case of categorical statements, where 'topic' is to be understood as the 'Subject of Predication' (as in Reinhart 1981).

[11] It is to be noted that the American English speakers consulted allow both meanings to be associated to the stress pattern in (19b).

structures where we expect variability in Germanic, depending on whether T is analyzed as metrically visible or not. If T is analyzed as metrically invisible, NS will be assigned to the subject by the S-NSR, as in (20). If T is analyzed as metrically visible, then NS will be recursively assigned to the rightmost constituent by the C-NSR, as in (21). Thus, *the grammar generates both patterns and which pattern is selected by the speaker will depend on whether (s)he wants to put forth a thetic or a categorical judgment.* In the former case, pattern (20) will be selected and in the latter case pattern (21) will be selected.[12,13]

(20)

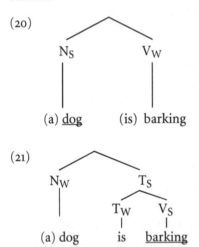

(21)

The same kind of analysis can be extended to the cases discussed by Bolinger (1972), such as those below. The (a) patterns arise if the infinitival tense

[12] J. Legate has brought to our attention the availability of NS on the subject in the case of subject-to-subject raising structures (e.g. *A dog seems to be barking*), in similar wide focus contexts. Such facts suggest that when *seem* functions as a raising verb, it has the status of a functional lexical item, rather than that of a main verb, along lines proposed by Cinque (2004) for Romance.

[13] Ladd (1996) also recognizes the primacy of arguments in Germanic NSR (as in (20)) and suggests that cases in which NS falls on the Verb (as in (21)) might be due to prosodic phrasing. These are said to involve two intermediate phrases, each with its own phrasal stress, with the last one as most prominent. Our experimental data indicates that this analysis is not correct. Indeed, 59% of the unergative SV tokens were pronounced by the ENC with NS on V (the rest with NS on the subject). Yet, in only 25% of the tokens with NS on V was the verb phrased separately from the subject. In all the other cases, the subject and the verb were phrased together. (Phrasing was determined in terms of perception and in terms of pitch-reset by two independent coders.) Further evidence for the possibility of analyzing SV intransitives with NS on the verb as one p-phrase is the availability of secondary stress retraction, which only occurs if the words with main and secondary phrasal stress are contained within the same p-phrase; e.g. *Ànnemarie bícycled* (example from Inkelas and Zec 1993). These comments also apply to the proposal put forth by Kratzer and Selkirk (2007) regarding phrasing and phrasal stress.

marker *to* is analyzed as metrically invisible; the (b) patterns if it is analyzed as metrically visible.[14]

(22) a. I can't go with you; I've got too many <u>things</u> to do.

  b. ...too many things to <u>do</u>.

(23) a. It's too heavy a <u>price</u> to pay.

  b. It's too heavy a price to <u>pay</u>.

(24) a. We're looking for a neighborhood where there are other <u>boys</u> to play with.

  b. ...where there are other boys to <u>play</u> with.

Note that none of the (a) patterns exist in the Romance languages (as noted by Ladd 1996 and Zubizarreta 1998), despite the fact that no word-order flexibility is available for such structures in any of the Romance languages, including Spanish (e.g. the Spanish counterpart of (23): *Es un precio muy alto para <u>pagar</u>* vs *Es muy alto para pagar un <u>precio</u>*). In other words, in Romance, and in particular in Spanish, only the C-NSR is active; it can't be otherwise because functional categories in these languages are always metrically visible.

14.3 Nuclear accent and its interaction with discourse and pragmatics

14.3.1 *(Un)expectedness and noteworthiness*

In a well-known 1972 article, Bolinger argued that there is no such thing as an unmarked phrasal stress pattern defined by the grammar, that phrasal stress in English is governed solely by relative notions of semantic weight and pragmatic predictability, and that ultimately one can predict the location of nuclear stress in English only if one is a mind reader. We have not adhered to that position because we think that if we maximize control of discourse factors as well as factors stemming from world knowledge, clear patterns do emerge (namely the ones outlined in the previous section).[15] Indeed, in the experiment reported in the next section, which included thirty English native

---

[14] Note that the examples in (24) also require analyzing the preposition *with* as metrically invisible.

[15] At the same time, we recognize that controlling for sentence grammar external factors 100% is a very difficult task, the main reason being that the question may prime some of the words in the answer to varying degrees and inferable words can trigger anaphoric deaccenting. Furthermore, inferences may vary from subject to subject. This is an issue that deserves further experimental investigation.

speakers (ENC), we found that in fairly neutral wide focus contexts, unaccusative SV sentences with change of location verbs (*come, enter, arrive, appear, escape, vanish*) were pronounced 97 percent of the time with main stress on the subject, and unaccusative SV sentences with change of state verbs (*break, close, open, die*) were pronounced 98 percent of the time with main stress on the subject. A sample of Q&A pairs is given below; see also (7).

(25)   How was the parade?
       Fun. The <u>band</u> came.

(26)   What's all the excitement in the stadium?
       The <u>football team</u> entered.

(27)   Why is that child crying?
       A <u>cat</u> died.

While unaccusatives seem to favor the eventive (or thetic) interpretation, which requires the pattern with NS on the subject (as discussed in the previous section), unaccusatives with NS on the verb are not excluded. In our protocol, we found NS on the verb with tokens that involved the change of location verbs *fell* and *disappear*; see the examples in (17). Out of twenty-eight tokens of type (17a), seven had NS on the subject and twenty-one on the verb; out of twenty-eight tokens of type (17b), thirteen had NS on the subject and fifteen on the verb. It seems that the unexpectedness (and therefore, noteworthiness) of the reported event favors the categorical interpretation and therefore NS on the verb (as suggested by Sasse op. cit.) This was further confirmed by the fact that the tokens *snow is falling/leaves have fallen* (tested with five ENCs) favored NS on the subject, in contrast with (17a).

   In the case of unergative SV sentences (*bark, roar, smile, talk, dance, swim, sing, run, cry, and sneeze*), we found a fair amount of variability within tokens and across subjects: 47 percent of tokens were pronounced with main stress on the subject and 53 percent with main stress on the verb. Some samples of Q/A pairs are given below.

(28)   How was your field trip?
       It was cool. A lion roared.

(29)   Why are those children screaming?
       Because a dog is barking.

(30)   What did they do to celebrate the new track at school?
       A student ran.

(31) How did the party end?
      A guest sang.

Yet, pragmatic factors may favor one prosodic pattern over the other. Thus, while 67 percent of the tokens had main stress on the subject in cases of 'expected' predicates (e.g. *a dog is barking, a dolphin is swimming*), 81 percent of the tokens were pronounced with main stress on the verb in cases of 'unexpected' predicates (e.g. *a dog is singing, a dolphin is talking*). The 'unexpected' nature of the predicate given world knowledge renders the latter highly 'noteworthy'.

Pragmatic factors such as '(un)expectedness' and 'noteworthiness' can also alter the placement of NS in cases where the grammar dictates an unequivocal location. Thus, we have found variability in the case of some transitives. While 100 percent of the token answers in the case of (32) and (33) were produced with main prominence on the object (as predicted by the NSR), there was variability in the case of (34). Two thirds of the token answers were produced with NS on the object, while the other third was produced with main stress on the verb and deaccented object. This is probably due to the fact that *movies* is a highly predictable object for the verb *watch*.

(32) Does Jason make good grades in school?
      No, he doesn't buy <u>books</u>.

(33) Do you have a hobby?
      Yes, I collect <u>stamps</u>.

(34) Is Ellen coming out with us tonight?
      No, Ellen doesn't watch <u>movies</u>. / Ellen doesn't <u>watch</u> movies.

We also found some variability in the case of ditransitive sentences. While 87 percent of the token answers in the case of (35) were produced with main stress on the PP object *covers* and 80 percent of the token answers in (36) were produced with main stress on the PP object *bed* (which is a robust result), 94 percent of the token answers in (37) were produced with main stress on the direct object *ice* and the PP deaccented. This may be due to the highly noteworthy presence of 'ice' on the road, more so than 'pictures' on covers, or 'toys' under the bed.[16]

---

[16] The same explanation can be give to the contrast between the German examples (i) (cited in Zubizarreta 1998) and (ii) (cited in Kahnemuyipour 2004 and attributed to Winkler and Göbel 2002). Indeed, a state of affairs involving a gun on a table is more noteworthy than one involving a book on a table.

(i)   Karl hat ein Buch in <u>Regal</u>   gestellt.
      Karl has a   book on the shelf put

(35)   Are you finished with the coloring books?
        No, I'm drawing pictures on the <u>covers</u>.

(36)   What did Lucy do before dinner?
        She hid her toys under the <u>bed</u>.

(37)   Why are all the cars slowing down?
        Because there is <u>ice</u> on the road.

14.3.2 *Anaphoric deaccenting*

As is well known, in English, anaphoric DPs are subject to deaccenting. Two types of anaphora must be distinguished: the case of pronouns and the case of previously mentioned or inferable lexical NPs. English pronouns are intrinsically weak elements (unless emphasized). Indeed, we found that pronouns, such as those in (38) and (39) are unstressed 100 percent of the time, with NS shifted onto the verb.

(38)   Do we have tomatoes?
        No, I didn't <u>buy</u> them.

(39)   Why is this bag so heavy?
        We put <u>sand</u> in it.

We may assume that, because English pronouns are inherently weak, they enter the metrical structure with a label *W*, thus bleeding the NSR from applying to it and its sister node. In other words, because the pronoun is inherently labeled *W*, its metrical sister is automatically labeled *S*.[17]

On the other hand, lexical NPs in English may be deaccented iff they have been previously mentioned implicitly or explicitly. As Ladd (1980) noted, the noun *book* in the answer to the question in (40) may count as previously mentioned, given the presence of *Don Quixote* in the context question (indeed a title of a book may prime the noun *book*).

(40)   Did John read Don Quixote?
        No, John doesn't <u>read</u> books.

(ii)   weil   er eine <u>Pistole</u> auf den Tisch gelegt hat.
        because he a   gun   onto the table put   has

[17] In a metrical grid notation, a pronoun lacks a word-level 'star' (i.e. it is inherently stressless) and therefore cannot support further 'star' assignment by the application of the NSR. This does not preclude pronouns (like other weak prosodic categories) from being assigned emphasis by a discourse-sensitive low-level rule, emphasis being a paradigmatic rather than a syntagmatic notion (Ladd 1996).

Therefore, we assume that in English, previously mentioned DPs may trigger A-deacc, a rule which applies to the output of the NSR. We leave the technical details of this rule vague.[18]

(41) Lexical Anaphora Deaccenting (A-deacc)
      A previously mentioned noun is deaccented, shifting stress onto its metrical sister node.

In a pilot study, we found that, although lexical anaphora deaccenting was indeed attested in the case of implicit mention, it was not very frequent. On the other hand, we found deaccenting of explicitly mentioned lexical nouns to be robust. Some examples from our experimental stimuli with transitives and ditransitives are given below. (See 14.4.3 for results in percentages.)

(42) Did Jason go to the book fair?
      No, he doesn't <u>buy</u> books.

(43) Why are you buying that old stamp?
      Because I <u>collect</u> stamps.

(44) Why are these notebooks missing their cover?
      Because I'm drawing <u>pictures</u> on the covers.

(45) Why was the racetrack closed down?
      Because there was <u>water</u> on the track.

Spanish, on the other hand, lacks anaphoric deaccenting entirely, both for pronouns, such as (39), and for previously mentioned lexical nouns as in (42)–(45). In all such cases, NS in Spanish falls on the last word of the phrase (cf. Cruttenden 1997; Ladd 1996; Zubizarreta 1998).

---

[18] More phonetic research is required on lexical (i.e. non-prominal) anaphora, to see whether its prosody is like that of pronominal anaphora or like that of 'secondary focus', discussed by Beaver et al. 2007. These authors show that there is a remnant of stress in secondary focus and suggest that this perception is due to the acoustic correlates of duration and intensity and not to an Fo event. If the case of lexical anaphora is more like 'secondary focus' than like unstressed pronouns, we should think of it, technically speaking, as a case of 'deaccenting' (rather than as 'destressing'), i.e. as a case of pitch-accent deletion, which then triggers stress-strengthening of the sister constituent (i.e. addition of 'stars' to the sister constituent) in the metrical grid. Under such a view, the NSR is an encapsulated high-level rule that assigns a rhythmic interpretation to a metrical structure, while A-deacc (like Emphasis) is a discourse-sensitive low-level rule which indirectly affects the metrical grid. Because we think that the latter analysis is probably the correct one, we refer to the phenomenon at hand as anaphoric deaccenting (rather than as anaphoric destressing, as proposed by Reinhart 2006).

14.4 A comparison of English native speech with the English of Spanish speakers

The English speech of Spanish speakers may be particularly revealing in our quest for empirical evidence that there are several sources to English Nuclear Stress (in particular the NSR and A-deacc). This is so because we expect that the speech of second language acquirers will reveal the existence of prosodic transfer:

(46) *Phrasal Prominence Transfer (PTT) Hypothesis*:
      Spanish speakers of English, in particular non-high proficiency speakers, transfer the NSR from their native language.

The above hypothesis predicts that:

(47) a. L1 Spanish speakers will place NS on the verb rather than on the subject in intransitive SV structures in English.

      b. L1 Spanish speakers will place NS on the verb rather than on the object in the English compound OV structures.

Furthermore, acquiring the Germanic NSR entails that Spanish native speakers have to restructure their native NSR. On the other hand, since Spanish has no counterpart to the A-deacc rule, acquiring the latter does not require restructuring a native algorithm. Alternatively, within a grammar-competition model (Yang 2002), we may assume that the L2 learner is faced with two competing NSR algorithms: the general C-NSR (active in the L1, as well as in the L2) and the specific S-NSR (active in the L2 grammar only). In contrast, since there is no A-deacc in Spanish, there is no competing L1 algorithm involved in the L2 acquisition of A-deacc. Therefore, we expect a delay in the acquisition of the Germanic NSR as opposed to Germanic A-deacc:

(48) Native speakers of Spanish will acquire A-deacc before they acquire the Germanic NSR (i.e. the S-NSR in (12)).

The hypothesis in (48) makes the following predictions:

(49) a. Speakers that have acquired the Germanic NSR would also have acquired A-deacc.

      b. Speakers that have acquired A-deacc may or may not have acquired the Germanic NSR.

The experiment reported in the following section was set up to test the above predictions, which, as we shall see, were borne out. We will furthermore see that the results of this experiment provides indirect support for the hypothesis that the non-phrase-final Germanic NS pattern is intimately related to the metrical invisibility of functional categories, as stated in (2)/(3).

14.4.1 *The experimental design*

The experiment was designed to elicit NS placement at the phrasal level. The participant and the experimenter engaged in a scripted dialogue based on a Question and Answer (Q&A) format. Each participant saw forty-five target stimuli, and an equal number of fillers, with the intention of varying the force and form of the sentences in the dialogue. There were two lists of test items constructed using a Latin square design. Stimuli included a variety of syntactic structures paired with different information-structure contexts, only a subset of which will be discussed here, namely those that are relevant to the present discussion. The relevant structures are listed below, all associated with wide focus contexts:[19]

(50) a. Unergative SV (12 tokens, 3 of which contained pragmatically unexpected predicates).

   b. Unacc. SV (12 tokens), Unacc. SAdvV (4 tokens), Unacc. SVAdv (4 tokens).

   c. Transitive OV compounds (4 tokens).

   d. Transitive SVO (4 tokens), Ditransitive SVOPP (4 tokens).

   e. Transitive SVO, with previously mentioned O (4 tokens); Ditransitive SVOPP, with previously mentioned PP (4 tokens).

   f. Transitive SVO, with pronominal O (2 tokens), Ditransitive SVOPP, with pronominal PP (2 tokens).

Participants' responses were recorded and analyzed using PitchWorks software program. The data were coded for the presence vs absence of pitch accent and for location of nuclear accent. Data coding was done by two independent coders, both native speakers of English, in order to ensure inter-rater reliability.

Two participant populations were tested: a control group of 30 adult, native English speakers (ENC), and a test group of 24 adult, L1Spanish/L2English

---

[19] We also included contexts with narrow focus (on the subject, on the object, and on the VP) to insure that the L2 speakers had the ability to associate NS with focus. Furthermore, fillers in general allowed us to control for participants' attention to context.

TABLE 14.1 Results Cloze test L2 participant population

Cloze test results	Range	Average
ENC	70–75	73
L2 High Proficiency	66–73	70
L2 Intermediate Proficiency	58–65	63

speakers. All participants were living in Los Angeles, California (where testing took place) at the time of the experiment. The test group completed a Cloze test (Oshita 1997) as an independent measure of proficiency. The test consisted of three passages with every fifth word left blank, giving us a total of seventy-five blanks with a score range from 0 to 75. Of the twenty-four participants in this group, twelve tested at the high proficiency level, and twelve at the intermediate proficiency level; see Table 14.1.[20]

In the following section we present and discuss the results of this experiment.

14.4.2 Results and discussion

14.4.2.1 *Germanic non-phrase final NS patterns*   The results for unaccusative verbs are presented in Table 14.2, with sample examples below. It is in the case of wide focus SV unaccusative structure where we see the greatest difference between the ENC and L2 populations, with the former producing NS on the subject 97 percent of the time, and the latter group only 13 percent of the time, a statistically significant difference. (Throughout this section, we annotate the tables with the relevant statistics.) We attribute this significant difference to the application of the S-SNR in the case of the ENC, and to the *transfer* of the C-NSR from Spanish into English in the case of the L2 speakers. However, we do not observe a significant difference in the case of the SAdvV or the SVAdv contexts. Indeed, for the SAdvV cases both populations place NS sentence-finally at the same rate (91 percent), and for the SVAdv the majority of NS placement was sentence-final for both groups. This is because the operative algorithm for this construction is the C-NSR, which is present in both English and Spanish.

---

[20] L2 participants were also asked to complete a background questionnaire, which provides information about age of testing, age of exposure to English, length of time in the US (or other English-speaking countries), and other relevant information.

TABLE 14.2 Unaccusative structures

Unaccusative	Prosodic pattern* [**S** v]	Prosodic pattern [S Adv **V**]	Prosodic pattern** [S V **Adv**][i]
ENC	97%	91%	80%
L2	13%	91%	94%

* $\chi^2 = 139.3$, $p < .0001$; ** $\chi^2 = .59$, $p = .443$
[i] The remaining 20% patterns for the SV Adv structure for English natives were mostly cases of NS on the verb, either with a clear prosodic boundary preceding the Adv or with the Adv deaccented.

(51)   SV unaccusative, wide focus
       Q: What was that crashing sound?
       a. A <u>glass</u> broke.   (ENC)
       b. A glass <u>broke</u>.   (L2)

(52)   SAdvV
       Q: What happened?
       a. A glass suddenly <u>broke</u>.   (ENC)
       b. A glass suddenly <u>broke</u>.   (L2)

Another structure where the S-NSR operates in English is the case of transitive compounds. As shown in Table 14.3, the data also reveals a significant difference between the control and L2 groups: ENCs placed NS on the argument 96 percent of the time, L2ers only 36 percent of the time. Again, L2 speakers show a strong tendency to transfer sentence-final NS.

(51)   Transitive compound
       Q: Does Jill like to visit parks?
       a. Oh yes. She's a <u>bird</u>-watcher.   (ENC)
       b. Oh yes. She's a bird-<u>watcher</u>.   (L2)

TABLE 14.3 Transitive compound structures

Transitive compound	Prosodic pattern* [S [**O** v]]
ENC	96%
L2	36%

* $\chi^2 = 45.43$, $p < .0001$

TABLE 14.4 Unergative structures

Unergative	Prosodic pattern* [S̲ v]	Prosodic pattern [s V̲]
ENC	41%	59%
L2	23%	77%

* $\chi^2 = 2.82$, p = .093

The above contrast between the ENC speakers and the L2 group validates the PTT Hypothesis in (46). We turn next to the results obtained for the unergative SV structures, which we think also supports the PTT hypothesis.

As mentioned in section 14.2, there are two possible metrical outputs available for unergatives, depending on whether the functional category T is analyzed as metrically visible or not. The former analysis yields NS on the verb and the latter yields NS on the subject. The general results obtained are given in Table 14.4 above.

When we remove the three tokens with pragmatically unexpected predicates (*A dolphin is talking, A dog is singing, A lion smiled*), a more balanced result is obtained for the ENC speakers; see Table 14.5. These results confirm that there is indeed a high degree of variability with respect to NS placement in English unergative SV sentences. Furthermore, we see a distinct difference between the ENC and the L2 speakers. The latter group produced a significantly higher number of tokens with NS on the verb than with NS on the subject. Again, this can be attributed to the effects of transfer.

(53)   Unergative structure (with pragmatically neutral predicate):
        Q: What was the noise in the waiting room?
        a.   A patient sneezed. A patient sneezed.   (ENC)
        b.   A patient sneezed.   (L2)

TABLE 14.5 Unergative structures (with pragmatically expected/neutral predicates)

Unergative	Prosodic pattern* [S̲ v]	Prosodic pattern [s V̲]
ENC	49%	51%
L2	23%	77%

* $\chi^2 = 25.39$, p < .0001

TABLE 14.6 Unergatives structures (with pragmatically unexpected predicates)

Unergative	Prosodic pattern* [$\underline{S}$ v]	Prosodic pattern [s $\underline{V}$]
ENC	19%	81%
L2	15%	85%

$\chi^2 = .87$, p $= .350$

The results for the three tokens with pragmatically unexpected predicates are given in Table 14.6. In this case, the results for ENC and L2 speakers are similar but possibly for different reasons. In the case of the ENC speakers, the preference for producing NS on the verb is due to pragmatics. In the case of the L2 speakers, it could be due to transfer.

(54)   Unergative structure (with pragmatically unexpected predicate):
    Q: Why does everybody look so surprised?
    a.   Because a dog is <u>singing</u>.   (ENC)
    b.   Because a dog is <u>singing</u>.   (L2)

We turn next to transitive and ditransitive structures in wide focus contexts, with and without previously mentioned material. The results are given in Table 14.7 below.

    The NSR algorithm predicts NS on the direct object in transitives and on the PP in ditransitives for both ENC and L2 speakers. As shown in columns 2 and 4 in Table 14.7, this was indeed what we obtained in the case of L2 speakers to a very high extent. On the other hand, the predicted results were less robust in the case of ENC, especially in the case of ditransitives. In the case of the transitives, the relatively lower percentage of NS production on the final

TABLE 14.7 Transitives: Wide focus with and without previously mentioned material (+/−PM)

Transitives	Pattern [S [v $\underline{O}$]] (−PM)	Pattern* [S [$\underline{V}$ o]] (+PM)	Pattern [S [V o $\underline{PP}$]] (−PM)	Pattern** [S [V $\underline{O}$ pp]] (+PM)
ENC	80%	82%	60%	80%
L2	98%	23%	93%	14%

* $\chi^2 = 35.54$, p $< .0001$; ** $\chi^2 = 26.57$, p $< .0001$

constituent by native speakers was due primarily to two test items, one of which was already commented on in section 14.3.2 and is repeated in (55). A third of the ENC speakers deaccented the object in this example, shifting NS to the verb. As mentioned earlier, this is possibly due to the highly predictable status of *movies* as object of the verb *watch*. The other relevant test item is given in (56), which was pronounced by almost half of the speakers with the deaccented object and NS on the verb. This is probably due to the particular verb used. In effect, in a previous pilot study, we also noted that the verb *hate* used in the same context produced similar results. It could be that emotionally loaded verbs (like *hate, love, like*) tend to attract emphasis.

(55)   Why don't you take Ellen to the movie festival?
       Because Ellen doesn't watch movies.

(56)   Did Barbara taste your dish?
       No, she doesn't <u>like</u> spinach.

As for the ditransitives in column 4, although we did find some variability in three out of the four ditransitives in wide focus contexts without previously mentioned PP, the low percentage of tokens pronounced with NS on the PP is due to a great extent to one test item, which we commented on in section 14.3.2 and which we repeat in (57) below. Eleven out of thirteen speakers pronounced this case with deaccented PP and NS on the object. As mentioned earlier, we may attribute the shifting of NS onto the object in this case to the highly noteworthy status of the object (or alternatively to the priming of *roads* by *cars*).

(57)   Why are all the cars slowing down?
       Because there is <u>ice</u> on the road.

The pragmatic factors of predictability vs unexpectedness and the related notion 'noteworthiness' are not easy to control for when these are not due solely to shared pragmatic knowledge and it undoubtedly deserves further more careful empirical investigation. Nevertheless, we contend that if we can manage to peel off the effects of pragmatics, we will find clean core patterns that emerge from the data.

We turn next to the transitives and ditransitives with previously mentioned material, i.e. the cases of anaphoric deaccenting. Differences in prosodic patterns between populations were predicted in such cases, given that English but not Spanish has the A-deacc rule (see section 14.3.2). These predictions were borne out, as can be seen by comparing the rows in columns 3 and 5 in Table 14.7. ENC speakers deaccented the object and placed NS on the verb

TABLE 14.8 Proficiency levels: L2 prosodic proficiency and Cloze test proficiency

Target-like NS	Target-like A-deacc	High proficiency	Intermediate proficiency
−	−	6	10
−	+	2	2
+	+	4	0
+	−	0	0

82 percent of the time in transitive structures, a rate significantly higher from that of the L2 population, which was 23 percent (a test item sample is given in (58)). Likewise significant, A-deacc was observed by ENC 80 percent of the time in ditransitive structures when the information in the PP was previously mentioned, and only 14 percent of the time by L2ers (a test item sample is given in (59)).

(58) Previously mentioned object
Q: Why are you buying that old stamp?
a. Because I <u>collect</u> stamps.   (ENC)
b. Because I collect <u>stamps</u>.   (L2)

(59) Previously mentioned PP
Q: Why are these notebooks missing their covers?
a. Because I'm drawing <u>pictures</u> on the covers.   (ENC)
b   Because I'm drawing pictures on the <u>covers</u>.   (L2)

We turn next to the data that speaks to the timing of acquisition of the specific Germanic NSR; see (48) and its related predictions in (49).[21] The relevant individual results are presented in Table 14.8.

This table shows the distribution of the acquisition of prominence patterns, cross-tabulated with Cloze test proficiency. There were six high proficiency and ten intermediate proficiency L2 speakers that have not acquired the Germanic NSR nor A-deacc. Two high proficiency and two intermediate proficiency L2 speakers have acquired A-deacc but have not acquired the

---

[21] We considered that a given L2 speaker has acquired the NSR or A-deacc if 75% of his/her relevant token items were target-like. While any cut-off point is arbitrary, 75% as cut-off point is a reasonable one, often used in studies on second language acquisition.

TABLE 14.9 Unstressed pronouns

Transitives	Prosodic pattern [S [$\underline{V}$ pro]]	Prosodic pattern [S [V $\underline{O}$ pro]]
ENC	100%	94%
L2	91%	68%

Germanic NSR. Finally, four high-proficiency speakers have acquired both the Germanic NSR and A-deacc. Crucially, the opposite order is not found, i.e. we do not find speakers who have acquired the Germanic NSR without having acquired A-deacc. Thus, the predictions made by hypothesis (48) are confirmed by the data in the present study.

As for pronouns, the results show that the L2 speakers were generally much more target-like than in the case of anaphoric lexical DPs. Compare columns 3 and 5 in Table 14.7 with the results in Table 14.9.

When we segregate the data according to proficiency level (shown in Table 14.10), we can clearly see that unstressed pronouns are indeed produced before deaccented lexical anaphora.

We attribute the above difference to the fact that English pronouns are inherently unstressed, while deaccenting of anaphoric lexical DPs is context-dependent. Indeed, the latter requires paying attention to detailed aspects of the linguistic material in the discourse, which we assume adds an extra level of processing complexity.

Finally, we turn to some indirect evidence that this experiment provides for the contention that the non-phrase-final NS patterns in Germanic is intimately connected to the possibility of analyzing its functional categories as metrically invisible. Recall that the cue to this property of Germanic functional categories is the fact that functional words are generally unstressed. This makes the following predictions regarding production of unstressed

TABLE 14.10 Deaccented lexical anaphora and unstressed pronouns

	NS A-deacc Pro − − −			NS A-deacc Pro − − +			NS A-deacc Pro − + +			NS A-deacc Pro + + +		
Interm.	3			7			2					
High	1			5			2			4		

TABLE 14.11 Copula reduction

ENC	98%
L2 G1	94%
L2 G2	62%
L2 G3	68%

copula and acquisition of the Germanic NSR by L1 Spanish/L2 English learners:

(60)   a.   L2 learners that have acquired the Germanic NSR use unstressed copula at comparable level as native speakers.

   b.   L2 learners that have not acquired the Germanic NSR use unstressed copula at significantly lower level than native speakers.

We counted the number of unstressed copulas for native speakers and the three groups of L2 speakers previously identified,[22] and we obtained the following results shown in Table 14.11. ENC is the native control group, L2 G1 is constituted of L2 speakers with target-like NS and target-like A-deacc, L2 G2 of L2 speakers with non-target-like NS but target-like A-deacc, and L2 G3 of L2 speakers with neither target-like NS nor target-like A-deacc.

   The above results show that the predictions in (60) were borne out. Only the L2 speakers that had acquired the Germanic NSR produced unstressed copulas at the same rate as native speakers, namely in the 90 percentile range, while the other speakers that had not acquired the Germanic NSR produced unstressed copulas in the 60 percentile range. It is particularly noteworthy that G2 (with target-like A-deacc) and G3 (with non-target-like A-deacc) patterned together. In other words, only target-like production of Germanic NS patterns correlate with a native-like level of copula deacc. These preliminary results, if on the right track, provide evidence for (2)/(3) and they furthermore show that the explanation for the late acquisition of Germanic NS patterns cannot be explained solely in terms of difficulties with using NS stress to encode the thetic vs categorical distinction. Note furthermore that such results provide us with an explanation for why all high-proficiency L2 learners have acquired A-deacc but not the S-NSR. Indeed, the acquisition of the Germanic NSR (but not the acquisition of A-deacc) has a pre-requirement: it requires certain aspects of the phonotactics of English to

---

[22] The analysis was based on 22 test items that contained copulas.

have been acquired, namely the vowel reduction characteristic of English unstressed syllables.

14.5 Conclusion

Based on the L2 data presented here, we can safely conclude that L2 learners start out computing NS on the basis of the general NSR (i.e. the C-NSR). In addition, we presented experimental evidence showing that learners acquire A-deacc before they acquire the Germanic NSR (i.e. the S-NSR). Thus, the L2 data discussed here and the resulting generalizations contribute to linguistic theory in that they provide independent evidence for a modular approach to Nuclear Stress: parts of NS are generated by the NSR (i.e. the S-NSR and the C-NSR) and parts of it are generated by A-deacc.

Furthermore, we have provided preliminary evidence based on L2 speech that the metrical invisibility of functional categories (cued by the stressless nature of the corresponding functional words) is what makes the Germanic NS patterns possible. We think that the latter is ultimately connected to the difference in rhythm between the two sets of languages: Spanish is classified as a syllable-timed language and English as a stress-timed language. This difference in rhythm arises from differences in language-specific phonotactics (Dauer 1983). On the connection between NS placement and rhythm, see Nava and Zubizarreta 2008.

15

Focus as a grammatical notion:
A case study in autism*

KRISZTA SZENDRŐI

15.1 The communicative function of focus and universal grammar

It is beyond reasonable doubt that focus marking in natural language has a communicative function. It obviously helps information exchange, if the speakers know which constituents are part of the background and which ones carry new information. In most languages, focus is marked by main stress and/or pitch accent. This is even true in Hungarian, where focus also has a designated syntactic position.[1]

However, this does not necessarily mean that focus marking is an extralinguistic, general communicative tool. In what follows, I will argue that focus is a specific grammatical concept that cannot be described in its entirety by its communicative role. Rather, it has language- and grammar-specific characteristics. This position is widely accepted amongst generative linguists, while it is sometimes questioned in the psycholinguistics literature. For instance, Cutler and Swinney (1986) claim that prosodic marking on focus (i.e. main stress or pitch accent) is at least in certain cases not part of the grammar, but is only there to draw our attention to the relevant constituent.[2] In this view,

* I thank Ilona Bedő for providing access to an autistic participant; Judit Gervai for drawing my attention to the work of Miklós Győri on language and autism; Reiko Vermeulen and Nomi Erteschik-Shir for helpful comments; and last but not least, L. for his cooperation. This work was financed by the Dutch Science Foundation (NWO) (No 048.011.047) whose help is gratefully acknowledged here.

[1] I have argued elsewhere that in the case of Hungarian focus, prosodic marking is fundamental and the syntacatic position is a consequence of the prosodic marking, but this is irrelevant here (see Szendrői 2001, 2003).

[2] To be precise, Cutler and Swinney (1986) formulate their claim for child language. They say that children at an early stage of their cognitive and linguistic development do not have a more sophisticated focus concept and simply use stress and pitch accent as an attention-drawing device. Here I will not go into why I think their claim is untenable even for child language, but see Szendrői (2004).

focus marking is similar to saying something louder so that the hearer has a better chance of understanding what we say. When the speaker applies focus marking on a constituent, he simply wants to draw the hearer's attention to the focal constituent. The hearer, in turn, notices the prosodically marked constituent and concludes that the speaker used this marking to draw his/her attention to this constituent.

In contrast, the generative position is that the concept of focus and focus marking is part of universal grammar (see e.g. Chomsky 1971; Reinhart 2006). In other words, every normally developing child knows what focus is and that languages mark focus prosodically (by main stress or pitch accent) due to their genetic endowment.

Although the literature abounds with theoretical support for the generative position, there is relatively scarce experimental evidence available. My aim here is to add to this body of work, hoping that such an endeavor helps interaction between theoretical and experimental linguistics and thus, in the long run, contributes to the making of a conceptually sound and psychologically realistic grammar.

An important difference between the two approaches to focus marking described above is that while in the generative approach production and comprehension of focus is the result of an automated, language-specific process, in the rival theory a pragmatic (or more general) deductive step is necessary. Namely, in order to be able to identify the communicative import of the stressed constituent, the hearer has to assume that it was the speaker's *intention* to signal this. In other words, this approach to focus assumes that communication is intentional in nature. Intentional communication means that the meaning of each communicative unit (e.g. an utterance) involves the effect that the speaker has on his/her audience due to the fact that the audience is aware that the speaker is not only delivering a message, but also trying to have an effect on his/her audience by his/her utterance (see Grice 1957; Sperber and Wilson 1995, etc.) Take an example: if a guest says to his host: *It's cold in here*, his intention is not only to make the host aware of this fact, but also, by uttering this sentence, he intends to have an effect; for instance, he wants to make the host turn on the heating. The host, in parallel, will not only acknowledge that according to her guest the temperature in the room is low, but also take into account that the guest had some aim in mind when uttering this statement, and so she will try to deduce this aim. In the specific case of focus, the speaker's intention is to get the hearer to interpret the focal constituent as new, relevant information, while the hearer, upon hearing the focal utterance, has to deduce this intention of the speaker.

This deductive step is not necessary if one adopts the generative standpoint. Here, the constituent bearing main stress will be automatically interpreted as focal, i.e. as new and relevant information, because this is what the focus-marking rule in the grammar prescribes. It is not necessary for the hearer to deduce the speaker's intention to mark the constituent as focus. Actually, it is irrelevant whether the speaker had any such intention when uttering a focal utterance.[3]

But how could we find evidence that would help us choose between these two approaches to focus marking? Introspection, the common tool of theoretical linguistics, is of little help in this matter. If we were to ask the speaker whether he had any intention to get the hearer to interpret the focal constituent as new information, he/she would of course claim that it was his/her intention to do so. The hearer, on the other hand, is of course capable of finding out that this was the speaker's intention. But this does not necessarily mean that speakers identify foci as a result of this thought process. However, the point where the two focus theories diverge is precisely the *method* they assume for the identification of a focal constituent: by using an automated grammatical rule, or by deducing the other's intention. If our aim is to investigate whether a specific focus-marking rule is truly available in the grammar of human languages, then we have to create an experimental setting where the deductive process is unavailable for some reason. If in such a situation, the speaker's ability to identify the focus did not diminish, then we could conclude that a language-specific tool is available to him/her; he/she does not have to rely on the communicative deduction process to identify the focus.[4]

---

[3] An important contribution on this issue is Erteschik-Shir's (1997) position. She defines focus in the pragmatic sense, as in (i). But she also states that 'For any sentence several focus assignments will generally be possible, one of which is realised in discourse. A sentence, in discourse, has only one main focus, which is *assigned to a syntactic constituent*. The constituent may be an NP, VP or the whole S' (Erteschik-Shir 1997: 11; my italics). The crucial point is that although she states that focus has a particular pragmatic function (as in (i)), it is grammatically encoded by assigning f-marking to a syntactic constituent.

(i) The Focus of a sentence S = the (intension of) a constituent c of S which the speaker intends to direct the attention of his/her hearer(s) to, by uttering S (Erteschik-Shir 1997: 11; originally from Erteschik-Shir 1973).

[4] Note that the reverse is not true. In an experimental setting where the grammar-specific focus-marking rule is blocked for some reason, we cannot conclude anything from the speaker's undiminished ability to identify the focus correctly. This is because the generative theory does not claim that the availability of the grammar-specific focus-marking rule *precludes* the ability to carry out a communicative deduction process. It only claims that the grammar-specific rule is available, presumably alongside general, communicative deductive mechanisms. In other words, if in this specific situation, the speaker relies on his/her deductive mechanisms to determine the focus, it does not follow that he/she would do the same were the grammar-specific rule available to him/her.

At this point, the psycholinguistic method appears to be useful. If we could identify a population where we have reason to believe that the communicative deductive steps that are necessary to identify the focus are not available to the speaker, we could investigate whether focus marking and focus identification are impaired in this population. In section 15.3, I will argue that people with autism constitute an adequate population to carry out this investigation. But first we need to introduce some basic notions that organize discourse.

15.2 Focus and background

Focus has an important role in the organization of discourse. When we speak, our sentences often contain constituents that have already been referred to, and also others that are new at that particular point of the discourse. Any answer to a question is relevant, new information. We thus take the focus of an utterance to be the constituent that answers an implicit or explicit question in a discourse. Accordingly, the most common focus test is the so-called *wh*-test. As shown in (1), the focus of the utterance is 'Snow white', as this is the constituent that provides an answer to the preceding question.

(1)   A: Who ate the apple?
      B: SNOW WHITE ate the apple.

In Hungarian, as opposed to English, focus has a designated syntactic position: it immediately precedes the verb, while the verbal particle is postverbal, as in (2). In addition, just as in other languages, the focal constituent is also prosodically marked: it gets main stress (indicated by small caps in the examples) and constituents that follow it undergo stress reduction (Kálmán and Nádasdy 1994).

The constituent that follows the moved focus is called the background:

(2)   focus   background
      HÓFEHÉRKE ette meg az almát.
      snow white ate PRT the apple-ACC
      'SNOW WHITE ate the apple.'

We could say that the most extreme form of deaccenting is when the deaccented constituent is erased completely, as in (3) (see Williams 1997).

(3) A: Ki ette meg az almát?
         'Who ate the apple?'

     B: Hófehérke.
         Snow white.

Of course, in everyday life we do not only converse using question-answer pairs. But there are other conversational situations where it is possible to reliably identify the focus of the utterance. For instance, if a speaker corrects the other speaker, then the relevant constituent is the focus of his/ her utterance:

(4) A: A herceg megkóstolta az almát.
         'The prince tasted the apple.'

     B: Nem. Hófehérke kóstolta meg az almát.
         no Snow.white tasted prt the apple-acc
         'No. Snow white tasted the apple.'

Note that in such situations it is inappropriate to omit the postfocal constituent:

(5) A: A herceg megkóstolta az almát.
         'The prince tasted the apple.'

     B: Nem. #Hófehérke.
         no   Snow.white
         'No. Snow white.'

To be more precise, omission of the postfocal constituent is only appropriate if the first speaker already used a marked focus on the agent, in other words, if the omitted constituent had been marked as background by the first speaker:[5]

(6) A: A herceg kóstolta meg az almát.
         the Prince tasted prt the apple-acc
         'The prince tasted the apple.'

     B: Nem. Hófehérke.
         no   Snow.white
         'No. Snow white.'

---

[5] Note that the same is true in English (cf. (i) and (ii)).

(i) A: The Prince tasted the apple.
     B: No. Snow white #(did).

(ii) A: The Prince tasted the apple.
     B: No. Snow white (did).

So far, we have demonstrated that in order to use focus and background marking properly in discourse, the speaker has to be aware of at least the following grammatical rules: (i) focus bears the main stress of the utterance, and in Hungarian, it immediately precedes the verb, (ii) the backround is destressed, (iii) the background can be omitted if it is the same as the background of the previous utterance.

15.3 Autism

Autism is a developmental disorder with genetic roots. Its most important symptoms are that a person with autism has an impairment in his/her ability (i) to create and maintain social relationships, (ii) to take part in interpersonal communication (both verbal and non-verbal), and (iii) to organize his/her interests and behavior in a flexible manner (WHO 1990). Autism is often accompanied by severe mental retardation, in which case linguistic abilities are often severely deficient. Autism that is not accompanied by mental retardation is called Asperger's syndrome, or high-functioning autism; some people with this form of autism may actually have higher than average IQs. The typical symptoms of high-functioning autism are (i) in the realm of social interactions—interactions are too formal, rigid, and often restricted to a stereotypical field of interest; (ii) in the realm of communication—formally sound, but pedantic speech, poor articulation, unusual tone, intonation and speed of speech, comprehension outperforms production; (iii) concerning stereotypical, repetitive behavior—intense interest in a narrow, stereotypical area (e.g. constant studying of the TV program) (Győri 2003: 68).

According to Győri (2003: 79), the hardest problem researchers investigating autism face is the heterogeneity of the syndrome in a range of different ways. A wide range of variation occurs in the causes of the onset of autism, in its neurobiological background, in the nature and extent of the cognitive deficit, in the make-up of the set of symptoms, and in the occurring developmental patterns. In spite of this, we know since seminal work by Baron-Cohen et al. (1985) that people with autism lack the fundamental cognitive ability of (naive) theory of mind, or mentalization.[6] It is this ability that allows us to ascribe mental states (belief, desire, emotional states, intentions) to different agents and to assume that such mental states are the root cause of the behavior of these agents. In other words, in everyday life it is our theory

---

[6] It is an open question whether people with autism have impairments concerning other cognitive functions, besides the impairment of their theory of mind. I will not go into this here, but see for instance Győri (2003: 115–25) for an overview of this issue.

of mind that allows us to interpret, explain, and to some extent foresee complex human behavior.

There is a well-established link between theory of mind and ability for verbal and non-verbal communication (see e.g. Sperber and Wilson 2001 and references there). Due to the intentional nature of interpersonal communication described above, speakers must be aware of the communicative intentions of their conversational partner. Evidently, they need to be able to regard them as creatures capable of mental processes, i.e. they must be able to assign mental states (such as belief) and intentions (such as will) to the other speakers.

Numerous experimental studies support the presence of a theory of mind deficit in people with autism (see e.g. Baron-Cohen et al. 1985; Perner et al. 1989; Happé 1993; Baron-Cohen 1995). As a result, these people form a population that provide an excellent opportunity for the investigation of issues regarding language use and pragmatics, and thus, consequently also the issue of focus marking.[7] More specifically, if focus were not marked by grammar-specific tools, we would expect that people with autism would find focus marking and focus identification problematic. This is so, because the general deductive process that would be necessary to determine the focus, which was described in the previous section, requires a theory of mind on the part of the speaker, which is not available for people with autism. Therefore, if we find that at least in certain conversational situations, focus marking and focus identification are not problematic for an autistic person, then we can conclude that focus marking follows grammar-specific rules.[8] This was the outcome of the case study described in the following section.

15.4 A case study

15.4.1 *The experimental participant*

L. was diagnosed with autism at a young age. At the time of the experiment, he was 13 years old. He had a normal (100) non-verbal IQ. According to the psychologist who treats him, he is a high-functioning autistic patient, as he

---

[7] This is a simplification. Győri (2003) showed that, although most people with autism have a severe theory of mind deficit, certain compensational strategies may significantly ameliorate their experimental results. Moreover, based on some of his experimental findings, Győri (2003: 12) concludes that certain autistic people actually have complex mentalizational abilities.

[8] As is standard in psycholinguistic research, this line of thought assumes that a neurologically impaired population does not possess (or hardly possesses) any abilities that are not available to the normal population. This is not an innocent assumption, but a necessary one, as otherwise we would not be able to make any predictions about the normal population based on experimental findings from a neurologically impaired population.

manages well in many complex situations in life (e.g. gets around town alone).

L.'s behavior shows many autistic symptoms: poor eye contact; stilted, too formal conduct; unexpected changes of subject while conversing; surprisingly detailed interest in particular areas (such as the public transportation system of Budapest). His speech is fluent, but 'dry'. His intonation is flat and he is liable to understand things literally. His linguistic abilities are without doubt very good: his sentences are often complex, his vocabulary is large. He commits few grammatical mistakes in his spontaneous speech. Some examples of these are an occasional topic drop (which is not allowed in Hungarian), or the use of indicative mood instead of the conditional in irrealis situations.[9]

Observing L.'s spontaneous behavior reveals a deficit in his functional mentalizational abilities. Due to lack of time, I could not acquire experimental proof of this. It can be regarded as anecdotal evidence for instance that while it posed no problems for L. to understand why fire extinguishers do not contain water (namely, because water cannot be used to put out fires involving electricity and at the moment of manufacturing it is impossible to know in advance for what kind of fire the extinguisher would be used), he was completely incapable of understanding that the fact that in Hungarian 'folklore' chimney sweepers bring luck is a superstitious belief (i.e. people believe it even though it is not really true).[10]

---

[9] It is interesting to note that the observed ungrammatical verbal mood inflection occurred in an irrealis situation, as in (i). This sentence was uttered after I showed a picture to L. where a lost dog was delivered to his owner by a policeman, and the dog, happy to see him again, licks his owner.

(i) L. *(laughing)*
    – Mi   lenne,   ha a   kutyus a   rendőrt   nyalná   meg, és   akkor
    what   be-COND   if the   doggy the   policeman-ACC lick-COND   prt   and   then
    [a   rendőr]   megijed*(-ne).
    the   policeman frightens(-COND)
    'Imagine if the doggy licked the policeman! Then he would be frightened!'

It is possible that this is not a coincidence but reflects L.'s difficulties in conceptualizing the situation. This would not be surprising, as it is likely that conceptualizing a situation like this would require theory of mind, as one must be able to assume that the policeman is capable of the mental state of being frightened. The issue whether lack of irrealis morphology reflects a conceptual difficulty would require further research.

[10] It was also interesting how L. told a story how he once switched off his mobile phone so that people could not disturb him, as he wanted to go see the terminus of the underground line after school. He got delayed and by the time he got home, his parents were really worried about him. In his narrative, his mother was worried that he had had an accident, but L. did not understand this, because he had not had an accident. This also shows that L. has difficulties assuming that another person, in this case his mother, could believe things to be true that are in fact not true. It is widely accepted that an ability to ascribe false belief to an agent requires mentalization.

15.4.2 *The experimental task*

In the course of the experiment L. carried out a bi-modal elicited production task, following Baltaxe (1984). The bi-modal stimulus involved the simultaneous presentation of a picture and an utterance uttered by the experimenter about the picture. The task of the participant was to determine whether the experimenter can see well what is on the picture, and if not, correct her. I made sure that it was plausible that the experimenter might make mistakes: the pictures were placed right in front of L. and relatively far away from the experimenter, so it was possible for her to claim that she did not see the picture properly. As a result, L. understood the experimental task to be a picture recognition task. This was a typical stimulus:

FIGURE 15.1 Picture for test item *The girl is stroking a cat.*

(7)   *Experimenter (E):*   –A   lány simogat egy cicát.
                              the girl strokes a   cat-ACC
                              'The girl is stroking a cat.'

       Expected answer: –Nem. A   lány EGY KUTYÁT simogat.
                              no   the girl a   dog-ACC strokes
                              'No. The girl is stroking A DOG.'

Both Baltaxe's original aim and my aim in this experiment was to use the stimuli to create a situation where the participant has to use focus.

TABLE 15.1 Number of correct responses

Test items (expected answer: NO + correction of experimenter)	84% (63/75)
Controls (expected answer: YES)	100% (15/15)

The theoretical basis for this method is the observation, described above in (3), that correction of an utterance involves focusing the corrected constituent.

15.4.3 *The conduct of the experiment*

The picture recognition game was introduced after a lengthy spontaneous conversation with L. The experiment lasted about one hour, including short interruptions of spontaneous discourse. During the experiment, L. received 90 test items (i.e. stimulus pairs), 17 percent (15/90) of which required no correction, while 83 percent (75/90) required correction of the statement uttered by the experimenter. As L. believed that the experimental task was picture recognition, I did not think it necessary to introduce extra fillers.

15.4.4 *Results and discussion*

L. did not make mistakes when there was no discrepancy between the picture and the utterance. In 84 percent of the cases where a discrepancy occurred, he correctly identified it. (see Table 15.1).

In the remaining 16 percent of cases, L. either could not conclude what exactly was in the picture, or he understood things too literally and was unable to use inference to deduce the nature of the discrepancy. The breakdown of incorrect responses is given in Table 15.2, while (8) provides an illustrative example.

(8) a. E: -...és sötétszínű   pólóban   van.
          and dark-coloured T_shirt-LOC is
        '...and he is wearing a dark T-shirt.'

TABLE 15.2 The breakdown of incorrect responses

Incorrect responses:	
a. L.: 'I can't see it properly.'	11% (8/75)
b. L. failed to notice the discrepancy	5% (4/75)
Total:	16% (12/75)

L: -Azt   nem lehet   tudni,   mert   itt
that-ACC not possible know-INF because here
fehérnek   tűnik   a   fekete- fehérben.
white-DAT appears the black- white-LOC
'It's impossible to tell, because it seems white in the black and
white [picture].'

E: -Akkor valószínű inkább világos színű,   ugye? Mert
then   likely   more   light   coloured TAG because
a   nadrágja,   az   sötét.
the trousers-POSS that dark
'Then it is more likely to be LIGHT coloured, isn't it? Because his
trousers, those are dark.'

L: -Igen, azt feketében jelzi.
yes   that-acc black-loc signals
'Yes. Those are signaled by black.'

b. E: -...és a   gyerek akinek megnézi a   fogát   az
and the child   whose sees   the tooth-ACC that
szőke hajú.
blond haired
'...and the child whose teeth he is looking at is blond.'

L. -SÁRGA színű.
yellow coloured
'It's YELLOW.'

E: -Sárga színű.   Nem lehet   megállapítani a
yellow coloured not possible state-INF   theLOC
képről,   hogy...
picture- that
'It's yellow. It is not possible to tell from the picture whether...'

L.: -Nem lehet.
not   possible
'It's not possible.'

It is not surprising that L. experienced difficulties both in picture recognition
and in interpretation, as certain picture recognition difficulties and a too
literal interpretation of pictures are both characteristic symptoms of autism
(see for instance Győri 2003).

The breakdown of correct responses is given in Table 15.3. Here we get a
better picture of the nature of the utterances L. intended as corrections.

TABLE 15.3 The breakdown of correct responses for test items

Correct responses:	
a. Pragmatically appropriate, elliptic answer with correct intonation	53% (40/75)
b. Pragmatically appropriate, syntactically correct full-sentence answer with correct intonation	19% (14/75)
c. Pragmatically inappropriate, elliptic answer with correct intonation	3% (2/75)
d. Pragmatically appropriate, elliptic answer with incorrect intonation	9% (7/75)
Total:	84% (63/75)

In more than half of the cases, L. gave an elliptic answer with focal stress that was appropriate in the discourse. Examples are given in (9). In (9a), nominative case indicates that the elided part is something like *That's a...* rather than the experimenter's utterance. Ellipsis is licensed here. In (9b) the presence of the copular verb in the experimenter's utterance licenses the ellipsis. In (9c), which follows on from previous discourse given in (10a) below, the experimenter's question provides the necessary licensing for the ellipsis. In all of these cases, the focal constituent bears focal stress, so these responses can be regarded as correct responses.

(9) a. E: -Itt egy televiziót látunk ahol a bemondónő
            here a   tv.set-ACC see-we where the presenter-woman
            épp a híreket   mondja.
            just the news-ACC says
            'Here we can see a telly, where the presenter[woman] is read-
            ing out the news.'

     L: -Bemondóbácsi!
         presenter-man
         'Presenter-MAN'

   b. E: -A kislánynak   kék nadrágja   van.
            the little.girl-GEN blue trousers-POSS is
            'The little girl has blue trousers.'

     L: -Piros
         red
         'RED [ones]'

   c. E: -Igen? Mit   tapaszt rá?
            yes   what-ACC glues   PRT
            'Yes? What does he glue on [the wall]?'

L: -A TÉGLÁT.
the brick-acc
'The BRICK.'

In a further 13 percent of the cases, L.'s response was a full sentence with focus on the relevant constituent, both syntactically and prosodically. In (10a) he utters an all-focus utterance, correctly stressing every constituent. In (10b) there is correct focus marking on both contrasted elements (teeth; dentist) and in (10c) the focus marking appears on the contrasted verbs (to begin to kick; to push out).

(10) a. E: -Ezen   a   kápen   EGY MUNKÁST   látunk
this-LOC the picture-LOC a   worker-ACC see-we
amint   éppen festi   a   falat.
as   just   paints the wall-ACC
'In this picture, we see a worker as he is painting the wall.'

L: -...RÁTAPASZTJA a   FALRA   a   HÁZÉPÍTÉSNÉL...
PRT-glues   the wall-LOC the house-building-LOC
'He glues [them] onto the wall while building a house.'

b. E: -Ezen   a   képen   egy orvost   látunk, aki
this-LOC the picture-LOC a   doctor-ACC see-we who
fülész   és   viszgálja a   gyereknek a   fülét.
ear.specialist and examines the child-GEN the ear-ACC
'In this picture we see a doctor. He is an ear specialist and he is examining the child's ear.'

L: -Nem, nem, nem, nem, nem.
'No, no, no, no, no, no.'

E: -Hanem?
'Rather?'

L: -Hanem a   FOGÁT   nézi meg egy FOGORVOS.
rather the tooth-ACC looks PRT a   dentist
'Rather, his TEETH are examined by a DENTIST.'

c. E: -Ezen   a   képen   egy focista   van és   éppen
this-loc the picture-loc a   footballer is   and just
áll   a   kapuban és kivédi   a   labdát.
stands the goal-loc   PRT-defends the ball-acc
'In this picture, we see a footballer as he is standing in goal and pushes the ball out.'

L: -Rúgni   kezdi.
      kick-INF begins
      'He begins to KICK [it].'

Note, however, that there were several cases, where L.'s utterance was pragmatically marginal, even though focus marking was correct. These were elliptic utterances, where the use of ellipsis was not appropriate.

(11)   a.   (In the picture there is a puppy with two plates. One has milk, the other water. The doggy splashes the milk around. He does not touch the water.)

E: -Na hát itt   viszont   ez   a   kiskutya itt
      PRT PRT here   in.contrast this the doggy   here
      rosszalkodik, mert   ahelyett, hogy meginná a
      behaves.bad   because   instead   that drink-COND the
      tejecskét, ahelyett kiönti.
      milk-DIM-ACC instead PRT-pours
      'Here the doggy is misbehaving: instead of drinking the milk he is splashing around with it.'

L: -Az INNIVALÓJÁT.
      the drink-POSS-ACC
      'His DRINK.'

E: -Mit?
      'What?'

L: -A VIZET.
      the water-ACC
      'The water.'

E: -A VIZET   önti ki.
      the water-ACC pours PRT
      'He is splashing around with the WATER.'

b.   E: -Na ezen   a   képen   viszont   nagyon rendesen
            PRT this-LOC the picture-LOC in.contrast very   nicely
            viselkedik és   megissza a   vizet.
            behaves   and PRT-drinks the water-ACC
            'Now, in this picture [the doggy] behaves himself and drinks the water.'

L: -A TEJET.
      the milk-ACC
      'The MILK.'

E: -A TEJET   issza   meg.
    the milk-ACC drinks PRT
    'He is drinking the MILK.'

As I already explained above (see (3)), the pragmatic condition for ellipsis is that the background status of the elided constituent is evident for both the speaker and the hearer. In (11a), the elided word (*kiönti* 'PRT-pours') is backgrounded, as the experimenter contrasts it with the verb *meginná* 'PRT-drink-COND'. But even in (11b), where no contrasting verb appears, the lack of background marking on the verb by the experimenter renders the ellipsis in L.'s utterance inappropriate. Of course, L.'s responses are perfectly comprehensible; they do not require more than a simple inference. It would be interesting to see in future research, however, whether these kinds of pragmatic errors are characteristic of autistic speech. This would tell us more about autism and also about such pragmatic phenomena.

Finally, I want to discuss those responses that can be described as incorrect. In 9 percent of the cases, L.'s response carried less stress or accent than what can be considered normal. These responses fit in with his general speech, which has a narrow range and a flat intonation, as does the speech of many autistic people. Nevertheless, cases where the utterance was also elliptic or where the contrast fell on the verb, as in (12), were counted as incorrect in the present experiment. This is because ellipsis makes the syntactic effect of focus invisible and in the case of verb focus there is no syntactic effect. One would need to rely on prosody alone to determine whether focus marking was correct and in these cases the necessary accent was judged to be lacking.

(12) E: -Itt egy lányt   látunk, aki   gyalogol.
          here a   girl-ACC see-we who   walks
          'Here we can see a girl who is walking.'

      L: -Fut.
          'Runs.'

15.5 Conclusions

It is clear from the above that L., despite the fact that he is autistic, used focus marking correctly in 75 percent of the cases when he had to correct a previous statement of the experimenter. It is needless to say that one cannot draw strong conclusions from a single case study, especially not in the case of such a heterogeneous syndrome as autism. But we can safely say that the results of this case study clearly point in the direction that focus marking is not an exclusively communicative device, but rather follows a language-specific rule.

Despite his knowledge of focus marking, L.'s language use differs from what is considered normal or average in many different ways. Even in the case of focus, we can only conclude that he used it correctly in a discourse situation where his task was to correct a previous statement uttered by the experimenter. We do not have proof that he would use focus in every discourse situation that non-autistic speakers would. (Note, however, that in L.'s spontaneous speech syntactic focus marking seemed normal.) We also saw that it is questionable whether other pragmatic devices, such as background marking and background identification, are equally available to him. It is also an open question whether the poor prosody of L.'s speech is connected to the impairment of his mentalizational abilities and to the consequent communicative deficit.

I hope that this case study has proved suggestive as to how psycholinguistic methodology can help us investigate issues in theoretical linguistics.

16

Intermodular argumentation: Morpheme-specific phonologies are out of business in a phase-based architecture

TOBIAS SCHEER

16.1 Setting the scene: Interactionism, selective spell-out, and modification-inhibiting no-look-back (PIC)

The minimalist focus on the interface has afforded a radical change in generative interface architecture. Since the 1960s (Chomsky 1965: 15ff), the inverted T model has stood unchallenged (aside from the generative semantics interlude): a concatenative device (morphosyntax) feeds two interpretative devices, PF and LF. This architecture was supplemented with a proviso which requires that all concatenation be done before any interpretation. That is, the morphosyntactic derivation is completed before the result (S-structure) is sent to PF and LF in one go.

An alternative view of the communication between morphosyntax and LF/PF was formulated in phonology in the early 1980s: the backbone of Lexical Phonology (Pesetsky 1979; Kiparsky 1982a,b), so-called interactionism, holds that concatenation and interpretation are intertwined. That is, first some pieces are merged, the result is interpreted, then some more pieces are concatenated, the result is again interpreted and so on.

While GB-syntax of that time hardly produced any echo, generative orthodoxy in phonology reacted to this violation of 'all concatenation before all interpretation': Halle and Vergnaud (1987) proposed a non-interactionist version of Lexical Phonology that restores the interface landscape of SPE to a large extent. Halle and Vergnaud (1987) also promote a new idea: selective spell-out. Since cyclic derivation was introduced by Chomsky et al. (1956: 75) and formalized in Chomsky and Halle (1968: 15ff), interpretation was held to run through the bracketed string (that is inherited from S-structure) from inside out; (roughly[1]) every morpheme break defined a cycle. Halle and Vergnaud dispense with this definition of what an interpretational unit is: they propose to grant cyclic status only to a subset of morphosyntactic divisions. That is, some nodes trigger interpretation, others do not.[2]

Halle and Vergnaud's (1987) selective spell-out is exactly what modern (syntactic) phase theory is about: in more familiar terminology, nodes may or may not be phase heads, hence their material may or may not be an interpretational unit. As far as I can see, the phonological heritage is left unmentioned in the syntactic literature since derivation by phase was introduced by Epstein et al. (1998), Uriagereka (1999), and Chomsky (2000, 2001b, et passim).

This is also true for interactionism: multiple spell-out and derivation by phase make the generative interface architecture interactionist, exactly along the lines that Lexical Phonology had laid out: first you do some concatenation, then some interpretation, then some more concatenation, etc. For (extralinguistic) reasons of computational economy regarding the limited availability of active memory, a costly cognitive resource (e.g. Chomsky 2000: 101, 2001b: 15), modern phase theory applies the interactionist world view. Here again, the phonological origin of the idea has gone unnoticed as far as I can see (let alone the anti-interactionist reaction of generative orthodoxy in the 1980s).

On the pages below, I examine a question that is closely related to selective spell-out and interactionism: critical for current syntactic phase theory is a device which guarantees that previously interpreted strings do not burden further computation—in Chomsky's terms, strings that are returned from interpretation are 'frozen' and 'forgotten' when concatenation resumes.

---

[1] In actual fact, SPE holds that all morphemic and syntactic divisions are cycles, except for sequences of morphemes that belong to the same major category: these cohabit in the same cycle (hence [[[theatr]$_N$ ic + al]$_A$ i + ty]$_N$, Chomsky and Halle 1968: 88f.).

[2] Of course the question associated with selective spell-out is how to decide just which subset of nodes is spelled out. The phonological take of Halle and Vergnaud (and of all other phonologists who practice selective spell-out) is that this depends on a lexical property of the piece (the affix) that is merged. In Halle and Vergnaud's terminology, there are cyclic (interpretation-triggering) and non-cyclic (interpretation-neutral) affixes. Under the header of phasehood, this is a top-ranked question on the agenda in current syntactic phase theory (den Dikken 2007 for example provides an overview of the large body of literature). Unlike in phonology where phasehood depends on a lexical property of affixes, the syntactic take is that it depends on the label of nodes (which of course is also a projection of a lexical property, but in a different sense): I call the two options node-driven vs piece-driven phase (Scheer 2008, forthcoming). This question, and an eventual unification of both options, cannot be discussed in the frame of this paper.

I discuss the history of no-look-back devices in generative theory, which begins with Chomsky's (1973) Conditions on Transformations, and whose offspring—until its recent revival in the coat of the Phase Impenetrability Condition (PIC)—was essentially phonological. No-look-back devices are designed in order to prevent computation from considering 'old' strings. Depending on their precise formulation, however, they have very different empirical effects, which correspond to the thing that the analyst wants the computation to be unable to do. I show that here again, Chomsky's PIC has a phonological precedent: unlike all other no-look-back devices that the literature has accumulated since 1973, Kaye's (1992, 1995) mechanism inhibits the modification of previously interpreted strings—which are thus 'frozen'.

Modification-inhibiting no-look-back is absolutely critical for current syntactic theory: it is a headstone of the interface-oriented minimalist programme. In contrast to GB where the completed morphosyntactic derivation was merely dumped into PF (and LF) with a 'good-bye and don't come back', phase theory establishes a two-way pipe between the morphosyntactic and the phonological (and semantic) module. Actors on both ends are not free anymore to do what they want: their theories and analyses may make predictions on the other end. The intermodular potential of phase theory, however, has not received much attention thus far. Syntacticians use Phase Impenetrability for syntax-internal purposes, and phase theory evolves at high speed without taking into account what happens when the parcel spends time on the phonological side. On the other hand, phonologists have barely acknowledged the existence of phase theory, let alone taken into account the predictions that it makes on the phonological side.

The argument that is made below builds on the fact that the chunks which are designated by the spell-out mechanism for computation at PF (interpretational units) must be the same on the syntactic and on the phonological side. Also, the phonological and syntactic computation of these identical portions of the string must be restricted by the PIC in the same way. A particular syntactic analysis thus makes precise predictions on the phonological side, and vice versa. A situation where a no-look-back device restricts the computation of 'old' strings in syntax, but not in phonology, or where it restricts them in different ways on both sides, is inconsistent.[3] Chomsky (2001b: 12f. see the quote in section 16.4) is actually explicit on the fact that the economy of active memory concerns phonological as much as syntactic computation.

On these grounds, competing phonological analyses of affix class-based phenomena are compared. Since Lexical Phonology, the most popular

---

[3] This issue is further examined in Scheer (2009).

solution is morpheme-specific phonologies, i.e. distinct computational systems that apply to strings according to their morphological composition (class 1 vs class 2 affixes). The modern offspring of this approach has been adapted to OT, where it runs under the banners of Stratal OT, DOT, co-phonologies, and indexed constraints. Halle and Vergnaud's (1987) aforementioned system that is based on selective spell-out proposes an alternative that works with only one computational system. Kaye (1992, 1995) has supplemented this approach with the aforementioned 'freezing' no-look-back device that is known as the PIC today.

It is shown that the PIC and morpheme-specific phonologies do the same labor in the analysis of affix-class-based phenomena: they organize underapplication. Therefore, I argue, no theory can afford to accommodate both devices: this would be redundant. If syntactic phase theory is on the right track, then present and past solutions that rely on morpheme-specific phonologies do not qualify: the PIC must exist in phonology. In other words, a core property of current syntactic theory, the PIC, is found to act as a referee for competing phonological theories.

I submit that intermodular argumentation provides stronger evidence than what can be produced by modular-internal reasoning: it offers the maximal degree of independent assessment that linguists can expect without leaving their discipline. Be it only for that reason, the new interactionist architecture that the minimalist orientation has installed is a good thing to have: after a long period of quasi-silence; syntacticians and phonologists can once more talk about things that are unrelated to the weather and to job openings.

Finally, it is worthwhile making explicit that this paper is not empirically oriented: while some contrasting empirical predictions that are made by competing theories are mentioned (namely in section 16.3.4), this is not what the argument relies on. No doubt the empirical record is important, no doubt theories need to be assessed according to empirical coverage, and also, of course, affix-class-based phenomena are not the only phenomena that inform the interface and cyclic derivation. All this needs to be pondered elsewhere, and typically is. The ambition of the following pages is merely to draw attention to the fact that the phase-based architecture offers a new opportunity for refereeing competing theories that has not been explored in the discussion thus far. This opportunity is intermodular in kind, and its discussion is based on a phenomenon that is surely not the only thing that can inform the interface, but which represents a core piece of the phonological evidence for cyclic derivation, and has played a key role in the historical development of the debate: morpheme-specific phonologies and, more generally speaking, the idea that there are several distinct computational systems in phonology, are around today because of affix-class-based phenomena (in English).

The roadmap is as follows. Section 16.2 introduces the approach that relies on morpheme-specific phonologies, as well as the variation that is afforded by different older and modern brands thereof. Section 16.3 presents the alternative account that builds on selective spell-out and just one computational system. The two representatives, Halle and Vergnaud (1987) and Kaye (1992, 1995), are shown to be different in that only the latter uses the PIC. Through a historical survey of the various no-look-back devices that have been proposed in the generative literature, section 16.4 shows that the PIC ('freezing' no-look-back) is unprecedented. Finally, section 16.5 gathers the strands and makes the argument: morpheme-specific phonologies have to go if derivation by phase is on the right track.

16.2 Morpheme-specific phonologies (two engines)

Let us start by introducing the relevant evidence regarding affix-class-based phenomena in English. Data and analyses have been extensively discussed in the literature. I therefore only introduce aspects that are critical for the argumentation. A more complete review appears in Scheer (forthcoming), of which the present paper is a piece.

16.2.1 *Morpheme-specific phonologies: The basic analysis of lexical phonology*

Affix classes are best studied in English (see Booij 2000: 297 for an overview of literature regarding other languages). Their existence was identified in SPE (Chomsky and Halle 1968: 84ff.); since then, the basic diagnostic for class membership is the behavior of affixes with respect to stress: they may be stress-shifting (class 1) or stress-neutral (class 2). While the former roughly correspond to the Romance stock of lexical material (e.g. *-ity, -ic, -ion, -ary, -al$_{adj}$*), the latter typically are of Germanic origin (e.g. *-ness, -less, -hood, -ship, -ful*). Relevant overview literature includes Kaisse and Shaw (1985), Giegerich (1999), McMahon (2000), and Bermúdez-Otero (forthcoming).

For example, a root such as *párent* appears with regular penultimate stress when it occurs in isolation; adding the stress-shifting affix *-al* produces *parént-al*, while the stress-neutral item *-hood* yields *párent-hood*. Another way of looking at the same facts is that both *párent* and *parént-al* bear transparent penultimate stress, while *párent-hood* illustrates an opaque non-penultimate pattern where stress behaves as if the suffix were not there. In other words, stress has been reassigned when *-al* has been added (stress-shifting), but reassignment was blocked upon the merger of *-hood*. The task for the analyst is thus to organize underapplication of the stress rule, which must somehow be prevented from reapplying to strings that are headed by class 2 affixes.

Table 16.1 below shows the solution that is proposed by Lexical Phonology.

The spine of Lexical Phonology is its stratal architecture: lexical entries contain underived roots, all class 1 affixes are concatenated at stratum 1 (level 1), while class 2 affixes join in at stratum 2 (level 2). After the concatenation is complete at each stratum, a stratum-specific phonology applies to the string as it stands. Rules are assigned to specific strata: in our example, the stress-assigning rule is a level 1 rule, which means that it is active at level 1, but absent from level 2. Another ground rule is that the derivation is strictly serial: given the order lexical entries → level 1 → level 2 (result: words), strings that are present at some point in this algorithm must run through all subsequent levels on their way to the surface. This means that they experience the computation at these levels.

In Table 16.1, then, /parent/ in isolation receives stress at level 1 where stress assignment is active. This is also true for /parent-al/ since -*al* has been concatenated in time. Stress assignment to /parent-hood/, however, concerns only /parent/ since -*hood* has not yet joined in at level 1. After its concatenation at level 2, stress does not move since the stress rule is absent from this stratum. Note that this is critical: otherwise *parént-hood* would be produced.

Underapplication of stress assignment at level 2 is thus achieved by the split of phonological computation into two morpheme-specific mini-grammars: one that assesses class 1 strings (where the stress rule is present), another that takes care of class 2 strings (where the stress rule is absent). The set of rules that applies at level 1 is thus necessarily distinct from the set of rules that applies at level 2—both phonologies specifically apply to a certain class of morphemes.

TABLE 16.1 *párent—parént-al* vs. *párent-hood* in Lexical Phonology

		parent	parént-al	párent-hood
lexicon		parent	parent	parent
level 1	concatenation	—	parent-al	—
	stress assignment	párent	parént-al	párent
level 2	concatenation	—	—	párent-hood
	rule application	—	—	—

16.2.2 *Modern implementations of the morpheme-specific strategy*

Morpheme-specific phonologies have been carried over from Lexical Phonology into the environment of OT—they are actually the only type of analysis that is practiced in this theory (i.e., there are no OT-incarnations of the alternative approach that is discussed in section 16.3).

Within OT, the two-engine approach falls into two varieties, serial and parallel. On the one hand, Stratal OT (Kiparsky 2000, 2003 Bermúdez-Otero forthcoming) and DOT (Rubach 1997 et passim) faithfully continue the stratal architecture of Lexical Phonology: strata are serially ordered, and any string that was present at stratum n-1 must run through stratum n and all subsequent strata. In OT, differences among grammars are expressed by means of a different ranking of the same universal constraint set. Morpheme-specific phonologies therefore incarnate as different constraint rankings. That is, constraints are re-ranked between strata.

The alternative implementation of the two-engine approach is parallel: class 1 strings are assessed by a computational system X, which is different from the computational system Y which applies to class 2 strings. In contrast to the serial solution, however, class 1 strings never meet class 2 computation, and vice versa: nothing is serially ordered, and hence strings that are headed by a class-specific affix do not run through other 'strata' (there are no strata in this approach) on their way to the surface. There are two competing representatives of this solution, co-phonologies (e.g. Itô and Mester 1995; Inkelas 1998; Anttila 2002) and indexed constraints. The latter were originally introduced by Prince and Smolensky (1993) for the purpose of alignment, but the idea was then generalized to other constraints (both faithfulness and markedness). This direction is represented by, among others, Itô and Mester (1999) and Pater (2000, forthcoming).

Figure 16.1 below depicts the three approaches discussed.

The difference between the two parallel solutions, co-phonologies and indexed constraints, is the number of constraint hierarchies that are involved. While the former provide for the existence of two independent rankings, the latter couch two (or more) computational systems in one single hierarchy. This is done by means of indices: the same constraint may appear several times, but with different indices that specify which type of string it exclusively considers. Strings are also indexed, and when EVAL assesses a candidate only those constraints are active that match this lexical index. All constraints continue to be freely interspersed across indices and with non-indexed constraints. The two distinct computational systems are thus made of two blocks of constraints, the x- and the y-family in Figure 16.1b.

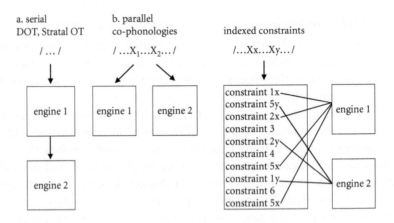

FIGURE 16.1   Morpheme-specific phonologies: different implementations in OT.

16.3 Selective spell-out and only one computational system (one engine)

16.3.1 *Halle and Vergnaud (1987): Selective spell-out*

In one way or another, all systems that have been discussed so far are based on morpheme-specific mini-phonologies. In all cases, this is the instrument that assures underapplication in the analysis of affix-class-based phenomena. Halle and Vergnaud (1987) have introduced an alternative that works with only one computational system.[4] The heart of their mechanism is selective spell-out. The idea has already been introduced in section 16.1: only some nodes of the morphosyntactic tree trigger spell-out. Whether or not a node dominates an interpretational unit (i.e., is a phase head or not) is decided by its head: affixes are lexically specified as interpretation-triggering (cyclic affixes in Halle and Vergnaud's terms) or interpretation-neutral (non-cyclic in their vocabulary). This property is then inherited by the node that they project, and the spell-out mechanism does or does not send off nodes to PF/ LF according to this characteristic.

---

[4] Halle and Vergnaud (1987) is a book about stress, not about the interface. The interface theory that it contains has only really emerged in subsequent work: Halle et al. (1991); Halle and Kenstowicz (1991); Odden (1993). Modern offspring includes Halle (1997), Halle and Matushansky (2006), and Halle and Nevins (forthcoming). I use Halle and Vergnaud (1987) as a cover term that refers to the entire line of thought, in recognition of the fact that this book appears to be the first source in print (except a manuscript of Halle's (1986) which to date I was unable to hunt down: Morris Halle does not have a copy, and a call on Linguist List also remained fruitless).

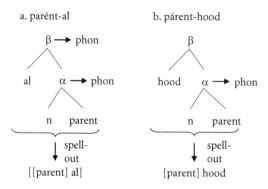

a. parént-al   b. párent-hood

FIGURE 16.2   Halle and Vergnaud (1987): analysis of affix-class-based stress.

In Figure 16.2a below, β triggers spell-out because it is projected by the class 1 affix *-al;* by contrast in Figure 16.2b, the stress-neutral class 2 affix *-hood* does not provoke the interpretation of its node.

An additional proviso is that all roots are interpretational units by themselves (Halle and Vergnaud 1987: 78). This is integrated into Figure 16.2 by the fact that the root node α is always spelled out. The difference between *parént-al* and *párent-hood*, then, is one of cyclic structure: in addition to the root, the former is subject to interpretation as a whole, while the latter is not. The input that enters phonology is thus /[[parent] al]/ vs /[parent] hood/.[5] Penultimate stress assignment then applies to each cycle: while the derivation ends for the latter item when [párent] has received stress (there is no further cycle), it reapplies to [párent al]; that is, stress is shifted to the right, and the result is *parént-al* vs *párent-hood* ([parent] in isolation of course comes out as *párent*).

This analysis achieves underapplication by selective spell-out: class 2 affixes do not trigger interpretation, which prevents the stress rule from reapplying. Two more ingredients, however, need to be made explicit: for one thing, it was already mentioned that roots are always spelled out by themselves—this is nothing that selective spell-out enforces per se. Also, class 1, rather than class 2 affixes, are interpretation-triggering—this additional choice is not a property of the model either.

In sum, then, Halle and Vergnaud achieve the same affix-class-based effect as Lexical Phonology (and modern incarnations thereof), but without

---

[5] Recall that Halle and Vergnaud are anti-interactionist, i.e. need to complete the morphosyntactic derivation before the full string, augmented with cycle-defining brackets, is sent to PF for interpretation.

TABLE 16.2 Differences between Halle and Vergnaud (1987) and Kaye (1995)

	Halle and Vergnaud	Kaye
a. the root is an interpretational unit	yes	no
b. the word is an interpretational unit	no	yes
c. interpretation-triggering affixes trigger the spell-out of	their own node	their sister
d. type of English affix-classes that triggers interpretation	class 1	class 2
e. underapplication is achieved by	cycles	cycles and no look-back

recurring to morpheme-specific phonologies: there is only one computational system that assesses all strings.[6]

16.3.2 *Kaye (1995): A different implementation of selective spell-out*

Kaye (1992, 1995) adopts selective spell-out and, like Halle and Vergnaud, rejects morpheme-specific phonologies. The implementation of selective spell-out, however, is significantly different given the 'secondary' choices that Kaye makes. A comparison appears in Table 16.2 above.[7]

Unlike with Halle and Vergnaud, the root is not an interpretational unit (i.e. a cycle) per se in Kaye's system. By contrast, the word is always an interpretational unit (while it is not with Halle and Vergnaud: /[parent]

---

[6] For the sake of completeness, it needs to be mentioned that the single computational system at hand only refers to the contrast with morpheme-specific multiple phonologies. We are not talking about chunk-specific phonologies, which apply only to a certain size of pieces and are a separate issue. The literature works with two well-identified chunk sizes for which specific computation has been proposed: word-level phonology (as opposed to smaller chunks) and sentence-level phonology (which assesses sequences of words, as opposed to sequences of morphemes). The former was introduced by SPE (in English for example, vowel reduction within a word is calculated with reference to main stress, which however is only determined after the last morpheme has been added), and is also provided for by Halle and Vergnaud (1987) (under the label of non-cyclic rules). The latter goes back to the Praguian distinction between word and sentence phonology, which has become a hallmark of Lexical Phonology (as far as I can see, the idea was introduced by Rubach 1981) where the set of lexical rules is distinct from the set of postlexical rules. Halle and Vergnaud (1987) reject this distinction.

[7] A formal property of Kaye's system that cannot be addressed in this paper is the ability of terminal elements to be spelled out in isolation. This contrasts with regular spell-out procedures (and with Halle and Vergnaud), which can only spell out nodes. Hence [[prefix] [root]] is a possible (actually: a necessary) structure in Kaye's system, which requires the prefix to be interpreted prior to its being merged. This is known as counter-cyclic merger (or late adjunction) in syntax (e.g. Stepanov 2001), a non-standard mechanism. Interestingly, though, a property of counter-cyclic merger in syntax is precisely that the item at hand is spelled out before being merged—exactly what Kaye's system requires. This parallel is further discussed in Newell and Scheer (2007) and Scheer (forthcoming).

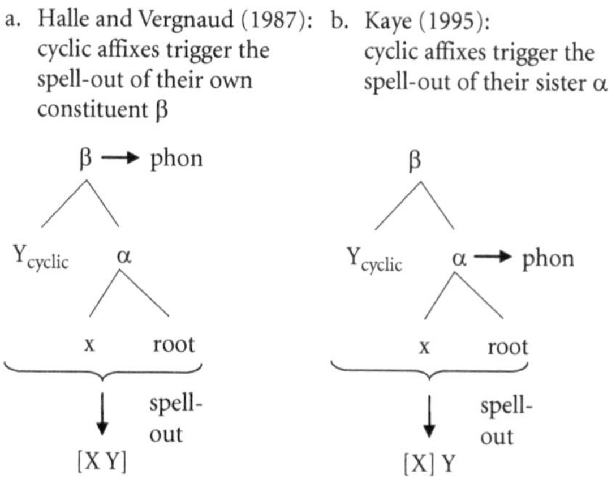

a. Halle and Vergnaud (1987):   b. Kaye (1995):
   cyclic affixes trigger the   cyclic affixes trigger the
   spell-out of their own   spell-out of their sister α
   constituent β

FIGURE 16.3   Interpretation-triggering affixes: what exactly is spelled out.

hood/). A third contrast is that with Kaye, class 2 affixes are interpretation-triggering, whereas this privilege was granted to class 1 affixes by Halle and Vergnaud. Finally, another important difference is that with Kaye the sister of the interpretation-triggering affix, rather than the node that dominates the affix itself, is spelled out.[8] Figure 16.3 above depicts this difference.

Given an interpretation-triggering (i.e. cyclic) affix Y and a root, two significantly distinct results are produced: /[root Y]/ vs /[root] Y/. Note that this is only the isolated result of the action of the affix, which needs to be supplemented with the computation-independent provisos in Table 16.2a,b: the root is always a cycle with Halle and Vergnaud, the word is always an interpretational unit in Kaye's system. This leaves us with identical structures: /[[root] Y]/ is produced on both sides.

It is not true, however, that the two different spell-out strategies return identical results. This is shown in Table 16.3 below where interpretation-neutral affixes are included.

The contrast between Halle and Vergnaud and Kaye thus concerns strings that bear an interpretation-neutral affix, and it is the result of the combined choices in Table 16.2a–c. These choices are hard-wired in the two systems, i.e. independent of the situation in particular languages. That is, the analyst must still identify which are the interpretation-triggering and which are the interpretation-neutral affixes in the particular language under study—theory will not help. The English situation is discussed in the following section.

---

[8] It will be mentioned in the conclusion that this is relevant when comparing the phonological mechanism with syntactic phase theory: spelling out the sister is the phonological version of Chomsky's phase edge.

TABLE 16.3 Result of the two spell-out strategies with interpretation-triggering and interpretation-neutral affixes. Below X is an interpretation- neutral, Y an interpretation-triggering affix

	Halle and Vergnaud	Kaye
a. root-X	[root] X	[root X]
b. root-Y	[[root] Y]	[[root] Y]

16.3.3 *Modification-inhibiting ('Freezing') no-look-back and the English situation*

It has already been mentioned that Halle and Vergnaud and Kaye have made opposite choices for English: while class 1, but not class 2 affixes trigger interpretation for the former, the reverse distribution is assumed by the latter. Table 16.4 below shows the configurations that are produced. It also mentions a set of data that has not been considered thus far, i.e. processes that require the underapplication to class 1 strings (rather than to class 2 strings). In Lexical Phonology, this type of process is called a level 2 rule (against stress assignment, which is a level 1 rule).

As may be seen, the additional factor regarding the (opposite) choice of interpretation-triggering affix classes produces structures on both sides that are systematically distinct.

Let us now look at how Kaye's system actually works. It was mentioned in Table 16.2e that Kaye uses a specific no-look-back device in addition to selective spell-out (while Halle and Vergnaud do not). Kaye's basic line of attack is to follow the observation that morphosyntactic boundaries may or may not be visible for phonological processes. We know that they are if a morphologically complex string shows a different behavior with respect to a monomorphemic item. This is the case of *párent-hood$_2$*, which deviates from

TABLE 16.4 English affix classes: comparison

		monomorphemic situation	root + class 1 affix	root + class 2 affix
a. level 1 rule	H&V	[parent]	[[parent] al]	[parent] hood
	Kaye	[parent]	[parent al]	[[parent] hood]
b. level 2 rule	H&V	[sign]	[[sign] ature]	[sign] ing
	Kaye	[sign]	[sign ature]	[[sign] ing]

the monomorphemic penultimate pattern (*párent*). By contrast, penultimate *parént-al₁* is indistinguishable from monomorphemic *párent*. The opacity (underapplication) of a process is thus indicative of the process being 'disturbed' by a morphological boundary. By contrast, phonological transparency witnesses that the boundary is invisible in phonology. Hence [parent al] vs [[parent] hood].

Stress assignment, then, is straightforward for [parent] and [parent al]: in both cases, the penultimate vowel is made tonic. The no-look-back device only enters the scene when embedded domains need to be computed in [[parent] hood]. Cycles are processed from inside out. The inner cycle thus receives regular penultimate stress on this pass: [párent]. On the outer cycle, the penultimate stress rule must be prevented from reapplying—otherwise *[parént hood] is produced. In Kaye's system, this is assured by the proviso that strings which have already been subject to interpretation cannot be modified by further computation on later cycles. That is, the previously assigned main stress of the first vowel of [párent] is 'frozen' on the outer cycle. Syntacticians will have recognized Chomsky's Phase Impenetrability (on which more shortly).

16.3.4 *English processes that require underapplication to class 1 strings (level 2 rules)*

Let us now turn to the other type of affix-class-sensitive processes in English, which are known as level 2 rules from Lexical Phonology. Abstracting away from theory-specific vocabulary that muddies the water, the empirical fact is that English features affix-class-based phenomena of two types: one that requires underapplication to class 2 strings (i.e. [root + class 2]: *párenthood₂*, level 1 rules in LP), another where the process underapplies to class 1 strings (i.e. [root + class 1], *si[g]n-ature₁*, level 2 rules in LP).

The latter is represented by a process that simplifies root-final clusters which involve a nasal. The phenomenon is well known and amply discussed in the literature (e.g. Mohanan 1986). It comes in several brands: /gN/ → [N] (*sign, sign-ing₂* vs *si[g]n-ature₁*), /mn/ → [m] (*damn, damn-ing₂* vs *dam[n]-ation₁*), /mb/, /ŋg/ → [m], [ŋ] (*sing, sing-ing₂* vs *lon[g]-er₁* (comparative of *long*), *bomb, bomb-ing₂* vs *bom[b]-ard₁*).[9]

Chomsky and Halle (1968: 85) have observed that 'the inflectional affixes which are neutral with respect to stress also characteristically affect final

---

[9] The latter process, postnasal plosive deletion, suffers from a number of exceptions (Bermúdez-Otero 2008) and is therefore not the best witness of the pattern.

clusters in the same way as word boundary does'. That is, clusters before class 2 affixes systematically behave as if they were word-final. That being final is a necessary condition for the application of the process is also shown by the fact that the clusters in question survive morpheme-internally: *i[g]nore, am[n]esia, fin[g]er, Ham[b]urg*.[10]

It is this additional condition on finality that makes the difference between processes that require underapplication to class 1 strings and those that underapply to class 2 strings. In any event, it may be seen in Table 16.4 that Kaye's (as much as Halle and Vergnaud's) system attributes identical cyclic patterns to all strings that have the same affix class-structure. Had the process itself not introduced an additional condition, Kaye's system would be unable to distinguish the two patterns.

Given the final condition, then, nasal clusters simplify under Kaye's analysis iff they are string-final upon phonological computation. 'Upon phonological computation' is an explicit formulation of 'cycle-final' (or phase-final in modern terms, domain-final in Kaye's terminology). Given this process, the cluster in [sign] and [[sign] ing] is simplified since at some point in the derivation it is string-final when phonological interpretation occurs. By contrast, the cluster in [sign ature] is never string-final when computation applies and therefore survives (the same goes for [ignore]).

We are now in a position to compare the empirical coverage of Halle and Vergnaud's and Kaye's implementation of selective spell-out—at least regarding the English pattern. As a matter of fact, Halle and Vergnaud's system coupled with the language-specific choice that class 1 rather than class 2 affixes are interpretation-triggering, is unable to account for processes that require underapplication to class 1 strings (i.e. level 2 rules, nasal cluster simplification). Given the cyclic structures /[sign]/, /[sign] ing$_2$/, and /[[sign] ature$_1$]/ (see Table 16.4) it is impossible to formulate a rule that simplifies the cluster in the two former, but not in the latter case. This is because of Halle and Vergnaud's specific choice according to which the root is always an interpretational unit (see Table 16.2a): if cluster simplification applies to [sign] (i.e. *sign*), it will also apply to /[sign] ing$_2$/ (which is fine), and to /[[sign] ature$_1$]/ (which is counterfactual).

The literature that has worked out Halle and Vergnaud's system (see n. 4) tacitly confesses that LP's level 2 rules cannot be covered: while it is explained

---

[10] Note that this fact has got nothing to do with derived environments: *sign* is just as underived as *i [g]nore*, but eliminates the cluster. What decides whether the cluster simplifies or not is its being root-final (in addition of the affix-class conditioning of course).

at length how level 1 rules are analyzed, as far as I can see there is no mention of the level 2 pattern at all.[11]

16.4 A short history of no look-back devices since Chomsky (1973)

We have seen that modification-inhibiting ('freezing') no-look-back is a critical ingredient of Kaye's system. This section shows that Kaye's version of no-look-back is unlike all others that have been proposed since Chomsky (1973), and that Chomsky's modern Phase Impenetrability was actually invented by Kaye (1992, 1995).

There is quite some confusion in the literature when it comes to the discussion of no-look-back devices. The most deeply rooted misconception is due to Kiparsky (1982a,b), who has scrambled derived environment effects with Chomsky's original requirement to use newly introduced material— while presenting his significantly modified package as a *version* of Chomsky's Strict Cyclicity.

The ancestor of all no-look-back devices is Chomsky's (1973) Strict Cycle Condition, which prevents rules from applying if they do not use material that has been introduced on the current cycle. The original formulation appears below.

Strict Cycle Condition (SCC)
'No rule can apply to a domain dominated by a cyclic node A in such a way as to affect solely a proper subdomain of A dominated by a node B which is also a cyclic node.'
                                                                    Chomsky (1973: 243)

The effect is that rules are blocked whose structural description is met by a string which is made exclusively of material that belongs to previous cycles. That is, given $[[AB]_i C]_j$, a rule that is triggered by AB can apply at cycle i, but not at cycle j. Or, in other words, multiple application of rules is prohibited.

Kean (1974) and Mascaró (1976) have applied Chomsky's SCC to phonology. Mascaró's (1976: 7) formulation talks about the 'proper' application of a rule, which means that 'improper' applications are blocked: 'for a cyclic rule

---

[11] Another empirical issue is so-called bracketing paradoxes, i.e. cases where—contrary to the affix-ordering generalization (Siegel 1974) that was a headstone of Lexical Phonology—class 2 affixes occur closer to the root than class 1 affixes. Examples are *govern-ment$_2$-al$_1$*, *organ-ize$_2$-ation$_1$*, and the celebrated *un$_2$-grammatic-al$_1$-ity$_1$* (which must be $[[un_2 [grammatic al_1]] ity_1]$) (see Aronoff and Sridhar 1983, 1987). The bankruptcy of affix ordering is an argument that Halle and Kenstowicz (1991: 459) and Halle et al. (1991: 142) make in order to dismiss the stratal architecture of Lexical Phonology. Unlike for the stratal system, bracketing paradoxes are not an obstacle for their model. Discussion regarding the reaction of Kaye's system cannot be provided in the frame of this paper. The issue is considered at greater length in Scheer (forthcoming).

to apply properly in any given cycle j, it must make specific use of information proper to (i.e. introduced by virtue of) cycle j.'

A derived environment effect is a phenomenon whereby a rule only applies to morphologically complex strings.[12] Paul Kiparsky has been on the track of this pattern since Kiparsky (1968–73). It is for sure that Chomsky's (and Kean's and Mascaró's) condition on the applicability of rules is entirely irrelevant for derived environment effects: it will not prevent rules from applying to monomorphemic strings since these have necessarily been introduced on the latest (the only) cycle. Thus Trisyllabic Shortening (*s[ej]ne - s[æ]n-ity*), a famous example, will happily apply to *n[aj]tingale* and *[aj]vory* under Chomsky's SCC.

Nonetheless, Kiparsky (1982a,b) introduces his version of the SCC as if it were just a restatement of Mascaró's.

'With some simplification, his [Mascaró's] proposal was:

(47)   Strict Cycle Condition (SSC):
    a.   Cyclic rules apply only to derived representations.
    b.   Def.: A representation φ is derived w.r.t. rule R in cycle j iff φ meets the structural analysis of R by virtue of a combination of morphemes introduced in cycle j or the application of a phonological rule in cycle j.'

Kiparsky (1982b: 153f.)

Derived environments have thus appeared overnight in what Kiparsky sells as Mascaró's slightly 'simplified' Strict Cycle Condition. Also, the notion of phonologically derived environment has joined in where Chomsky and Mascaró were only talking about morphological conditions.

Kiparsky's attempt to kill two birds ('use new material!' and derived environment effects) with one stone (his scrambled SCC[13]) was considered an important achievement in the 1980s, but turned out to lead into a dead end: ten years later, Kiparsky (1993) himself declared the bankruptcy of his version of the SCC.[14]

Another (anecdotal) aspect of this dossier is that the combination of Chomsky's SCC with derived environment effects was actually not done by Kiparsky (1982a,b), which is always given credit in the literature, but by Halle

---

[12] Or to monomorphemic strings which however are the result of the application of a previous rule (phonologically derived environments).

[13] Cole (1995: 72) is also explicit on the fact that what Kiparsky's SCC actually does is to combine two very different patterns.

[14] From a post-hoc perspective, Bermúdez-Otero's (forthcoming) interpretation is that all the adornment that the practitioners of the 1980s were inveigled to add to the basic stratal idea—namely Kiparsky's SCC (together with structure preservation and brackets)—lured Lexical Phonology on to decline. Stratal OT is now about to reinitialize the motion on the grounds of the original set-up, which is freed from the disastrous patches of the 1980s.

(1978) in an article that nobody quotes.[15] Unlike Kiparsky, Halle (1978: 131) is explicit on the fact that 'the version of the constraint on cyclic rule application that I propose below is a combination of certain suggestions made by Kiparsky (1973: 60), with others due to Mascaró (1976: 9).' His formulation is reproduced below.

'A cyclic rule R applies properly on cycle j only if either a) or b) is satisfied:
a)   R makes specific use of information, part of which is available on a prior pass through the cyclic rules, and part of which becomes first available on cycle j. [. . .]
b)   R makes specific use of information assigned on cycle j by a rule applying before R.'   Halle (1978: 131)

Halle's version of the SCC does exactly the same labor as Kiparsky's. The critical modification with respect to Chomsky's SCC is that instead of imposing only new material to be used by rules, Halle requires that new *and* old material be accessed.

The historical survey of the question notwithstanding, the goal of this section is not historiographic; rather, what I intend to show is that (the significant confusion regarding the various versions of the SCC laid aside) Kaye's no-look-back device is unlike all others that have been proposed since Chomsky (1973). What Kaye introduces is the idea that previously interpreted strings cannot be modified by computation on subsequent cycles: modification-inhibiting no-look-back.[16]

Chomsky's (2000, 2001b, et passim) Phase Impenetrability does exactly the same thing: previously interpreted phases are 'frozen in place' (Chomsky

---

[15] I am aware of two exceptions: Rubach (1981: 18ff.) and Szpyra (1989: 17). Halle (1978) is absent from Kiparsky (1982b); it is mentioned in the reference section of Kiparsky (1982a), but does not appear in the text (or the notes) of this article.

[16] Due to space restrictions, two issues need to be rejected into this footnote. For one thing, Kaye (1992: 142, 1995: 307) makes explicit reference to Chomsky (1973), Kean (1974), and Mascaró (1976) when he introduces his no-look-back mechanism, which is supposed to do the same job. His actual practice, however, is different: Kaye applies modification-inhibiting no-look-back, which has got nothing to do with Chomsky's SCC: 'when phonology is done on the external domain, an empty onset is available for the n. However, the principle of *strict cyclicity* states that the association created in the inner domain cannot be undone in an external domain. The association remains and the *n* also links to the available onset' Kaye (1995: 307, emphasis in original). Like other voices around the SCC, Kaye was thus confused, and 'freezing' no-look-back was introduced incognito, as it were.

The other thing that needs to be mentioned for the sake of completeness is a no-look-back device which has not been discussed in the main text because it does not interfere with the SCC. In order to account for level 2 rules (underapplication to class 1 strings), Lexical Phonology uses brackets and bracket erasure, which are due to Mohanan (1982, 1986). On this count, all morphemes are enclosed by brackets upon concatenation, and rules can make reference to these brackets, which are however erased at the end of each stratum. Hence *si[g]n-ature*$_i$ is [[sign][ature]$_1$] at stratum 1, but enters stratum 2 as [sign ature] after bracket erasure. G-deletion then is a level 2 rule and sensitive to brackets (g → ø / __n]); it therefore does not apply to [sign ature] (but simplifies the cluster of [[sign][ing]$_2$], which has 'fresh' brackets).

2001b: 6). It was mentioned in section 16.1 that Chomsky's PIC is the instrument which frees active memory from the unnecessary burden of old strings. This extralinguistic motivation is reflected in the quote below, which is also explicit on the fact that the economy effect is supposed to apply to phonological as much as to syntactic memory.

The whole phase is 'handed over' to the phonological component. The deleted features then disappear from the narrow syntax. [. . . Uninterpretable features] have been assigned values (checked); these are removed from the narrow syntax as the syntactic object is transferred to the phonology. The valued uninterpretable features can be detected with only limited inspection of the derivation if earlier stages of the cycle can be 'forgotten'—in phase terms, if earlier phases need not be inspected. The computational burden is further reduced if the phonological component too can 'forget' earlier stages of derivation. These results follow from the Phase-Impenetrability Condition (PIC) (MI [Minimalist Inquiries, i.e. Chomsky 2000], (21)), for strong phase HP with head H,

(7) The domain of H is not accessible to operations outside HP; only H and its edge are accessible to such operations.   Chomsky (2001b: 12f.)

The current syntactic literature on phase theory in general and Chomsky (2000, 2001b, et passim) himself in particular is not very historically oriented. Of course there is nothing wrong with that—it is strange to see, though, that Chomsky makes no reference at all to previous no-look-back devices that the generative literature has produced, and actually not even to his own (1973) paper where the idea was launched. That the syntactic literature does not mention the fact that modification-inhibiting no-look-back was introduced by Kaye (1992, 1995) is less surprising: Kaye's work is in phonology, and on top of that does not belong to the phonological mainstream.

16.5 Conclusion

Given the preceding, the argument now is quite simple: if current phase theory is on the right track, 'freezing' (i.e. modification-inhibiting) no-look-back must also be in place in phonology—exactly what Kaye (1992, 1995) proposes. This is an intermodular argument: the PIC exists for extralinguistic and syntax-internal reasons, but the new interactionist architecture of grammar makes a prediction to the end that it restricts phonological as much as syntactic computation. Otherwise the global architecture is inconsistent.

The necessary presence of the PIC in phonology, then, discriminates between competing theories of PF which are based on phonology-internal evidence only. This has a direct impact in the area of affix-class-based phenomena, for which two families of competing analyses exist: on the one hand, those that are based on morpheme-specific computational systems (Lexical Phonology and its serial or parallel offspring in present-day OT); on the other hand, those that rely on selective spell-out and have strings of whatever morphological composition assessed by the same computational system at PF. Among the latter, Kaye's system uses the PIC, while Halle and Vergnaud's does not (nor does it use any other no-look-back device for the analysis of affix-class-based phenomena). Kaye's approach is thus selected: it is the only one that implements the syntactically warranted PIC.

Now it could be argued that this does not disqualify the other theories: the intermodular argument only requires that the PIC be active somewhere in phonology—not specifically in the analysis of affix-classes. That is, approaches that are based on morpheme-specific phonologies could still be correct: the PIC restricts phonological computation, but happens not to be responsible for affix-class-based phenomena. This argument, however, is flawed: the simultaneous presence of morpheme-specific phonologies and the PIC is not an option because both devices do the same job. It was shown that underapplication is achieved by morpheme-specific phonologies on the one hand, and by the combined action of selective spell-out and the PIC on the other. No theory can thus afford to accommodate both devices—that would be redundant. Either morpheme-specific phonologies or selective spell-out and the PIC are correct. Syntactic phase theory then referees: the former has to go.

A last word on Kaye's visionary skills. It was mentioned in Table 16.2c that what the merger of an interpretation-triggering affix actually triggers is the spell-out of its sister rather than of its own node. This is exactly what is called the phase edge in current syntactic theory: given a phase head XP, spell-out of XP only triggers the interpretation of the complement; the head and Spec, XP (the edge of the phase) are spelled out only at the next higher phase (see the quote from Chomsky (2001b) in section 16.4, also Chomsky 2000: 108; this parallel is discussed at length in Scheer 2008). The same transmodular logic holds as before: since the definition of interpretational units is done only once upon spell-out of morphosyntactic structure, syntax is as much engaged as phonology. A situation where phonological and syntactic evidence requires the definition of different interpretational chunks would call the entire architecture into question. Rather, it is expected that phonology and syntax single out the same interpretational units and require the same spell-out mechanism. This is what Kaye's system offers with respect to current syntactic phase theory.

References

Abu-Fadl, F. (1961). *Volkstuemliche Texte in arabischen Bauerndialekten der aegyptischen Provinz Sharqiyya*. Muenster: University of Muenster.

Åfarli, T. A. (1995). 'A note on the syntax of adverbial phrases'. *Norsk Lingvistisk Tidsskrift* 13: 23–40.

—— (1997). 'Dimensions of phrase structure: The representation of sentence adverbials', *Motskrift* 2: Institutt for nordistikk og litteraturvitenskap, NTNU, 91–113.

—— (2008). Frames and Predication. Ms. NTNU, Trondheim.

Alexiadou, Artemis (1997). *Adverb Placement. A Case Study in Antisymmetric Syntax*. Amsterdam: John Benjamins.

—— (2001). 'Adjective syntax and noun raising: word order asymmetries in the DP as the result of adjective distribution'. *Studia Linguistica* 55: 217–48.

Allan, R., Holmes, Philip, and Lundskær-Nielsen, T. (1995). *Danish: A Comprehensive Grammar*. London: Routledge.

Anderson, Stephen R. (2005). *Aspects of the Theory of Clitics*. Oxford: Oxford University Press.

Anttila, Arto (2002). 'Morphologically conditioned phonological alternations'. *Natural Language and Linguistic Theory* 20: 1–42.

Aronoff, Mark and Sridhar, S. (1983). 'Morphological levels in English and Kannada, or Atarizing Reagan', in J. Richardson, M. Marks, and A. Chukerman (eds), *Chicago Linguistics Society 19, Papers from the Parasession on the Interplay of Phonology, Morphology and Syntax*. Chicago: Chicago Linguistics Society, 3–16. Reprinted (1987) in Edmund Gussmann (ed.), *Rules and the Lexicon*, Lublin: Katolicki Universytet Lubelski, 9–22.

Aslin, R. N., Saffran, J. R., and Newport, E. L. (1998). 'Computation of conditional probability statistics by human infants'. *Psychological Science* 9: 321–4.

Baayen, R. H., Piepenbrock, R., and Gulikers, L. (1995). The CELEX Lexical Database (CD-ROM). Linguistic Data Consortium, University of Pennsylvania, Philadelphia, PA.

Bader, M. and Frazier, L. (2005). 'Interpreting leftward-moved constituents'. Special issue of *Linguistics* 43 (1): 49–87.

Baker, Mark (1985). 'The Mirror Principle and morphosyntactic explanation'. *Linguistic Inquiry* 16, 373–415.

—— (2001). *The Atoms of Language: The Mind's Hidden Rules of Grammar*. New York: Basic Books.

Baltaxe, C. (1984). 'The use of contrastive stress in normal, aphasic, and autistic children'. *Journal of Speech and Hearing Research* 27: 97–105.

Barbiers, S. (1995). 'The syntax of interpretation'. Doctoral dissertation. Holland Institute of Generative Linguistics.

Baron-Cohen, S. (1995). *Mindblindness: An Essay on Autism and Theory of Mind.* Cambridge, MA: MIT Press.

——Leslie, A., and Frith, U. (1985). 'Does the autistic child have a "theory of mind"?'. *Cognition* 21: 37–46.

——Tager-Flusberg, H. and Cohen, D. J. (2000). *Understanding Other Minds.* New York: Oxford University Press.

Bayer, J. (2004). 'Decomposing the left periphery—dialectal and cross-linguistic evidence', in L. Horst and S. Trissler (eds), *The Syntax and Semantics of the Left Periphery.* Berlin: Mouton de Gruyter, 59–95.

——(2005). 'That-trace without reference to the subject'. Invited lecture. 20th Comparative Germanic Syntax Workshop, Tilburg.

Beaver, D. and B. Clark (2002). 'The proper treatments of focus sensitivity', in L. Mikkelsen and C. Potts (eds), *WCCFL 21 Proceedings.* Somerville, MA: Cascadilla Press, 15–28.

——and Clark, B. (2003). 'Always and only: why not all focus sensitive operators are alike'. *Natural Language Semantics* 11 (4): 323–62.

—— ——Flemming, E., Jaeger, F., and Wolters, M. (2007). 'When semantics meets phonetics: acoustical studies of second occurrence focus'. *Language* 83 (2): 245–76.

Becker-Christensen, C. (ed.) (1995). *Nudansk Ordbog & Sprogbrugsleksikon.* 15th edn. Copenhagen: Politikens Forlag.

Beckman, M. E. and Pierrehumbert, J. B. (1986). 'Intonational structure in Japanese and English'. *Phonology Yearbook* 3: 255–309.

Beghelli, Filippo and Stowell, Tim (1997). 'The syntax of distributivity and negation', in Anna Szabolcsi (ed.), *Ways of Scope Taking*, Dordrecht: Reidel, 71–108.

Behaghel, Otto (1932). *Deutsche Syntax*, IV. Heidelberg: Carl Winters.

Belletti, A. and Rizzi, L. (1988). 'Psych-verbs and θ-theory', *Natural Language and Linguistic Theory* 6: 291–352.

Benmamoun, E. (2000). *The Feature Structure of Functional* Categories, Oxford Studies in Comparative Syntax. Oxford: Oxford University Press.

van den Berg, Rob, Gussenhoven, Carlos, and Rietveld, Toni (1992). 'Downstep in Dutch: implications for a model', in Gerhard Docherty and D. Robert Ladd (eds), *Papers in Laboratory Phonology II: Gesture, Segment and Prosody.* Cambridge: Cambridge University Press, 335–67.

Berman, Arlene and Szamosi, Michael (1972). 'Observations on sentential stress'. *Language* 48: 304–25.

Bermúdez-Otero, Ricardo (2008). 'Evidence for Chung's generalization'. Paper presented at 16th Manchester Phonology Meeting, Manchester, 22–4 May.

——(forthcoming). *Stratal Optimality Theory.* Oxford: Oxford University Press.

Besten, Hans den (1983). 'On the interaction of root transformations and lexical deletive rules', in Werner Abraham (ed.), *On the Formal Syntax of the Westgermania.* Amsterdam: Benjamins, 47–131.

Billings, Loren and Rudin, Catherine (1996). 'Optimality and superiority: a new approach to multiple *wh*-ordering', in Jindřich Toman (ed.), *Formal Approaches to Slavic Linguistics: The College Park Meeting, 1994.* Ann Arbor: Michigan Slavic Publications, 35–60.

Bion, R. H., Benavides, S., and Nespor, M. (submitted). 'Acoustic markers of prominence influence infants' and adults' memory for speech sequences'.

Bloom, L. (1970). *Language Development: Form and Function in Emerging Grammars.* Cambridge, MA: MIT Press.

Bobaljik, J. D. (1995). 'Morphosyntax: the syntax of verbal inflection'. Ph.D. dissertation, MIT.

——(2001). 'Floating quantifiers: handle with care', in Lisa Cheng and Rint Sybesma (eds), *The Second Glot International State-of-the-Article Book.* Amsterdam: Mouton de Gruyter, 107–48.

——(2002). 'A-chains at the PF interface: copies and "covert" movement'. *Natural Language & Linguistic Theory* 20 (2): 197–267.

—— and Carnie, A. (1996). 'A minimalist approach to some problems of Irish word order', in R. Borsley and I. Roberts (eds), *The Syntax of the Celtic Languages: A Comparative Perspective.* Cambridge: Cambridge University Press, 223–40.

—— and Jonas, D. (1996). 'Subject positions and the roles of TP'. *Linguistic Inquiry* 27: 195–236.

Boeckx, C. (2008). *Bare Syntax.* Oxford: Oxford University Press.

Boersma, P. and Weenink, D. (2006). 'Praat: doing phonetics by computer (Version 4.5.2)'.

Bolinger, D. (1972). 'Accent is predictable (if you're a mind-reader)'. *Language* 48: 633–44.

Bolton, T. L. (1894). 'Rhythm'. *American Journal of Psychology* 6: 145–238.

Booij, Geert (2000 [1996]). 'The phonology-morphology interface', in Lisa Cheng and Rint Sybesma (eds), *The First Glot International State-of-the-Article Book.* Berlin: Mouton de Gruyter, 287–305. May be downloaded at <http://www.unice.fr/dsl/tobias.htm>.

Bošković, Željko (2001). *On the Nature of the Syntax–Phonology Interface.* Amsterdam: Elsevier.

——(2002a). 'Clitics as nonbranching elements and the linear correspondence axiom'. *Linguistic Inquiry* 33 (2): 329–40.

——(2002b). 'On multiple wh-fronting'. *Linguistic Inquiry* 33 (3): 351–83.

——(2004a). 'Be careful where you float your quantifiers'. *Natural Language and Linguistic Theory* 22: 681–742.

——(2004b). 'Clitic placement in South Slavic'. *Journal of Slavic Linguistics* 12 (1–2): 37–90.

——(2007). 'On the locality and motivation of Move and Agree: an even more minimal theory'. *Linguistic Inquiry* 38 (4): 589–644.

Bowers, J. (1993). 'The syntax of predication'. *Linguistic Inquiry* 24: 591–656.

Brandner, E. (2004). 'Head-movement in minimalism, and V/2 as force-marking', in H. Lohnstein and S. Trissler (eds), *Syntax and Semantics of the Left Periphery.* Berlin: Mouton de Gruyter.

Brassai, Sámuel (1863–5). 'A magyar mondatról [About the Hungarian sentence] II-III', *Akadémiai Értesítő* [Academic Newsletter] 3: 3–128, 173–409.

Bresnan, Joan (1971). 'Sentence stress and syntactic transformations'. *Language* 47: 257–81.

—— (1972). 'Stress and syntax: a reply'. *Language* 48: 326–42.

Brisson, C. (1998). 'Distributivity, maximality, and floating quantifiers'. Doctoral dissertation, Rutgers University.

Brody, M. (1990). 'Remarks on the order of elements in the Hungarian focus field', in Istvan Kenesei (ed.), *Approaches to Hungarian*. Szeged, Hungary: Jozsef Attila Tudomanyegyetem, 395–122.

—— (1997). *Mirror Theory*. UCL Working Papers in Linguistics, 9. University College London.

—— and Szabolcsi, Anna (2003). 'Overt scope in Hungarian'. *Syntax* 6, 19–51.

Brown, R. (1973). *A First Language: The Early Stages*, Cambridge, MA: Harvard University Press.

Brustad, K. (2004). *The Syntax of Spoken Arabic: A Comparative Study of Moroccan, Egyptian, Syrian and Kuwaiti Dialects*. Washington, DC: Georgetown University Press.

Bruce, Gösta (1977). 'Swedish word accent in sentence perspective'. *Travaux de l'Institut de Linguistique de Lund* 12. Lund: Gleerup.

Buchstaller, I. and Traugott, E. (2006). '"The lady was all demonyak." Historical aspects of adverbial *all*. *English Language and Linguistics* 10: 345–70.

Carlson, G. (1977) 'Reference to kinds in English'. Ph.D. dissertation, University of Massachusetts, Amherst.

Carlson, K., Clifton, C., Jr, and Frazier, L. (2001). 'Prosodic boundaries in adjunct attachment'. *Journal of Memory & Language* 45: 58–81.

Castro, A. (2006). 'On possessives in Portuguese'. Doctoral dissertation, Universidade Nova de Lisboa & Université Paris VIII.

—— and Costa, J. (2003). 'Weak forms as X°: prenominal possessives and preverbal adverbs in Portuguese', in Ana Teresa Pérez-Leroux and Yves Roberge (eds), *Romance Linguistics: Theory and Acquisition*. Amsterdam and Philadelphia: John Benjamins, 95–110.

Chahal, D. (2003). 'Phonetic cues to prominence in Arabic'. *Proceedings of the 15th International Congress of Phonetic Sciences*: 2067–70.

—— and Hellmuth, S. (forthcoming). 'Comparing the intonational phonology of Lebanese and Egyptian Arabic'. *Prosodic Typology. Volume 2*. Oxford: Oxford University Press.

Cheng, Lisa (1991). 'On the typology of wh-questions'. Cambridge, MA: MIT Working Papers in Linguistics.

Chomsky, Noam (1965). *Aspects of the Theory of Syntax*. Cambridge, MA: MIT Press.

—— (1971). 'Deep structure, surface structure and semantic interpretation', in D. Steinberg and L. Jakobovits (eds), *Semantics: An Interdisciplinary Reader in Philosophy, Linguistics and Psychology*. Cambridge: Cambridge University Press, 183–216.

Chomsky, Noam (1973). 'Conditions on transformations', in Stephen Anderson and Paul Kiparsky (eds), *A Festschrift for Morris Halle*. New York: Holt, Rinehart & Winston, 232–86.

——(1981). *Lectures on Government and Binding*. Dordrecht: Foris.

Chomsky, Noam (1984) *Modular Approaches to the Study of the Mind*. San Diego: State University Press.

——(1993). 'A minimalist program for linguistic theory', in K. Hale and S. J. Keyser (eds), *The View From Building 20: Essays in Linguistics in Honor of Sylvain Bromberger*. Cambridge, MA: MIT Press, 1–52.

——(1995). *The Minimalist Program*. Cambridge, MA: MIT Press.

——(2000). 'Minimalist inquiries: the framework', in Roger Martin, David Michaels, and Juan Uriagereka (eds), *Step by Step. Essays on Minimalist Syntax in Honor of Howard Lasnik*, Cambridge, MA: MIT Press, 89–155.

——(2001a). 'Beyond explanatory adequacy', *MIT Occasional Papers in Linguistics 20*. Cambridge, MA.: MITWPL, Department of Linguistics and Philosophy, MIT.

——(2001b). 'Derivation by phase', in Michael Kenstowicz (ed.), *Ken Hale: A Life in Language*, MIT Press: Cambridge, MA: MIT Press, 1–52.

——(2004). 'Beyond explanatory adequacy', in A. Belletti (ed.), *Structures and Beyond: The Cartography of Syntactic Structures, Volume 3*. Oxford: Oxford University Press, 104–31.

——and Halle, M. (1968). *The Sound Pattern of English*. New York: Harper and Row.

————and Lukoff, Fred (1956). 'On accent and juncture in English', in Morris Halle, Horace Lunt, Hugh McLean, and Cornelis van Schooneveld (eds), *For Roman Jakobson. Essays on the Occasion of his Sixtieth Birthday*. The Hague: Mouton, 65–80. May be downloaded at <http://www.unice.fr/dsl/tobias.htm>.

Christophe, A., Dupoux, E., Bertoncini, J., and Mehler, J. (1994). 'Do infants perceive word boundaries? An empirical study of the bootstrapping of lexical acquisition'. *Journal of the Acoustical Society of America* 95: 1570–80.

——Mehler, J., and Sebastián-Gallés, N. (2001). 'Perception of prosodic boundary correlates by newborn infants'. *Infancy* 2: 385–94

——Millotte, S., Bernal, S., and Lidz, J. (2008). 'Bootstrapping lexical and syntactic acquisition'. *Language and Speech* 51: 61–75

——Nespor, M., Dupoux, E., Guasti, M.-T., and Ooyen, B. v. (2003). 'Reflections on prosodic bootstrapping: its role for lexical and syntactic acquisition'. *Developmental Science* 6 (2): 213–22.

——Peperkamp, S., Pallier, C., Block, E., and Mehler, J. (2004). Phonological phrase boundaries constrain lexical access: I. Adult data. *Journal of Memory and Language* 51: 523–47.

Cinque, G. (1993). 'A null theory of phrase and compound stress'. *Linguistic Inquiry* 24: 239–97.

——(1994). 'On the evidence for partial N movement in the Romance DP', in G. Cinque, J. Koster, J.-Y. Pollock, L. Rizzi, and R. Zanuttini (eds), *Paths Toward Universal Grammar*. Georgetown: Georgetown University Press.

—— (1999). *Adverbs and Functional Heads: A Cross-Linguistic Perspective.* Oxford: Oxford University Press.

Cinque, G. (2004). ' "Restructuring" and functional structure', in A. Belletti (ed.), *The Cartography of Syntactic Structures. Vol. 3, Structures and Beyond.* Oxford: Oxford University Press, 132–91.

Clahsen, H. and Eisenbeiss, S. (1993). 'The development of DP in German child language'. Paper presented at the SISSA Encounters in Cognitive Science, Trieste.

Clements, G. N. (1981). 'The hierarchical representation of tone features', in G. N. Clements (ed.), *Harvard Studies in Phonology*, II, 50–108.

Clifton, C., Jr, Frazier, L., and Carlson, K. (2006). 'Tracking the What and Why of speakers' choices: prosodic boundaries and the length of constituents'. *Psychonomic Bulletin & Review* 13: 854–61.

Cohen, A. and Erteschik-Shir, N. (2002). 'Topic, focus and the interpretation of bare plurals'. *Natural Language Semantics* 10: 125–65.

Cole, Jennifer (1995). 'The cycle in phonology', in John Goldsmith (ed.), *The Handbook of Phonological Theory.* Oxford: Blackwell, 70–113.

Collins, C. (1997). *Local Economy.* Cambridge: MIT Press

Comrie, B. (1981). *Language Universals and Linguistic Typology: Syntax and Morphology.* Oxford: Blackwell.

Cooper, G. and Meyer, L. (1960). *The Rhythmic Structure of Music.* Chicago: University of Chicago Press.

Costa, J. (1998). 'Word order variation. A constraint-based approach'. Ph.D. dissertation, Leiden University.

—— (2002). 'VOS in Portuguese: Arguments against an analysis in terms of remnant movement', in A. Alexiadou, E. Anagnostopoulou, S. Barbiers, and H.-M. Gärtner (eds), *Dimensions of Movement.* Amsterdam: John Benjamins, 69–89.

—— (2004). *Subject Positions and Interfaces. The Case of European Portuguese.* Berlin: Mouton de Gruyter

—— (2008). 'A focus-binding conspiracy. Left-to-right merge, scrambling and binary structure in European Portuguese'. Ms., Universidade Nova de Lisboa.

—— (2009). 'A focus-binding conspiracy. Left-to-right merge, scrambling and binary structure in European Portuguese'. Forthcoming in J. van Craenenbroeck (ed.), *Alternatives to Cartography.* Berlin: Mouton de Gruyter.

—— and Szendroi, K. (2006). 'Acquisition of focus marking in European Portuguese. Evidence for a unified approach', in V. Torrens and L. Escobar (eds), *The Acquisition of Syntax in Romance Languages.* Amsterdam: John Benjamins, 319–29.

Cruttenden, A. (1997). *Intonation.* Cambridge: Cambridge University Press.

Csirmaz, Anikó (2006). 'Particles and a two-component theory of aspect', in Katalin É. Kiss (ed.), *Event Structure and the Left Periphery. Studies on Hungarian.* Dordrecht: Springer, 107–28.

Cutler, A., Dahan, D., and Donselaar, W. A. van (1997). 'Prosody in the comprehension of spoken language: a literature review'. *Language and Speech* 40 (2): 141–202.

Cutler, A. and Swinney, D. (1986). 'Prosody and the development of comprehension'. *Journal of Child Language* 14: 145–67.

Dauer, R. (1983). 'Stress timing and syllable timing reanalyzed'. *Journal of Phonetics* 11: 51–62.

Davies, M. (2008). *The Corpus of Contemporary American English (COCA): 385 million words, 1990-present*. Available online at <http://www.americancorpus.org>.

Dayal, Veneeta (2003). 'Bare nominals: non-specific and contrastive readings under scrambling', in Simin Karimi (ed.), *Word Order and Scrambling*. London: Blackwell, 67–90.

Dehé, N. (2005). 'The optimal placement of *up* and *ab*: a comparison'. *Journal of Germanic Linguistics* 8: 185–224.

Diesing, M. (1988). 'Bare plural subjects and the stage/individual contrast', in M. Krifka (ed.), *Genericity in Language: Proceedings of the 1988 Tübingen Conference*. Tübingen: University of Tübingen.

Diesing, Molly (1992). *Indefinites*. Cambridge, MA: MIT Press.

Dik, S.et al. (1981). 'On the typology of focus phenomena', in T. Hoekstra (ed.), *Perspectives on Functional Grammar*. Dordrecht: Foris.

Dikken, Marcel den (2007). 'Phase extension: contours of a theory of the role of head movement in phrasal extraction'. *Theoretical Linguistics* 33: 1–41.

Doetjes, J. (1997). *Quantifiers and Selection: On the Distribution of Quantifying Expressions in French, Dutch, and English*. HIL Dissertations 32. The Hague: Holland Academic Graphics.

Dowty, D. (1987). 'A note on collective predicates, distributive predicates and "all"', in F. Marshall, A. Miller, and Z.-S. Zhang (eds), *Proceedings of the Third Eastern State Conference on Linguistics*. Columbus, OH: Ohio State University.

——and Brodie, B. (1984). 'A semantic analysis of "floated" quantifiers in a transformationless grammar', in Mark Cobler, Susan MacKaye, and Michael Wescoat (eds), *Proceedings of the Third West Coast Conference on Formal Linguistics*. Stanford: CSLI, 75–90.

Dryer, M. S. (1992). 'The Greenbergian word order correlations'. *Language* 68(1): 81–138.

——(2005). 'Order of subject, object and verb', in M. Haspelmath, M. S. Dryer, D. Gil, and B. Comrie (eds), *The World Atlas of Language Structures Online*. Munich: Max Planck Digital Library, ch. 81. Available online at <http://wals.info/feature/81>. Accessed on July 8, 2009.

Duarte, I. (1987). 'A construção de Topicalização em Português Europeu: Regência, Ligação e Condições sobre Movimento'. Ph.D. dissertation, Universidade de Lisboa.

Du Bois, J. W., Chafe, W. L., Meyer, C., and Thompson, S. A. (2000). *Santa Barbara Corpus of Spoken American English*, Part 1. Philadelphia: Linguistic Data Consortium.

————————and Martey, N. (2003). *Santa Barbara Corpus of Spoken American English*, Part 2. Philadelphia: Linguistic Data Consortium.

——and Englebretson, R. (2004). *Santa Barbara Corpus of Spoken American English*, Part 3. Philadelphia: Linguistic Data Consortium.

Dupoux, E. and Peperkamp, S. (2002). 'Fossil markers of language development: phonological deafnesses in adult speech processing', in B. Laks and J. Durand (eds), *Phonetics, Phonology, and Cognition*. Oxford: Oxford University Press, 168–90.

Egedi, Barbara (2008). 'Adverbial (dis)ambiguities. Syntactic and prosodic features of ambiguous predicational adverbs', in Katalin É. Kiss (ed.), *Adverbs and Adverbial Adjuncts at the Interfaces*. Berlin: Mouton de Gruyter.

É. Kiss, Katalin (1987). *Configurationality in Hungarian*. Dordrecht: Reidel.

—— (1991). 'Logical structure in syntactic structure: the case of Hungarian', in James C.-T. Huang and Robert May (eds), *Logical Structure and Syntactic Structure*. Dordrecht: Kluwer, 111–47.

—— (1994). 'Sentence structure and word order', in Katalin É. Kiss and Ferenc Kiefer (eds), *Hungarian Syntax*. New York: Academic Press, 1–90.

—— (2002). *The Syntax of Hungarian*. Cambridge: Cambridge University Press.

—— (2006). 'Focussing as predication', in Valéria Molnár and Susanne Winkler (eds), *Architecture of Focus*. Berlin: Mouton de Gruyter, 169–96.

—— (2008a). 'Free word order, (non-)configurationality, and phases'. *Linguistic Inquiry* 39: 441–75.

—— (2008b). 'Substitution or adjunction? Quantifiers and adverbials in the Hungarian sentence'. *Lingua*, forthcoming.

—— (2008c). 'The Hungarian VP revisited', in Christopher Piñón and Szilárd Szentgyörgyi (eds), *Approaches to Hungarian 10, Papers from the Veszprém Conference*. Budapest: Akadémiai Kiadó, 31–58.

É. Kiss, Katalin (ed.), (2008d). *Adverbs and Adverbial Adjuncts at the Interfaces*. Interface Explorations. Berlin: Mouton de Gruyter.

El Zarka, D. (2008). 'Leading, linking and closing tones and tunes in Egyptian Arabic—what a simple intonation system tells us about the nature of intonation'. Paper presented at the annual meeting of the Arabic Linguistics Society, Michigan, March 2008.

Endress, A. D., Dehaene-Lambertz, G., and Mehler, J. (2007). 'Perceptual constraints and the learnability of simple grammars'. *Cognition* 105 (3): 577–614.

—— and Mehler, J. (under review). 'Primitive computations in speech processing'.

—— Scholl, B. J., and Mehler, J. (2005). 'The role of salience in the extraction of algebraic rules'. *Journal of Experimental Psychology: General* 134 (3): 406–19.

Engberg-Pedersen, E., et al. (eds), (2005). *Dansk Funktionel Lingvistik: En Helhedsforståelse af Forholdet mellem Sprogstruktur, Sprogbrug og Kognition*. København: Kopiservice Humaniora, Københavns Universitet.

Engdahl, E. and Vallduví, E. (1994). 'Information packaging and grammar architecture: a constraint-based approach', in E. Engdahl (ed.), *Integrating Information Structure into Constraint-Based and Categorial Approaches*. DYANA-2 Report R.1.3.B. Amsterdam: HLLC, 39–79.

Epstein, Samuel, Groat, E. M., Kawashima, R., and Kitahara, H. (1998). *A Derivational Approach to Syntactic Relations*. Oxford: Oxford University Press.

Ernst, T. (2002). *The Syntax of Adjuncts*. Cambridge: Cambridge University Press.

Erteschik-Shir, N. (1973). 'On the nature of island constraints'. Ph.D. thesis, MIT, Cambridge, MA.

——(1979) 'Discourse constraints on dative movement'. *Syntax and Semantics* 5 (12). Also in T. Givón (ed.), *Discourse and Syntax*. New York: Academic Press, 441–67.

——(1997). *The Dynamics of Focus Structure*. Cambridge: Cambridge University Press.

——(2005a). 'The sound patterns of syntax: the case of object shift'. *Theoretical Linguistics* 31 (1/2): 47–94.

——(2005b). 'What is syntax?'. *Theoretical Linguistics* 31 (1/2): 263–74.

——and Strahov, Natalia (2004). 'Focus structure architecture and P-syntax'. *Lingua* 114 (3): 301–23.

Estling Vannestål, M. (2004). 'Syntactic variation in English quantified noun phrases with *all, whole, both* and *half*'. Doctoral dissertation, Växjö Universitet.

Fanselow, Gisbert (2004). 'Cyclic phonology-syntax interaction: movement to first position in German'. *Information Structures* 1. ISIS: Working Papers of the SFB 632. Potsdam, 1–42.

——and Lenertová, Denisa (2008). 'Left peripheral focus: mismatches between syntax and information structure'. Ms., University of Potsdam and University of Leipzig.

Féry, C. (2006). 'The fallacy of invariant correlates of information structure', in C. Féry, G. Fanselow, and M. Krifka (eds), *The Notions of Information Structure*, Interdisciplinary Studies on Information Structure, 6. Potsdam: Universitaetsverlag Potsdam.

——and Drenhaus, Heiner (2008). 'Single prosodic phrasing', in *Interdisciplinary Studies in Information Structure* 10. Working Papers of the SFB 632. Potsdam: Universitaetsverlag Potsdam, 1–44.

——Fanselow, G., and Krifka, M. (2006). 'The notions of information structure', in *Interdisciplinary Studies on Information Structure*, 6. Potsdam: Universitaetsverlag Potsdam.

——and Herbst, L. (2004). 'German sentence accent revisited', in S. Ishihara, M. Schmitz, and A. Schwarz (eds), *Interdisciplinary Studies on Information Structure (ISIS)*. 1. Potsdam: Universitätsverlag Potsdam.

——and Ishihara, Shinichiro (2009a). 'How focus and givenness shape prosody', in M. Zimmermann and C. Féry (eds), *Information Structure from Different Perspectives*. Oxford: Oxford University Press.

————(2009b). 'The phonology of second occurrence focus'. *Journal of Linguistics* 45 (2).

——and Ketner, Gerrit (2008). 'The prosody of grouping names in German and Hindi'. Ms. Potsdam.

——and Kügler, Frank (2008). 'Pitch accent scaling on given, new and focused constituents in German'. *Journal of Phonetics* 36: 680–703.

——Paslawska, Alla, and Fanselow, Gisbert (2007). 'Nominal split constructions in Ukrainian'. *Journal of Slavic Linguistics* 15 (1): 3–48.

—— and Samek-Lodovici, Vieri (2006). 'Focus projection and prosodic prominence in nested foci', *Language* 82 (1): 131–50.

—— and Truckenbrodt, Hubert (2005). 'Sisterhood and tonal scaling', in *Studia Linguistica* special issue 'Boundaries in intonational phonology', 59 (2/3): 223–43.

Fisher, C. and Tokura, H. (1996). 'Prosody in speech to infants: direct and indirect acoustic cues to syntactic structure', in E. Morgan, L. James, and Katherine E. Demuth (eds), *Signal to Syntax: Bootstrapping from Speech to Grammar in Early Acquisition*. Hillsdale, NJ: Lawrence Erlbaum, 343–63.

Fitzpatrick, J. (2006). 'The syntactic and semantic roots of floating quantification'. Doctoral dissertation, MIT.

Fox, Danny (2003). 'On logical form', in R. Hendrick (ed.), *Minimalist Syntax*. London: Blackwell.

—— and Pesetsky, David (2005). 'Cyclic linearization of syntactic structure'. *Theoretical Linguistics* 31 (1–2): 1–46.

Franks, Steven (1998). 'Clitics in Slavic'. Position paper presented at the Comparative Slavic Morphosyntax Workshop, Spencer, Indiana, June 1998. Available online at <http://www.indiana.edu/~slavconf/linguistics/download.html>.

—— (2000). 'Clitics at the interface', in Frits Beukema and Marcel den Dikken (eds), *Clitic Phenomena in European Languages*. Amsterdam: John Benjamins, 1–46.

—— (2005). 'Adverb interpolation in the Bulgarian clitic cluster', in Robert Rothstein, Ernest Scatton, and Charles Townsend (eds), *A Festschrift for Charles Gribble*. Bloomington, IN: Slavica, 117–33.

—— (2006a). 'Agnostic movement', in C. Davis, A. R. Deal, and Y. Zabbai (eds), *Proceedings of NELS XXXVI*, 1: 267–78.

—— (2006b). 'Another look at *li* placement in Bulgarian'. *The Linguistic Review* 23 (2): 161–211.

—— (2007). 'Deriving discontinuity', in Franc Marušić and Rok Žaucer (eds), *Studies in Formal Slavic Linguistics*. Frankfurt-am-Main: Peter Lang, 103–20.

—— (2008). 'Clitic placement, prosody, and the Bulgarian verbal complex'. *Journal of Slavic Linguistics* 16 (1): 91–137.

—— and Bošković, Željko (2001). 'An argument for Multiple Spell-Out'. *Linguistic Inquiry* 32 (1): 174–83.

—— and King, Tracy Holloway (2000). *A Handbook of Slavic Clitics*. Oxford: Oxford University Press.

Frascarelli, M. (2000). *The Syntax-Phonology Interface in Focus and Topic Constructions in Italian*. Dordrecht: Kluwer.

Frazier, L., Carlson, K., and Clifton, C. (2006). 'Prosodic phrasing is central to language comprehension'. *TICS* 10 (6): 244–9.

Frey, Werner (2004). 'A medial topic position for German'. *Linguistische Berichte* 198: 153–90.

Frota, S. (1999). 'Prosody and focus in European Portuguese'. Ph.D. dissertation, Universidade de Lisboa.

Frota, S. and Vigário, M. (2002). 'Efeitos de peso no Português Europeu', in M. H. Mateus and C. N. Correia (eds), *Saberes no Tempo. Homenagem a Maria Henriqueta Costa Campos*. Lisboa: Colibri, 315–33.

Gary, J. O. and Gamal-Eldin, S. (1981). *Cairene Egyptian Colloquial Arabic*. London: Croom Helm.

Gervain, J., Macagno, F., Cogoi, S., Peña, M., and Mehler, J. (2008). 'The neonate brain detects speech structure'. *PNAS* 105 (37): 14222–7.

——— Nespor, M., Mazuka, R., Horie, R., and Mehler, J. (2008). 'Bootstrapping word order in prelexical infants: A Japanese-Italian crosslinguistic study'. *Cognitive Psychology* 57: 56–74.

Giegerich, Heinz (1999). *Lexical Strata in English*. Cambridge: Cambridge University Press.

Golden, Marija and Milojević Sheppard, Milena (2000). 'Slovene pronominal clitics', in Frits Beukema and Marcel den Dikken (eds), *Clitic Phenomena in European Languages*. Amsterdam: John Benjamins, 191–207.

Gordon, P. C., Grosz, B. J., and Gilliom, L.A. (1993). 'Pronouns, names, and the centering of attention in discourse'. *Cognitive Science* 17: 311–47.

Gout, A., Christophe, A. and Morgan, J. (2004). 'Phonological phrase boundaries constrain lexical access: II. Infant data'. *Journal of Memory and Language* 51: 547–67.

Greenberg, J. (1963). 'Some universals of grammar with particular reference to the order of meaningful elements', in J. Greenberg (ed.), *Universals of Language*. Cambridge, MA: MIT Press, 73–113.

Grice, H. P. (1957). 'Meaning'. *The Philosophical Review* 66: 377–88.

Grice, M., D'Imperio, M., Savino, M. and Avesani, C. (2005). 'Strategies for intonation labelling across varieties of Italian', in S.-A. Jun (ed.), *Prosodic Typology: The Phonology of Intonation and Phrasing*. Oxford: Oxford University Press: 362–89.

Gundel, J. K. (1988). 'Universals of topic-comment structure', in M. Hammand, E. Moravcsik, and J. Wirth (eds), *Studies in Syntactic Typology*. Amsterdam: John Benjamins, 209–39.

Gussenhoven, Carlos (1983a). 'Testing the reality of focus domains'. *Language and Speech* 26: 61–80.

——— (1983b). 'Focus, mode and the nucleus'. *Journal of Linguistics* 19: 377–417.

——— (1984). *On the Grammar and Semantics of Sentence Accents*. Dordrecht: Foris.

——— (1992). 'Sentence accents and argument structure', in I. Roca (ed.), *Thematic Structure: Its Role in Grammar*. Berlin and New York: Foris, 79–106.

——— (2004) *The Phonology of Tone and Intonation*. Cambridge: Cambridge University Press.

Győri, M. (2003), *Domain Specificity in Cognition and Language: Understanding Irony in High-Functioning Autism*. Doctoral dissertation, ELTE University Budapest.

Haider, H. and Prinzhorn, M. (eds), (1986). *Verb Second Phenomena in Germanic Languages*. Dordrecht: Foris.

Hale, K. and Keyser, J. (2002). *Prolegomenon to a Theory of Argument Structure*. Cambridge, MA: MIT Press.

Halle, Morris (1978). 'Formal vs. functional considerations in phonology'. *Studies in the Linguistic Sciences* 8: 123–34. Reprinted in B. Brogyányi (ed.), *Studies in Diachronic, Synchronic any Typological Linguistics: Festschrift for O. Szemerényi.* Amsterdam: Benjamins, 325–41.

—— (1986). 'On the phonology-morphology interface'. Ms., MIT.

—— (1997). 'On stress and accent in Indo-European'. *Language* 73: 275–313.

—— Harris, James, and Vergnaud, Jean-Roger (1991). 'A reexamination of the stress erasure convention and Spanish stress'. *Linguistic Inquiry* 22: 141–59.

—— and Kenstowicz, Michael (1991). 'The Free Element Condition and cyclic versus non-cyclic stress'. *Linguistic Inquiry* 22: 457–501.

—— and Matushansky, Ora (2006). 'The morphophonology of Russian adjectival inflection'. *Linguistic Inquiry* 37: 351–404.

—— and Nevins, Andrew (forthcoming). 'Rule application in phonology', in Eric Raimy and Charles Cairns (eds), *Architecture and Representations in Phonological Theory.* Cambridge, MA: MIT Press.

—— and Vergnaud, J.-R. (1987). *An Essay on Stress.* Cambridge, MA: MIT Press. May be downloaded at <http://www.unice.fr/dsl/tobias.htm>.

Halliday, M. (1967). 'Notes on transitivity and theme in English, part II'. *Journal of Linguistics* 3: 199–244.

—— (1970). *A Course in Spoken English: Intonation.* Oxford: Oxford University Press.

Hamblin, C. L. (1973). 'Questions in Montague English', *Foundations of Language* 10: 41–53.

Happé, F. (1993). 'Communicative competence and theory of mind in autism: a test of relevance theory'. *Cognition* 48: 101–19.

Harada, K. (1972). 'Constraints on Wh-Q Binding'. *Descriptive and Applied Linguistics* 5: 180–206.

Haspelmath, M., Dryer, M. S., Gil, D., and Comrie, B. (eds) (2005). *The World Atlas of Language Structure.* Oxford: Oxford University Press.

Hay, J. S. and Diehl, R. L. (2007). 'Perception of rhythmic grouping: testing the iambic/trochaic law'. *Perception & Psychophysics* 69 (1): 113–22.

Hayes, B. (1986). *A Metrical Theory of Stress Rules.* New York: Garland Press.

—— (1989). 'The prosodic hierarchy in meter', in P. Kiparsky and G. Youmans (eds), *Phonetics and Phonology. Rhythm and Meter.* New York: Academic Press, 201–60.

—— (1995). *Metrical Stress Theory.* Chicago: Chicago University Press.

Helgå, H. B. (2008). 'Negasjon i norsk som andrespråk'. Master's thesis. NTNU, Trondheim.

Hellan, L. (1994). 'A note on clitics in Norwegian', in *Clitics: Their Origin, Status and Position. EUROTYP Working Papers (Theme Group 8),* 6. Programme in Language Typology, European Science Foundation, 80–90.

Hellmuth, S. (2005). 'No de-accenting in (or of) phrases: evidence from Arabic for cross-linguistic and cross-dialectal prosodic variation', in S. Frota, M. Vigario, and M. J. Freitas (eds), *Prosodies (with Special Reference to Iberian Languages).* Phonetics and Phonology Series. Berlin: Mouton de Gruyter, 99–121.

Hellmuth, S. (2006a). 'Focus-related pitch range manipulation (and peak alignment effects) in Egyptian Arabic', in R. Hoffmann and H. Mixdorff (eds), *Proceedings of Speech Prosody 2006*. Dresden: TUD Press Verlag der Wissenschaften GmbH, 410–13.

——(2006b). 'Intonational pitch accent distribution in Egyptian Arabic'. Unpublished Ph.D. thesis, SOAS.

——(2007a). 'The foot as the domain of tonal alignment of intonational pitch accents'. *Proceedings of the 16th ICPhS*, Saarbruecken, Germany.

——(2007b). 'The relationship between prosodic structure and pitch accent distribution: evidence from Egyptian Arabic'. *The Linguistic Review* 24: 291–316.

Hendriks, P. (2004). '*Either, both* and *neither* in coordinate structures', in A. ter Meulen and W. Abraham (eds), *The Composition of Meaning: From Lexeme to Discourse*. Amsterdam: John Benjamins, 115–38.

Heycock, C. (1994). 'Focus projection in Japanese'. *Proceedings of the North East Linguistic Society* 24: 157–71.

——(2008). 'Japanese -*wa*, -*ga*, and information structure', in S. Miyagawa and M. Saito (eds), *The Oxford Handbook of Japanese Linguistics*. New York: Oxford University Press, 54–83.

Higginbotham, J. (1993). 'Questions', in K. Hale and J. Keyser (eds), *The View from Building 20*. Cambridge, MA: MIT Press.

Hirsh-Pasek, K., Kemler, D., Nelson, G., Jusczyk, P. W., Cassidy, K. W., Druss, B., and Kennedy, L. (1987). 'Clauses are perceptual units for young infants'. *Cognition* 26 (3): 269–86.

Holmberg, A. (1993). 'Two subject positions in IP in Mainland Scandinavian', *Working Papers in Scandinavian Syntax* 52. Department of Scandinavian Linguistics, University of Lund, 29–41.

——and Platzack, C. (1995). *The Role of Inflection in Scandinavian Syntax*. Oxford: Oxford University Press.

Hooper, J. B. and Thompson, S. A. (1973). 'On the applicability of root transformations'. *Linguistic Inquiry* 4: 465–79.

Hornstein, Norbert, Nunes, Jairo, and Grohmann, Kleanthes (2005). *Understanding Minimalism*. Cambridge: Cambridge University Press.

Horvath, Julia. 2006. 'Separating "Focus Movement" from focus', in V. S. S. Karimi et al. (eds), *Clever and Right: A Festschrift for Joe Emonds*. Berlin: Mouton de Gruyter.

Hualde, J. I. (2007). 'Stress removal and stress addition in Spanish'. *Journal of Portuguese Linguistics* 6: 58–89.

Huang, C.-T. J. (1982). 'Logical relations in Chinese and the theory of grammar'. Ph.D. dissertation, MIT.

Hyman, L. M, Katamba, F., and Walusimbi, L. (1987). 'Luganda and the Strict Layer Hypothesis'. *Phonology Yearbook* 4: 87–108.

Ibrahim, O. A. G., El-Ramly, S. H., and Abdel-Kader, N. S. (2001). 'A model of Fo contour for Arabic affirmative and interrogative sentences'. Mansoura University, Egypt: 18th National Radio Science Conference, 517–24.

Inkelas, Sharon (1998). 'The theoretical status of morphologically conditioned phonology: a case study of dominance effects'. *Yearbook of Morphology* 1997: 121–55.

——and Zec, D. (1993). 'Auxiliary reduction without empty categories: a prosodic account'. *Working Papers of the Cornell Phonetics Laboratory* 8: 205–53.

Ishihara, Shinichiro (2007). 'Major phrase, focus intonation and multiple spell-out (MaP, FI, MSO)'. *The Linguistic Review* 24: 137–67.

——and Féry, Caroline (in prep.). 'Syntactic and prosodic realization of information structure in German, Hungarian and Japanese'. Ms. Potsdam.

Itô, Junko and Mester, Armin (1995). 'Japanese phonology', in John Goldsmith (ed.), *The Handbook of Phonological Theory*. Oxford: Blackwell, 816–38.

————(1999). 'The phonological lexicon', in Natsuko Tsujimura (ed.), *The Handbook of Japanese Linguistics*. Oxford: Blackwell, 62–100.

————(2007). 'Prosodic categories and recursion'. Handout of a talk presented at WPSI3, Indiana University, September 14, 2007.

Jackendoff, R. (1972). *Semantic Interpretation in Generative Grammar*. Cambridge, MA: MIT Press.

Jacobs, Joachim (1993). 'Integration', in Marga Reis (ed.), *Wortstellung und Informationsstruktur*. Tübingen: Niemeyer, 63–116.

Jaeger, F. and Wagner, M. (2003). 'Association with focus and linear order in German'. *The Semantics Archive*, 26 pp.

Jelinek, E. (2002). 'Agreement, clitics and focus in Egyptian Arabic', in J. Ouhalla and U. Shlonsky (eds), *Themes in Arabic and Hebrew Syntax*. Studies in Natural Language and Linguistic Theory. Berlin: Springer, 71–105.

Johannessen, J. B. (2005). 'The syntax of correlative adverbs'. *Lingua* 115: 419–43.

Jun, S.-A. (2005). 'Prosodic typology', in S.-A. Jun (ed.), *Prosodic Typology: The Phonology of Intonation and Phrasing*. Oxford: Oxford University Press, 430–58.

Jun, S.-A. (ed.), (2005). *Prosodic Typology. The Phonology of Intonation and Phrasing*. Oxford: Oxford University Press.

Jusczyk P. W., Hirsh-Pasek, K., Nelson, D. G., Kennedy, L. J., Woodward, A., and Piwoz, J. (1992). 'Perception of acoustic correlates of major phrasal units by young infants'. *Cognitive Psychology* 24 (2): 252–93.

——and Krumhansl, C. L. (1993). 'Pitch and rhythmic patterns affecting infants' sensitivity to musical phrase structure'. *Journal of Experimental Psychology and Human Perception Performance* 9 (3): 627–40.

Kahnemuyipour, Arsalan (2004). 'The syntax of sentential stress'. Unpublished Ph.D. dissertation, University of Toronto.

Kaisse, Ellen and Shaw, Patricia (1985). 'On the theory of Lexical Phonology'. *Phonology Yearbook* 2: 1–30. May be downloaded at <http://www.unice.fr/dsl/tobias. htm>.

Kálmán, L. and Nádasdy, Á. (1994). 'A hangsúly' [Stress], in Ferenc Kiefer (ed.), *Strukturális magyar nyelvtan 2, Fonológia* [Structural Hungarian Grammar 2, Phonology]. Budapest: Akadémiai Kiadó, 393–467.

Karimi, Simin. (2003). 'On object positions, specificity, and Scrambling in Persian', in Simin Karimi (ed.), *Word Order and Scrambling*. London: Blackwell, 91–124.

Karins, K., Liberman, M., McLemore, C., and Rowson, E. (2002). CallHome Egyptian Arabic Speech Supplement LDC2002S37. Philadelphia, Linguistic Data Consortium.

Kaye, Jonathan (1992). 'On the interaction of theories of Lexical Phonology and theories of phonological phenomena', in Uli Dressler, Hans Luschützky, Oskar Pfeiffer, and John Rennison (eds), *Phonologica 1988*. Cambridge: Cambridge University Press, 141–55. May be downloaded at <http://www.unice.fr/dsl/tobias.htm>.

——(1995). 'Derivations and interfaces', in Jacques Durand and Francis Katamba (eds), *Frontiers of Phonology*. London and New York: Longman. Also in *SOAS Working Papers in Linguistics and Phonetics* 3 (1993): 90–126, 289–332. May be downloaded at <http://www.unice.fr/dsl/tobias.htm>.

Kayne, R. S. (1994). *The Antisymmetry of Syntax.* Cambridge, MA: MIT Press.

Kean, Mary-Louise (1974). 'The strict cycle in phonology'. *Linguistic Inquiry* 5: 179–203.

Keating, P., Cho, T., Fougeron, C., and Hsu, C. (2003). 'Domain-initial articulatory strengthening in four languages', in J. Local, R. Ogden, and R. Temple (eds), *Phonetic Interpretation*. Cambridge, MA: Cambridge University Press, 143–61.

Kemler, D., Nelson, G., Hirsh-Pasek, K., Jusczyk, P., and Wright-Cassidy, K. (1989). 'How the prosodic cues in motherese might assist language learning'. *Journal of Child Language* 16 (1): 55–68.

Keyser, S. J. (1968). 'Review of Sven Jacobson "Adverbial positions in English"'. *Language* 44: 357–74.

Kiparsky, Paul (1968–1973). 'How abstract is phonology?' in Osamu Fujimura (ed.), Manuscript circulated since 1968 and published 1973 in *Three Dimensions of Linguistic Theory*. Tokyo: TEC, 5–56.

——(1982a). 'From cyclic phonology to lexical phonology', in Harry van der Hulst and Norval Smith (eds), *The Structure of Phonological Representations I*. Dordrecht: Foris, 131–75. May be downloaded at <http://www.unice.fr/dsl/tobias.htm>.

——(1982b). 'Lexical morphology and phonology', in In-Seok Yang (ed.), *Linguistics in the Morning Calm*, Seoul: Hanshin, 3–91. May be downloaded at <http://www.unice.fr/dsl/tobias.htm>.

——(1993). 'Blocking in nonderived environments', in Sharon Hargus and Ellen Kaisse (eds), *Studies in Lexical Phonology*. San Diego: Academic Press, 277–313.

——(2000). 'Opacity and cyclicity'. *The Linguistic Review* 17: 351–65.

——(2003). 'Syllables and moras in Arabic', in Caroline Féry and Ruben van de Vijver (eds), *The Syllable in Optimality Theory*. Cambridge: Cambridge University Press, 147–82.

Kiss, K. (1998). 'Identificational focus versus informational focus'. *Language* 74 (2): 245–73.

Kisseberth, C. W. and Abasheikh, M. I. (1974). 'Vowel length in Chi Mwi:ni—a case study of the role of grammar in phonology', in A. Bruck, A. Fox, and M. W. La Galy (eds), *Papers from the Parasession on Natural Phonology*. Chicago: Chicago Linguistic Society, 193–209.

Kjelgaard, M. M. and Speer, S. R. (1999). 'Prosodic facilitation and interference in the resolution of temporary syntactic closure ambiguity'. *Journal of Memory & Language* 40: 153–94.

Kornfilt, Jaklin 2003. 'Scrambling, subscrambling, and case in Turkish', in Simin Karimi (ed.), *Word Order and Scrambling*. London: Blackwell, 125–54.

Koster, J. (1975). 'Dutch as an SOV Language'. *Linguistic Analysis* 1: 111–36.

Kratzer, A. (1988). 'Stage-level and individual-level predicates', in M. Krifka (ed.), *Genericity in Language: Proceedings of the 1988 Tübingen Conference*. Tübingen: University of Tübingen.

—— and Selkirk, Elizabeth O. (2007). 'Phase theory and prosodic spellout: The case of verbs'. *The Linguistic Review* 24: 93–135.

Krifka, M. (2006). 'Basic notions of information structure', in C. Féry, G. Fanselow, and M. Krifka (eds), *The Notions of Information Structure*. Interdisciplinary Studies on Information Structure 6. Potsdam: Institutsverlag Universitaet Potsdam.

Krifka, Manfred (1984). *Fokus, Topik, syntaktische Struktur und semantische Interpretation*. Ms., University of Tübingen.

Krumhansl, C. L. and Jusczyk, P. W. (1990). 'Infants' perception of phrase structure in music'. *Psychological Science* 1: 70–3.

Kuno, S. (1973). *The Structure of the Japanese Language*. Cambridge, MA: MIT Press.

Kuroda, S.-Y. (1965). 'Generative grammatical studies in the Japanese language'. Ph.D. dissertation, MIT.

—— (1972). 'The categorical and the thetic judgment: evidence from Japanese syntax'. *Foundations of Language* 9: 153–85.

—— (1988) 'Whether we agree or not: a comparative syntax of English and Japanese'. *Linguisticae Investigationes* 12: 1–47.

Ladd, D. R. (1980). *The Structure of Intonational Meaning: Evidence from English*. Bloomington, IN: Indiana University Press.

—— (1988). 'Declination "reset" and the hierarchical organization of utterances'. *Journal of the Acoustical Society of America* 84: 530–44.

—— (1990). 'Metrical representation of pitch register', in J. Kingston and M. Beckman (eds), *Papers in Laboratory Phonology I: Between the Grammar and Physics of Speech*. Cambridge: Cambridge University Press, 35–57.

—— (1996). *Intonational Phonology*. Cambridge: Cambridge University Press.

Laenzlinger, Christopher 2005. 'A feature-based theory of adverb syntax', in J. R. Austin, S. Engelberg, and G. Rauh (eds), *The Interplay between Meaning, Context, and Syntactic Structure*. Amsterdam: John Benjamins, 205–52.

Lakoff, George (1972). 'The global nature of the Nuclear Stress Rule'. *Language* 48, 285–303.

Lambova, Mariana (2004). 'On information structure and clausal architecture: evidence from Bulgarian'. Doctoral dissertation, University of Connecticut.

Lambrecht, K. (1994). *Information Structure and Sentence Form*. Cambridge: Cambridge University Press.

——(2001). 'A framework for the analysis of cleft constructions'. *Linguistics* 39 (3): 463–516.

Laniran, Yetunde O. and Clements, George N. (2003). 'Downstep and high raising: interacting factors in Yoruba tone production'. *Journal of Phonetics* 31: 203–50.

Lasnik, Howard (1999). 'On feature strength: Three minimalist approaches to overt movement'. *Linguistic Inquiry* 30 (2): 197–217.

Lebeaux, D. (1988) 'Language acquisition and the form of the grammar'. Ph.D. dissertation, University of Massachusetts, Amherst.

Legendre, Geraldine (2003). 'What are clitics? Evidence from Balkan languages'. *Phonological Studies* 6: 89–96.

Lehiste, I. (1973). 'Phonetic disambiguation of syntactic ambiguity'. *Glossa* 7: 107–22.

Liberman, M. (1975 [1978/9]). 'The intonational system of English', Ph.D. dissertation, MIT, Cambridge, MA (published by Indiana University Linguistic Club, Blooming-ton, IN, 1978; Garland, New York/London, 1979).

——and Pierrehumbert, J. (1984). 'Intonational invariance under changes in pitch range and length', in M. Aronoff and R. T. Oehrle (eds), *Language Sound Structure*. Cambridge, MA: MIT Press, 157–233.

——and Prince, A. (1977). 'On stress and linguistic rhythm'. *Linguistic Inquiry* 8 (2): 249–336.

Low, E. L. and Grabe, E. (2002). 'Durational variability in speech and the rhythm class hypothesis', in C. Gussenhoven and N. Warner (eds), *Laboratory Phonology 7* Berlin and New York: Mouton de Gruyter, 515–46.

Mahajan, A. (1990). 'The A/A-bar distinction and movement theory'. Ph.D. dissertation, MIT.

Marácz, László. 1989. 'Asymmetries in Hungarian'. Ph.D. dissertation, Groningen University.

Marslen-Wilson, W. D., Tyler, L. K., Warren, P., Grenier, P., and Lee, C. S. (1992). 'Prosodic effects in minimal attachment'. *Quarterly Journal of Experimental Psychology* 45A (1): 73–87.

Martins, F. and Mascarenhas, I. (2004), 'Efeitos de Peso: Uma Nova Perspectiva', in *Actas do XIX Encontro Nacional da Associação Portuguesa de Linguística*. Lisboa: APL, 535–45.

Mascaró, Joan (1976). 'Catalan phonology and the phonological cycle'. Ph.D. dissertation, MIT.

McCarthy, John J. and Prince, Alan S. (1990). 'Foot and word in prosodic morph-ology: the Arabic broken plural'. *Natural Language and Linguistic Theory* 8: 209–83.

McCloskey, J. (1996). 'On the scope of verb-movement in Irish'. *Natural Language and Linguistic Theory* 14: 47–104.

——(2005). 'Questions and questioning in a local English', in R. Zanuttini et al. (eds), *Cross-Linguistic Research in Syntax and Semantics: Negation, Tense and Clausal Architecture*. Washington, DC: Georgetown University Press.

McMahon, April (2000). *Lexical Phonology and the History of English*. Cambridge: Cambridge University Press.

Mehler, J., Lambertz, G., Jusczyk, P. W., and Amiel-Tison, C. (1987). 'Discrimination de la langue maternelle par le nouveau-né'. *C. R. Académie des Sciences de Paris* 303 (15): 637–40.

——————————(1988). 'A precursor of language acquisition in young infants'. *Cognition* 29: 143–78.

——and Nespor, M. (2003). Linguistic rhythm and the acquisition of language, in A. Belletti (ed.), *Structures and Beyond*. Oxford: Oxford University Press.

Meinunger, A. (2005). 'Remarks on the verb second phonomenon, the nature of volitional predicates, "konjunktiv" and speculations on illocution'. Berlin: ZAS.

——(2006), 'The discourse status of subordinate sentences and some implications for syntax and pragmatics', in V. Molnár and S. Winkler (eds), *The Architecture of Focus*. Berlin: Mouton de Gruyter.

Meisel, J. M. (ed.), (1992). *The Acquisition of Verb Placement. Functional Categories and V2 Phenomena in Language Acquisition*. Dordrecht: Kluwer Academic Press.

Merchant, Jason (2001). *The Syntax of Silence: Sluicing, Islands, and the Theory of Ellipsis*. Oxford: Oxford University Press.

——(2007). 'Three kinds of ellipsis: syntactic, semantic, pragmatic?' Ms. University of Chicago.

Millotte, S. (2005). 'Le rôle de la prosodie dans le traitement syntaxique adulte et l'acquisition de la syntaxe'. Unpublished Ph.D. thesis, Ecole des Hautes Etudes en Sciences Sociales, Paris.

——René, A., Wales, R., and Christophe, A. (2008). 'Phonological phrase boundaries constrain the on-line syntactic analysis of spoken sentences'. *Journal of Experimental Psychology: Learning, Memory & Cognition* 34: 874–85.

——Wales, R., and Christophe, A. (2007). 'Phrasal prosody disambiguates syntax'. *Language and Cognitive Processes* 22: 898–909.

Mitchell, T. F. (1993). *Pronouncing Arabic 2*. Oxford: Clarendon Press.

Mittwoch, A. (1976). 'Grammar and illocutionary force'. *Lingua* 40: 21–42.

——(1977). 'How to refer to one's own words: speech-act modifying adverbials and the performative analysis'. *Journal of Linguistics* 13: 153–368.

——(1979). 'Final parentheticals with English questions—their illucutionary function and grammar'. *Journal of Pragmatics* 3: 401–12.

Miyagawa, S. (2001). 'The EPP, scrambling, and wh-in-situ', in M. Kenstowicz (ed.), *Ken Hale: A Life in Language*. Cambridge, MA: MIT Press, 293–338.

——(2003). 'A-movement scrambling and options without optionality', in S. Karimi (ed.), *Word Order and Scrambling*. Oxford: Blackwell, 177–200.

Mohanan, Karuvannur (1982). 'Lexical phonology'. Ph.D. dissertation, MIT. May be downloaded at <http://www.unice.fr/dsl/tobias.htm>.

——(1986). *The Theory of Lexical Phonology*. Dordrecht: Reidel. May be downloaded at <http://www.unice.fr/dsl/tobias.htm>.

Moon, C., Cooper, R. P., and Fifer, W. (1993). 'Two-day-olds prefer their native language'. *Infant Behavior and Development* 16: 495–500.

Morgan, J. L. (1994). 'Converging measures of speech segmentation in preverbal infants'. *Infant Behavior and Development* 17: 387–400.

——and Demuth K. (eds) (1996). *Signal to Syntax: Bootstrapping from Speech to Grammar in Early Acquisition.* Hillsdale, NJ: Lawrence Erlbaum.

Moro, Andrea (2000). *Dynamic Antisymmetry.* Linguistic Inquiry Monograph 38. Cambridge, MA: MIT Press.

Mughazy, M. (2009). 'The information structure of existential sentences in Egyptian Arabic', in J. Owens and A. Elgibali (eds), *Information Structure in Spoken Arabic.* Oxford: Routledge.

Müller, K. E. (1998). 'German focus particles and their influence on intonation'. Doctoral dissertation, University of Stuttgart.

Nakanishi, K. (forthcoming). 'Semantic properties of Split Topicalization in German', in C. Maienborn and A. Woellstein-Leisten (eds), *Events in Syntax, Semantics, and Discourse.* Tübingen: Niemeyer.

Nava, E. and Zubizarreta, M. L. (2008). 'Order of acquisition of prosodic prominence patterns: evidence from L1 Spanish/L2 English Speech'. Paper presented at *Generative Approaches to Language Acquisition (Galana)* 3, University of Connecticut, Storrs (September 4–6, 2008).

Nazzi, T., Bertoncini, J., and Mehler, J. (1998). 'Language discrimination by newborns: toward an understanding of the role of rhythm'. *Journal of Experimental Psychology: Human Perception and Performance* 24 (3): 756–66.

——Kemler-Nelson, D., Jusczyk, P., and Jusczyk, A. (2000). 'Six-month-olds' detection of clauses embedded in continuous speech: effects of prosodic well-formdness'. *Infancy* 1 (1): 123–47.

Neeleman, Ad and Reinhart, T. (1998). 'Scrambling and the PF-Interface', in W. Geuder and M. Butt (eds), *Projecting from the Lexicon.* Standford, CA: CSLI Publications.

————(1999). 'Scrambling and the PF Interface', in Miriam Butt and Wilhelm Geuder (eds), *The Projection of Arguments: Lexical and Compositional Factors.* Stanford, CA: CSLI Publications.

Nemoto, N. (1993). 'Chains and case positions: a study from scrambling in Japanese'. Ph.D. dissertation, University of Connecticut.

Nespor, M., Guasti, M. T., and Christophe, A. (1996). 'Selecting word order: the Rhythmic Activation Principle', in U. Kleinhenz (ed.), *Interfaces in Phonology.* Berlin: Akademie Verlag, 1–26.

——Peña, M., and Mehler, J. (2003). 'On the different roles of vowels and consonants in speech processing and language acquisition'. *Lingue & Linguaggi* 2: 203–31.

——Shukla, M., Vijver, R. van de, Avesani, C., Schraudolf, H., and Donati, C. (2008). 'Different phrasal prominence realization in VO and OV languages'. *Lingue e Linguaggio* 7 (2): 1–28.

Nespor, M. and Vogel, I. (1982). 'Prosodic domains of external sandhi rules', in H. v. d. Hulst and Norval Smith (eds), *The Structure of Phonological Representations*. Dordrecht: Foris, 225–55.

——— (1983). 'Prosodic structure above the word', in A. Cutler and D. R. Ladd (eds), *Prosody: Models and Measurements*. Berlin: Springer-Verlag, 123–40.

——— (1986 [2008]). *Prosodic Phonology*. Berlin. Mouton de Gruyter. (Reedition of Nespor and Vogel (1986), Dordrecht: Foris, with a new Introduction.)

Newell, Heather and Scheer, Tobias (2007). 'Procedural first'. Paper presented at the 38th Poznań Linguistic Meeting, Poznań, 13–16 September. May be downloaded at <http://www.unice.fr/dsl/tobias.htm>.

Nishigauchi, T. (1990). *Quantification in the Theory of Grammar*. Dordrecht: Springer.

Norlin, K. (1989). 'A preliminary description of Cairo Arabic intonation of statements and questions'. *Speech Transmission Quarterly Progress and Status Report* 1: 47–9.

O'Connor, J. D. and Arnold, G. F. (1961). *The Intonation of Colloquial English*. London: Longman.

Odden, David (1993). 'Interaction between modules in lexical phonology', in Sharon Hargus and Ellen Kaisse (eds), *Studies in Lexical Phonology*. New York: Academic Press, 111–44.

Olsvay, Csaba. 2000. 'Formális jegyek egyeztetése a magyar nemsemleges mondatokban' [Agreement features in non-neutral Hungarian sentences], in László Büky and Márta Maleczki (eds), *A mai magyar nyelv leírásának újabb módszerei* [New Methods in Analyzing Modern Hungarian] 4. Szeged: Szegedi Tudományegyetem, 119–51.

Oshita, H. (1997). 'The unaccusative trap: L2 acquisition of English intransitive verbs'. Unpublished doctoral dissertation, USC.

Østbø, C. B. (2003). 'Generativ analyse av norske setningsadverbialer: et kritisk blikk'. Hovedfagsoppgave. NTNU, Trondheim.

Pater, Joe (2000). 'Nonuniformity in English stress: the role of ranked and lexically specific constraints'. *Phonology* 17: 237–74.

——— (forthcoming). 'Morpheme-specific phonology: constraint indexation and inconsistency resolution', in Steve Parker (ed.), *Phonological Argumentation: Essays on Evidence and Motivation*. London: Equinox.

Peña, M., Bion, R. H., and Nespor, M. (in progress). 'How modality-specific is the iambic-trochaic law? Evidence from vision'.

——— Bonatti, L., Nespor, M., and Mehler, J. (2002). 'Signal-driven computations in speech processing'. *Science* 298: 604–7.

Peperkamp, S., Le Calvez, R., Nadal, J. P., and Dupoux, E. (2006). 'The acquisition of allophonic rules: statistical learning with linguistic constraints'. *Cognition* 101: B31–B41.

Pereltsvaig, Asya (2007). 'Split phrases in colloquial Russian: a corpus study', in Richard Compton et al. (eds), *Formal Approaches to Slavic Linguistics: The Toronto Meeting*. Ann Arbor: Michigan Slavic Materials, 245–63.

Perlmutter, D. (1972). 'Evidence for shadow pronouns in French relativization', in Paul Peranteau et al. (eds), *The Chicago Which Hunt*. Chicago: Chicago Linguistic Society, University of Chicago, 73–105.

Perner, J., Frith, U., Leslie, A., and Leekam, S. (1989). 'Explorations of the autistic child's theory of mind: knowledge, belief, and communication'. *Child Development* 60: 689–700.

Pesetsky, David (1979). 'Russian morphology and lexical theory'. Ms, MIT. Available at <http://web.mit.edu/linguistics/www/pesetsky/russmorph.pdf>.

Peti-Stantić, Anita (2007). 'Wackernagelovo pravilo—norma ili mogućnost', in Branko Kuna (ed.), *Sintaktičke kategorije*. Zagreb: Institut za hrvatski jezik i jezikoslovlje, 173–87.

Pierrehumbert, J. (1980). 'The phonology and phonetics of English intonation'. Ph.D. dissertation, MIT.

——and Beckman, Mary E. (1988). *Japanese Tone Structure*. Cambridge, MA: MIT Press.

——and Hirschberg, J. (1990). 'The meaning of intonational contours in the interpretation of discourse', in Philip R. Cohen, Jerry Morgan, and Martha E. Pollack (eds), *Intentions in Communication*. Cambridge, MA: MIT Press, 271–311.

Pinón, Christopher (1995). 'Around the progressive in Hungarian', in István Kenesei (ed.), *Approaches to Hungarian 5*. Szeged: JATE, 155–9.

Pitt, M. A., Dilley, L., Johnson, K., Kiesling, S., Raymond, W., Hume, E., and Fosler-Lussier, E. (2006). Buckeye Corpus of Conversational Speech Columbus, OH: Department of Psychology, Ohio State University.

Pollock, J.-Y. (1989). 'Verb movement, universal grammar, and the structure of VP'. *Linguistic Inquiry* 20: 365–424.

Poser, William J. (1984). 'The phonetics and phonology of tone and intonation in Japanese'. Ph.D. dissertation. MIT, Cambridge, MA.

Prince, A. and P. Smolensky (1993). *Optimality Theory: Constraint Interaction in Generative Grammar*. Rutgers University Center for Cognitive Science Technical Report 2.

Ramus, F. (2002). 'Acoustic correlates of linguistic rhythm: perspectives', in *Proceedings of Speech Prosody 2002. Aix-en-Provence, France*.

——Hauser, M. D., Miller, C., Morris, D., and Mehler, J. (2000). 'Language discrimination by human newborns and by cotton-top tamarin monkeys'. *Science* 288 (5464): 349–51.

——Nespor, M., and Mehler, J. (1999). 'Correlates of linguistic rhythm in the speech signal'. *Cognition* 73 (3): 265–92.

Reinhart, T. (1981). 'Pragmatics and linguistics: An analysis of sentence topics'. *Philosophica* 27, Special Issue on Pragmatic Theory.

——(1995). *Interface Strategies*. OTS Working papers in Linguistics, Utrecht University.

——(1999). 'The processing cost of reference-set computation: guess patterns in acquisition'. OTS Working Papers in Linguistics.

——(2006). *Interface Strategies: Optimal and Costly Computation*. Cambridge, MA: MIT Press.

Reis, M. (1995). 'Extractions from verb-second clauses in German?', in U. Lutz and J. Pafel (eds), *On Extraction and Extraposition in German*. Amsterdam: Benjamins, 45–88.

—— (1997). 'Zum syntaktischen Status unselbständiger Verbzweit-Sätze', in C. Dürscheid and K.-J. Ramers (eds), *Sprache im Fokus. Festschrift für Heinz Vater zum 65. Geburtstag.* Tübingen: Niemeyer, 121–44.

Riemsdijk, H. van, and Williams, E. (1981). 'NP-structure'. *The Linguistic Review* 1: 171–217.

Rifaat, K. (1991). 'The intonation of Arabic: an experimental study'. Unpublished Ph.D. thesis, University of Alexandria.

Rizzi, L. (1986). 'Null Objects in Italian and the Theory of pro'. *Linguistic Inquiry* 17: 501–57.

—— (1997). 'The fine structure of the left periphery', in L. Haegeman (ed.), *Elements of Grammar: Handbook of Generative Syntax.* Dordrecht: Kluwer, 281–337.

Roach, P. (1982). 'On the distinction between "stress-timed" and "syllable-timed" languages', in D. Crystal (ed.), *Linguistic Controversies.* London: Edward Arnold, 73–9.

Roberts, Ian (1998). '*Have/Be* raising, Move F, and procrastinate'. *Linguistic Inquiry* 29: 113–25.

—— (2005). *Principles and Parameters in a VSO Language: A Case Study in Welsh.* Oxford: Oxford University Press.

Rochman, Lisa (2007a). 'Motivating floated quantifiers', in Ronald P. Leow, Héctor Campos, and Donna Lardiere (eds), *GURT Proceedings.* Washington, DC: Georgetown University Press.

—— (2007b). 'Phonological effects in floating quantifier placement', in Peter Reich, Bill Sullivan, and Arle Lommel (eds), *Proceedings of Linguistic Association of Canada and the United States Forum.* Houston, TX: Linguistic Association of Canada and the United States.

—— (forthcoming). 'Motivating floated quantifiers', in Ronald P. Leow, Héctor Campos, and Donna Lardiere (eds), *GURT Proceedings.* Washington, DC: Georgetown University Press.

—— (in prep.). 'The role of focus structure and intonation in quantifier floating'. Ph.D. dissertation, Ben Gurion University of the Negev.

Ronat, M. (1982). 'Logical Form and discourse islands', *Journal of Linguistic Research* 2: 33–48.

Ross, John Robert (1970). 'On declarative sentences', in R. A. Jacobs and P. S. Rosenbaum (eds), *Readings in English Transformational Grammar* (Waltham, MA: Blaisdell).

Rubach, Jerzy (1997). 'Extrasyllabic consonants in Polish: Derivational Optimality Theory', in Iggy Roca (ed.), *Derivations and Constraints in Phonology.* Oxford: Clarendon, 551–81.

—— (1981). *Cyclic Phonology and Palatalization in Polish and English.* Warsaw: Wydawnictwa Uniwersytetu Warszawskiego.

Rubin, E. J. (2003). 'Determining pair-merge'. *Linguistic Inquiry* 34: 660–8.

Rudnickaya, Elena (2000). 'The derivation of Yes–No *Li* questions in Russian: Syntax and/or phonology?', in Tracy H. King and Irina Sekerina (eds), *Formal Approaches* to *Slavic Linguistics: The Philadelphia Meeting, 1999*. Ann Arbor: Michigan Slavic Materials, 347–62.

Saffran, J., Aslin, R., and Newport, E. (1996). 'Statistical learning by 8-month-old infants'. *Science* 274 (5294): 1926–8.

Saito, M. (1985). 'Some asymmetries in Japanese and their theoretical implications'. Ph.D. dissertation, MIT.

—— (1989). 'Scrambling as semantically vacuous A'-movement', in M. Baltin and A. Kroch (eds), *Alternative Conceptions of Phrase Structure*. Chicago: University of Chicago Press, 182–200.

—— (2003). 'A derivational approach to the interpretation of scrambling chains'. *Lingua* 113: 481–518.

—— (2005) 'Further notes on the interpretation of scrambling chains', in J. Sabel and M. Saito (eds), *The Free Word Order Phenomenon: Its Syntactic Sources and Diversity*. Berlin: Mouton de Gruyter, 335–76.

Salverda, A. P., Dahan, D., and McQueen, J. M. (2003). 'The role of prosodic boundaries in the resolution of lexical embedding in speech comprehension'. *Cognition* 90: 51–89.

Samek-Lodovici, Vieri (2005). 'Prosody syntax interaction in the expression of focus'. *Natural Language & Linguistic Theory* 23: 687–755.

Sasse, H.-J. (1987). 'The thetic/categorical distinction revisited'. *Linguistics* 25: 511–80.

Scheer, Tobias (2008). 'Spell out your sister!' in Natasha Abner and Jason Bishop (eds), *Proceedings of the 27th West Coast Conference on Formal Linguistics*. Somerville: Cascadilla, 379–87. May be downloaded at <http://www.unice.fr/dsl/tobias.htm>.

—— (2009). 'Intermodular argumentation and the word-spell-out-mystery', in Kleanthes Grohmann (ed.), *Explorations of Phase Theory: Interpretation at the Interfaces*. Berlin: Mouton de Gruyter, 23–66.

—— (forthcoming). *How Morpho-syntax Talks to Phonology. A Survey of Extra-Phonological Information in Phonology since Trubetzkoy's Grenzsignale*. Berlin: Mouton de Gruyter.

Schmerling, S. (1976). *Aspects of English Sentence Stress*. Austin: University of Texas Press.

Seidl, A. and Johnson, E. (2006). 'Infant word segmentation revisited: edge alignment facilitates target extraction'. *Developmental Science* 9: 565–73.

Selkirk, E. (1984). *Phonology and Syntax: The Relation between Sound and Structure*. Cambridge, MA: MIT Press.

—— (1986). 'On derived domains in sentence phonology'. *Phonology Yearbook* 3: 371–405.

—— (1995). 'Sentence prosody: intonation, stress, and phrasing', in John Goldsmith (ed.), *The Handbook of Phonological Theory*. Cambridge, MA: Blackwell, 550–69.

—— (2000). 'The interaction of constraints on prosodic phrasing', in M. Horne (ed.), *Prosody: Theory and Experiment*. Dordrecht: Kluwer, 231–61.

Selkirk, E. (2002). 'Contrastive FOCUS vs. presentational focus: prosodic evidence from right node raising in English', in B. Bel and I. Marlin (eds), *Speech Prosody 2002: Proceedings of the First International Speech Prosody Conference*. Aix-en-Provence: Laboratoire Parole et Langage, 643–6.

Shlonsky, U. (1997). *Clause Structure and Word Order in Hebrew and Arabic*. New York: Oxford University Press.

Shukla, M., Nespor, M., and Mehler, J. (2007). 'An interaction between prosody and statistics in the segmentation of fluent speech'. *Cognitive Psychology* 54 (1): 1–32.

—————— (in prep.). 'Grammar on a language map'.

Siegel, Dorothy (1974). 'Topics in English morphology'. Ph.D. dissertation, MIT.

Sigurðsson, Halldór Ármann (2004). 'Meaningful silence, meaningful sounds'. *Linguistic Variation Yearbook* 4: 235–59.

Skopeteas, S., Fiedler, I., Hellmuth, S., Schwarz, A., Stoel, R., Fanselow, G., Féry, C., and Krifka, M. (2006). 'Questionnaire on Information Structure (QUIS)'. *Interdisciplinary Studies on Information Structure (ISIS): Working Papers of SFB632 University of Potsdam*, 4.

Slobin, D. (1973). 'Cognitive prerequisites for the development of grammar', in C. A. Ferguson and D. Slobin (eds), *Studies of Child Language Development*. New York: Holt, Rinehart & Winston, 175–208.

Snedeker, J. and Yuan, S. (2008). 'Effects of prosodic and lexical constraints on parsing in young children (and adults)'. *Journal of Memory & Language* 58 (2): 574–608.

Soares, Carla (2003). 'The C-domain and the acquisition of European Portuguese: The case of wh-questions'. *Probus* 15: 147–76.

Soderstrom, M., Seidl, A., Kemler Nelson, D. G., and Jusczyk, P. W. (2003). 'The prosodic bootstrapping of phrases: evidence from prelinguistic infants'. *Journal of Memory and Language* 4: 249–67.

Sosa, J. M. (1999). *La entonación del español*. Madrid: Cátedra.

Sperber, D. and Wilson, D. (1995). *Relevance. Communication and Cognition*. 2nd edn. Cambridge, MA: Harvard University Press.

—————— (2001), 'Pragmatics, modularity and mind-reading'. *Mind and Language* 17: 3–23.

Speyer, Augustin (2005). 'Topicalization and the trochaic requirement'. *Penn Working Papers in Linguistics* 10 (2), 243–56.

Sportiche, D. (1988). 'A theory of floating quantifiers and its corollaries for constituent structure'. *Linguisic Inquiry* 19: 425–49.

Stechow, Arnim von and Uhmann, Susanne (1986). 'Some remarks on focus projection', in Werner Abraham and S. de Meij (eds), *Topic, Focus, and Configurationality*. Amsterdam: John Benjamins, 295–320.

Stepanov, A. (2001). 'Late adjunction and minimalist phrase structure'. *Syntax* 4: 94–125.

Sternefeld, Wolfgang (2006). *Syntax. Eine morphologisch motivierte generative Beschreibung des Deutschen*. Tübingen: Stauffenburg Verlag.

Stjepanović, Sandra (2007). 'Free word order and copy theory of movement', in Norbert Corver and Jairo Nunes (eds), *The Copy Theory of Movement*. Amsterdam: John Benjamins, 219–48.

Suñer, M. (1982). *Syntax and Semantics of Spanish Presentational Sentence-Types*. Washington, DC: Georgetown University Press.

Surányi, Balázs (2006). 'Scrambling in Hungarian'. *Acta Linguistica Hungarica* 53: 393–432.

Swerts, M. (2007). 'Contrast and accent in Dutch and Romanian'. *Journal of Phonetics* 35: 380–97.

——Krahmer, E., and Avesani, C. (2002). 'Prosodic marking of information status in Dutch and Italian: a comparative analysis'. *Journal of Phonetics* 30 (4): 629–54.

Szabolcsi, Anna (1997). 'Strategies for scope taking', in Anna Szabolcsi (ed.), *Ways of Scope Taking*. Dordrecht: Reidel, 109–55.

Szendrői, K. (2001). 'Focus and the syntax-phonology interface'. Doctoral dissertation, University College London.

—— (2003). 'A stress-based approach to the syntax of Hungarian focus'. *The Linguistic Review* 20 (1): 37–78.

—— (2004). 'Acquisition evidence for an interface theory of focus', in J. van Kampen and S. Baauw (eds), *Proceedings of GALA 2003, Volumes 1–2*. Utrecht: LOT, 457–68.

Szpyra, Jolanta (1989). *The Phonology–Morphology Interface*. London & New York: Routledge.

Tada, H. (1993). 'A/A-bar partition in derivation'. Ph.D. dissertation, MIT.

Thráinsson, H. (2001). 'Object shift and scrambling', in M. Baltin and C. Collins (eds), *The Handbook of Contemporary Syntactic Theory*. Malden: Blackwell, 148–202.

Trehub, S. (2003). 'Toward a developmental psychology of music'. *Annals of the New York Academy of Science* 999: 402–13.

Truckenbrodt, Hubert (1995). 'Phonological phrases: their relation to syntax, focus, and prominence'. Unpublished Ph.D. thesis, MIT.

—— (1999). 'On the relation between syntactic phrases and phonological phrases'. *Linguistic Inquiry* 30 (2): 219–55.

—— (2002). 'Upstep and embedded register levels'. *Phonology* 19: 77–120.

—— (2004). 'Final lowering in non-final position'. *Journal of Phonetics* 32: 313–48.

—— (2005). 'A short report on intonation phrase boundaries in German', *Linguistische Berichte* 203: 273–96.

—— (2006a). 'Phrasal stress', in Keith Brown (ed.), *The Encyclopedia of Languages and Linguistics, Volume 9*. 2nd edn. Oxford: Elsevier, 572–9.

—— (2006b). 'On the semantic motivation of syntactic verb movement to C in German', *Theoretical Linguistics* 32 (3): 257–306.

—— (2007a). 'Upstep of edge tones and of nuclear accents', in Carlos Gussenhoven and Tomas Riad (eds), *Tones and Tunes. Volume 2: Experimental Studies in Word and Sentence Prosody*. Berlin: Mouton, 349–86.

—— (2007b). 'The syntax phonology interface', in Paul de Lacy (ed.), *The Cambridge Handbook of Phonology*. Cambridge: Cambridge University Press, 435–56.

Uhmann, Susanne (1991). *Fokusphonologie*. Tübingen: Niemeyer.

Uriagereka, Juan. (1999). 'Multiple spell-out', in Samuel Epstein and Norbert Hornstein (eds), *Working Minimalism*. Cambridge, MA: MIT Press, 251–82.

Vallduví, E. (1991). 'The role of plasticity in the association of focus and prominence'. *Proceedings of the Eastern States Conference on Linguistics (ESCOL) 7*: 295–306.

—— (1992). *The Informational Component*. New York: Garland.

—— (1995). 'Structural properties of information packaging in Catalan', in K. Kiss, (ed.), *Discourse Configurational Languages*. Oxford: Oxford University Press.

Vergnaud, J. R. and Zubizarreta, M. L. (2005). 'The representation of focus and its implications: towards an alternative account of some "intervention effects"', in H. N. Corver, R. Huybregts, U. Kleinhenz, and J. Koster (eds), *Organizing Grammar: Linguistic Studies in Honor of Henk van Riemsdijk*. Berlin and New York: Mouton de Gruyter: SSG 86.

Vikner, Sten (1995). *Verb Movement and Expletive Subjects in the Germanic Languages*. Oxford: Oxford University Press.

Wackernagel, Jacob (1892). 'Über ein Gesetz der indogermanischen Wortstellung'. *Indogermanische Forschungen* 1: 333–436.

Wagner, Michael (2005). 'Prosody and recursion'. Doctoral dissertation, MIT, Cambridge, MA.

Warren, P (1996). 'Prosody and parsing: an introduction'. *Language and Cognitive Processes* 11 (1–2): 1–16.

Watson, J. C. E. (2002). *The Phonology and Morphology of Arabic*. Oxford: Oxford University Press.

Wechsler, Stephen (1991). 'Verb second and illocutionary force', in Katherine Leffel and Denis Bouchard (eds), *Views on Phrase Structure*. Dordrecht: Kluwer, 177–91.

WHO (World Health Organization) (1990). *International Classification of Diseases (10th revision) Chapter 5: Mental and behavioural disorders (including disorders of psychological development). Diagnostic criteria for research*. Geneva: WHO.

Wightman, C., Shattuck-Hufnagel, S., Ostendorf, M., and Price, P. (1992). 'Segmental durations in the vicinity of prosodic phrase boundaries'. *Journal of the Acoustical Society of America* 91 (3): 1707–17.

Williams, Edwin. (1997). 'Blocking and anaphora'. *Linguistic Inquiry* 28: 577–617.

Winkler, Susanne and Göbbel, Edward (2002). 'Review Article: Zubizarreta, M. L. (1998) Prosody, Focus, and Word Order, Linguistic Inquiry Monograph 33. Massachusetts: MIT Press'. *Linguistics* 40 (6): 1185–243.

Woodrow, H. (1951). 'Time perception', in S. S. Stevens (ed.), *Handbook of Experimental Psychology*. New York: Wiley, 1224–36.

Xu, Y. (1999). 'Effects of tone and focus on the formation and alignment of Fo contours'. *Journal of Phonetics* 27: 55–105.

Yang, C. (2002). *Knowledge and Learning in Natural Language*. New York: Oxford University Press.

Zubizarreta, M. L. (1998). *Prosody, Focus and Word Order*. Cambridge, MA: MIT Press.
—— and Vergnaud, J.-R. (2005). 'Phrasal stress, focus, and syntax', in M. Everaert and H. van Riemsdijk (eds), *The Syntax Companion*. Cambridge: Blackwell.
Zwart, C. Jan-Wouter (1997). *Morphosyntax of Verb Movement. A Minimalist Approach to the Syntax of Dutch*. Dordrecht: Kluwer.
Zwicky, A. (1977). *On Clitics*. Bloomington, IN: Indiana University Linguistics Club.

Author Index

Subject Index

OXFORD STUDIES IN THEORETICAL LINGUISTICS

Lightning Source UK Ltd.
Milton Keynes UK
UKHW021030300122
397914UK00002B/171